Economics for Business

Second edition

Economics for Business

Second edition

David Begg
Damian Ward

The **McGraw·Hill** Companies

London Boston Burr Ridge, IL · Dubuque, IA Madison, WI New York San Francisco
St. Louis Bangkok Bogotá Caracas Kuala Lumpur Lisbon Madrid Mexico City
Milan Montreal New Delhi Santiago Seoul Singapore Sydney Taipei Toronto

Economics for Business second edition
David Begg and Damian Ward
ISBN 13 978-0-07-711451-0
ISBN 10 0-07-714515

Published by McGraw-Hill Education
Shoppenhangers Road
Maidenhead
Berkshire
SL6 2QL
Telephone: 44 (0) 1628 502 500
Fax: 44 (0) 1628 770 224
Website: www.mcgraw-hill.co.uk

British Library Cataloguing in Publication Data
A catalogue record for this book is available from the British Library

Library of Congress Cataloguing in Publication Data
The Library of Congress data for this book has been applied for from the Library of Congress

Acquisitions Editor: Kirsty Reade
Development Editor: Hannah Cooper
Marketing Manager: Marca Wosoba
Production Editor: Beverley Shields

Text Design by Jonathan Coleclough
Cover design by Ego Creative
Typeset by MCS Publishing Services Ltd, Salisbury, Wiltshire
Printed and bound in Spain by Mateu Cromo Artes Graficas

First edition published in 2004 by McGraw-Hill Education

ISBN 13 978-0-07-711451-0
ISBN 10 0-07-7114515

Dedication

For my beloved Jen
D. Begg

For Mel, Lucy, Emily and Oscar
D. Ward

Brief Table of Contents

Detailed Table of Contents

This book is for students interested in business. It is not an economics book with some business applications. Instead, we highlight problems faced by real businesses and show how economics can help solve these decision problems.

Our approach

This approach is new, and focuses on what as a business student you really need. It is issue driven, utilizing theories and evidence only after a problem has been identified. Business decisions are the focus on the screen, and economic reasoning is merely the help button to be accessed when necessary. Of course, good help buttons are invaluable ... .

Our coverage

Our book offers a complete course for business students wanting to appreciate why economics is so often the back-up that you require. After a brief introduction, we help you to understand how markets function and how businesses compete, then we train you to evaluate problems posed by the wider economic environment, both nationally and globally.

As a business student, you do not need to know, nor should you want to master, the whole of economics. Your time is scarce and you need to learn how to manage it effectively. *Economics for Business* gets you off to a flying start by focusing only on the essentials. We discuss only what you can comfortably cover during a single term course.

Cases and examples

Business does not stand still and neither should you. You need a course embracing topical examples from the real world as it evolves. Whether we are discussing the pricing of Louis Vuitton handbags, the business model behind the A380 super-jumbo, or how fast the Chinese economy can grow, we aim to bring you the business issues of the day and challenge you to think about how you would respond to them.

Strategic learning

Business students want an instant picture of where they are, what the problem is, and how an intelligent response might be devised. Each chapter begins with the executive summary 'What you need to know at a glance' and concludes with a summary and learning checklist. Providing an informative link in the flow of ideas.

You are thus encouraged to become a 'strategic learner', accessing resources that support your particular lifestyle and learning pattern. You can follow the order that we propose, but you can also browse and move from one topic to another, as you might on the Internet. Active learning both engages your interest and helps you remember things.

Online of course

Our online supplements include both an Instructor Centre and a Student Centre. The Instructor Centre provides key teaching aids to help your lecturers impress you.

The Student Centre offers readers a testbank for self-assessment, a glossary of terms you may wish to check, a moving update of Economics in the News, and links to other interactive economics tools.

Summing up

We were prompted to write this book because fewer and fewer students are studying economics for its own sake. More and more students are switching to courses that study business as a whole.

This creates a market opportunity. Instead of trying to convert books designed for economics courses into books that will suffice for business students, we aimed to write a book that asks what business students want and meets your needs directly.

Identifying market opportunities, and deciding how to respond, is of course a large part of what *Economics for Business* is about. We hope you get as much fun out of reading it as we had in writing it.

David Begg
Damian Ward

May 2006

Acknowledgements

Our thanks go to the following reviewers for their comments at various stages in the text's development:

Adam Blake, University of Nottingham
Tom Craven, University of Ulster
Sougand Golesorkhi, Lancaster University
Rob Haywood, University of Brighton
Ronald Mahieu, Erasmus University, Rotterdam
Pedro Martins, Queen Mary, University of London
Gareth Myles, University of Exeter
Mike Walsh, Coventry University
Pam Whisker, University of Plymouth

Every effort has been made to to trace and acknowledge ownership of copyright and to clear permission for material reproduced in this book. The publishers will be pleased to make suitable arrangements to clear permission with any copyright holders whom it has not been possible to contact.

Technology to enhance learning and teaching

Online Learning Centre (OLC)

After completing each chapter, log on to the supporting Online Learning Centre website. Take advantage of the study tools offered to reinforce the material you have read in the text, and to develop your knowledge of economics for business in a fun and effective way.

Resources for students include:

- Virtual tour of OLC features
- Short contemporary cases
- Glossary
- Weblinks
- Crosswords & self-test questions
- Animated exercises

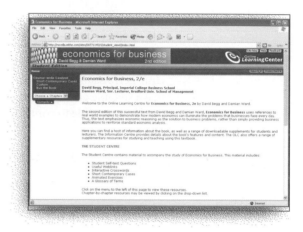

Also available for lecturers:

- PowerPoint slides
- Technical worksheets
- Topical worksheets
- Case study worksheets
- Testbank

EZTest, a new computerized testbank format from McGraw-Hill, is available with this title. EZTest enables you to upload testbanks, modify questions and add your own questions, thus creating a testbank that's totally unique to your course! Find out more at: http://mcgraw-hill.co.uk/he/eztest/.

Lecturers: Customize Content for your Course using the McGraw-Hill Primis Content Centre

Now it's incredibly easy to create a flexible, customized solution for your course, using content from both US and European McGraw-Hill Education textbooks, content from our Professional list including Harvard Business Press titles, as well as a selection of over 9000 cases from Harvard, Insead and Darden. In addition, we can incorporate your own material and course notes.

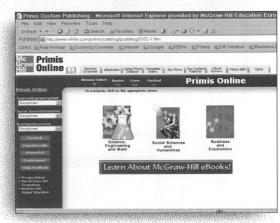

For more information, please contact your local rep who will discuss the right delivery options for your custom publication – including printed readers, e-Books and CDROMs. To see what McGraw-Hill content you can choose from, visit **www.primisonline.com**.

Study Skills

Open University Press publishes guides to study, research and exam skills, to help undergraduate and postgraduate students through their university studies.

Visit **www.openup.co.uk/ss/** to see the full selection of study skills titles, and get a **£2 discount** by entering the promotional code study when buying online!

Computing Skills

If you'd like to brush up on your Computing skills, we have a range of titles covering MS Office applications such as Word, Excel, PowerPoint, Access and more.

Get a £2 discount off these titles by entering the promotional code **app** when ordering online at **www.mcgraw-hill.co.uk/app**

Guided Tour

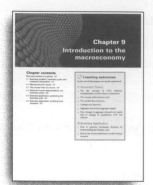

Learning outcomes

Each chapter opens with a set of learning outcomes, summarizing what you will learn from each chapter

Key terms

These are highlighted throughout the chapter, so that you can clarify key terms as you work through the topics

Figures and tables

Each chapter provides a number of figures and tables which will help you to visualize the various economic models, and illustrate and summarize important concepts

Business applications

Throughout the book these contemporary applications bring the economic theory to life by applying topics to real life business situations

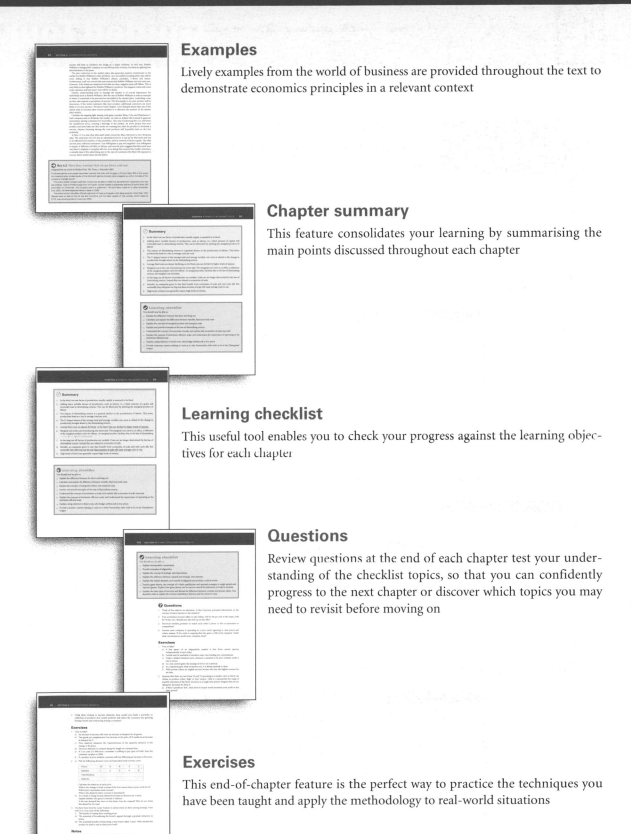

Examples

Lively examples from the world of business are provided throughout the text to demonstrate economics principles in a relevant context

Chapter summary

This feature consolidates your learning by summarising the main points discussed throughout each chapter

Learning checklist

This useful tool enables you to check your progress against the learning objectives for each chapter

Questions

Review questions at the end of each chapter test your understanding of the checklist topics, so that you can confidently progress to the next chapter or discover which topics you may need to revisit before moving on

Exercises

This end-of-chapter feature is the perfect way to practice the techniques you have been taught and apply the methodology to real-world situations

Section I
Introduction

Section contents

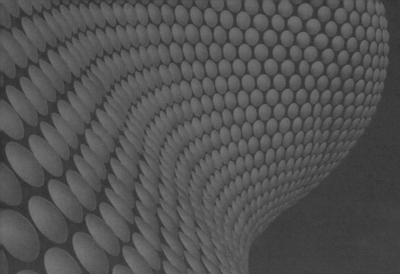

Chapter 1
Economics
for business

Chapter contents

 Learning outcomes

By the end of this chapter you should understand:

Economic Theory

- Economics is the study of how society resolves the problem of scarcity

- The concept of opportunity cost

- The difference between microeconomics and macroeconomics

- The difference between market and planned economies

Business Application

- How firms operate within microeconomic and macroeconomic environments

Economics for business at a glance

The issue

What is economics and how does economics relate to business?

The understanding

Economics seeks to understand the functioning of market places. Microeconomics examines consumers, firms and workers within markets, seeking to understand why prices change for particular products, what influences the costs of firms and in particular what will influence a firm's level of profitability. Macroeconomics examines the whole economy as one very large market. Macroeconomics seeks to address how the government might manage the entire economy to deliver stable economic growth. Through the development of the production possibility frontier and an initial discussion of markets the basic economic concepts will be introduced to you.

The usefulness

Firms operate within an economic environment. The revenue they receive from selling a product is determined within a market. Furthermore, the cost that the firm has to pay for its labour, raw materials and equipment are also priced within markets. Microeconomics addresses the various market influences that impact upon a firm's revenues and costs. Macroeconomics addresses the economy level issues which similarly affect a firm's revenues and costs. Understanding, reacting to, and possibly even controlling micro- and macroeconomic influences on the firm are crucial business skills.

1.1 What is economics?

Think about everything you would like to own, or consume. Table 1.1 contains a list of material items as examples, but it could equally contain items such as a healthy life and peace in the world.

Table 1.1 Wish list

Big house	Luxury restaurant meals
Luxury car	Designer clothes
Top of the range mobile phone	Membership of a fitness club
Holiday in an exotic location	A case (or two) of fine wine
Designer shoes	Plasma TV
Swiss watch	Games console
Digital camcorder	Tickets to the Monaco Grand Prix

Now list the resources that might contribute to paying for these desirable items; Table 1.2 shows ours.

Table 1.2 Resources list

Salary	Royalties from book
Consulting fees	Generous friends

You will be quick to note that the wish list is significantly longer than the resources list and there will be a significant gap between the expense required by the wish list and the likely yield of the resources list.

So we have a problem: we have a wish list that is very long and a resources list that is very short. What will we spend our resources on and what will we decide to leave in the shops? This problem is economics, one which recognizes the difference between **infinite wants** and **finite resources**.

Infinite wants are the limitless desires to consume goods and services.

Finite resources are the limited amount of resources that enable the production and purchase of goods and services.

We as individuals would all like to consume more of everything; bigger houses, bigger cars. But we only have finite resources with which to meet all our wants.[1] Firms also have infinite wants. They would like to be operating in more countries, selling larger product ranges. But firms are limited by their access to shareholders' funds and good labour. Governments too have infinite wants, providing more healthcare and better education, but are limited by their access to tax receipts.

Factors of production

Factors of production are resources needed to make goods and services: land, labour, capital and enterprise.

Economists start their analysis by focusing on the entire economy and noting that there are a variety of wants from individuals, firms and governments, and only a limited number of resources, or **factors of production**, which economists group into four categories: land, labour, capital and enterprise.

Land is where raw materials come from: oil, gas, base metals and other minerals. Labour is the ability of individuals to work. Capital is production machinery, computers, office space or retail shops. Enterprise is the final factor of production that brings land, labour and capital together and organizes them into units that can produce products in the pursuit of profit.

In spotting new market opportunities entrepreneurs are often innovators and risk-takers, committing resources to commercial projects, which may flourish or, alternatively, perish. Box 1.1 provides a bizarre example, but proven entrepreneurs might include Richard Branson of Virgin and Bill Gates of Microsoft; and in fact any individual who successfully sets up in business, whether it be as a car mechanic, a business consultant, or a hairdresser. They all organize resources in the pursuit of profit.

Production possibility frontier

The **production possibility frontier** shows the maximum number of products that can be produced by an economy with a given amount of resources.

The production possibility frontier is an important illustrative tool because it can be used to highlight important economic concepts. These are:

1 Finite resources

2 Opportunity costs

Box 1.1 **Business profile: 'It was all or bust'**

Adapted from the Daily Telegraph, 16 October, 2005

Michelle Mone, the creator of the Ultimo bra staked everything on building the better bra.

'I went to a dinner, and I was wearing a Wonderbra, and it was really uncomfortable. I was wearing a low-cut dress and the bra was pushing my boobs together and up, and it hurt. Then I got it. I knew what I was going to do – invent the perfect bra. I told my husband that night. He said I was mad. "For God's sake, what do you know about bras?" '

The answer was very little at first. But she learned quickly, working with scientists to create a bra that was a sort of strap-on bosom-amplifier. But inventing, patenting, producing and marketing a bra in the face of big competitors was very tough, and she and her husband almost went under. '[However], the thing is, I can do the research. I do the research all the time because I've got boobs and you haven't.' She offers a smile of impregnable certainty and tinks a teaspoon against her coffee cup.

The Ultimo has been a commercial success helped by high profile wearers such as Julia Roberts.

3   Macro- and microeconomics

4   Planned, market and mixed economies. We will discuss each in turn.

Finite resources

Figure 1.1 shows the production possibility frontier for an imaginary economy that only produces two goods, pizza and beer, and highlights the constraint created by access to only a finite amount of resources. With a fixed quantity of resources an infinite amount of beer, or pizzas, cannot be produced. If all resources were allocated to the production of

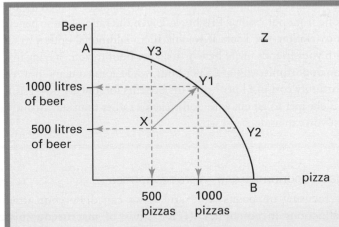

Figure 1.1 **Production possibility frontier**

The production possibility frontier shows the maximum amounts of beer and pizza that can be produced with a fixed amount of resources. At Y1 1000 litres of beer and 1000 pizzas can be produced. At Y3 more beer can be produced but some pizza production has to be sacrificed, while at Y2 beer can be sacrificed in order to produce more pizzas. Z cannot be achieved with current resource levels and X represents unemployment with production of beer and pizzas below the optimal levels attainable on the frontier, such as Y1, Y2 and Y3 beer, then we would be at point A on the diagram, with a maximum amount of beer being produced and no pizzas. But if all resources were allocated to pizzas, then we would be at point B, with a maximum number of pizzas being produced and no beer. The curve between points A and B indicates all the maximum combinations of beer and pizza that can be produced. The frontier shows what it is possible to produce with a limited amount of resources.

Operating on the frontier is optimal, all finite resources are employed. Operating at a point such as Z is currently impossible. The economy does not have the resources to produce at Z. Operating at X is inefficient, because some resources must be unemployed. More output could be produced by employing all factors of production and moving towards the frontier.

Opportunity costs

Opportunity costs are the benefits forgone from the next best alternative.

If pizza production is reduced in order to make more beer, then the **opportunity cost** consists of the benefits that could have been received from the pizzas that have not been made. Opportunity costs give the production possibility frontier a negative slope; simply, more pizzas must mean less beer. Reading this book now has an opportunity cost. You could be watching TV. Recalling that the economic problem is one of infinite wants and finite resources, ideally you will try to make your opportunity cost as low as possible. With your limited resources you will try to maximize your gains from consumption. This way you are sacrificing the least amount of benefit.

◎ Maximizing gains

If the benefit of reading this book to you can be estimated at £1 per hour and the benefit of watching TV can be estimated at £0.50 per hour, then the opportunity cost of reading this book, rather than watching TV is £0.50, the benefit you have given up. In contrast, if you watched TV, then the opportunity cost would be £1, the benefit forgone from not reading this book. Given the ratio of these benefits, you can minimize your opportunity cost by reading this book. If we add in an additional option to reflect the true student lifestyle, a night out with your friends might be worth £5 per hour to you. Staying in and reading this book would then represent an opportunity cost of £5 per hour, while going out and not reading the book would only represent an opportunity cost of £1 per hour, the benefits forgone by not reading this book. In terms of opportunity cost it is cheaper to go out with your friends rather than stay in and read this book. If you fail this module, at least you can understand why.

Macroeconomics and microeconomics

Macroeconomics is the study of how the entire economy works.
Microeconomics is the study of how individuals make economic decisions within an economy.

By focusing on points X, Y and Z we can draw your attention to two important distinctions in economics, (i) the study of **macroeconomics** and (ii) the study of **microeconomics**.

Macroeconomics

Points X and Z represent mainly macroeconomic problems. At point X the economy is not operating at its optimal level; we said point X was likely to be associated with unemployment. This occurs during a recession. Part of macroeconomics is in understanding what creates a recession and how to remedy a recession. Governments and the central bank adjust interest rates, taxation and government spending to try to move the economy from point X towards point Y. Point Z is also a macroeconomic issue. The economy cannot achieve point Z now, but in the future the economy could grow and eventually attain point Z. How do we develop policies to move the economy over the long term to point Z? This question has been the recent focus of economic policymakers with the focus placed upon the issue of 'sustainable economic growth'.

Microeconomics

Microeconomics places the focus of analysis on the behaviour of individuals, firms or consumers. Rather than looking at the economy as a whole, it attempts to understand why consumers prefer particular products. How will changes in income, or prices influence consumption patterns? In relation to firms, micro-economists are interested in the motives for supplying products. Do firms wish to maximize sales, profits, or market share? What factors influence costs and how can firms manage costs? What determines the level of competition in a market and how can firms compete against each other?

By focusing on individual consumers, firms and the interaction between the two, the economist is particularly interested in the functioning of markets. This particular aspect of economics can be highlighted by examining movements along the production possibility frontier. Point Y1 on the frontier has been described as being efficient. But points Y2 and Y3 are also on the frontier and are, therefore, equally efficient. At Y1 the economy produces a balanced mix of pizza and beer. At Y2 the economy specializes more in pizza and at Y3 the economy specializes more in beer production. How will the economy decide between operating at Y1, Y2 and Y3? The answer lies in understanding resource allocation mechanisms.

Planned, market and mixed economies

Planned economy

In a **planned economy** the government plans whether the economy should operate at point Y1 or another point. Until the last decade these systems were common in the former Soviet Bloc and China.

In a **planned economy**, the government decides how resources are allocated to the production of particular products.

Market economy

In a **market economy** there are two important groups, consumers that buy products and firms that sell products. Consumers buy products because they seek the benefits associated with the consumption of the product. For example, you eat food because it stops you feeling hungry; and you drive a car because it helps you to travel between various locations. Similarly, firms sell products in order to make a profit.

In the market place information is exchanged between consumers and firms. This information relates to the prices at which consumers are willing to buy products and similarly the prices at which firms are willing to sell. For any particular product you will have a maximum price at which you are willing to buy. The more desirable you find the product, the greater will be your maximum price. In contrast, firms will have a minimum price at which they are willing to sell. The easier, or cheaper, it is to make the good, the lower this minimum price will be. If the minimum price at which firms are willing to sell is less than consumers' maximum willingness to pay, then the potential for a market in the good exists. Firms can make the product in the clear expectation of making a profit.

Firms are likely to move their productive resources – land, labour, capital and enterprise – to the markets that present the greatest opportunities for profit. Given our discussion above, profits will vary with the willingness of consumers to pay and the costs

In a **market economy**, the government plays no role in allocating resources. Instead markets allocate resources to the production of various products.

incurred by firms. If consumers are willing to pay higher prices, or production costs fall, then profits will increase. Increasing profits will lead firms to move resources into the market. In contrast, as consumers reduce their willingness to buy a product, or if firms' costs increase, profits will fall and firms will look to reallocate their resources into more profitable markets.

 Pizza and beer

In our pizza and beer example, let us consider the following: we are at point Y1 and suddenly scientists show that beer is very good for your health. Following this news, we would expect consumers to buy more beer. As beer increases in popularity, beer producers are able to sell for a higher price and make greater profits. As consumers allocate more of their income to beer, pizza producers would begin to lose sales and profits. Over time pizza-makers would recognize that consumers have reduced their consumption of pizzas. In response, pizza producers would begin to close down their operations and move their resources into the popular beer market. The economy moves from Y1 to Y3 in Figure 1.1.

Comparing command and market economies

Market economies rely on a very quick and efficient communication of information that occurs through prices. Firms ordinarily set a price that indicates their willingness to sell. Consumers communicate their willingness to buy by purchasing the product at the given price. The problem of what should be produced and what should not be produced is solved by the price system.

The command (or planned) economy, in setting production levels for various goods and services, requires similar market-based information regarding the costs of production and the consumption requirements of consumers. But how would you go about setting food, clothing, drink, transport and education output levels for an economy? You might conduct a questionnaire survey asking consumers to rank the different products by level of importance. But this has a number of problems. It is costly, the respondents might not represent the views of all consumers and it might not be timely with the questionnaire only being carried out every couple of years. The collection of information required for effective planning is very complicated and costly within a command economy, especially when compared with the simple and efficient exchange of information in the market economy through the pricing system. It is of little surprise that in recent years, planned economies have become less popular.

Mixed economy

In a **mixed economy** the government and the private sector jointly solve economic problems.

In reality many economies function as a mixture of planned and market economies.

For example, within many modern economies the sale of groceries is a purely market solution with private firms deciding what they will offer to consumers within their own supermarkets. The provision of public health care is an example of the government deciding what healthcare treatments will be offered to the population. Economies differ in the degree to which they are mixed. The US has arguably less planned provision of goods and services than some member states of the EU. At the other extreme, economies such as Cuba are more dependent upon planning, with only a few (but perhaps an increasing number of) private enterprises.

In summary, economics studies how individuals, firms, governments and economies deal with the problem of infinite wants and finite resources. Microeconomics examines the economic issues faced by individuals and firms, while macroeconomics studies the workings and performance of the entire economy. We will now indicate why an understanding of economics can provide an essential understanding for business.

1.2 **Why study economics for business?**

Business and management draw upon a number of different disciplines including, but not exclusively, accounting and finance, human resource management, operations management, marketing, law, statistics and economics. Each discipline has a particular focus and set of issues that it specializes in understanding.

The economist's analysis of business begins with a simple assumption: firms are in business to make profits for their owners. Moreover, firms are in business to maximize profits, or make the highest amount of profit possible. The assumption that firms are profit maximizers is clearly a simplification. Firms represent a collection of workers, managers, shareholders, consumers and perhaps individuals living within the locality of the firm's operations. Each of these groups may have a different interest within the firm. For example, shareholders may seek greater profit, but workers and managers may seek increased wages. These conflicts generate complexity within the organizational environment of firms. Economists try to simplify the complex nature of reality. Therefore, rather than attempt an understanding of all the complex interrelationships within a firm, economists simply assume that the firm is in business to maximize profits. Economists are not arguing that the complex interrelationships between the various interest groups within a firm are not important. However, economists are assuming that without profits, firms would find it difficult to survive financially. Therefore, while subjects such as human resource management, organization theory, and corporate social responsibility focus upon how the firm might manage the conflicting relationships between the competing interest groups of shareholders, workers and wider society, business economists have focused upon an understanding of firms' profits.

Firms, as profit-making organizations, can be viewed as a combination of revenue-based cash flows going in, and cost-based cash flows going out. Within this view of firms, economics for business can be simplified to an analysis of the economic influences that enhance revenues and reduce costs, thereby increasing firm-level financial performance or, more directly, profit.

In Figure 1.2 the firm is positioned between its revenue and its costs. In placing the firm in the middle of the diagram it is also recognized that the firm operates within micro and macroeconomic environments. The micro and macro environments are covered in detail by the various chapters within this book but, importantly, and perhaps simplistically, each chapter adds to an understanding of how the firm can improve its revenue and/or cost position. Broad areas of interest and importance are now discussed.

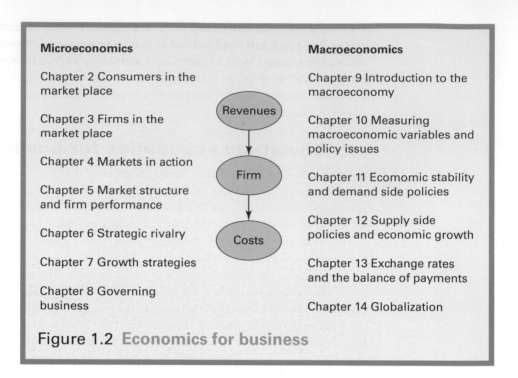

Microeconomics

Chapter 2 Consumers in the market place

Chapter 3 Firms in the market place

Chapter 4 Markets in action

Chapter 5 Market structure and firm performance

Chapter 6 Strategic rivalry

Chapter 7 Growth strategies

Chapter 8 Governing business

Macroeconomics

Chapter 9 Introduction to the macroeconomy

Chapter 10 Measuring macroeconomic variables and policy issues

Chapter 11 Ecomomic stability and demand side policies

Chapter 12 Supply side policies and economic growth

Chapter 13 Exchange rates and the balance of payments

Chapter 14 Globalization

Figure 1.2 **Economics for business**

Markets and competition

The particular focus of economics is on the functioning of markets. Markets are important for firms in a number of ways. First, a market place is where a firm will sell its product and, therefore, generate revenue. Second, a firm's inputs – land, labour, capital and enterprise – are all purchased through markets and, therefore, markets influence a firm's level of costs. The level of competition varies across markets: some are highly competitive, others are not. Throughout life, if you wish to be a winner, it is easier to achieve success when the competition is weak; and business is no different. In highly competitive business environments prices will fall, while in low competitive environments price competition will be less severe. If interested in enhancing revenues, it is important to understand how to recognize issues likely to promote competition and influences that will enable competition to be managed and controlled. It is also important to understand how a firm can change its mode of operations in order to improve its competitive advantage. Growth by acquisition of a rival clearly reduces competition, but growth by the purchase of a raw material supplier into the industry also places your rivals at a disadvantage, because you then own what your rivals need. Good business people understand how to manage and exploit competitive opportunities.

Government intervention

Governments can also intervene in markets. Society, or government, does not view excessive pollution of the environment as desirable. Some pollution may be an unavoidable consequence of beneficial production. In order to manage pollution the government can attempt to influence the commercial activities of firms. This usually involves increased taxes for firms that pollute, and subsidies, or grants, for firms that attempt to operate in a more environmentally friendly manner. Therefore, the government can seek to influence firms' costs and revenues, boosting them when the firm operates in the interest of society, and reducing profits when the firm operates against the public interest. Firms need to be able to understand when their activities are likely to attract the attention of government, or pressure groups, and what policies could be imposed upon them.

Globalization

Finally, firms do not operate within singular markets; rather, they function within massive macroeconomic systems. Traditionally such systems have been the national economy but, more recently, firms have begun to operate within an increasingly global environment. Therefore, in order for firms to be successful they need to understand how macroeconomic events and global change will impact on their current and future operations.

National economies have a tendency to move from economic booms into economic recessions. If a firm's sales, and therefore revenues, are determined by the state of the macroeconomy, then it is important for the firm to understand why an economy might move from a position of economic prosperity, to one of economic recession. Similarly, during a recession firms struggle to sell all of their output. Price discounts can make products and inputs – such as labour, raw materials and capital equipment – cheaper, thereby reducing a firm's costs.

While understanding the state of the macroeconomy is important, it is also beneficial to have an understanding of how the government might try to manage the economy. How will changes in taxation affect consumers, firms and the health of the economy? How will interest rate changes influence inflation and the state of the economy? These are common governmental policy decisions with important implications for business.

Moreover, within the global economy matters of international trade, exchange rates, European Monetary Union and the increasing globalization of business all impact upon the operations and competitive position of business. Operating internationally may enable a firm to source cheaper production, or access new market and revenue streams. However, equally, international firms can access UK markets, leading to an increase in competition for UK domestic producers. Successful companies will not only recognize these issues but, more importantly, they will also understand how these issues relate to themselves and business generally. From this, strategies will be developed and the firm will attempt to manage its competitive environment.

In order to develop your understanding of these issues, this book is separated into a number of parts that build on each other. In Section II you will be introduced to the workings of market places. Section III will develop an understanding of competition in markets. This will then be followed by an overview of firm governance by shareholders and government. This will conclude the microeconomic section of the book. Macroeconomics is split into two obvious parts: macroeconomics in the domestic economy and macroeconomics in the global economy. At the domestic level you will be introduced to how the macroeconomy works, the factors leading to the level of economic activity and the options available to a government trying to control the economy. At the global level you will be provided with an understanding of international trade and the workings of exchange rates. This will lead to the important issue of European Monetary Union. Finally, an assessment of globalization and the implications for business will be provided.

In order to highlight the relevance of economics to business, each chapter begins with a business problem. Theory relevant to an understanding of the problem is then developed. Each chapter closes with two applications of the theory to further highlight the relevance of the theory to business and management. In this way economic theory is clearly sandwiched between real-world business issues and practices, highlighting for you that economics, where appropriate, is a subject to be applied in the understanding of business problems.

1.3 **Appendix: the economist's approach**

Economics as a subject has a number of characteristics associated with it and, to aid your learning, it is worth pointing them out to you.

Language

The economist makes use of terms and phrases that are particular and peculiar to economics. For example, from the above discussion economics is the study of why you cannot have everything. But the economist talks about infinite wants, finite resources, opportunity costs and production possibility frontiers. Using the economic terminology will help you. Economists use particular terminology because it helps them to understand each other when communicating ideas. Succinct terms, such as opportunity cost, once understood, convey complex ideas quickly to anyone else who understands the phrase.

Abstract models

Models or **theories** are frameworks for organizing how we think about an economic problem.

Economists think about the world in terms of **models** or **theories**.

Economists recognize that the world is extremely complicated and, therefore, prefer to make models using simplifying assumptions. The complexity of the real world is stripped out in favour of a simple analysis of the central, or essential, issues. As an example, consider the box opposite, where we discuss how an economist might approach how David Beckham bends free kicks.

Normative and positive economics

Positive economics studies objective or scientific explanations of how the economy works.
Normative economics offers recommendations based on personal value judgements.

A **positive economics** question and a **normative economics** statement will help to clarify the differences:

Positive question: what level of production will maximize the firm's profits?
Normative statement: firms should maximize profits.

The positive question seeks to address a technical point – can economics identify the output level where firms will make the largest profit? The normative statement, in contrast, seeks to assert the opinion that profit maximization is best – it is making a value judgement. In the case of the positive question economists can make a response with theory consisting of a set of accepted rational arguments that provide a technical answer to the question. However, in respect of the normative statement, economists can only reply with similar, or alternative value statements: for example, firms should not focus entirely on profit maximization; I believe they should also consider the needs of wider stakeholders such as workers, the environment, suppliers and customers.

This is an important distinction. Positive economics is the technical and objective pursuit of economic understanding. As a subject it seeks to provide answers to questions and propose solutions to problems. Normative economics is different in that it does not seek to answer questions; rather, it seeks to assert and represent particular beliefs – which are difficult, if not impossible, to provide positive answers to.

Bend it like Beckham

In modelling David Beckham's ability to bend free kicks, economists would strip out the complex issues, such as natural talent, good practice and high-pressure championship experience, and take the simplifying assumption that David Beckham behaves like a world-class physicist. David Beckham must behave like a highly accomplished physicist because he can clearly calculate all the angles and force needed to bend a free kick and score a goal.

In reality David Beckham probably has no more understanding of physics than many of us. So, to say that David Beckham behaves like a physicist seems peculiar. However, the important point is that the theory *predicts*; it need not *explain*. The theory does not *explain* why David Beckham can bend free kicks and score goals with such accuracy. But it does *predict* that David Beckham will score spectacular goals if he behaves like a world-class physicist. This is because a leading physicist, indeed any physicist, could use the Newtonian laws of motion to work out the perfect angle and trajectory for the football to travel in a spectacular arc into the back of the net. But why should economists wish to develop strange abstract assumptions about reality, leading to theories that predict, as opposed to theories that can explain?

The answer to this question is that economists try to keep things simple and extract only the important points for analysis. The world is very complex, so what we try to do as economists is to simplify things to the important points. David Beckham is probably a football player because of some natural talent, a good deal of practice, championship experience and perhaps some poorer opponents. All these would explain why David Beckham can score great goals. But to keep things simple we will assume he behaves like a leading physicist. If theoretically true, then David Beckham will also be an amazing free kick specialist. Therefore, the predictive approach is a theoretical short cut that enables economists to simplify the complex nature of reality. So, whenever you come across a theory in this book that is not a true reflection of reality, do not worry. We are happy in our little fantasy world where people like David Beckham double up as Einstein.

Economics is not peculiar in exhibiting a tension between objective and subjective approaches to reason. In art, the positive approach may centre on a technical understanding of various media. But the use of these media, the choice of images to create and how to interpret them are all normative, value laden and subjective; as highlighted by the controversy surrounding the winner of the Turner Prize (see Box 1.2).

 Box 1.2 Forget painting, Turner Prize is awarded to an old boatshed

Adapted from an article by Nigel Reynolds, the Daily Telegraph, 6 December, 2005

The Turner Prize was awarded last night to Simon Starling, a conceptualist whose installations are so odd and difficult to analyse that he is known on the art circuit as 'the nutty professor'. His victory may at least do something to promote the ancient craft of carpentry with his entry Shedboatshed.

He bought and dismantled a shed, built a boat from some of its planks and loaded the remaining ones into the boat, which he then rowed to Basle in Switzerland, where he was having an exhibition. He dismantled the boat and faithfully rebuilt the boathouse and put it on display.

The Tate's selection panel, having scoured the country over the past dozen years to find transvestite potters, dirty beds and sliced cows, was possibly too exhausted to whip up headlines again. Shedboatshed, described by Richard Dorment, the *Daily Telegraph*'s art critic, as 'a parable about ecology, about recycling, about saving materials and energy', is a typical piece. Critics are divided over his work. Dorment has praised Shedboatshed, but Tom Lubbock in the *Independent* condemned it as 'really boring'.

Diagrams

Quickly flick through all the pages of this book. How many diagrams did you see? Economists like diagrams. For the economist diagrams are an effective way of communicating complex ideas. In order to develop your understanding of economics you will need to develop your competence in this area, as it is almost impossible to manage without them, which is disappointing for any of you who detest them with a passion.

As a brief reminder a diagram, at least as we will be using them, provides a visual indication of the relationship between two variables. For example, consider a fridge and an oven. Neither are currently switched on. When we do switch them on we are interested in seeing how the temperature inside the oven and the fridge changes the longer each appliance is on. This is not rocket science: the fridge will get colder and the oven hotter. A maths teacher would say that there is a **positive relationship** between time and temperature in the cooker.

In our example of the oven, as time increases – 1 minute, 2 minutes, etc. – the temperature of the oven also increases. Our two variables, time and temperature, increase together.

In contrast, the maths teacher would say that there is a **negative relationship** between time and temperature in the fridge.

In our example of the fridge, as time increases, the temperature of the fridge decreases. Figure 1.3 is a diagram showing the positive relationship between time and temperature within the oven, while Figure 1.4 is a diagram of the negative relationship between time and the temperature inside the fridge.

We will be doing nothing more complicated than this. We might reasonably argue that as prices increase consumers will buy less; we therefore expect to see a negative relationship between the price of a product and the amount of the product purchased by consumers. Similarly, in the case of a positive relationship we might argue that consumer expenditure increases as income levels rise. Essentially the diagrams are a simple visual illustration of the relationship between two variables. The more you try to understand them and gain confidence in using them, the easier economics becomes.

> A **positive relationship** exists between two variables if the values for both variables increase and decrease together.

> A **negative relationship** exists between two variables if the values for one variable increase (decrease) as the value of the other variable decreases (increases).

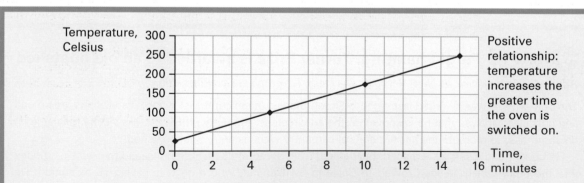

Figure 1.3 **Positive relationship: oven temperature against time**

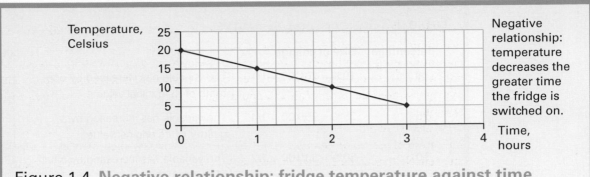

Figure 1.4 **Negative relationship: fridge temperature against time**

Economic data

Economists make use of data to examine relationships between variables. Data can be categorized into **time series data** and **cross-sectional data**.

For example, the price of a cinema ticket recorded for each year between 1990 and 2008 is an example of one variable measured at various points in time. The time period between each observation is usually fixed. So, in the case of cinema tickets, the variable, price, is measured once every year. However, time series can be measured in a variety of periods – yearly, monthly, daily, hourly, or by the minute. The price of shares on the London stock market is measured in all of these formats.

The profits of individual companies in the supermarket industry in 2008 would be an example of cross-sectional data, with profits of different companies being measured at the same point in time.

Rather than measure the profits of individual supermarkets in 2004 we could also measure individual companies' profits in 2007, 2006, 2005 and so on. This way we are combining cross-sections and time, thus providing us with **panel data**.

> **Time series data** are the measurements of one variable at different points in time.
>
> **Cross-sectional data** are the measurements of one variable at the same point in time across different individuals.

> **Panel data** combines cross-sectional and time series data.

Using data

In using data economists employ a number of simple mathematical techniques, including calculations of percentages and the use of index numbers. Both are simple to understand, but a refresher may help your understanding.

In order to measure the change in a variable we can use **percentages**.

We can use Table 1.3 to understand how big a particular percentage change is.

Since a percentage measures the rate of change in a variable, we need both the variable's original and new value.

> A **percentage** measures the change in a variable as a fraction of 100.

We calculate the percentage as the absolute change divided by the original number, then multiplied by 100:

$$\frac{(\text{New value} - \text{Original value})}{\text{Original value}} \times 100$$

For example, the share price of Company A was £2.00 in 2007 and £3.00 in 2008. The percentage change is therefore:

$$\frac{(\pounds3.00 - \pounds2.00)}{\pounds2.00} \times 100 = 50\%$$

Table 1.3 Percentage changes

Percentage	Size of change	
10	10% = 10/100 = 1/10.	The variable has increased by one tenth of its original value
25	25% = 25/100 = 1/4.	The variable has increased by a quarter of its original value
50	50% = 50/100 = 1/2.	The variable has increased by a half of its original value
100	100% = 100/100 = 1.	The variable has increased by the same amount as its original value; it has doubled in size
200	200% = 200/100 = 2.	The variable has increased by twice its original value; it has tripled in size
500	500% = 500/100 = 5.	The variable has increased by five times its original size

Index numbers

Index numbers are used to transform a data series into a series with a base value of 100.

As an example of the use of **index numbers** take the data series in Table 1.4, which measures the price of a pint of beer.

Table 1.4 Index numbers

Year	Price of beer	Index
2005	£1.50	100
2006	£1.60	107
2007	£1.80	120
2008	£2.00	133

The price of beer is in pounds sterling. To convert this data series into a unitless series with a base value of 100, we first need to select the base year. In Table 1.4 we have selected 2005 as the base year. In order to generate the index we simply take the price of beer in any year, divide by the base year value and times by 100. So in 2005 we have (£1.50/£1.50) × 100 = 100. In 2006 we have (£1.60/£1.50) × 100 = 107.

A sensible question is to ask why we use index numbers? There are a number of reasons. The first is to recognize that since we have a base value of 100 it is very easy to calculate the percentage change in the variable over time. From Table 1.4 we can readily see that between 2005 and 2008 beer has increased by 33 per cent.

The second reason is that index numbers facilitate averaging. Assume we are interested in how prices across the economy are rising. If an index was created not only for beer prices but also for car prices, cigarettes and in fact all products that are commonly sold, then an average of all the indices would enable an assessment of average price rises in the UK.

The Retail Price Index does exactly this. It is an average of many individual product price indices. The average is weighted by the importance of the product within the average household's consumption. For example, since housing costs represent a major element of household consumption, the house price index receives a higher weight in the Retail Price Index than the price index for sweets and confectionery. The FTSE 100 is another example of an index and combines as an average the prices of all shares in the FTSE 100. The value of the index increases (decreases) if on average shares in the FTSE 100 increase (decrease).

In summary, index numbers are used to create data series that are unitless. They have a base year of 100 and can be used to calculate percentage changes from the base year with ease. By virtue of having a common base year value of 100, index numbers can also be used to create averages from many different indices, such as price level indices or stock market indices.

Summary

1 Economics assumes that everybody would like to consume more of everything, but we only have a limited amount of resources with which to facilitate such consumption.

2 Economic factor resources are split into four categories: land, labour, capital and enterprise.

3 The production possibility frontier is used by economists to provide an illustration of finite resources. The production possibility frontier shows the maximum total output that can be produced using the limited amount of factor inputs. As more of one good is produced, less of the remaining good can be produced

4 Opportunity cost is measured as the benefits forgone from the next best alternative.

5 Operating on the frontier represents full employment and is defined as productively efficient. Operating inside the frontier is inefficient as the output of both goods can be increased by making an efficient utilization of the underemployed factor resources. Operating outside the frontier is currently impossible. However, over time the economy may become more productively efficient, producing more output for a given level of input; or the economy may gain access to additional factor inputs, also enabling output to increase.

6 Macroeconomics is an examination of the economy as a whole and, therefore, considers issues such as the level of economic activity, the level of prices, unemployment, economic growth, and international trade and exchange rates.

7 Microeconomics focuses upon the economic decision-making of individuals and firms. Microeconomics examines how individual markets function and how firms compete with one another.

8 Where on the frontier an economy operates, producing more beer than pizza, or vice versa, depends upon the resource allocation mechanism. In command economies the government plans how much of each good to produce. In market economies the interaction of consumers and firms through the pricing system of the market directs resources away from non-profitable markets and towards profitable ones.

9   Economics has a language and terminology; this aids communication of ideas and should be mastered.

10 Economics uses abstract models. In reality the world is very complex. In economics simplifying assumptions are deployed in order to make the world simple. As a consequence, an explanation of reality is often sacrificed for prediction.

11 Positive economics seeks to address objective questions with theory. Normative economics seeks to assert value judgements on what is preferable economic behaviour.

12 Economists place an emphasis on diagrams when explaining ideas and theories. A positive relationship exists between two variables if both variables increase together. A negative relationship between two variables exists when as one variable increases the other decreases.

13 Economic data can be time series, cross-sectional or a combination of the two (panel data). Time series data are the measurements of one variable at various points in time. Cross-sectional data are the measurements of one variable at the same point in time, but across a number of firms or individuals.

14 A percentage measures the change in a variable as a fraction of 100. You can calculate a percentage change as (New value − Original value)/Original value × 100.

15 An index converts a variable into a unitless data series with a base year of 100. This is achieved by dividing each value by the base year value and then multiplying by 100.

16 Index numbers can be combined to create averages. Common examples are the retail price index and the FTSE 100. Changes in the individual price indices then lead to changes in the average indices.

 ## Learning checklist

You should now be able to:

- Explain the economic problem of scarcity
- Understand the concept of opportunity cost
- Explain the difference between microeconomics and macroeconomics
- Highlight the differences between market and planned economies
- Explain why an understanding of economics is important for business

 ## Questions

1   List goods, or services, that compete for your income. Similarly, list activities that compete for your time. In deciding what you will spend your income on and how you will allocate your time, do you minimize your opportunity costs?

2   Which of the following statements relate to macro or microeconomics? (a) During the last 12 months average car prices have fallen; (b) inflation for the past 12 months has been 3.5 per cent; (c) strong sales in the housing market have prevented the Bank of England from reducing interest rates.

3   Why does business need to understand the functioning of markets?

4   Why does business need to understand the functioning of the economy?

Questions 5 and 6 relate to material within the appendix

5   Which of the following is positive and which is normative? (a) It is in the long-term interest of the UK to be a member of the Euro; (b) Will entry into the Euro reduce UK inflation?

6   Using the data listed below, plot house prices on the Y axis and time on the X axis. Is there a positive or negative relationship between time and house prices? Convert the data series on house prices into an index using 2000 as the base year.

Year	Average price of a house
2000	£60 000
2001	£75 000
2002	£80 000
2003	£90 000
2004	£110 000
2005	£120 000

Calculate the percentage increase in house prices for the following periods: 2000–01, 2001–02, 2002–03, 2003–04, 2004–05.

Exercises

1   True or False?
    a)   Economics is about human behaviour and so cannot be a science.
    b)   An expansion of the economy's productive capacity would be reflected in an outward movement of the production possibility frontier.
    c)   China is an example of a command economy in which private markets play no part.
    d)   When you make a choice there will always be an opportunity cost.
    e)   Firms should operate in the interests of their wider stakeholders is an example of a normative economic statement.
    f)   Economists assume that business operates in a purely economic environment.

2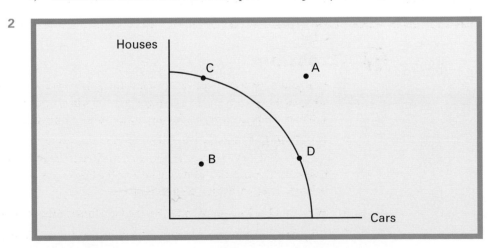

a) Which combination of goods can be produced, with surplus resources being unemployed?
b) Which combination of goods would represent full employment, with resources mainly allocated to the production of houses?
c) Which combination of goods cannot currently be achieved?
d) Which combination of goods represents full employment, with resources mainly allocated to the production of cars.
e) How might the level of output identified in c) be achieved in the future?
f) Can you envisage circumstances under which the production possibility frontier could move to the left?

Notes

1 This is true at least at one point in time. In the future capital could be expanded by firms investing in additional capital.

Section II
Understanding markets

Section contents

Chapter 2
Consumers in the market place

Chapter contents

 Learning outcomes

By the end of this chapter you should understand:

Economic Theory

- Demand curves

- Factors leading to a change in demand

- The price elasticity of demand

- Cross price and income elasticity

Business Application

- How measures of elasticity can lead to improved management of total revenue

- How an appreciation of consumer surplus can lead to enhanced pricing strategies

Demand theory at a glance

The issue

Setting the price for a product is crucial for the product's and a company's success. But what is the best price for a particular product?

The understanding

As a product becomes more expensive, consumers will begin to demand less. In some markets consumers will be very sensitive to a change in price. In others they may not react at all. This reaction is measured using elasticity. An examination of demand theory and the concept of elasticity will develop these ideas more fully.

The usefulness

If the price of the product can be made to rise at a quicker rate than the decline in demand, then total revenue will rise. Therefore, by understanding how consumers respond to price changes we can optimize the price charged.

2.1 Business problem: what is the best price?

If, as suggested in Box 2.1, pricing is so important, what is the best price? The best price is determined by the firm's objectives. The following provides a common list of objectives for a firm:

1   Maximize the amount of profit made by the firm

2   Maximize the market share for the firm's product

3   Maximize the firm's total revenues

 Box 2.1 **Pricing and profits**

Choosing the wrong pricing strategy can be a costly mistake

Published 4 June 2003, Wharton Business School

According to Raju and Zhang from Wharton Business School, research suggests that pricing strategies can have a huge influence on company profits. They cite a study of more than 2400 companies by McKinsey in 1992 showing the impact that various decisions would have on the bottom line: a 1% reduction in fixed costs improves profitability by 2.3%; a 1% increase in sales volume will result in a 3.3% increase in profit; a 1% reduction in variable costs will prompt a 7.8% rise in profit; but a 1% hike in pricing can boost profitability by 11%.

'In recent years, business people have paid attention to many things that can influence their companies' success,' Zhang says. 'They've looked at organizational behavior, downsizing, benchmarking and reengineering, and companies have done a lot to cut costs. But they haven't spent as much time thinking about the best possible pricing strategies. I think the picture painted by McKinsey is still pretty much true today. There's a lot of room for profit improvement through better pricing strategies.'

These are all commercial objectives. Firms could also adopt non-commercial objectives, such as reducing environmental impact or being a socially responsible employer. But for the purpose of this chapter we will concentrate on the three objectives listed above. It is generally not possible for a firm to choose more than one of these objectives. For example, in order to maximize market share, a firm might reasonably be expected to reduce its prices in order to attract more customers. But by dropping its prices, the firm could be sacrificing profit. Therefore, we will assume that a firm seeks to maximize one of our three objectives[1] and the best price can be defined as the one that enables the firm to meet its preferred objective.

How are prices set? Take the case of supermarkets. When walking around a supermarket have you as a consumer ever set the price for a product? The answer is probably not. Now compare the case of supermarkets with buying a house, or a car. When we purchase a house, or a car we might make an opening offer to the vendor as part of a negotiation over the price. At the supermarket, by contrast, we would never consider negotiating over a trolley full of shopping; nor would we negotiate in many other types of shop, such as a clothing retailer. Admittedly, we may have an indirect effect on prices by refusing to buy a product that we consider too expensive but in the main it appears that supermarkets, retailers and perhaps even the producers of the products are controlling the prices that we have to pay.

As business students it is important to recognize the position of product suppliers. This is because control is essential when seeking to set the best price and achieve the firm's objectives. But herein lies the business problem: what is the best price? To illustrate the problem consider the following: very high sales can be generated with low prices, while very high prices will tend to generate low sales. But which option is preferable? As an example, we can show that these alternative scenarios can be similar. If a low price of £5 generates 10 sales, then total revenue is £50; if a high price of £10 generates only 5 sales, then total revenue is also £50. Given that these options are identical, a businessperson would really like to know if there is a pricing option of around £8 selling to 8 customers, making a total revenue of £64.

Whether £8 is the best price, or indeed whether £8.25 is even better, is a difficult question to address. When a national supermarket chain is selling beer, soap powder, or even oven chips by the hundreds of thousands, a small change in the price can generate huge changes in total revenue. By the end of this chapter you will understand how you assist the supermarkets in finding the best price. Every time you pass through the till at the supermarket, scanner data are stored and matched with promotional offers such as 'Buy One Get One Free'. This is then modelled and used to address strategic price changes.

It is clearly important to recognize that firms will price items relative to their cost structures. If a firm wishes to make a profit, then the price must be greater than costs. If the firm wishes to maximize market share, while not making a loss, then the price cannot fall below the cost of making the product. While recognizing the importance of costs, in this chapter we will simply focus on the interaction between pricing and consumers' willingness to buy a particular product. Through Chapters 3, 4 and 5 we will develop a fuller understanding of pricing decisions by recognizing both firms' cost structures and consumers' willingness to purchase. In this chapter we begin this analysis by developing a clear understanding of demand theory.

2.2 Introducing demand curves

The **demand curve** illustrates the relationship between price and quantity demanded of a particular product.

In attempting to understand consumer behaviour, economists use a very simple construct known as the **demand curve**.

Figure 2.1 is an example of a demand curve, where the line Q_D represents quantity demanded. The slope of the demand curve Q_D is negative. This simply depicts the rather obvious argument that as prices fall, more of a product will be demanded by consumers. Using our previous example, at a price of £10 the demand curve indicates that consumers across the market are willing to demand 5 units in total. But if the company dropped the price to £5 then it might expect to sell 10 units.

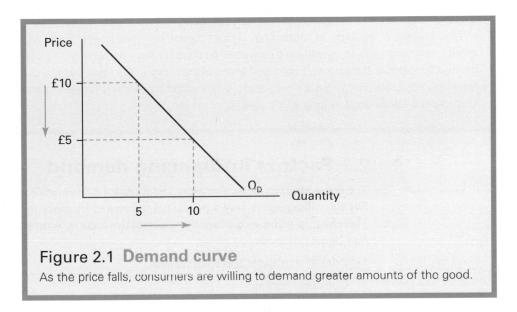

Figure 2.1 Demand curve
As the price falls, consumers are willing to demand greater amounts of the good.

The negative relationship between price and quantity demanded is often exploited by businesses. For example, Figure 2.1 could be an example of a 'buy one get one free' offer. Firms use such offers because they are sometimes reluctant to reduce the price of their product. This is because overt price reductions could lead to a retaliatory price war from rivals. Lower prices may also provide a signal to the market that the product is of an inferior quality. A 'buy one get one free' offer allows the published price to stay the same, but the effective price for consumers is halved. Under such an offer, consumers are more willing to demand the product and, not surprisingly, companies use such promotions to boost sales and gain market share.

Furthermore, we all like end-of-season sales at our favourite clothing retailers. But sales simply represent an attempt by the retailer to shift stock that we as consumers would not buy at the higher price and are, therefore, another example of the demand curve in action.

In Box 2.2 we have a business example of price cutting to attract demand. Even though consumers may prefer branded Cola, a price reduction by a rival brand will increase consumers' willingness to demand.

Box 2.2 Pricing and demand

Rival Big Cola is a big pain for Coke in Mexico

Adapted from an article by Marla Dickerson, New York Newsday, 2 January 2006

Big Cola has grabbed 5 per cent of Mexico's $6.5 billion soft-drink trade. And it has forced titans Coke and PepsiCo Inc. to lower prices in a country where they have long reaped some of their fattest profits.

Big Cola has done it without big-budget advertising, fancy trucks or an extensive product line. The secret: lots of cola for a little money. A 3.3-liter container of its flagship Big Cola brand sells for about $1.12, and sometimes as little as 86 cents on special.

The low-price strategy is attracting budget-conscious consumers such as Carlos Lopez. The construction worker was recently in a convenience store buying a monster bottle of Big Cola to share with his buddies back at the job site. Lopez said some of them prefer the Real Thing, and he admitted a lifelong fondness for Coke. But when it's his turn to buy a round, economics prevail. 'It's cheap,' he said of Big Cola. 'And it tastes good as long as it's cold.'

2.3 Factors influencing demand

The demand curve shows a negative relationship between price and quantity demanded. But the willingness to buy a product is influenced by more factors than simply price. Therefore, in order to capture these alternative factors, economists make reference to four broad categories:

1   Price of substitutes and complements

2   Consumer income

3   Tastes and preferences

4   Price expectations

Price of substitutes and complements

Substitutes are rival products; for example, a BMW car is a substitute for a Mercedes, or a bottle of wine from France is a substitute for a bottle from Australia.

Substitutes are competing products in the same market place, seeking to gain customers from their rivals. So, if French wine producers decided to reduce the price of their wine, they would hope to gain some of the Australian wine producers' customers. As a result, the Australians sell less wine for the same price. This is depicted in Figure 2.2 with the demand curve for Australian wine moving in to the left to Q_{D2} and Australian wine consumption decreasing from 1000 to 500 units at a constant price of £5 per bottle. Clearly the opposite will also be true. If the French increased their prices, then they might expect to lose customers to the Australians. This would be depicted as a rightward shift in the demand curve from Q_{D0} to Q_{D1}.

In Box 2.3 we have the example of supermarkets embarking on price promotions to lure customers away from their rivals. Those who are successful reap the benefits of increased demand and increased market share.

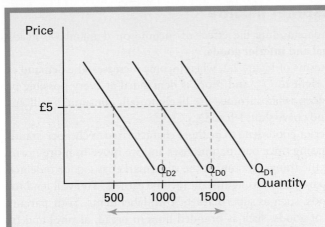

Figure 2.2 Movements in demand

Demand shifts to the left following: (i) a reduction/increase in the price of a substitute/complement product; (ii) a reduction/increase in income if the good is normal/inferior; (iii) a fall in consumers' preferences for the product.

Demand shifts to the right following: (i) an increase/reduction in the price of a substitute/complement product; (ii) an increase/reduction in income if the good is normal/inferior; (iii) an improvement in consumers' preferences for the product.

 Box 2.3 Price strategies

Asda chief threatens new price war in move to catch up Tesco

Adapted from an article by Julia Finch, the Guardian, 14 December 2005

Andy Bond, Asda's chief executive, threatened a new price war yesterday in an effort to close the sales gap with Tesco. He set out a plan to fight back, with lower prices. 'Asda has always been about being the lowest-priced retail brand and I'm going to be more aggressive next year', Mr Bond said.

The price war between Tesco and Asda has been fierce in recent years, with food prices being cut at 1%–2% a year. Asda has consistently topped surveys to find the cheapest grocery prices, but in recent months both Tesco and J Sainsbury have beaten it. Asda's market share, meanwhile, has fallen to 16.6% – nearly half that of Tesco – and it is expected to lose its position as Britain's no. 2 grocer to Sainsbury's in the coming months.

Complements are products that are purchased jointly. Beer and kebabs would be a youthful and modern example; another would be cars and petrol.

Complements are products that are demanded together. For example, if you buy a car, then you will have to buy petrol. This, therefore, means that the demand for the two products is related. If cars become cheaper, then more cars will be demanded. As a consequence, more petrol will also be demanded. If Figure 2.2 represents demand for petrol, then a reduction in the price of cars will lead to increased demand for cars. This increased demand for cars will lead to a higher demand for petrol. The demand curve for petrol will shift to the right from Q_{D0} to Q_{D1}, with more petrol being demanded at the existing price of £5 per gallon.

Consumer income

Normal goods are demanded more when consumer income increases and less when income falls.

Inferior goods are demanded more when income levels fall and demanded less when income levels rise.

In understanding the effect of income on demand we need to distinguish between **normal** and **inferior goods**.

In terms of Figure 2.2, when income increases, the demand curve for Australian wine shifts right to Q_{D1} and more is demanded at every possible price. However, during a recession, when incomes are likely to fall, consumers will cut back on wine and the demand curve shifts left to Q_{D2}.

Inferior goods tend to be those characterized as cheaper brands – products that we stop purchasing once our income rises and we move to more normal type of goods. Think about the things you buy at the supermarket as a poor indebted student and the things your parents buy as significant income earners. You will tend to be buying inferior types of goods, such as supermarkets' own label items. Your parents will be buying normal types of goods, such as branded lines in bread, alcohol and frozen foods. In terms of Figure 2.2, as income rises the demand curve for an inferior good would shift left to Q_{D2}. When income falls the demand curve for an inferior good would shift right to Q_{D1}. In brief, the behaviour of the demand curve for normal goods is opposite to that of inferior goods.

Tastes and preferences

Tastes and preferences reflect consumers' attitudes towards particular products. Over time these tastes and preferences are likely to change. Fashion is an obvious example: what might be popular this year will be out of fashion next year. Technological development might be another. Mobile phones capable of sending images and connecting to the Internet are becoming increasingly popular. We can survive quite well without such technology but, through advertising, companies try to influence our tastes and preferences for such advanced capabilities.

In order to represent a positive improvement in tastes and preference for a product, in Figure 2.2 the demand curve would shift right to Q_{D1}, with more products being sold at any given price, while a reduction in consumer backing for a product would lead to a leftward shift in the demand curve, with less being sold at any given price. For example, in recent times flat-screen, high-definition televisions have begun to replace cathode-ray televisions, reflecting changed tastes and preferences for flat-screen technologies and, therefore, lower demand at all prices.

The role of advertising

Advertising can play at least one of two roles in demand theory. First, it provides consumers with information about products. Advertising informs consumers that new products have arrived on the market, that a product has new features, or that a product is being offered at a lower price. In this way advertising plays a very valuable informational role for firms and for consumers. Demand for products increases simply because consumers are informed about the nature and availability of the product. Therefore, when advertising plays an informational role, the demand curve for the product shifts out to Q_{D1} as more consumers become informed about the existence of the product.

There is, however, another role for advertising. If adverts are simply about informing consumers about the existence of products, why are they played repeatedly over very long periods of time? Moreover, why do product suppliers hire well-known celebrities to appear in their adverts? How many adverts do you see on the television, or in the press, that provide information about the product's characteristics, price or availability?

Advertising is also about trying to change consumers' tastes and preferences. We all know that mobile phones are capable of sending pictures and video, so why would we be interested in knowing that celebrities use such technology? We all know that a Swiss watch looks good and can keep reasonable time, so why would we be interested in knowing which celebrities wear such watches? One possible answer is that the product provider is not simply selling a product. Instead they are selling you a desirable lifestyle. We do buy technologically advanced mobile phones because they are useful; but we also buy such phones because we believe that they say something positive about who we are. By emphasizing these less tangible aspects of a product, it is possible to build additional differentiation into the product. Two mobile phones might provide the same functions, but only one is used by a world-class footballer. Accordingly, advertising is not simply about informing consumers about what they *can* buy; it is also about informing them about what they *should* buy. Whether advertising is providing information, or developing consumers' tastes and preferences, the overriding aim is to shift the demand curve from Q_{D0} to Q_{D1}, while at the same time shifting the competitors' demand curves from Q_{D0} to Q_{D2}.

Price expectations

Price expectations are beliefs about how prices in the future will differ from prices today.

If you expect prices to fall in the future, then it may be wise to wait and delay your purchase. For example, recently launched computers, televisions and DVD systems are often sold in the market at premium prices. Within three to six months, newer models are brought out and the old versions are then sold at lower prices. If you do not have a taste or preference for cutting edge technology, you can cut back on consumption today in the expectation that prices will fall in the future. In terms of our demand curves, if we expect prices to fall in the future, then demand today will be reduced, shifting back to Q_{D2}. But the demand curve for three to six months' time will shift right to Q_{D1}.

The opposite can also be true. It is possible to believe that in the future prices will rise. Property may be more expensive in the future, share prices might increase, or oil will be more expensive in six months' time. Therefore, if you expect prices to rise in the future, you are likely to bring your consumption forward and purchase now. In terms of our demand curves, your demand for now shifts out to Q_{D1}, but your demand in the future shifts back to Q_{D2}.

We now understand that the demand for a product is influenced by (i) its own price, (ii) the price of substitutes and complements, (iii) the level of consumer income, (iv) consumers' tastes and preferences, and (v) price expectations. We are now in a position to introduce the **law of demand**.

The **law of demand** states that, *ceteris paribus*, as the price of a product falls, more will be demanded (*Ceteris paribus* means all other things being equal).

Accordingly, as long as (ii) the price of substitutes and complements, (iii) the level of consumer income, (iv) consumers' tastes and preferences, and (v) price expectations remain constant, there must be a negative relationship between price and quantity demanded.

Do higher prices attract higher demand?

The negative relationship between price and quantity demanded can cause students and business managers problems. For example, designer clothes and perfumes would not be purchased if they were cheap. So, does a positive relationship exist between price and willingness to demand luxury items? While it remains an appealing idea, the answer to this question is still no, since all products have a negative demand curve. This is because even when you are very rich you still have a budget constraint.

Assume you are fortunate to have an annual expense account of £500 000. Your designer clothes cost £300 000 per year, champagne is another £100 000; and the private jet another £100 000. If your favourite designer suddenly increases their prices by £50 000, you are faced with a choice. If you continue to buy the same quantity of clothes, they will now cost £350 000, and you will have to cut back on the champagne and the jet. Alternatively, you could cut back on your clothes and maintain the same amount of champagne and the private jet. However, most probably you will reduce some of your demand for designer clothes, perhaps buying fewer clothes at the higher price of £325 000, as opposed to the £350 000 it would cost to buy the same quantity as last year. The extra £25 000 might come from reducing your flights and the amount of champagne that you drink.

It is important to understand, from the example above that higher prices for one product limit how much money you can spend on *all* goods and services that you like to consume. The demand curve for designer clothes should have a negative slope, because you will decrease the quantity of clothes purchased in order to retain consumption of the champagne and jet travel.

Therefore, for luxury items, how do we explain the positive relationship between price and quantity demanded? Some consumers prefer products that have an element of exclusivity. A high price not only ensures exclusivity, but also signals that the product is special. A low price would not create the same image. Therefore, the high price attracts particular consumers into the market. This leads to the demand curve shifting out to the right in Figure 2.2 and means that the positive relationship between price and quantity is associated with a change in tastes and preferences. As such, the positive relationship of price and demand is best described as a shift of the demand curve, rather than a movement along the curve.

These points are picked up in Figure 2.3, with product providers such as Louis Vuitton keen to avoid their product being sold at discount prices. The high price of the product and the distribution of the product through licensed clothing retailers is deliberately managed in a way to promote the product's high-quality image. Consumers' tastes and preferences have been developed by Louis Vuitton to the extent that consumers expect Louis Vuitton bags to be expensive and more exclusive than cheaper alternatives. Louis Vuitton will be concerned to protect the high price image of its product, fearful that a low price would have a detrimental effect on consumers' tastes and preferences. The demand curve for Louis Vuitton will shift to the left, reducing the number of bags sold.

In Figure 2.3, Q_{D1} represents the demand for Louis Vuitton handbags among consumers who have a strong taste and preference for expensive and exclusive bags. At a price of £1000 demand is Q_D high price. Q_{D2} is the demand for Louis Vuitton among consumers who do not have a strong taste and preference for expensive and exclusive bags. We can see that at a price of £1000 none of these consumers will buy – the line from £1000 does not touch Q_{D2}. However, at a discounted price of £100 consumers represented by Q_{D2} are willing to buy Louis Vuitton. The demand curves Q_{D1} and Q_{D2} both have a negative slope. However, if we were to focus mistakenly on points A and B, and draw a line connecting the two points, then we might be led to believe that increases in price lead to increases in demand. This would be a mistake, because it is the differing tastes and preferences for cheap and exclusive brands that leads to the shift between the two points A and B.

However, the real problem facing the purveyors of luxury goods around the world, is that income levels have risen such that individuals of modest incomes can indulge in conspicuous consumption, see Box 2.4. This has led to Bobos in Paradise, or the super rich wearing drab clothes and driving beaten-up cars, pursuing conspicuous-inconspicuous consumption.

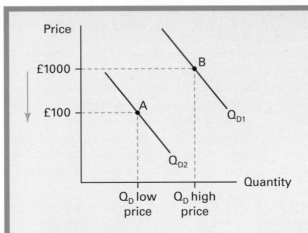

Figure 2.3 Demand for Louis Vuitton

Q_{D1} and Q_{D2} are the demand curves for Louis Vuitton bags. Under Q_{D1} stores are not allowed to sell Louis Vuitton bags at discount prices, while under Q_{D2} stores are able to sell Louis Vuitton bags at a discounted price. Consumers with a taste and preference for expensive and exclusive bags are willing to buy bags at £1000. But once discounting by stores makes Louis Vuitton bags become cheap and not exclusive, then consumers are less willing to buy bags. Demand shifts from Q_{D1} to Q_{D2} and fewer bags are purchased. The reason we sometimes think there is a positive relationship between price and willingness to demand is because we only focus on points A and B. If we joined up these two points, we would see a positive relationship between price and quantity demanded. But this is a mistake, as we really need to focus on the shifts in the demand curves reflecting a change in tastes and preferences.

 Box 2.4 Managing prices

Inconspicuous consumption

Adapted from an article in The Economist, 20 December 2005

Now that luxury has gone mass market, how are the super-rich to flaunt their wealth? The recently reopened Louis Vuitton store on the Champs Elysées is a deliberate exercise in democratic luxury. On its new, opulent art deco terraces, elegant French ladies of a certain age – the epitome of the traditional consumer of luxury fashion – rub padded shoulders with jeans-and-tee-shirt sporting rap singers and a gaggle of British working-class hen-weekenders.

It seems likely that Louis Vuitton's still-exquisite handbags, shoes and other indulgences are not as exclusive as before. Products and services that were once the preserve of a very wealthy few are increasingly becoming accessible, if not to everyone, then certainly to millions of people around the world. This may be upsetting to those super-rich folk who have long been able to afford luxury, and may in one crucial respect even regard it as a necessity.

As Thorstein Veblen noted over a century ago in *The Theory of the Leisure Class* – the book in which he coined the phrase 'conspicuous consumption' – spending lavishly on expensive but essentially wasteful goods and services is 'evidence of wealth' and the 'failure to consume in due quantity and quality becomes a mark of inferiority and demerit'. But in the 21st century, 'being a conspicuous consumer is getting harder and harder'. What does a billionaire have to do to get noticed nowadays?

Being a millionaire, for instance, is becoming commonplace. In 2004 there were 8.3 million households worldwide with assets of at least $1 million, up by 7 per cent on a year earlier, according to the latest annual survey by Merrill Lynch and Capgemini. The newly wealthy are often desperate to affirm their status by conspicuously consuming the favoured brands of the already rich. In developed countries this can be seen, in its extreme form, in the rise of 'Bling' – jewellery, diamonds and other luxuries sported initially by rappers – and Britain's unsophisticated Burberry-loving 'chavs'. (Burberry is considered unusually successful at tapping a broader market. But even it now understands that not every new customer is desirable: in January it withdrew its distinctive checked baseball caps because of their popularity with chavs.)

The number of luxury buyers in the developed world is also being swelled by two other trends. First, consumers are increasingly adopting a 'trading up, trading down' shopping strategy. Many traditional mid-market shoppers are abandoning middle-of-the-range products for a mix of lots of extremely cheap goods and a few genuine luxuries that they would once have thought out of their price league.

Demand for luxury is also soaring from emerging economies such as Russia, India, Brazil and China. Antoine Colonna, an analyst at Merrill Lynch, estimates that last year Chinese consumers already accounted for 11% of the worldwide revenues of luxury-goods firms, with most of their buying done outside mainland China. He forecasts that, by 2014, they will have overtaken both American and Japanese consumers, becoming the world's leading luxury shoppers, yielding 24% of global revenues.

For the already rich, strategies such as splashing out on ever bigger houses, longer yachts or getting special treatment from luxury-goods firms does not contribute much marginal conspicuousness.

But, perhaps the true symbol of exalted status in the era of mass luxury is conspicuous non-consumption. This is not just the growing tendency of the very rich to dress scruffily and drive beaten-up cars, as described by David Brooks in 'Bobos in Paradise'. It is showing that you have more money than you know how to spend.

2.4 **Measuring the responsiveness of demand**

You have been introduced to the demand curve and the factors that cause demand to shift. However, for the businessperson it is not enough to know that the demand for a product is determined by (i) its own price, (ii) the price of substitutes and complements, (iii) the level of consumer income, (iv) consumers' tastes and preferences, and (v) expectations regarding future prices. As a person in the market place making real pricing decisions, the businessperson needs to know the impact of price changes on the quantity demanded.

Elasticity is a measure of the responsiveness of demand to a change in price.

Figure 2.4 provides an illustration of **elasticity**. In Figure 2.4a a small change in the price leads to a much bigger change in the quantity demanded. But in Figure 2.4b a very large change in the price leads to a small change in the quantity demanded. So, we might say that in Figure 2.4a demand is responsive to a change in price, while in Figure 2.4b demand is not very responsive to a change in price. While the demand curve in 2.4a is flatter than the demand curve in 2.4b, the slope of the demand curve is not the only determinant of how responsive demand is to a change in price. We will return to this point shortly. But first let us consider why some products have demand that is responsive to a change in price while others do not.

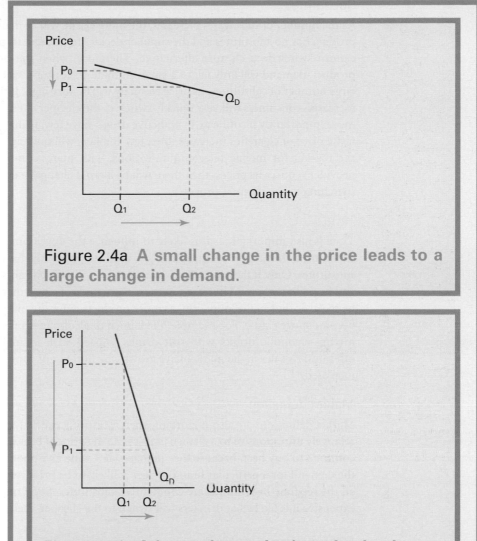

Figure 2.4a A small change in the price leads to a large change in demand.

Figure 2.4b A large change in the price leads to a small change in demand.

Figure 2.4 Price and quantity changes

Determinants of elasticity

The elasticity of a product is determined by a number of factors:

1   Number of substitutes

2   Time

3   Definition of the market

Substitutes

As the number of substitutes increases, the more elastic will be demand. For example, if a product has no substitutes and the supplier decides to increase its prices, then consumers cannot switch to a cheaper alternative. Therefore, when the price increases for this product, demand will only fall by a small amount. In contrast, when a product has a very large number of substitutes, its price elasticity will be very high. If the price of the product increases, consumers will very quickly switch to the cheaper alternatives. Cigarettes – and more importantly nicotine as an addictive drug – have few, if any, substitutes. Therefore, if the price of cigarettes increases, then few smokers will quit cigarettes. Alternatively, in the market for mobile telecommunications, with many competing suppliers, if one provider reduces its prices, then there will be a rapid change in demand, with consumers switching to the cheapest provider.

Time

Time is also important, as it is likely to influence the development and introduction of substitutes. Initially, new products or markets will only have a small number of substitutes. Only if these products are successful will new entrants come into the market and begin to compete. Therefore, in the early periods of a new market demand is likely to be inelastic, but in the long term, as more products enter the market, demand is likely to become more elastic. For example, the launch of alcoholic drinks for the youth market, mixing alcoholic drinks with soft drinks, started with a small number of product offerings. As sales in the market have grown, the number of competing products has also increased.

Market definition

Market definitions are also important when measuring elasticity. The demand for beer is relatively unresponsive to a change in price. As the price of beer increases, consumers still continue to buy beer, because they perhaps view wine as a poor alternative. In contrast, the demand for a particular brand of beer is likely to be price responsive. This is because all the separate beer brands are competitive substitutes. So, if one brand becomes more expensive it is likely that drinkers will switch to the cheaper alternatives.

Measuring elasticity

Mathematically, economists can measure elasticity, or the responsiveness of demand to a change in price, using the following formulas:

Formula   **Elasticity**

One $$\varepsilon = \frac{\text{Percentage change in quantity demanded}}{\text{Percentage change in price}}$$

$$=$$

Two $$\frac{\text{Change in quantity demanded}}{\text{Change in price}} \times \frac{\text{Price}}{\text{Quantity demanded}}$$

The value of ε for elasticity will lie between zero and infinity $(0 < \varepsilon < \infty)$.[2] This is a very large number range, so economists break the range down into regions that they can describe and utilize. Using the first formula, each of these regions is described in Table 2.1.

Table 2.1 Important elasticity measures

	Percentage change in price	Percentage change in demand	Numerical calculations	Elasticity value	Description
1	10	0	$\frac{0}{10} = 0$	$\varepsilon = 0$	Perfectly inelastic
2	10	5	$\frac{5}{10} = \frac{1}{2}$	$\varepsilon < 1$	Inelastic demand
3	10	10	$\frac{10}{10} = 1$	$\varepsilon = 1$	Unit elasticity
4	10	20	$\frac{20}{10} = 2$	$\varepsilon > 1$	Elastic demand
5	10	Infinitely large		$\varepsilon =$	Perfectly elastic

Where elasticity $\varepsilon < 1$ demand is described as **inelastic**, or a change in the price will lead to a proportionately smaller change in the quantity demanded. When $\varepsilon = 1$ demand has **unit elasticity**, or demand is equally responsive to a change in price. Where $\varepsilon > 1$ demand is described as **elastic**, or demand is responsive to a change in price. **Perfectly elastic demand** exists when $\varepsilon = \infty$. In other words, demand is very responsive to a change in price.

We will begin with an easy example. If the price of cigarettes increased by 10 per cent, how many smokers would cut back on the number of cigarettes smoked? Many smokers would continue smoking. In an extreme situation a 10 per cent change in the price of cigarettes could lead to no change in the quantity demanded. (In reality this would not happen, but the example provides a reasonable description of a theoretical extreme.)

In economic terms demand is said to be perfectly inelastic when $\varepsilon = 0$; that is, demand does not respond to a change in price. This is detailed in the first row of Table 2.1.

Clearly *perfectly inelastic demand* is an extreme situation. So in the second row of Table 2.1 we consider the situation where a 10 per cent change in the price leads to a 5 per cent change in demand.

The demand for Coca-Cola may well be **inelastic**. If Coke increased its prices by 10 per cent we might expect it to lose a small, rather than large number of customers. So, demand is not very responsive to a change in price.

In row 3 we have the situation where a 10 per cent change in the price leads to a 10 per cent change in the quantity demanded – **unit elasticity**.

In row 4 we consider the situation where a 10 per cent change in the price leads to a much bigger change in quantity demanded, in this case 20 per cent, resulting in **elastic demand**.

Consider the price of mobile phone contracts; nearly all competing networks offer very similar menus and prices. One of the reasons for this is because demand is reasonably elastic. If one company raised its prices, then over time many of its subscribers would switch to another network. Therefore, similar prices are offered because each network recognizes that demand is responsive to price differences.

Finally in row 5 we consider **perfectly elastic demand**. In this case the change in price is 10 per cent and, in response, demand changes by a very large amount. The London financial markets come close to a situation of perfectly elastic demand. If the market price of shares in Shell is £10 then you can sell all of your holdings at £10. But if you offered to sell at £10.01 you would not sell a single share, as potential buyers would move to the many other sellers offering to sell at £10.

Elasticity and the slope of the demand curve

We mentioned above that the slope of the demand curve is only an indication of how elastic demand is. In fact we can now show that the elasticity of demand changes all the way along a particular demand curve. We will do this by using the second formula for elasticity (see Figure 2.5).

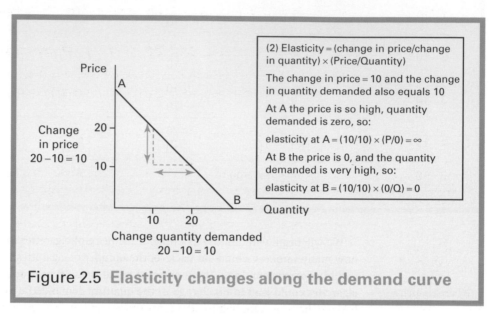

Figure 2.5 Elasticity changes along the demand curve

During a basic maths course you will have been told that to measure the slope of a line, you need to draw a triangle next to the line. The slope, or gradient, of the line is then the change in the vertical distance divided by the change in the horizontal distance. In our case the gradient is the change in price (the vertical) divided by the change in quantity demanded (the horizontal). For our second formula we need the 'inverse' of the slope, that is we need the change in quantity demanded (horizontal) divided by the change in price (vertical). But what we can say is that the slope of the line is constant, so the inverse of the slope is also constant. We have measured the slope and the inverse in the middle of the line and it is equal to $10/10 = 1$. In fact, in our example, because the slope is constant, it does not matter where we measure the slope – it is always $10/10 = 1$.

We can now calculate the elasticity of demand at two special points, A and B. At A the demand line just touches the vertical axis. The price is so high that demand is zero. At B the demand line just touches the horizontal axis. The price is zero and demand is very high.

Using our second formula for elasticity, at A the elasticity is:

$(10/10) \times (\text{price}/0) = \text{infinity} = \infty$

Because at A the demand is zero, the elasticity of demand must be infinite. We know that this means that demand is perfectly elastic.

The elasticity at B is:

$(10/10) \times (\text{quantity demanded}/0) = 0$

Because at B the price is zero, the elasticity of demand must be zero. We know that this means that demand is perfectly inelastic.

Therefore, all the way along the demand curve the elasticity changes from being perfectly elastic to perfectly inelastic, even though the slope has remained constant. This is because the elasticity of demand is influenced by the slope of the demand line; *and* by the ratio of price and quantity demanded. When the price is very high, a small reduction in the price will generate a proportionately bigger change in demand. But when the price is very low, a small change will not generate a proportionately bigger change in demand.

In simple terms, consumers react to price reductions when a product is very expensive. But they are less motivated by price reductions when a product is already very cheap. Therefore, demand is more elastic at higher prices than at lower ones.

2.5 Income and cross price elasticity

Income elasticity measures the responsiveness of demand to a change in income. **Cross price elasticity** measures the responsiveness of demand to a change in the price of a substitute or complement.

Before considering the application of this knowledge it is also worth introducing you to two related measures: **income elasticity** and **cross price elasticity**.

$$\text{Income elasticity} = Y\varepsilon = \frac{\text{Percentage change in demand}}{\text{Percentage change in income}}$$

For normal goods, income elasticity is above zero because as consumers' income rises, say during an economic boom, more normal types of goods will be produced. If $Y\varepsilon < 1$, the product is described as income inelastic, or demand will grow at a slower rate than income, while if $Y\varepsilon > 1$ demand is income elastic, or demand will grow at a faster rate than income. The recent UK and US housing booms are a reflection of positive income elasticity, with consumers being more willing to spend money on property as their incomes increased within a prosperous economy.

For inferior goods, income elasticity lies between zero and minus infinity because as incomes rise, consumers buy fewer inferior goods. This time demand is income inelastic if $Y\varepsilon$ lies between zero and -1, or is income elastic if $Y\varepsilon$ is smaller than -1, e.g. -5.

$$\text{Cross price elasticity} = XY\varepsilon = \frac{\text{Percentage change in demand of product X}}{\text{Percentage change in the price of product Y}}$$

If X and Y are substitutes or rivals then, as the price of Y increases, the demand for X will increase, so $XY\varepsilon$ for substitutes lies between zero and plus infinity. If X and Y are complements, then as the price of Y becomes more expensive, less X will also be purchased; $XY\varepsilon$ must lie between zero and minus infinity.

In Box 2.5 we have examples of price, cross price and income elasticity for bus travel. With a price elasticity of demand equal to 0.1, demand is price inelastic. A drop in prices would not generate many more bus travellers. A cross price elasticity of +0.3 indicates that buses and cars are substitutes and, since the value is less than 1, the relationship is inelastic. Therefore, even if cars became more expensive few drivers would opt for buses instead. The income elasticity of −2.4 suggests that bus travel is an inferior good and highly income elastic. Therefore, even a small rise in income will cause bus travellers to cut their demand for bus travel, and perhaps move to car travel.

 Box 2.5 Elasticity measures for bus travel

Price elasticity	(−) 0.1
Cross price elasticity (with cars)	+0.3
Income elasticity	−2.4

2.6 Business application: Pricing Strategies I – exploiting elasticities

Finding the best price was this chapter's business problem. After introducing demand theory and the concept of elasticity we are now able to return to this particular problem.

Cost-plus pricing

A rather simple approach to pricing is to simply take the costs of producing the product and add a mark-up, such as 30 per cent. This might cover some stray, unaccounted-for costs and also the required profit margin. The benefit of this approach is in its computational simplicity only requiring a basic idea of costs and a grasp of a desirable profit margin. It may also appear to be fair. Who would begrudge a firm asking for a 30 per cent mark-up? After all, they are taking a risk and they should be able to generate a decent financial return.

Unfortunately, while appealing, cost-plus pricing neglects almost everything we have introduced you to in this chapter. That is, it fails to take account of consumers' willingness to demand. There is no guarantee that consumers will be willing to buy your product when the mark-up is 30 per cent. Alternatively, 30 per cent may not be a sufficiently high enough mark-up. Consumers may exhibit a very keen preference for your product and a low elasticity of demand. While 30 per cent appears fair, you might be able to gain good sales volumes with a mark-up of 50–100 per cent. It therefore appears that we need to also consider demand theory when setting prices.

'Buy one get one free' – discounting or price experiment?

In simple terms the need to find the best price stems from a broader need to generate revenues. At the beginning of this chapter in the business problem example it was suggested that at a price of £5 we might sell 10 units, making £50 of revenue. But at a price of £8 we might sell 8 units, making a total revenue of £64. This looks like a better option. But how can we be sure that moving from £5 to £8 is a good idea? We might have ended up selling only 6 units, making a total revenue of only £48 (see Table 2.2).

Table 2.2 Total revenue

Price	Quantity	Total Revenue
£5	10	£50
£8	8	£64
£8	6	£48

Price elasticity measures the response of demand to a change in price. We face two outcomes when changing the price: demand falls to 8 or 6 units. Falling from 10 to 8 units is a small response to a change in price or, in our new terminology, demand is inelastic. But when demand falls to 6 units the response is much bigger and demand can be described as elastic. But what happens to total revenues? When demand is inelastic, total revenues have increased to £64. But when demand is price elastic, total revenues have fallen to £48. We can expand upon these simple ideas using Figure 2.6.

In Figure 2.6a we have a price elastic demand curve. So, at a price of P_0 we can expect to sell Q_0 units. Therefore, **total revenue** is represented by the rectangle defined by the P_0 and Q_0.

If we drop the price to P_1 then sales increase to Q_1 and total revenue is now equal to the new rectangle defined by P_1 and Q_1.

The impact of a price reduction on total revenue is the difference in size between the two rectangles. By selling at a lower price we lose some total revenue. For example, if we were selling at £10 and now we are only asking for £8, we are losing £2 per unit. But by

Total revenue is price multiplied by number of units sold.

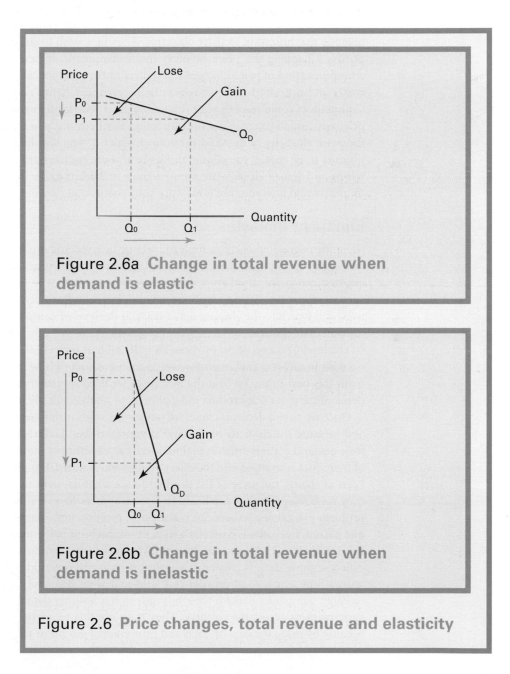

Figure 2.6a **Change in total revenue when demand is elastic**

Figure 2.6b **Change in total revenue when demand is inelastic**

Figure 2.6 **Price changes, total revenue and elasticity**

reducing the price we will also gain some total revenue by selling to more customers – in this example Q_1 as opposed to Q_0 customers. Hence, when demand is price elastic, selling at a lower price will boost total revenues. In contrast, if we examine the case of inelastic demand in Figure 2.6b we see that reducing the price leads to a drop in total revenues.

We now have economic guidance for business. If demand is elastic then dropping prices raises total revenues; but if demand is inelastic, prices should be increased in order to increase total revenues.

If we return to our business problem, the best price occurs when price elasticity equals 1, which is exactly in between the elastic and inelastic region. With unit elasticity a 10 per cent increase in the price leads to a 10 per cent change in quantity demanded. Total revenue does not change; the maximum has been found.

Admittedly, firms may not always target a price elasticity equal to 1. They may not have revenue maximization as their objective. They may wish to maximize market share or profits. Changing the price involves the development of new pricing plans and the communication of price changes to retailers of the product. As a result, change can be costly and not offset by improvements in revenue. Change can also represent a risk. Competitors could react to your price changes. A reduction in your price could lead to a price war, which you may not find attractive. Furthermore, you may not fully understand the price elasticity of demand for your product. If you consider the demand for your product to be elastic, you should think about reducing your price. But if you have got it wrong and demand is inelastic, your revenues will fall, not rise. It is, therefore, important to understand how you might measure your elasticity of demand.

Elastic or inelastic?

Cigarettes were used as an example of inelastic demand and mobile phone networks were used as an example of elastic demand. Cigarettes have few substitutes: if all cigarettes become expensive, smokers will not switch to another type of vice, as there are few sources of nicotine. If one telephone network increases its prices, however, mobile phone users can switch to the cheaper networks. It is the level of competition for a product that influences its elasticity.

The level of competition provides an indication of how elastic demand is. However, if we wish to target unit elasticity we will need a measure of how far our current pricing is from this best price. To find the best price we need to gather data that will enable the demand curve for our product to be plotted, or mathematically modelled.

Once we have a demand curve, we can see the relationship between price and quantity and measure the elasticity of demand at various prices. Unfortunately the data required for a demand curve is difficult to find. Ideally an experiment should occur where the price of a product is changed and the effect on demand is noted, but product suppliers are not keen to change the price of the product to see what happens to the demand. Indeed, if they raise the price they are likely to lose customers to a rival brand. Recognizing this problem market researchers can make use of promotional exercises. For example, a 'buy one get one free' offer is basically a 50 per cent discount in the market. A 'buy two get the third free' offer is a 33 per cent discount. When you buy a product at the supermarket, so-called 'scanner data' is created. Therefore, for any given period of time the supermarket knows how much soap powder was sold and what discounts were on offer. Market research companies make it their business to buy scanner data from a large selection of supermarkets across the country. They then use this to advise companies on pricing, because by using the data on sales and promotional discounts they can begin to estimate the elasticity of demand. For each price at which the product is sold, the market researchers also note down how many units of the product are sold at the tills. They then plot this as in Figure 2.7. The plot shows a negative relationship between price and quantity demanded. To smooth out this relationship the researchers then use a computer to calculate the trend line, as in Figure 2.8. The trend line is in fact the demand curve that we have been using throughout this chapter.

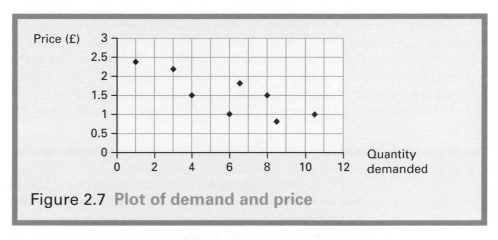

Figure 2.7 Plot of demand and price

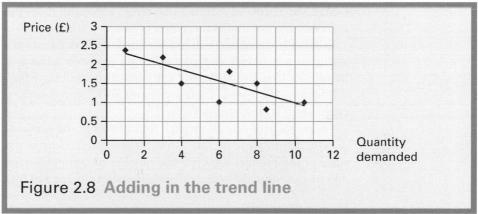

Figure 2.8 Adding in the trend line

By using mathematical techniques known as econometrics, the trend line can be analysed and manipulated to provide an estimate of the price elasticity of demand. Knowing that unit elasticity is optimal, product managers can then make an informed decision about whether to raise or lower prices. In your working lives you are unlikely ever to calculate the elasticity of demand for a product, but being able to understand the concept will be very important (see Box 2.6).

Product life cycle and pricing

The preceding discussion analysing elasticity and total revenue for the most part neglects the time-varying nature of competition and elasticity. When a new and innovative product emerges onto the market, it faces very few competitors. At launch the Sony Portable Play Station, in as much as it was able to play movies, music, access the Internet and play games, faced limited competition from Nintendo's GameBoy. However, this is unlikely to last: Nintendo and other electronics manufacturers will enter the market with

Box 2.6 Up close with Stelios Haji-Ioannous

Adapted from an article by Rupert Steiner, In Edge, the Institute of Leadership and Management, April, 2005

Mr easyJet's no-frills approach in business has carved a niche in hawking low cost, functional services, which has created him an 'easy' fortune in the process. Stelios is quick to acknowledge his debt to education. I specifically remember the economics class where we studied the simple concept of elasticity of demand – customers who want the flexibility of leaving it later to pay for products pay more than those who can commit earlier.

'While it was not a ping moment, some years later when I started the airline and had to come up with a pricing strategy, I knew it made more sense to vary the price rather than fix it. That one lesson was crucial to easyJet's success. When I started easyJet, airlines flew at 70% capacity – now we run at 85%. We have lifted occupancy by 15% which, multiplied by 600 flights a day with exactly the same costs, is a big boost to our margins.'

improved models. Motorola and its Razr mobile phone radically redirected the design and development of mobile phones. Cilitbang is a revolutionary cleaning product. While, in the automobile industry Renault were the first to convert a Mégane into a Scénic and create the MPV segment of the market. Citroën soon followed with a Picasso, Ford have a C Max and Toyota have their Verso range. Successful innovation spawns imitation and aggressive competition as the market grows.

Eventually consumers will become tired of old designs and concepts. Newer models and ideas will emerge and sales will track the latest fashion. Demand for Sony's PSP, Motorola's Razr and MPVs will fall, competitors will leave the market and competition will become less severe. These arguments are captured in the concept of a product life cycle, which is illustrated in Figure 2.9.

Successful products go through four phases of the product life cycle: introduction, growth, maturity and decline. (Unsuccessful products never pass introduction). At each stage of the product life cycle the number of competitors is different. This leads to differing substitutability and differing elasticities of demand for the products.

Pricing at launch

In the introduction stage an innovative product is likely to be unique and face few if any competitors. For early adopters who wish to be seen with the latest technology, demand will be price inelastic. Firms could, therefore, seek to price high in order to capture the high demand from this set of consumers.

Pricing during growth

In the growth phase, companies who have witnessed the success of the innovative product also join the market. This increases competition and substitutability and increases the elasticity of demand. Recognizing the inverse relationship between price and consumers' willingness to demand, firms can seek to gain a dominant position by cutting prices in the hope of gaining market share. Under this strategy firms are trading a revenue-maximizing strategy for a sales-maximizing strategy. This could be temporary: maximizing sales and market coverage in the short run and winning the hearts and minds of customers, only to then exploit this commercial position in the long run with a strategy which maximizes revenues.

Pricing during maturity

The ferocity of competition is most acute during the mature phase of the cycle, sales are at a peak and the market can be supplied by the largest number of competitors. The potential for a high degree of price elasticity in the mature phase of the cycle provides a basic rationale for the sales-maximization strategy during the growth phase. Gain market share, cut out competition, or face the consequences of merciless price competition in the mature phase of the cycle. High price elasticity means little control over pricing, as competitive pressures force the price down to the lowest possible level.

Pricing during decline

In the decline phase of the market consumers will begin to leave the market. In response some firms will also exit, seeking better commercial opportunities elsewhere. Competition will fall and the degree of price sensitivity among consumers will diminish. Firms remaining in the market will see the elasticity of demand begin to become more inelastic, and an element of price stability and hopefully price rises might occur.

Therefore, throughout the product life cycle the pricing strategy has to be reactive to the changing competitive nature of the market.

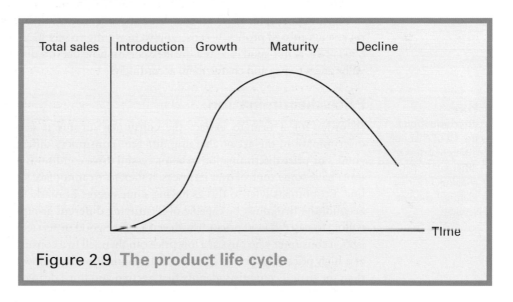

Figure 2.9 The product life cycle

2.7 Business application: Pricing Strategies II – extracting consumer surplus

Consumer surplus – the island of lost profits

Consumer surplus is the difference between the price you are charged for a product and the maximum price that you would have been willing to pay.

Here is a true but curious thought: when you buy a product you are nearly always willing to pay *more* for it. This is the concept of **consumer surplus**.

For example, you may have been willing to pay £750 for a flight to Australia, but you manage to find a flight for £500. Your consumer surplus is £250.

Figure 2.10 illustrates the idea of consumer surplus using the demand curve. You are charged £500, but you are willing to pay £750. Indeed, in the market there may be some consumers who would be willing to pay even more than you. The entire amount of consumer surplus in the market is the area under the demand line down to the price charged of £500. This area represents the amount each consumer would be willing to pay in excess of the price charged.

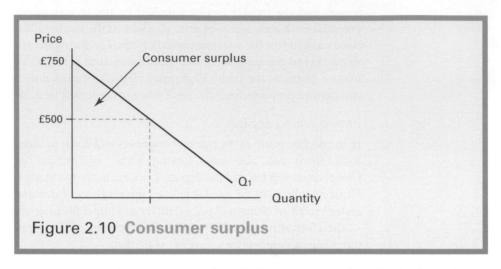

Figure 2.10 **Consumer surplus**

Consumer surplus represents a benefit for consumers, but clearly for a firm it represents missed profits, because you were willing to pay £750 and were only charged £500. This is not good. So, as a businessperson how do you discover a consumer's true willingness to pay and charge them accordingly?

Price discrimination

> **Price discrimination** is the act of charging different prices to different consumers for an identical good or service.

In order for a firm to extract the consumer surplus it needs to undertake price discrimination, the act of charging different consumers different prices for the same good. For price discrimination to be successful three conditions must exist. First the firm must have some control over its prices: it therefore cannot face a perfectly elastic demand line. Economists refer to this as having some degree of market power in setting prices. Second, the firm must be capable of identifying different groups of consumers who are willing to pay different prices. Third, resale of the good or service must be prohibited. If it isn't, a consumer who buys at a low price can then sell to a consumer who is willing to buy at a high price. The profits from price discrimination then flow to the consumer, rather than the firm. Economists identify first, second and third degree price discrimination.

First-degree price discrimination

Under first-degree price discrimination each consumer is charged exactly what they are willing to pay for the good or service. This is unlikely to work in practice because it would involve each customer freely admitting to the top price that they would be willing to pay. For example, an airline might line up all of its passengers and ask them to write on a large card the price they would be willing to pay to fly on the aircraft. The passengers would then be admitted onto the aircraft in price order. Highest first, lowest last. Those who bid too low may not fly if the aircraft is full. However, passengers might not write a truthful price and why should they? In addition, the entire process is very costly in terms of time and administration to carry out.

First-degree price discrimination is therefore seen to be difficult to carry out in practice. Instead, a seller looks for cues or signals of a consumer's willingness to pay. For example, a builder, plumber, or electrician might charge for work based on the type of car parked on the drive. Car sales people are trained to look at items worn by a potential buyer, such as the watch, the coat, clothes and even areas where they live. These all provide reasonable, but imperfect, signals of someone's ability to pay and perhaps willingness to pay. Finally, there is the use of auctions, where each potential buyer is forced to bid for an item. In bidding each buyer is communicating their willingness to pay. The highest bidder wins when the price is above every other bidder's willingness to pay – that is, every other bidder has no consumer surplus. However, auctions are costly to organize, only one sale at a time occurs and there is no guarantee that bidders will attend.

Second-degree price discrimination

Under second degree price discrimination, consumers are charged according to the number of units they buy. For example, gas, electricity and telephones tend to be offered under two part tariffs. The first part is a fixed element to cover the cost of the infrastructure. The second part covers the cost of using additional units of electricity gas, etc. If the fixed element is £10 per month and each unit costs £0.1, then a user of 100 units a month is charged £10 + (100 × £0.1) = £20. Taking account of the fixed element the cost per unit is £20/100 = £0.2. Now consider someone who uses 200 units: their monthly bill is £10 + (200 × £0.1) = £30, which equates to a cost per unit of £30/200 = £0.15. The higher user gains a discount of 25 per cent. But how does this extract the consumer surplus? The listed unit cost of £0.1 per unit is the price charged to all consumers. The fixed price element is set to extract the consumer surplus. Because the consumer surplus is not constant across all consumers, the fixed element can also be varied across consumers through the provision of pricing menus. High users with a presumably high willingness to pay are offered a high fixed access price, but a low cost per unit. Low users with a presumably low willingness to pay select a low fixed access price but a high cost per unit. These pricing strategies are also used beyond the utility industry – for example, membership of gyms and golf clubs often includes a fixed and variable element.

Third-degree price discrimination

Finally, we have third degree price discrimination where each consumer group is charged a different price. This tends to occur where firms can identify different market segments for a similar product or service. In the case of airlines, young students are fairly flexible when it comes to flying around the world. If the plane is full on Monday, they can fly on Tuesday. In fact, demand by young travellers is elastic, as different days of travel provide substitutes. A business traveller is more likely to have very specific needs. The overseas meeting will take place on a specific date and they will need to be back in the UK very quickly to attend more meetings. These travellers are less sensitive to price and so exhibit price-inelastic demand.

Therefore, rather than offering each traveller the same product at the same price, you can segment the market. Offer two different products at different prices. Cheap economy tickets with no frills to the student; and expensive business-class tickets to the businessperson, with comfortable seats, good food and access to airport lounges.

Premium television channels use the same idea. Instead of paying one fee for all digital channels, consumers are offered a menu. The base price includes the standard assortment of channels. The sport and movie channels are additional extras. Consumers that value sport highly will pay the higher price.

This is known as de-bundling the product. If the product is composed of many different parts, in our case various television channels, the offering is not sold as one bundle; rather, it is sold as a number of separate bundles, each with an individual price.

This stripping-out of valued products from the standard range enables companies to deal with the problem of consumer surplus by targeting customers with the combination of products that they value the most.

 Box 2.7 Sony targets big boys with all-singing and dancing games gadget

Adapted from an article by David Derbyshire, the Daily Telegraph, 31 August 2005.

Priced at £180, the Sony PSP is being promoted as more than just a games machine. Unlike its nearest rival, the Nintendo DS, it plays full-length movies, downloads and plays songs and video, and surfs the Internet.

Unlike previous consoles, such as the Playstation, the PSP will not be a loss leader for Sony. In the past, the company has sold consoles at less than cost price, knowing that it could recoup money from the strictly licensed games made by third-party companies. But in order to make its new format for games and films – UMD – popular, it has loosened its controls over the format and put up the price of the player. By Christmas, there will be about 50. Future software includes a conversion kit to turn it into a satellite navigation device, and TalkMan – a Star Trek-style voice recognition programme that translates a phrase into another language

---

In Box 2.7 Sony PSP is a handheld console, with add-ons: movies, games, music, downloads, satellite navigation. It is a de-bundled product and the pricing strategy reflects this. Previously, non-portable consoles have been sold at a loss, reflecting the competitive and therefore price-elastic nature of the market between Sony, Microsoft and Nintendo. Once a consumer buys a Sony console they are then forced to buy licenced product for the machine; demand is now inelastic and so the price increases. So, why change the strategy for the PSP? First, the console is innovative and unique in playing movies while on the move. The PSP therefore faces inelastic demand and Sony quite correctly have exploited this by selling at a premium. Second, by loosening control over the UMD format, it can promote increased supply of movies for its console, thus promoting competition and price elasticity for add-ons. This should help adopters of the PSP. The important point for business managers is that Sony have recognized that the demand characteristics for the PSP should be different from the stand-alone PlayStation and the means of raising revenue and extracting consumer surplus have changed.

 Summary

1 A key characteristic of modern economic life is that companies set prices. With companies in such a powerful position, what is the optimal price to set for a product?

2 The demand curve shows consumers' willingness to demand a product at various prices. As the price increases consumers are less willing to demand the product.

3 Demand is also seen to be influenced by the price of substitutes and complements.

4 Substitutes are rivals; complements are products that are purchased together. As a substitute becomes more expensive, demand for the rival product will increase. As the price of a complement rises, demand for the remaining product will fall.

5   Rising income will lead to an increase in demand for normal goods. But it will lead to a fall in demand for inferior goods.

6   The tastes and preferences of consumers change over time. As goods become popular, consumers move into the market. As products become unfashionable, consumers leave the market and demand falls.

7   Price elasticity, income elasticity and cross price elasticity measure how much demand changes when price, income or the price of a substitute or complement changes.

8   If the percentage change in demand is greater than the percentage change in price, then demand is said to be elastic. If the percentage change in demand is less than the percentage change in price, demand is said to be inelastic.

9   Companies use the concept of elasticity when setting prices. If demand is elastic, reducing prices will lead to a rise in total revenue. When demand is inelastic, raising prices will lead to an increase in total revenue.

10   Companies measure the elasticity of demand by analysing mathematically what happens to sales when they offer promotional discounts in the market.

11   Consumer surplus is the difference between the price charged and how much a consumer would have been willing to pay. This difference represents lost profits.

12   It is possible to capture some consumer surplus by de-bundling product offerings. Consumers can be offered a base package but extras are offered at much higher prices.

 Learning checklist

You should now be able to:

◆   Draw a demand curve for a good or service

◆   Understand how changes in income, the price of substitutes and complements, tastes and price expectations shift the demand curve left or right

◆   Explain the concept of price elasticity of demand and understand the distinction between elastic and inelastic demand

◆   Explain how total revenue can be improved by understanding how elastic demand is for a good or service

◆   Explain how firms can develop strategies to access consumer surplus

Questions

1   List five products that you think are price elastic. List five products that you think are price inelastic.

2   Is consumer surplus greater under elastic or inelastic demand?

3   How would you advise a company to go about changing the elasticity of demand for one of its products?

4   Using ideas relating to income elasticity, how would you build a portfolio or collection of products that would perform well when the economy was growing during a boom and contracting during a recession?

Exercises

1   True or False?
   a) An increase in income will cause an increase in demand for all goods.
   b) Two goods are complements if an increase in the price of X results in an increase in demand for Y.
   c) Price elasticity measures the responsiveness of the quantity demand to the change in the price.
   d) The price elasticity is constant along the length of a demand line.
   e) If a car costs £15 000 and a consumer is willing to pay upto £18 000, then the consumer surplus is £3000.
   f) If a product is price inelastic, revenues will rise following an increase in the price.

2   a) Plot the following demand curve and associated total revenue curve.

Price £	10	8	6	4	2
Demand	1	2	3	4	5
Total Revenue					
Elasticity					

   Calculate the elasticity at each price.
   What is the change in total revenue if the firm moves from a price of £8 to £4?
   Which price maximizes total revenue?
   What is the elasticity when revenue is maximized?
   b) As a result of rising income demand increases at all prices by 5 units.
   Explain whether this good is normal or inferior.
   Is the new demand line more or less elastic than the original? Why do you think this should be the case?

3   You have been hired by Louis Vuitton to advise them on their pricing strategy. Your brief is to cover each of the following:
   i)   The benefit of raising their existing prices.
   ii) The potential of broadening the brand's appeal through a gradual reduction in prices.
   iii) The potential benefits of launching a new brand called 'Louis'. Who should this product be sold to and at what price level?

Notes

1 We will examine the objectives of a firm more fully in Chapters 5 and 7.
2 You will shortly understand that elasticity must lie between zero and minus infinity. This is because if we increase prices then quantity demanded will decrease. So a negative change in demand will be divided by a positive change in the price. So the elasticity measure will always be negative. Economists ignore the negative sign and simply look at the numerical value for elasticity.

Chapter 3
Firms in the market place

Chapter contents

 Learning outcomes

By the end of this chapter you should understand:

Economic Theory

- The difference between the short and long run

- The difference between variable, fixed and total costs

- The concepts of marginal product and marginal costs

- The law of diminishing returns

- Economies of scale

- The concept of minimum efficient scale

Business Applications

- Why low pricing and high volume sales strategies, deployed by budget airlines, reflect high fixed costs

- Why qualification for the Champions' League by leading football clubs is a strategy for dealing with the high cost of owning and employing footballers

Cost theory at a glance

The issue

World class footballers cost in excess of £30 million, and the Super Jumbo A380 costs $264 million. Neither are cheap. So how does a business make money when using such expensive assets?

The understanding

Such assets represent costs that do not vary with the level of output. The way to exploit such assets is to make them productive. The more games Ronaldinho plays, the cheaper per game he becomes. The more flights a plane flies, the cheaper per flight the plane becomes. Unfortunately, over short periods of time, volume may come up against a problem known as the 'law of diminishing returns', while in the long run firms can encounter an additional problem known as 'diseconomies of scale'. By the end of this chapter you will understand each of these problems; and how costs can be managed in the short and long run.

The usefulness

This chapter will enable you to understand why successful airlines sell their seats at low prices, why teams such as Manchester United are desperate to stay in the Champions' League and why R&D intensive technology products need to conquer world markets.

3.1 Business problem: managing fixed and variable costs

Economists categorize costs as being fixed or variable.

Fixed costs are constant. They remain the same whatever the level of output. **Variable costs** change or vary with the amount of production.

Supermarket stores represent **fixed costs**. If the store attracts one shopper or 1000 shoppers per day, the cost of developing and maintaining the store is fixed. However, the number of checkout staff does change with the number of shoppers and, therefore, represents a **variable cost**. The cost of developing Windows XP was a fixed cost. Development costs do not increase if more copies of the product are sold. Rather, the costs of burning CDs with the program increase and so the distribution of the program represents a variable cost. Universities are a vast collection of fixed costs. The cost of lecture theatres, lecturers, library resources, central administration units and computer facilities are not hugely influenced by the number of recruited students. For example, the cost of lecturing to 50 students is the same as lecturing to 250 students.

The nature of fixed and variable costs has enormous implications for business. As an example, consider the contrasting differences between employing burger flippers and professional footballers.

Burger flippers at fast food restaurants are perhaps paid no more than £6 per hour. The majority of employed hours are on weekends, evenings or lunchtimes, periods when consumer demand is highest. This is because the employment of burger flippers is linked to the demand for burgers. More burger flippers are employed at lunchtimes and weekends when demand and, therefore, the production of burgers is highest. As a result, the cost of employing burger flippers is a predominantly variable cost. The wages paid rise and fall with the level of output. Ultimately, if demand for burgers drops dramatically, restaurants can generally terminate the employment of its burger flippers by giving one month's notice.

Professional footballers can be paid £100 000 a week when they play a game. This may fall by a fraction if they are on the substitutes' bench or when they are injured. Similarly, the wage may increase with bonuses if goals are scored or after a specified number of first team appearances. It is important to remember that the bulk of a professional footballer's wages is not linked directly to the creation of output, namely football games. Playing games or sitting on the subs' bench only leads to relatively small changes up or down in the wages paid to the player. The cost of employing professional footballers is, therefore, a predominantly fixed cost. A club's wages bill is changed very little by the number of games played. Furthermore, because footballers' contracts are fixed for anything up to five years, if the club wishes to terminate the employment of the player two years into the contract, they would have to pay three years' worth of compensation. These employment differences between footballers and burger flippers are crucial.

The business problem associated with employing footballers, or fixed costs, is *not that* they cost huge sums of money, but that the *nature* of the cost *does not change* with *output* and *revenues.*

If the revenues received from fans and television rights drop, clubs still have to honour their contractual obligations with their players. In contrast, fast food restaurants can change the number of burger flippers when demand falls. The transfer of football players between clubs is both the transfer of an asset and a liability. The buying club gains what it believes is a good player, but at the same time it also commits itself to an increase in its fixed costs.

The ideas in Box 3.1 provide a tantalizing glimpse into the relationship between a firm's cost structure, its financial performance and ultimately its share value. It is, therefore, important for businesses to recognize the various components of their cost structures and to differentiate between fixed and variable costs. By doing so they can then develop business models that accommodate the financial commitment associated with fixed costs. By the end of this chapter you will understand how to manage such cost structures highlighted by our initial discussion and the concepts within Box 3.1. But in order to achieve this we need to develop a broader understanding of cost theory.

➔ Box 3.1 Operational gearing

Adapted from an article in Investors Chronicle, 29 December 2005

Awareness of a company's operational gearing enables us to fill a yawning knowledge gap between turnover and profits. That is because operational gearing captures the relationship between a company's fixed and variable costs. Broadly speaking, a company with high operational gearing has high fixed costs and relatively low variable costs, while a company with low operational gearing has low fixed cost and comparatively high variable costs.

It is important to understand that operational gearing reveals the sensitivity of profits to changes in sales, and can tell us how close a company is to operational distress. If sales drop by 1%, net income could fall by 50% if a company has high operational gearing. On the other hand, a highly operationally geared company that is growing strongly could reap a rich harvest, as a large proportion of sales would flow through into profits and shareholders' returns.

The **short run** is a period of time where one factor of production is fixed. We tend to assume that capital is fixed and labour is variable.

The **long run** is a period of time when all factors of production are variable.

3.2 The short and long run

We will begin by considering a firm that employs two factors of production: labour in the form of workers and capital in the form of computers and office space.

If a firm needs to increase its level of output, it is fairly easy to employ more workers. Agencies specializing in temporary employment are able to offer suitable candidates within a day, or even an hour. In contrast, it is not as easy to expand the amount of office space. It takes time to find additional buildings, arrange the finance to purchase the buildings, and then fit the buildings with suitable furniture and equipment. The problem also exists when trying to downsize. It is fairly easy to lay off workers, but it takes time to decommission a building and sell it to some other user. Therefore, only in the **long run** are all factors of production seen to be variable.

Given our business problem we should not confine our thinking to capital as the only fixed factor of production. Clearly the nature of employment can make labour fixed. Contracts signed by footballers, company chief executives and many academics are for a fixed period of time. Contracts for burger flippers and many other types of work are open ended, with the employer and employee given the right to terminate the relationship with, typically, one month's notice. In the latter case, the employment of labour is reasonably variable, whereas for footballers labour is fixed.

A reasonable question is: how long is the long run? The answer is that it depends. For some companies it can be very long. Airlines place orders with aircraft suppliers up to five years in advance, while an Internet company might be able to buy an additional Internet server system within a week and double its output capacity.

However, an important issue is to understand how costs behave in the short and long run. In the next two sections we will see how in the short run costs are determined by the fixed amount of capital being exploited by more workers, while in the long run costs are influenced by varying the amount of capital.

3.3 The nature of productivity and costs in the short run

Productivity in the short run

If we are interested in knowing how the level of costs changes with the level of output, then we need to consider more than just the cost of employing labour and capital. We are also interested in understanding how the productivity of labour and capital change. If labour becomes more productive, then output increases for any given amount of cost.

In assessing productivity we need to distinguish between **total product** and **marginal product**.

Total product is the total output produced by a firm's workers. **Marginal product** is the addition to total product after employing one more unit of factor input.

Consider the following. An online supplier of electrical goods has two vans for deliveries, the fixed factor of production. The firm can also employ up to ten workers, the variable component. The total product and marginal product at each level of employment are detailed in Table 3.1. When the firm employs one worker, total product is 40 delivered items per day. This worker has to collate the orders, pick the items from the warehouse, package them for delivery, print off invoices, load the van, deliver the items and then deal with any enquiries and returned items. When the firm employs a second worker total output increases. This second worker can utilize the additional van and may specialize in dealing with enquiries and returns. When the third worker is employed, they do not have access to a van, but they could help by specializing in

Table 3.1 Total and marginal product of labour with a fixed amount of capital

Labour input (workers)	Output (total product)	Marginal product of labour
1	40	40
2	90	50
3	145	55
4	205	60
5	255	50
6	295	40
7	325	30
8	345	20
9	355	10
10	360	5

Task specialization occurs where the various activities of a production process are broken down into their separate components. Each worker then specializes in one particular task, becoming an expert in the task and raising overall productivity.

The law of diminishing returns states that as more of a variable factor of production, usually labour, is added to a fixed factor of production, usually capital, then at some point the returns to the variable factor will diminish.

collating orders, picking and packing. This again would help to raise output. The fourth worker might load vans and print invoices. The fifth worker might then help the third by specializing in picking orders from the warehouse; and so on and so on. The important point is that task specialization helps to raise productivity, as evidenced by the increasing marginal product for workers, 2, 3, 4, but thereafter diminishes. There is only so much **task specialization** that can occur without leaving a worker with a full day's work. Workers 5, 6, 7 and onwards will be filling the remainder of their working day, answering emails, checking their text messages, making coffees and collecting sandwiches for lunch. Activities which do not raise the total product of the firm.

The productivity of all the workers in our example is constrained by the number of vans the firm uses. With only two vans there is an upper limit to how many orders can be met per day, no matter how much task specialization occurs at the warehouse.

Most working environments are characterized by a mixture of workers and capital, in various forms: lecturers and lecture theatres, office staff and computers, burger flippers and burger grills. The relationship depicted in Figures 3.1 and 3.2 are therefore very important and economists know it as the **law of diminishing returns**.

The law of diminishing returns is highlighted by the marginal product of labour (see Figure 3.2). When we have a fixed factor of production, such as capital, and we add workers to the production process, these workers can exploit an underutilized resource. So, the marginal product rises. When we begin to over-resource the production process with too much labour, there is no more capital to utilize. As a result, the marginal product begins to fall. This is the point at which the law of diminishing returns occurs. In our particular example, additional workers are able to exploit the vans and become more productive. But once we begin to employ more workers, and there are not enough vans, the productivity of labour must begin to fall.

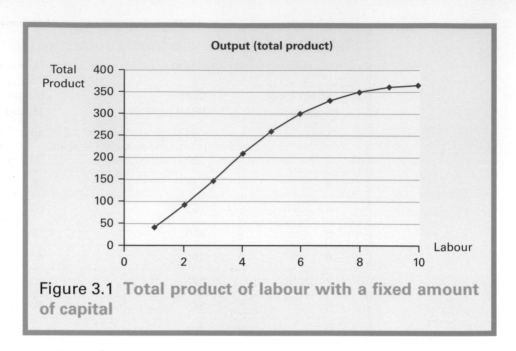

Figure 3.1 **Total product of labour with a fixed amount of capital**

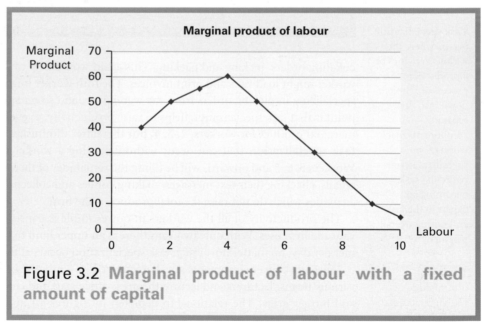

Figure 3.2 **Marginal product of labour with a fixed amount of capital**

Variable costs are costs associated with the use of variable factors of production, such as labour.

Fixed costs are associated with the employment of fixed factors of production, such as capital.

Total costs are simply fixed costs plus variable costs.

Costs in the short run

Now that we have an understanding of how productivity changes, we need to begin to think about how costs behave. In the short run we have three types of cost: **variable, fixed** and **total costs.**

Variable costs change with the level of output. This was picked up when we discussed the burger flippers. The higher the level of output, the more labour we employ and the higher the amount of variable cost.

Fixed costs do not change with the level of output. If we produce nothing, or a very large amount of output, fixed costs remain the same.

Each of these costs is listed in Table 3.2 for various levels of output and plotted in Figure 3.3.

Table 3.2 Short-run costs

Output	SRFC (short-run fixed costs)	SRVC (short-run variable costs)	SRTC (short-run total costs)
0	30	0	30
40	30	22	52
90	30	38	68
140	30	48	78
180	30	61	91
210	30	79	109
235	30	102	132
255	30	131	161
270	30	166	196
280	30	207	237

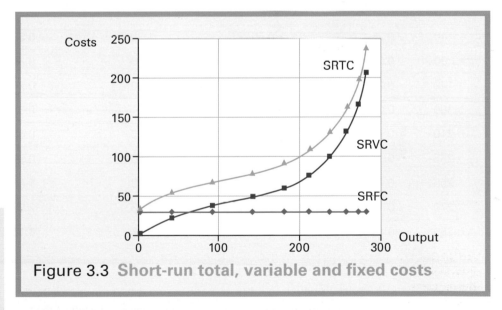

Figure 3.3 Short-run total, variable and fixed costs

Fixed costs are represented as the dark blue line, which is horizontal. In this example, fixed costs are constant at £30. Variable costs rise, slowing, then, as output increases, the variable costs begin to rise quicker. This simply reflects the law of diminishing returns. As additional workers become less productive, costs rise quicker than output. The total cost line in light blue is simply fixed plus variable costs.

Average costs

The next step is to consider how the cost per unit changes with the level of output. We measure the cost per unit using **average cost**.

Average total cost is calculated as total cost divided by the number of units produced. **Average variable cost** is calculated as total variable cost divided by the number of units produced. **Average fixed cost** is calculated as total fixed costs divided by the number of units produced.

Marginal cost is the cost of creating one more unit.

In addition to the average costs we also examine the **marginal costs**, calculated as:

Change in total cost

Change in output

(Since the marginal cost is the cost of producing one more unit, the change in output should be 1.)

However, firms rarely increase output by one unit and in our example output initially increases from 0 to 40 units of output: therefore, by dividing the change in total cost by the change in output of 40 we can approximate the marginal cost, or the cost of making one more unit:

Marginal cost $= (52 - 30)/(40 - 0) = 0.55$

The calculations for average and marginal costs are listed in Table 3.3 and plotted in Figure 3.4.

Table 3.3 Short-run average and marginal costs

Output	SRAFC (short-run average fixed costs)	SRAVC (short-run average variable costs)	SRATC (short-run average total costs)	SRMC (short-run marginal costs)
0				
40	0.75	0.55	1.30	0.55
90	0.33	0.42	0.76	0.32
140	0.21	0.34	0.56	0.20
180	0.17	0.34	0.51	0.33
210	0.14	0.38	0.52	0.60
235	0.13	0.43	0.56	0.92
255	0.12	0.51	0.63	1.45
270	0.11	0.61	0.73	2.33
280	0.11	0.74	0.85	4.10

The average variable and average total cost curves are both U-shaped. This simply reflects the law of diminishing returns. Towards the left of the figure the output is low. At this low level of output we have a small number of workers using the fixed capital. As we employ more workers, productivity increases and costs per unit fall. As the number of workers continues to increase, however, the law of diminishing returns predicts that productivity will fall. As a consequence, the cost per unit will increase. This point is also picked up in the marginal cost curve, which is the cost of producing one more unit. As labour becomes less productive, then costs of producing additional units must rise.

Relationship between the average and marginal

It should also be noted that the marginal cost curve cuts through the minimum points of

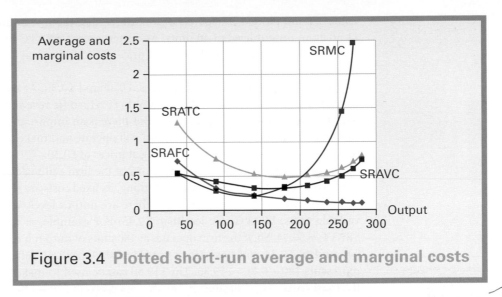

Figure 3.4 **Plotted short-run average and marginal costs**

the average total and average variable cost curves. This is because of a simple mathematical relationship between the marginal and the average. Assume your average examination score is 50. Your next exam is your marginal exam. If you gain a score of 70, then your average will increase. But if you gain a score of 20, your average will come down. Therefore, whenever the marginal is lower than the average, the average will move down; and whenever the marginal is higher than the average, the average will rise. Therefore, the marginal cost curve has to cut through the average cost curves at their minimum point.

Average fixed costs

The average fixed cost curve is different. It is always falling as output increases. This reflects simple mathematics. If fixed costs are £100 and we produce ten units, the average fixed costs are £100/10 = £10. But if we increase output to one hundred units, then average fixed costs become £100/100 = £1. Accountants refer to this as 'spreading the overhead'. As fixed costs are spread over a larger level of output, the fixed costs per unit will fall.

This relationship has important implications for managers. Consider the case of the Super Jumbo Airbus A380. Development costs have been estimated at €12 billion. If we assume Airbus finds two customers to buy the A380 the average fixed cost will be €12bn/2 = €6 billion. Therefore, in order for Airbus to break even, it will require its two customers to pay at least €6 billion; and then there is the cost of making the aircraft! Airbus has orders for just over 100 A380s, which helps to reduce the fixed cost per unit. But at a list price of €250 million, Airbus will have to sell many more A380s in order to recoup its variable costs of manufacturing and its fixed costs of development.

3.4 **Output decisions in the short run**

Now that we have an understanding of how costs behave in the short run we can begin to examine the firm's output decisions. In Chapter 5 we will see how we can find the level of output that will maximize the firm's profits. However, at this point we merely wish to show you when the firm will produce and when it will close down.

If the output is being sold at the same price to all consumers for £1.50, then the average revenue is also £1.50. If we now re-examine the short-run average total costs, SRATC in

Table 3.3 and plotted in Figure 3.4, we can see that the maximum value for SRATC is £1.30 at an output level of 40 units. As output grows, SRATC drops to a minimum of £0.51. Clearly, therefore, at the current price of £1.50 the firm can make a profit at any output level.

Now consider two much lower prices, £0.45 and £0.30. At both prices the firm will make a loss as its minimum SRATC is only £0.51, so its revenues will never be greater than its costs at either of these prices. But there is an important difference between the two scenarios. In the short run, the firm will operate and make a loss at prices of £0.45, but it will shut down and cease operating at prices of £0.30.

The understanding rests on whether or not the firm can make a positive contribution to its fixed costs. If the firm produces nothing, its fixed costs are £30 and its losses will also be £30. However, if the price is £0.45 there are output levels where the firm's average variable costs, SRAVC, are less than £0.45. For example, at an output of 180 units, SRAVC = £0.34. So, if the firm operates at 180 units of output it can cover its variable cost per unit of £0.34 and have £0.45 − £0.34 = £0.11 per unit left over. Selling 180 units represents 180 × 0.11 = £19.80. The £19.80 can be used to make a contribution towards the fixed costs. So, by producing 180 the loss drops to £30 − £19.80 = £11.20, as opposed to a loss of £30 (the fixed costs) if it produced nothing.

However, when the price drops to £0.30 the firm cannot cover any of its variable costs. Therefore, if it did decide to operate, then, not being able to cover its entire wage bill, it would be adding to the losses generated by its fixed costs. Hence, the best the firm can do is to shut down and incur only the fixed-cost losses of £30.

We can now go one step further. The marginal cost is the cost of producing one more unit. If the firm can receive a price that is equal to or greater than the marginal cost then it can break even or earn a profit on the last unit. If the firm maximizes profits, clearly, it will supply an additional unit of output when the price is equal to or greater than marginal cost. If we couple this argument with the previous point, that firms will not operate below short-run average variable cost, we can show, as in Figure 3.5, that the

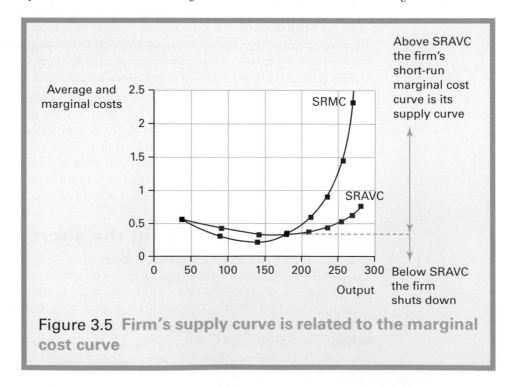

Figure 3.5 Firm's supply curve is related to the marginal cost curve

firm's supply curve is in fact the firm's short-run marginal cost curve above short-run average variable costs.

Theme parks

Theme parks offering thrilling roller coaster rides often close down during the winter. We can now offer an economic explanation for why they close. The rides are capital and represent fixed costs. The staff who operate the rides and keep the theme park clean are the variable costs. During the summer months many people are willing to go to a theme park and pay the entrance fee. The revenues generated cover the theme park's fixed and variable costs. However, in the winter, when it is cold and wet, very few people are willing to go to the theme park. The revenues generated by the theme park would be unlikely to cover the wages it would have to pay to its staff to open the park. It is, therefore, best for the theme park to close and incur no variable costs during the winter; and simply incur its fixed costs. If the theme park decided to stay open during the winter, its losses would rise since the wage bill would not be covered by the small number of paying visitors to the park. Firms, therefore, are only willing to supply output if revenues are greater than variable costs.

3.5 Cost inefficiency

Our discussion so far has assumed that firms are operating on the cost curve. This is troublesome, since some firms are more cost effective than their rivals; and in addition some firms are better at raising productivity over time. This is clearly the case with Mercedes Benz, described in Box 3.2. We therefore need to extend our framework in order to encapsulate these ideas.

If firms have the same productive technology, they have the same knowledge and manufacturing know-how. As such they are assumed to share the same cost curves. However, if one firm pays more for its workers, or uses them less effectively, then this firm will operate off its cost curve, as illustrated in Figure 3.6.

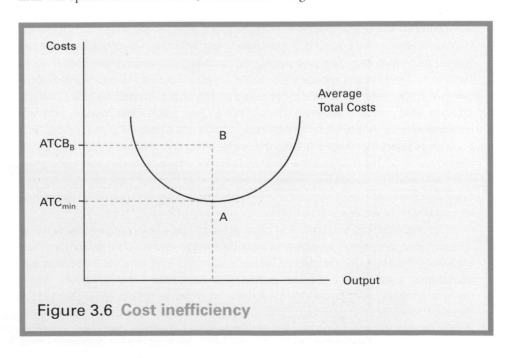

Figure 3.6 Cost inefficiency

Box 3.2 **Mercedes' new boss rolls up his sleeves**

Adapted from an article by Gail Edmondson in BusinessWeek, 17 October 2005

Only four weeks into the job, Mercedes Car Group chief Dieter Zetsche stunned employees on 28 September by ramming through a program to cut 8500 jobs at the German auto maker – 9% of its German workforce. 'Mercedes has become flabby', says Garel Rhys, director of the Centre for Automotive Industry Research at Cardiff University Business School in Wales. 'Management has woken up to the fact that they have to tackle their cost base.'

Although the vaunted Mercedes brand still commands a price premium of roughly 5% over luxury rivals, that is far too little to cover the yawning cost spread it has with the likes of BMW, Audi, and Lexus. 'A long hard road lies before us. Our costs in every part of the production chain are clearly higher than those of our best competitors', Zetsche said in a 28 September letter to employees. While auto makers do not reveal the actual numbers, industry experts estimate the cost of producing a car at Mercedes now runs $2400 to $3000 higher on average than at No. 1 luxury car-maker BMW. Ferdinand Dudenhöfer, director of the Center For Automotive Research in Gelsenkirchen, figures the gap represents 7% to 10% of total production costs on average. Mercedes insiders say the difference runs up to 22% on some models, such as the trouble-plagued E-Class. 'Mercedes' whole mantra has been: "We build the best luxury cars in the world – at any cost" ', says Morgan Stanley analyst Adam Jonas in London.

With Zetsche in the driver's seat, those days are over. The job cuts are a key step in bringing Mercedes' costs down and pushing productivity up. Mercedes lost $1.1 billion in the first half of 2005 and is likely to finish the year with a loss. But analysts say savings from the job cuts give momentum to Mercedes' efforts to save $5.6 billion by 2007. That target was set to help restore an operating margin of 7%, up from analysts' forecast of negative 0.8% this year.

Downsizing the workforce is just the first step. Zetsche's German plants lag a generation behind rivals BMW and Toyota Motor Corporation in cutting-edge factory design and processes, say analysts, and its labor and shift agreements are too rigid. Production lines in the Sindelfingen plant, for example, stop during the lunch hour, while BMW uses staggered lunch breaks to keep its line flowing. 'From a capacity-utilization point of view, a production-line stop is deadly', said a manager.

A former Daimler executive who spoke to *BusinessWeek* on background says Mercedes' costs started veering off track in 1999 when problems with Chrysler Corporation blew up and management attention was diverted. 'We stopped doing the tiny, constant things to get productivity gains each time a new model is introduced, such as investing in new equipment, adopting new processes, and reducing the number of workers on each new line', he says. 'By contrast, those guys [at BMW] worked on [productivity] constantly. Now the gap is huge. At a minimum, Mercedes has 10 000 workers too many.'

While BMW's plants run at 95% of capacity, Mercedes' German factories operate at around 80%, say analysts. One reason is declining sales of the E-Class and C-Class models, both of which have suffered quality problems. A face-lift for the E-Class in 2006 and a new C-Class expected in late 2007 should help buoy weak sales. But union contracts that make Mercedes workers' work rules less flexible than rivals' are also to blame for the relatively low output. At BMW, employees work less during periods of slow demand and then bank the unused hours, paying them back during peak periods, thus eliminating a lot of overtime pay. Mercedes recently instituted more flexible schedules and got union agreement to shuttle workers among plants, long a practice at BMW.

Improving quality is also vital. The drive to lead in new technologies has resulted in cars packed with different electronic systems, which all must be integrated into a core system that functions harmoniously, a devilishly hard task. By contrast, BMW has sought to install common electronics backbones across many model lines. It also saves money by sharing more components among models. 'Mercedes overinvested in the wrong things', says Stephen B. Cheetham, a London-based analyst at Sanford C. Bernstein & Co. 'The competition figured out you don't have to design an entirely new car to offer something new.' Mercedes insists its cars use the same electronic architecture but admits that many components vary across the wide array of models.

Firms A and B are both operating at the output level which is associated with the lowest short-run average total cost. However, only A is operating on the curve and achieving minimum average total cost ATC_{min}. B has much higher costs and this reflects a significant degree of cost inefficiency and as such A has a cost advantage over its rival. The reasons why this can occur are numerous, and in the case of Mercedes relate to the employment of too many workers and the poor development of electronic components. It is also suggested that Mercedes plants run at 80 per cent capacity, compared with BMW's 95 per cent. This means that BMW is nearer to point A and Mercedes is not only higher than A, but also to left of point A. This means that even if they could operate on the curve, their costs would still be higher than BMW's.

3.6 The nature of productivity and costs in the long run

In the long run both capital and labour are variable. Firms can change the number of machines, or the amount of office space that they use. Therefore, the law of diminishing returns does not determine the productivity of a firm in the long run. This is simply because there is no fixed capital in the long run to constrain productivity growth. So, in the long run productivity and costs must be driven by something else. This something else is termed **returns to scale**.

> **Returns to scale** simply measures the change in output for a given change in the inputs.

Increasing returns to scale exist when output grows at a faster rate than inputs. Decreasing returns exist when inputs grow at a faster rate than outputs. Constant returns to scale exist when inputs and outputs grow at the same rate.

This is not complicated. Look at Figure 3.7: in quadrant 1 we have the short-run average total cost curve, SRATC, with which we are familiar. Now consider adding more capital and labour to the production process.

In so doing we have changed the scale of operation and we now have a new cost curve. In quadrant 2 we have the situation where the new cost curve $SRATC_2$ moves down and to the right. The company can now produce the same level of output Q_1 for the lower average cost of AC_2. This is increasing returns to scale. As we increase inputs, outputs grow faster, so the cost per unit must fall. In quadrant 3, increasing the scale moves the cost curve $SRATC_2$ to the right and leaves average costs constant, a case of constant returns to scale. In quadrant 4, increasing scale leads to the new cost curve $SRATC_2$ shifting upwards and to the right, leading to an increase in costs, a case of decreasing returns to scale.

What economists tend to find in practice is that firms experience increasing, then constant and finally decreasing returns to scale: that is, firms move through quadrants, 2, 3 and 4 in order. Therefore, the family of short-run cost curves can be put together and the long-run cost curve can be derived, as in Figure 3.8.

The long-run average total cost curve, LRATC, is a frontier curve. It shows all the lowest long-run average costs at any given level of output and is really nothing more than a collection of short-run cost curves. What we can clearly see, however, is that as we increase the scale of operation, the long-run average cost initially falls and then begins to increase. So, the long-run cost curve is also U-shaped. However, the reason for the U-shape is not the law of diminishing returns; rather, in the long run economies of scale are the important issue.

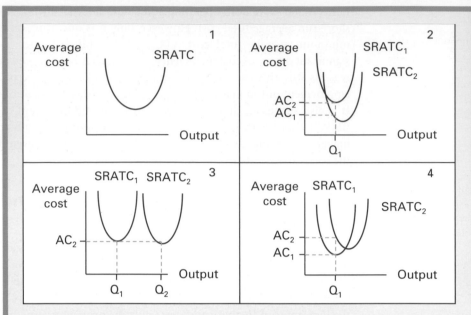

Figure 3.7 **Changing the capital input and impact on short-run cost curves**

When a firm changes its level of capital, e.g. machines, number of offices or shops, it moves to a new short-run cost curve. If the investment in capital makes the firm more efficient, then the cost curve will move down to the right, as in quadrant 2. If investment in capital leaves productivity unchanged, as in quadrant 3, then there is no change in average costs. If capital investment makes the firm less productive then average costs will increase, as in quadrant 4.

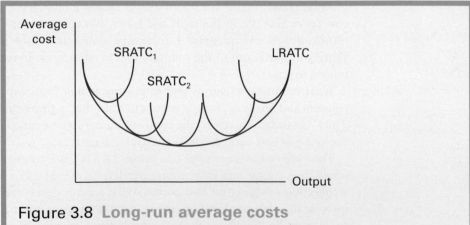

Figure 3.8 **Long-run average costs**

The long-run average cost curve is simply a collection of short-run average cost curves, illustrating how costs change as fixed inputs.

Economies of scale: production techniques

Economies of scale. Long-run average costs fall as output increases.

Economies of scale exist for a number of reasons. Consider the production process associated with making Fords and Ferraris. At a Ford production facility they might be capable of making 1000 cars in a 24-hour shift. Ferrari may only make 1000 cars in a year. At massive levels of scale, Ford employ mass production techniques; one person is responsible for fixing tyres, another for exhausts. This task specialization aids productivity and cuts costs. At Ferrari it is not possible to use mass-production techniques. The scale of operation is much lower. Therefore, as firms change their level of scale, they also change their production process and long-run costs fall.

Indivisibilities

Indivisibilities are assets that cannot be divided into smaller units.

In order to operate as a commercial airline you have to buy a jumbo jet. Assume the jumbo has 400 seats and you plan to fly between Manchester and Dubai, but only manage to find 300 passengers a day. You cannot chop off the back of the plane to cut your costs! But if you increase your scale and buy a second plane and use this to fly between Dubai and Hong Kong, you might find another 100 passengers who wish to fly Manchester to Hong Kong, via Dubai. In essence, this is nothing more than spreading fixed costs. The same arguments can be made regarding professional corporate staff. A company may only need one accountant, one lawyer and one marketing executive. In a small company there are not many accounts to manage, many contracts to negotiate and sign, or many marketing campaigns to organize. However, as the scale of the company grows the utilization of these expensive professional staff improves. The accountant manages more accounts and the lawyer oversees more contracts and, as a result, the cost per unit of output falls. Box 3.3 discusses the world's tallest building Taipei 101, so called after its number of floors. The indivisibility is land space. Once this has been purchased it can be increasingly exploited by building more floors. Air space is free, land space is not. Therefore, while often being monuments to engineering ingenuity and visually appealing, skyscrapers rest on the economic foundations of economies of scale. This is very true in areas of high population density and where land prices are high. New York, Shanghai, Taipei – all places where skyscrapers are popular.

 Box 3.3 Taipei 101 declared world's tallest building

Adapted from an article by Justin McCurry in the Guardian, 1 January 2005

It resembles a giant bamboo shoot, can carry people more than a kilometre skyward in less than 40 seconds, and yesterday it was officially declared the world's tallest building. The 508-metre-tall building in Taipei's Hsinyi district is 56 metres taller than the previous record holder, the Petronas Towers in Kuala Lumpur.

Made from concrete and steel, and wrapped in a double layer of heat-reducing glass, the structure houses a five-storey shopping mall and offices for 12 000 people. More than 30% of the 198 000 square metres of office space has been bought. The $1.8bn (£938m) skyscraper has become a matter of local pride. At yesterday's opening ceremony, Taiwan's president, Chen Shuibian, called it one of the most successful examples of construction the island had ever seen.

Geometric relationships

Have you ever noticed that bubbles are always round? Engineers and business managers have. Bubbles are round because they provide the biggest volume for the smallest surface area. More specifically, volume grows at a faster rate than the surface area. Volume is a measure of storage capacity. So, if we need to create a tank to brew beer, and we decide to double the volume of the tank, the material needed to cover the surface area, the sides and bottom, will not double in size. Instead, it will grow at a slower rate. Hence, it becomes proportionately cheaper to build larger tanks than it does to build smaller tanks. Look around your lecture theatre – we expect it will be big.

Diseconomies of scale

Long-run average costs will eventually begin to rise. The most obvious reason is that as companies increase in size they become more difficult to control and co-ordinate. More managerial input is required to run the business and managers themselves require additional management. So, as the scale of the company increases, the average cost also increases. Excessive bureaucracy now offsets any productivity gains.

Competitive issues

The issue of long-run costs has important insights for a competitive assessment of one firm against another. The lowest point on the long-run average total cost curve is defined as the **minimum efficient scale**. This is illustrated in Figure 3.9.

> The **minimum efficient scale** (MES) is the output level at which long-run costs are at a minimum.

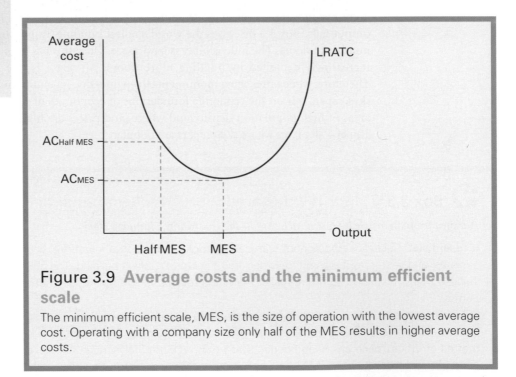

Figure 3.9 Average costs and the minimum efficient scale

The minimum efficient scale, MES, is the size of operation with the lowest average cost. Operating with a company size only half of the MES results in higher average costs.

If a company operates at a level of scale significantly below the minimum efficient scale, then it is likely to be uncompetitive, with higher average costs.

The size of this cost disadvantage varies. In some industries, economies of scale are small and the long-run average cost curve is fairly flat across all output ranges. In other industries economies of scale are significant and the long-run cost curve is markedly U-shaped. As a general rule, industries that are capital intensive generate higher fixed costs and lead to higher minimum efficient scale. Supermarkets, banking and car manufacturing all require large capital inputs and therefore exhibit high minimum efficient scale. In contrast, hairdressing, firms of solicitors and window cleaners do not require significant capital inputs. Minimum efficient scale in these industries is less of an issue.

In order to deal with an uncompetitive cost base companies can try to do a number of things. First, they might merge with another company in the same line of business. Clearly the new company will be bigger than the two separate parts and economies of scale should be realized. The merger of Air France and KLM falls into this category, as does the marriage of Telefonica and O_2. Managers often propose mergers as a way of pursuing cost economies. But they could just as well be pursuing market power. A merger effectively reduces the amount of competition in the market. This lowers the price elasticity of demand for the merged company's product. The bigger company has one less competitor and, therefore, has more scope to raise its prices.

3.7 Business application: linking pricing with cost structures

Fixed costs have been a dominant feature of this chapter. Professional footballers were shown in the business problem to be fixed costs. The development of the Airbus A380 was seen as a fixed cost; and the indivisibility of a skyscraper was also seen as a fixed cost.

In every example the fixed cost is a major component of total costs. Because an Airbus A380 without fuel weighs around 280 tonnes, the cost of moving the plane between two airports massively outweighs the cost of moving you and your suitcase. In fact, most airlines would let you fly between London and Sydney for as little as £30 – the same amount as many cheap flights from the UK to some European destinations. This trivial amount is again the variable cost and this time is associated with the cost of issuing tickets, handling your luggage and feeding you en route. This is nothing more than the marginal cost of carrying you between two cities. Prices above £30 are a bonus. Using this cost-based knowledge we can now explore the commercial decisions faced by the airlines which have ordered A380 and which are alluded to in Box 3.4.

 Box 3.4 Passenger volumes in the airline industry

Airbus big bird keeps its secrets

Adapted from an article in the South China Morning Post, 18 November 2005

The giant Airbus A380 aircraft visited Asia for the first time last week giving the media a sneak preview, but the European manufacturer and the hosts, Singapore Airlines did not surrender many of its secrets.

The vast interior of the US$292-million aircraft is certified to carry 853 passengers. Singapore Airlines have ordered seating configurations of 480 and the highest configuration to be ordered by any airline so far is 585. With an expected delivery of one a month, analysts are expecting a glut in seating capacity on long-haul routes, such as the Kangaroo route between Europe and Australia.

A senior Airbus executive described the A380 as the 'lowest ticket price aircraft around'. With a 17% lower seat-mile costs than the rival B747, Airbus chief commercial officer John Leahy mused that an all-economy configuration could make it cheaper to fly 2.5 hours from Mumbai to Bangalore than it would to take the train, a journey that takes 2.5 days.

More than any other commercial aircraft the A380 is a fixed cost for its operators, and moving the huge airframe between airports represents the bulk of the operator's costs. Interestingly, the aircraft is certified to carry 853 passengers, yet airlines appear to be ordering seating configurations between 480 and 580, presumably filling the free space with extra leg room, bars, gyms and other in-flight leisure facilities. However, we know that volume is crucial when fixed costs are high, because additional volume helps to spread the fixed cost over additional units of output. This lowers cost per unit sold, which ultimately lowers prices. With a simple piece of economic knowledge it is easy to envisage airlines very quickly moving towards 850 seats on A380s in the pursuit of a cost advantage over their rivals. History also provides a precedent. When the Boeing 747 was first launched, no one knew what to place inside the front end 'bubble'. Ideas of gyms and bars were discussed, before operators decided on extra seating.

Discount airlines, while not yet flying A380s, gain competitive advantage by being cost efficient. They know how to keep variable costs down through no frills service and they are extremely effective in dealing with their fixed costs. Load factor is reported by all discount carriers such as Ryanair and easyJet on a monthly basis. Load factor measures how good the airline is at selling all its available seats and discount carriers can often achieve a load factor of 85 per cent, beating their scheduled rivals by 20 percentage points. As suggested earlier, the aircraft is a fixed cost of many millions of pounds. But also, as a scheduled airline, the company has committed to fly between two cities on any given day. So, if it flies with no passengers, or a full plane, the airline will still incur fuel costs, staff costs and airport fees. In a sense these costs are also fixed, as they do not vary with the level of output, in this case the number of passengers carried. In the case of no frills easyJet, the variable costs are exceptionally low as no meals are offered and all tickets are electronic. Therefore, with such high fixed costs, airlines need to utilize their assets. They have to push volume through the aircraft and fill as many seats as possible. Each passenger makes a contribution to paying the huge fixed costs. The more passengers you carry, the more likely it is that you will be able to pay all of your fixed costs. Once this is achieved you start to make profits.

How do you drive volume through an aircraft? The simple answer is volume itself. For example, if it costs £10 000 to fly a jet between Manchester and Amsterdam and the plane carries 50 passengers, then the average fixed cost per passenger is £10 000/50 = £200. Then the company needs to charge at least £200 per passenger and this is only for a one-way ticket! But if the plane carries 150 passengers then the average fixed cost is £10 000/150 = £67.

From demand theory we know that we can generate higher demand at lower prices. So, we can drive volume by dropping the price. In part easyJet tries to achieve this with a twist. If you want to book a flight three months in advance the price will be very cheap. This is because easyJet have lots of seats available and they have a higher need to drive volume. Once momentum picks up in the market and the flight date approaches, they raise the price and begin to extract profits from late bookers. But, crucially, what can be observed from a business perspective is that easyJet is using a fine-tuned pricing strategy to deal with a cost-based problem.

However, we should not be fooled into thinking that in ordering A380s with only 480 seats the likes of Singapore Airlines have got it all wrong. This is because Singapore Airline bums are worth more money; easyJet succeeds in driving the load factor forward by sacrificing revenue. Its heavy discounts in the market place are used to drive sales volumes. But driving volumes through price reduction damages revenue yields, and easyJet counters this revenue strategy by also minimizing its costs. It is a no-frills airline.

So, no meals, no reissue of the ticket if you miss the flight, plus the use of unpopular airports where the landing fees are lower. In contrast, Singapore Airlines uses popular airports. It undertakes extensive brand development. It provides meals and drinks onboard. It will assist passengers who have missed their flight. In summary, Singapore Airlines provides more than simply a means of transport between two points. It also provides extras such as late checking, drinks and meals during the flight and rerouting if you miss your flight. In addition, as the first operator of the A380 Singapore Airlines will be able to offer its customers a unique experience. With few other operators owning an A380 at least in the early years after launch, the demand for a flight on an A380 will be price inelastic. The added extras of gyms and bars are designed to exploit this demand. However, in 10 years time when the world is awash with A380s 850 seats is likely to be common; and do not be surprised if easyJet or Ryanair own one, or two, for short hops into Europe.

3.8 Business application: footballers as sweaty assets

A common business term for making your fixed inputs work harder is 'to sweat the assets' and this is exactly what easyJet are trying to do by making their planes operate at maximum capacity. But how are Premiership football teams utilizing their very expensive football stars?

Few football clubs are looking at the huge expense of footballers as a problem that requires a pricing solution. Admittedly pricing may play a role. Football fans are willing to pay a higher price to watch a top Premiership side than, say, a First Division one. But the real and most obvious solution for Premiership sides is to increase the volume of games played.

In Figure 3.10 we have the demand for tickets at football games. Assuming the ticket price is £35, the demand curve for Premiership games indicates how many fans will buy at £35. Total revenue from Premiership games is illustrated by rectangle A. If the team qualify for the Champions' League then more games are played and ticket demand rises. Assuming a similar ticket price of £35, rectangle B defines the additional total revenue. In the recent past Manchester United have been very successful in using this strategy. By focusing on qualifying for the Champion's League and progressing within the competition they can literally sweat their assets, namely the players. Furthermore, by selling TV rights to their games, replica team kits and other merchandizing products, Manchester United do not only rely on the revenue streams from the turnstiles. However, once they fail to progress within the Champions' League then a financial hole appears in their business model (see Box 3.5). Players are utilized less, resulting in less TV revenue and gate receipts. Moreover, the value of the brand and the worth of merchandise decreases. Exposure and utilization of the players is a critical success factor for the business model underpinning the club.

Whether the problem is easyJet's, or Manchester United's, it is the same problem: one of exploiting fixed costs. Economics provides you with an ability to identify this type of problem and suggests some possible solutions. Implementing and managing the strategic solution is perhaps a more challenging problem.

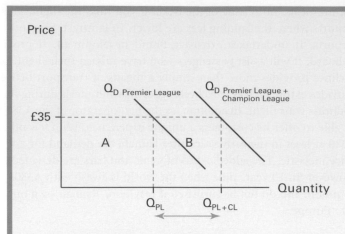

Figure 3.10 Demand for Premiership games and the Champions' League

Higher output resulting from more football games played yields more total revenue. This can go to paying the large fixed costs associated with employing top-class footballers.

 ## Box 3.5 Glazer family about to discover the true cost of coming up short

Adapted from an article by Nils Pratley, the Guardian, Friday 9 December 2005

What will be the financial cost for Manchester United of the team's failure to progress in the Champions League? You can take your pick from £2m, £15m or even, as advanced by one business school professor yesterday, up to £100m.

The figure of £2m is irrefutable representing gate receipts and television revenues. The £15m hit relates to potential lost revenues from winning the competition. However it is the potential damage to United as a brand that will be of more concern and United's owners the Glazers may soon be able to measure any repercussions. Talks to secure a shirt sponsor to replace Vodafone are already well advanced. They have already said they expect more than the £9m a year Vodafone was paying. The sustained and continued presence in the Champions League, especially in the later stages, has helped the big clubs to drive up the value of their sponsorship deals; but with United now squeezed by Chelsea for automatic access into the Champions League, the Glazers look to have a financial headache ahead.

An additional problem faced by the Glazers is the amount of debt which they raised in order to buy the club. Reportedly this stands at an astonishing £540 million. The interest on this loan is a fixed cost. Whether the team plays, or not, lenders will keep adding interest to the debt mountain. At an assumed interest rate of 6% per year the interest alone is £32m, which tops the club's 2004 profits of £27m. The Glazers have structured their debt in such a way that some of the interest can be added to the debt and therefore does not need repaying immediately. This helps to reduce the fixed-cost nature of the debt. Nonetheless, with an expensive team, an expensive manager, and an expensive mountain of debt to pay, all of which are fixed, it is imperative that Manchester United deliver on the volume of games and that means progression in numerous cup competitions. To fail on the pitch is financial suicide.

Summary

1   In the short run one factor of production, usually capital, is assumed to be fixed.

2   Adding more variable factors of production, such as labour, to a fixed amount of capital will eventually lead to diminishing returns. This can be illustrated by plotting the marginal product of labour.

3   The impact of diminishing returns is a gradual decline in the productivity of labour. This lower productivity leads to a rise in average costs per unit.

4   The U-shaped nature of the average total and average variable cost curve is related to the change in productivity brought about by the diminishing returns.

5   Average fixed costs are always declining, as the fixed costs are divided by higher levels of outputs.

6   Marginal cost is the cost of producing one more unit. The marginal cost curve is, in effect, a reflection of the marginal product curve for labour. As marginal product declines due to the law of diminishing returns, the marginal cost increases.

7   In the long run all factors of production are variable. Costs are no longer determined by the law of diminishing returns. Instead they are related to economies of scale.

8   Initially, as companies grow in size they benefit from economies of scale and unit costs fall. But eventually they will grow too big and diseconomies of scale will cause average costs to rise.

9   High levels of fixed costs generally require high levels of volume.

 Learning checklist

You should now be able to:

◆   Explain the difference between the short and long run

◆   Calculate and explain the difference between variable, fixed and total costs

◆   Explain the concepts of marginal product and marginal costs

◆   Explain and provide examples of the law of diminishing returns

◆   Understand the concept of economies of scale; and explain why economies of scale may exist

◆   Explain the concept of minimum efficient scale; and understand the importance of operating at the minimum efficient scale

◆   Explain, using reference to fixed costs, why budget airlines sell at low prices

◆   Provide economic reasons relating to costs as to why Premiership clubs wish to be in the Champions' League

❓ Questions

1 In the short run why do average total costs initially fall and then increase?

2 What are economies of scale and what are considered to be the main source of economies of scale?

3 From a cost perspective, why do you think ice cream is on special offer in November, but not in July?

4 Is it ever sensible to operate at prices below average fixed costs?

5 Do economies of scale offer a competitive advantage?

Exercises

1 True or false?
   a) Specialization can lead to economies of scale.
   b) Holding labour constant while increasing capital will lead to diminishing returns.
   c) The long-run cost curve meets the bottom of each short-run cost curve.
   d) Pursuit of minimum efficient scale can be a reason for merger.
   e) A rising marginal cost is a result of diminishing returns.
   f) Investing in brands represents a fixed cost.

2 A firm faces fixed costs of £45 and short-run variable costs SAVC as shown in Table 3.4

Table 3.4 Short-run costs of production

	Output	SAVC	SAFC	SATC	STC	SMC
1	17					
2	15					
3	14					
4	15					
5	19					
6	29					

   a) Fill in the remainder of the table, where SAFC is the short-run average fixed cost. SATC is the short-run average total cost. STC is the short-run total cost; and SMC is the short-run marginal cost.
   b) Plot SAVC, SAFC, SATC and SMC, checking that SMC goes through the minimum points of SAVC and SATC.
   c) The firm finds that it is always receiving orders for six units per week. Advise the firm on how to minimize its costs in the long run.
   Now consider Table 3.5

Table 3.5 **Short and long run decisions**

	Short-run decision			Long-run decision		
Price	Produce at a profit	Produce at a loss	Close down	Produce at a profit	Produce at a loss	Close down
18.00						
5.00						
7.00						
13.00						
11.50						

Cost conditions are such that LAC is £12; SATC is £17 (made up of SAVC £11 and SAFC £6). In Table 3.5 tick the appropriate short- and long-run decisions at each price.

3   Referring to Box 3.3 and the case of Mercedes consider the following questions:
   a) On the same diagram draw short-run average cost curves for Mercedes and BMW, depicting BMW's cost advantage.
   b) How might BMW exploit this advantage?
   c) If BMW and Toyota are using cutting-edge production facilities and flexible employment patterns do they share the same cost curve as Mercedes?
   d) Under what circumstances could you envisage the long-run average cost curve moving down? Hint: think about the role of productive technology and the comment of 'those guys [at BMW] worked on [productivity] constantly'.

Chapter 4
Markets in action

Chapter contents

 Learning outcomes

By the end of this chapter you should understand:

Economic Theory

- The concept of market equilibrium

- How changes in demand and supply lead to changes in the market equilibrium

- How price elasticity influences the size of changes in market price and output

- Market shortages and surpluses as instances of market disequilibria

- The difference between pooling and separating disequilibria

Business Application

- How firms can try to manage a market shortage to boost sales; and product, or brand, awareness

- The importance of being able to assess short- and long-run influences on demand, supply, market output and prices in the short and long run

Market theory at a glance

The issue

The price and the amount of goods and services traded change over time. But what causes these changes in particular product markets?

The understanding

Price changes in all markets, whether it is beer, entrance to a nightclub or the price of a DVD, stem from changes in supply and demand. Sometimes the price may change simply because demand or supply have changed. In more complex cases demand and supply could change together. Understanding how and why supply and demand change and the implications for market prices are important business skills.

The usefulness

Markets with upward price expectations will look more attractive than markets with downward price projections. If businesses can appreciate how competing factors will influence the price for their products or of key inputs, they can begin to develop successful strategies for the firm.

4.1 Business problem: picking a winner

How does a firm, or businessperson, know which product to promote and sell, and which to leave alone? Take Box 4.1 where the market for digger tyres has not followed producers' forecasts. High demand for metal commodities, such as iron ore and copper, has led to increased demand for diggers and their associated tyres. Unfortunately, the supply of digger tyres has lagged behind demand, leading to a shortage of tyres and perhaps this will be reflected in higher prices for the tyres that are already spoken for in 2006. Once additional productive capacity in tyre production is built, the boom in demand for metal ores maybe over. The demand for tyres will fall and the tyre industry could be left with a surplus of tyres, or at least a surplus of digger tyre-making capacity.

The central message is that the volumes and prices at which the tyres trade are a reflection of consumers' willingness to demand the product and firms' willingness to

 ### Box 4.1 Shortage of giant digger tyres puts brake on miners

Adapted from an article by Christopher Hope in the Daily Telegraph, 12 December 2006

A global shortage of enormous digger tyres, costing $20 000 each and a day to make is helping to keep the cost of metals and minerals artificially high. Typically Rio Tinto spends $100m (£57m) on 5000 tyres every year. But it warned that 'inventory levels have been extensively drawn down, producers say every large tyre produced into 2006 is already spoken for'.

John McGagh, head of Rio Tinto procurement, said: 'A supply/demand imbalance will last for at least the medium term'. Between 2003 and 2004 demand for large tyres jumped 20% but production levels had stayed flat since 1999 due to fixed capacity. New factories are not scheduled to come onstream until the end of next year. Prashant Prabhu, president of Michelin Earthmover Worldwide, said: 'This demand is unprecedented in the history of the industry and was unanticipated by the industry. Market growth has simply outpaced all expectations.'

supply the product. In essence, market places are an interaction of supply and demand. But accurately predicting the drivers of demand and supply is not always easy.

The problem of predicting future prices and volumes is not just limited to digger tyres. Consider your own futures. Some of you may wish to supply yourselves as marketing executives, others as accountants and perhaps some as business economists. The wage or price at which you will be hired will depend upon how many other workers wish to supply themselves to your chosen occupation; and how many firms demand such types of workers. Greater supply will increase competition and the price or wage rate will fall, while higher demand by firms will lead to higher wages. You, therefore, have to decide if the supply of workers into your chosen profession will rise or fall, and whether or not demand will rise or fall. Predicting correctly can potentially lead to higher income levels in the future.

The discussion in this chapter will present you with an economist's understanding of the market place. Explicitly highlighting the link between demand and supply in market places and illustrating how changes in demand and supply lead to changes in the market price of a product. By the end of the chapter you will have an understanding of how markets work and, more importantly, how business managers might try to make markets work for them.

4.2 Bringing demand and supply together

In Chapter 2, where we examined the price set in the market, we cheated by simply focusing on the willingness to demand. When considering markets and price setting we also need to think about firms and their willingness to supply at various prices. In Chapter 3, when examining the short-run costs of firms, we argued that the firm's supply curve is its marginal cost curve at prices above short-run average variable cost. We are now at a point where we can explore the supply curve more fully.

In Figure 4.1 we have a **supply curve** for the firm and the industry. Unlike the demand curve, the supply curve has a positive slope. In Chapter 3, when discussing short-run costs, we showed in Section 3.4, Figure 3.7, that the supply curve is the firm's marginal cost curve, at prices above average variable cost. As a summary, if the firm wishes to maximize profits, then it will be willing to supply additional units of output if the price it receives is greater, or equal to, the marginal cost. Since the marginal cost increases as output increases, higher prices are needed in order to induce additional supply. Therefore, the supply curve shows a positive relationship between price and output.

A **supply curve** depicts a positive relationship between the price of a product and firms' willingness to supply the product.

At each price Firm B is willing to supply more output than Firm A. This is because the marginal cost at each output level is lower for Firm B. At a price of £5, B is willing to supply 1500 units; A is only willing to supply 1000 units. Therefore, at all prices B is more willing to supply than A. The industry's willingness to supply is equal to the sum of A and B's willingness to supply.

Therefore, at a price of £5, the industry willingness to supply is 1000 + 1500 = 2500.

The industry supply curve in Figure 4.1 is the sum of each firm's willingness to supply at each possible price.

Just as we discussed with the demand curve, we also need to think about the factors that will lead to a shift in supply:

1   If more firms enter the market, then supply must shift out to the right with more industry output being offered for sale at any given price. Conversely, if firms close down and exit the market, then the supply curve must shift in to the left, with less industry output being sold at any given price.

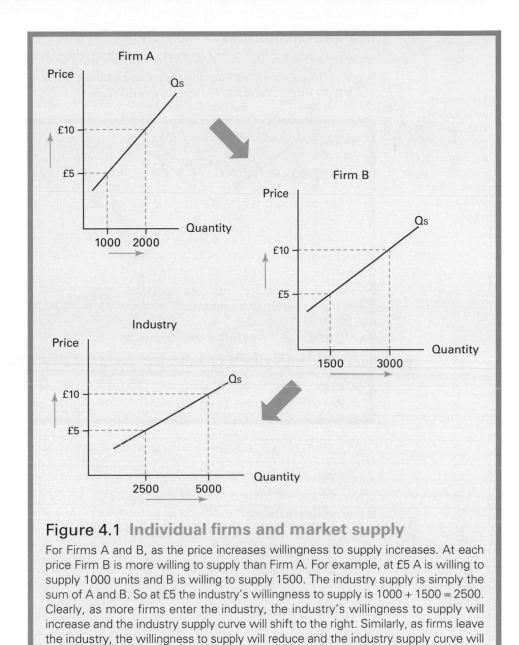

Figure 4.1 Individual firms and market supply

For Firms A and B, as the price increases willingness to supply increases. At each price Firm B is more willing to supply than Firm A. For example, at £5 A is willing to supply 1000 units and B is willing to supply 1500. The industry supply is simply the sum of A and B. So at £5 the industry's willingness to supply is 1000 + 1500 = 2500. Clearly, as more firms enter the industry, the industry's willingness to supply will increase and the industry supply curve will shift to the right. Similarly, as firms leave the industry, the willingness to supply will reduce and the industry supply curve will shift to the right.

2   If the costs of labour, or other inputs increase, profits must fall. As the potential to make profits decreases, then firms will be less willing to supply and so the supply curve will move in to the left. Conversely, if input prices fall, then the ability to make a profit increases and supply will shift out to the right.

3   If a new technology is invented that enables firms to be more productive, then their costs will fall. This makes profits increase and firms are willing to supply more. The supply curve will then move out to the right.

Market equilibrium

In order to understand the market place we now need to bring consumers and firms together. In Figure 4.2 we have the supply and demand curve together. Where demand and supply meet is known as the **market equilibrium**.

The **market equilibrium** occurs at the price where consumers' willingness to demand is exactly equal to firms' willingness to supply.

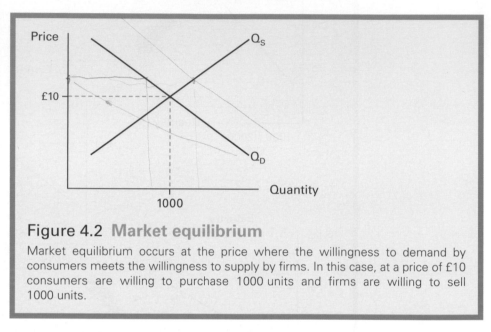

Figure 4.2 Market equilibrium

Market equilibrium occurs at the price where the willingness to demand by consumers meets the willingness to supply by firms. In this case, at a price of £10 consumers are willing to purchase 1000 units and firms are willing to sell 1000 units.

As a more realistic example, consider buying a second-hand car. Assume the seller (supplier) offers to sell the car for £5000. You examine the car and make an offer to buy at £4000. This is not equilibrium as you and the seller are willing to buy and sell at different prices. A trade will not occur because you cannot agree on the price. But assume the seller is now willing to reduce the asking price to £4500 and you accept. This is the equilibrium – you have both agreed a price at which you are willing to buy and the owner is willing to sell. As such, a trade will occur.

Before moving on it is worth making a few comments about the equilibrium. First, we assume that the equilibrium is unique. The demand and supply curve only intersect at one point. Given the condition of *ceteris paribus*, all other things being equal, the equilibrium is a stable position as there are no forces acting to move the price away from the equilibrium. In the case of our car, both the seller and the buyer are happy to trade at the agreed price of £4500. Second, any other combinations of price and quantity that are not the equilibrium values are described as market **disequilibria**.

In situations of **disequilibria**, at the current price the willingness to demand will differ from the willingness to supply.

Third, if the market is in disequilibrium then, as with the case of our car traders, negotiations and resulting price changes will push the market towards its equilibrium position. We will explain these points as we develop your understanding of the market.

4.3 Changes in supply and demand

The business problem concerned how market prices are likely to develop in the future. Now that we have a model of the market we can use our understanding of the factors that shift demand and supply to examine how the market reacts to these changes. We will begin by considering changes in demand.

Demand shifts to the right:

- for a normal good when income increases, or if an inferior good when income falls
- following an increase in the price of the substitute
- following a reduction in the price of a complement
- when tastes and preferences for this good improve.

Figure 4.3 illustrates a shift in demand to the right. At the initial equilibrium point 1000 units are traded at a price of £10. But as demand shifts out to the right a new equilibrium is achieved and now 2000 units are sold at a higher price of £20.

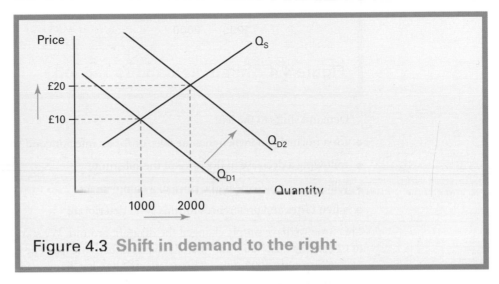

Figure 4.3 Shift in demand to the right

In part this has occurred in the UK housing market. Housing is likely to be an income-elastic good. Therefore, as UK consumers' incomes have risen during a period of economic growth, the willingness to demand homes will shift to the right, as in Figure 4.3. Moreover, the cost of borrowing has become much less as interest rates have fallen to record lows. Homes and mortgages are complements, because ordinarily you need a mortgage to finance the purchase of a home. As a result, the reduction in the price of mortgages will lead to an increase in the demand for mortgages and homes. Therefore, the falling price of mortgages also leads to a shift to the right in the demand for homes, again as shown in Figure 4.3.

Price expectations relate to views on future prices: will prices rise or fall in the future?

We can also bring **price expectations** into the analysis. If you think prices are going to rise in the future, then you will bring forward your consumption. The demand curve for consumption now, as opposed to consumption in the future, shifts to the right. Taking income, the price of complements and price expectations together, we can understand the increasing equilibrium price of houses in the UK as a consequence of three separate factors which have raised the demand for homes at all price levels. In terms of Figure 4.3, the demand curve for homes has shifted to the right because of income, cheaper mortgages and higher price expectations.

We can now explore what happens when demand shifts to the left, as in Figure 4.4.

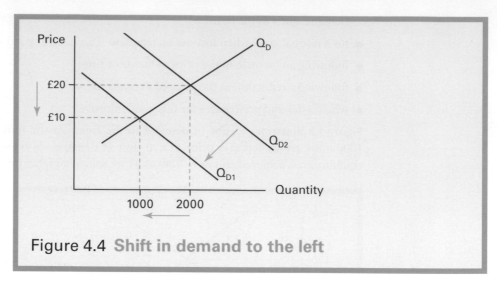

Figure 4.4 **Shift in demand to the left**

Demand shifts to the left:

- for a normal good when income falls, or for an inferior good when income rises
- following a decrease in the price of the substitute
- following an increase in the price of a complement
- when tastes and preferences for this good deteriorate

This time we have simply changed the diagram around. We start at an equilibrium price of £20 selling 2000 units and then demand shifts to the left. The equilibrium price falls to £10 selling only 1000 units. This is effectively what happened to the stock market as investors no longer wished to own dot.com shares. A change in tastes and preferences results in a lower valuation of the shares. This is also what happened to the airline industry after 11 September 2001. Commuters around the world lost the appetite to travel by jumbo jet. Coupled with a slowing global economy, falling corporate incomes reduced the demand for business travel. Fewer seats are sold at lower prices. Now let us consider supply. Supply shifts to the right:

- if more firms enter the market
- if the cost of inputs, such as labour, becomes cheaper
- if technological developments bring about productivity gains

In Figure 4.5 supply has shifted to the right. The equilibrium moves from a price of £20 selling 1000 units to £10 selling 2000 units. If we assume that the supply has moved to the right because more firms are competing in the market, then this outcome appears sensible.

Increased competition should lead to a drop in prices and more consumers taking up the product. The Internet is a significant technological development and it effectively cuts the costs of being a product provider. For example, rather than having to buy or lease many high-street shops, a new retailer can deal with its customers over the Internet. This significantly reduces its costs. Hence the market price, in major Internet areas such as travel, should fall. Lower prices mean lower profits and therefore economists predicted the dot.com crash with ease. We will return to Internet-based business in the business applications at the end of the chapter.

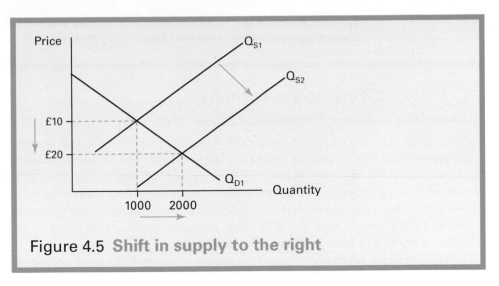

Figure 4.5 Shift in supply to the right

Let us now examine a shift in supply to the left. Supply shifts to the left:

- if firms exit the market
- if the cost of inputs, such as labour, become expensive

If supply shifts to the left, as in Figure 4.6, then the equilibrium price moves from £10 selling 2000 units to £20 selling 1000 units. This might occur if one firm exited the market or took steps to reduce its capacity. The airline industry after 11 September 2001 would be a suitable example. Taking aircraft off unpopular routes, or swapping large jumbos for smaller ones, reduces supply on particular routes. As this happens the cost of running the airline drops and the market price for tickets increases. The airline is then more likely to make a profit.

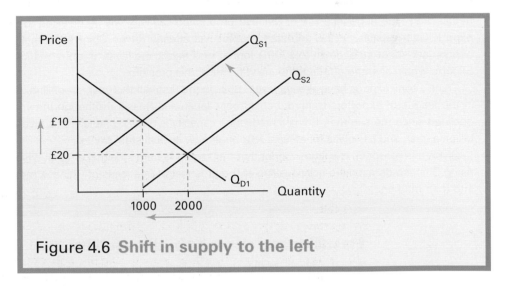

Figure 4.6 Shift in supply to the left

It is important to note that demand and supply may not always change on their own, they can also change at or around the same time. The discussion in Box 4.2 discusses the changing demand and supply conditions for steel on global markets. Under rising demand, the price of steel has increased. Following behind has been an expansion in capacity, particularly in China. However, whenever demand dips below capacity, the Chinese increase supply to the world and cause prices to fall.

 Box 4.2 Forging a new shape

Adapted from an article in The Economist, 8 December 2005

Steel today is dominated by the economic explosion that is China. The country now produces and consumes more than a quarter of world steel output. China's soaring demand lifted the whole industry out of the doldrums in late 2003. At the time, America was imposing import duties to stop meltdown in the mid-west as one American steel company after another toppled into bankruptcy. As China sucked in every available tonne, prices soared. Hot-rolled coil, for instance, the sheet steel for cars and fridges, rose from around $200 a tonne to more than $600. Steel companies saw operating margins rise to a fabulous 30% in some cases, as they made profits of $150–250 per tonne.

This spectacular boom encouraged a succession of mergers that is still underway. The latest twist is a bidding war for Canada's Dofasco between Arcelor, a European multinational that last month launched a hostile takeover, and Germany's ThyssenKrupp which trumped Arcelor with a higher agreed bid, worth €3.5 billion ($4.1 billion). The wave of consolidation started in 2001, when the top companies in France, Spain and Luxembourg combined to form Arcelor, which became the world's number one. Arcelor was toppled from its leading position earlier this year when Mittal, the London-based steel empire, 88% owned by Lakshmi Mittal and his family, bought America's International Steel Group.

In 1994 China's steelmaking capacity was only 11% of the world total, now it accounts for roughly 25%. The country's production has tripled since 2000 and consumption has more than doubled – every monthly twitch of demand sends ripples through markets round the world. Last autumn, and again in the spring, China was briefly a net exporter of steel. Coil steel prices slumped from $600 per tonne in March to $440 in early summer. Though prices recovered somewhat during the autumn, the abrupt decline showed China's influence over all markets.

The worry on every steelman's mind is that as the growth in demand for steel slows from its recent hectic rates, the huge increase in Chinese production capacity will be diverted to turning out steel for export. Over-capacity in the domestic market has already driven China's internal steel prices for the benchmark sheet steel down to $300 a tonne, well below the levels in other markets such as America. Exports would seem to offer a tempting way out of this problem.

China's total exports have already leapt 185% in the first half this year, propelling it from eighth position in the league of exporters to third, behind only Japan and Russia – although the volume of exports has declined since the summer. China's production capacity is growing rapidly. It is investing at a rate of $35 billion a year, and has plans for at least four huge new coastal steel plants.

Given this prospect, it is little wonder that the same western steelmakers that have done so well out of rising Chinese demand are now quaking at the prospect of fleetloads of Chinese metal steaming straight into their markets.

Elasticity and changes in the equilibrium

It is also worth noting that the elasticity of supply and demand will influence how the equilibrium changes. In Figure 4.7 we have an inelastic and an elastic supply curve and we can observe what happens to the equilibrium when we shift demand to the right.

Under inelastic supply we should expect that supply will not react strongly to a change in the price and this is what we observe. The price rises from £10 to £30, but output only increases from 100 to 200 units. In the case of elastic supply, the increase in demand

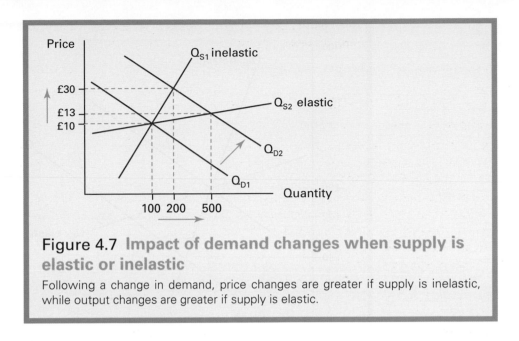

Figure 4.7 Impact of demand changes when supply is elastic or inelastic

Following a change in demand, price changes are greater if supply is inelastic, while output changes are greater if supply is elastic.

brings about a large change in output, 100 to 500 units, but only a small rise in the price, from £10 to £13.

In the real world there are lots of examples where successful business people engineer supply to be inelastic, as opposed to elastic, as this leads to price rises, as opposed to output rises. Lawyers and accountants restrict supply into their professions through the need to pass professional exams in order to act as a lawyer or an accountant. Some people comment that lawyers and accountants have a licence to print money and, in part, you now know why.

Sport is also a successful industry. Formula 1 motor racing strictly controls the number of teams in the sport and the number of races in a season. It also controls television rights for the F1 season and it can thereby limit the means by which the races are supplied to the viewing public. This is all done with the objective of running a commercially profitable sporting event. Premiership football is the same. Television access to games is strictly controlled by the Football Association, which sells television rights to Sky. The alternative would be for each club to sell its games on an individual basis. For example, one week Manchester United might sell their game with Liverpool to the BBC, while the week after they could sell their game with Chelsea to ITV. Instead Sky controls the supply of Premiership games and out of 400 games a season they only show around 60. So, by making the product scarce, or by engineering inelastic supply, the price in the market for Premiership games will rise.

In Figure 4.8 we consider how a change in supply affects the equilibrium when demand is elastic or inelastic. When demand is elastic, the increase in supply brings about a small change in the price, dropping from £30 to £22, with output increasing from 100 to 500 units. In the case of inelastic demand, the increase in supply generates a large drop in the price from £30 to £10, but only a small change in output from 100 to 200 units.

The clear lesson from this example is that, if faced with inelastic demand for your product, do not increase your production capacity and thereby increase supply, because the price will drop quicker than output increases and your total revenues will fall. However, if you are faced with elastic demand, do consider increasing your capacity and

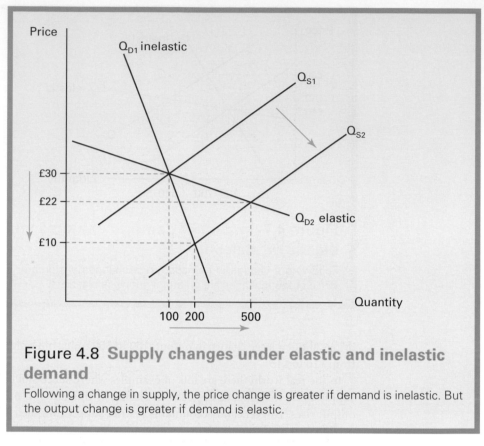

Figure 4.8 Supply changes under elastic and inelastic demand

Following a change in supply, the price change is greater if demand is inelastic. But the output change is greater if demand is elastic.

supplying more to the market, as output grows at a faster rate than the declining price and so total revenues will rise.

4.4 Disequilibrium analysis

So far we have only considered the market to be in equilibrium, where demand equals supply. In reality markets may never be in equilibrium; they may instead always be moving between equilibrium positions. First, let us consider a situation in which the price is higher than the equilibrium.

In Figure 4.9 the current market price of £10 is higher than the equilibrium price of £8. At a price of £10 consumers are willing to demand 1000 units, but firms are willing to supply 2000 units. This is clearly not an equilibrium position. With supply exceeding demand by 2000 − 1000 = 1000 units, the market is said to be running a surplus. In effect, firms will be left with excess stock in their warehouses. We suggested earlier that natural forces would push the market towards the equilibrium, so how might this happen?

If the firm has too much stock then, in accounting terms, its working capital is tied up. The firm has spent money making the product and it now needs to sell the product in order to free its cash for future production. The only way to sell the excess stock is to begin discounting the price until everything is sold. The more excess stock a firm has, the bigger the discount it has to offer. You will have noticed the trick used by clothing retailers: '50% off' is written large but 'on selected ranges' is written much smaller. The goods that are discounted by 50 per cent will almost certainly be those that few, if any, people wanted at the original price. The biggest discounts are generally offered on the

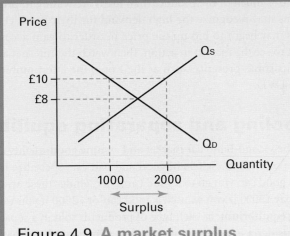

Figure 4.9 A market surplus

When the price is set above the equilibrium, firms are very willing to supply, but consumers are not willing to demand. As a consequence more is supplied than demanded. Firms are left with excess stock. In this case, at a market price of £10, firms supply 2000 units but consumers only demand 1000 units, leaving a surplus of 1000 units.

products where the retailer has observed the biggest difference between its willingness to supply and consumers' willingness to demand. Therefore, the biggest discounts are offered on the products where the retailer has the biggest level of unwanted stock.

Figure 4.10 illustrates the opposite situation, a market shortage. This time we have the market price of £8, which is below the market equilibrium price of £10. At £8 we can see that consumers are willing to demand 2000 units, but firms are only willing to supply 1000 units. We now have a shortage of 2000 − 1000 = 1000 units. Consumers would like

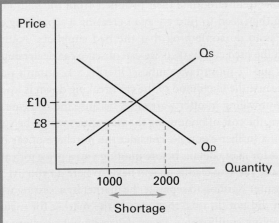

Figure 4.10 A market shortage

When the price is set below the equilibrium, firms are less willing to supply, but consumers are very willing to demand. As a consequence more is demanded than supplied. In this case, at a market price of £8, firms supply 1000 units but consumers demand 2000 units, leaving a shortage of 1000 units.

to buy twice as much of the product than firms are willing to provide. Two responses are likely. Firms may recognize the high demand for their products and raise the price. Or consumers may begin to bid up the price in order to gain access to the product. If you really want to see the market in action, then watch the Internet auction sites for the most popular Christmas presents, such as the Xbox, the latest mobile phones or recent film releases on DVD.

4.5 **Pooling and separating equilibriums**

Consider the second-hand car market and assume good-quality cars cost £5000 and bad-quality cars cost £2500. Sellers of good and bad cars specialize in each type of car. So, if you want a good car, you go to a good car seller. Under these arrangements you would be willing to pay £5000 if you wanted a good car, or £2500 if you wanted a bad car. This is a **separating equilibrium**, as each type of product is sold in a separate market.

Now consider a more realistic situation where good and bad cars are sold together. This is a **pooling equilibrium**, where the consumer finds it difficult to differentiate between good and bad products. So, unlike the separating equilibrium, both types of car are sold in the same market.

When you arrive at the dealership you are offered the following option. In a cloth bag are a number of car keys: 50 per cent open up good cars, 50 per cent open up bad cars. How much would you be willing to pay to put your hand in the bag and drive away with a car?

The statistical approach is to work out the expected value of the car. You have a 0.5 chance of gaining a good car worth £5000 and a 0.5 chance of ending up with a bad car worth £2500. The expected value is therefore $0.5 \times £5000 + 0.5 \times £2500 = £3750$.

So all cars are sold at the pooling equilibrium price of £3750. If this permeates across the market, sellers of bad cars gain an extra £1250, while suppliers of good cars lose £1250. Over time more bad cars will come to the market and good cars will leave the market. This is known as **Gresham's Law**, where bad products drive out good products.

Suppliers of good-quality cars under a pooling equilibrium are disadvantaged because they are unable to differentiate their products from the bad offerings. In order to solve this problem they need to find a way of creating a separating equilibrium. The way to achieve this is to do something that the bad suppliers would be unwilling to copy. Therefore, in the used car markets we can observe car dealerships offering cars with 100-point checks and 12-month warranties. Offering a 12-month warranty is cheap for good car sellers because the likelihood of the car breaking down is low. In contrast, the bad car suppliers are unwilling to offer warranties because the bad cars are likely to break down and, therefore, the cost of honouring the warranties would be very high.

In terms of a further example, consider the purchase of car insurance. The insurance company asks for many details before quoting you a price for car insurance. How old are you? How many years no claims do you have? Where do you live? What type of car do you drive? The insurer is trying to separate the market by assessing whether you are a good, or bad risk. If it did not do this, then clearly the market for insurance risks would move towards a pooling equilibrium. Every driver would be charged the same price for car insurance. However, in such a market bad drivers with high accident, or theft rates, pay less than they should, while good drivers, with low accident and theft rates, pay more than they should. Therefore, by separating the market the insurance company is able to charge the right insurance premiums for good and bad drivers.

A **separating equilibrium** is where a market splits into two clearly identifiable sub-markets with separate supply and demand.

A **pooling equilibrium** is a market where demand and supply for good and poor products pools into one demand and one supply.

Gresham's Law states that an increasing supply of bad products will drive out good products from the market.

4.6 Business application: marketing pop concerts – a case of avoiding the equilibrium price

The preceding discussion argued that markets will always find the equilibrium. So-called market forces push the market to a state where demand equals supply. This seems fairly reasonable, but how might a firm manage its market for strategic benefit? Or, can a firm control market forces? A successful businessperson would more than likely answer this last question with a yes.

Take, for example, the task of managing a pop star. Whether or not you like Robbie Williams he is undoubtedly a megastar. Some of his status stems from his talent, but some also stems from his personal management. By way of an example, assume Robbie Williams is going on tour to promote his new album and you are overseeing the task of pricing tickets for various venues.

An arena being used by Robbie Williams holds 20 000 people. The supply of seats at this venue is fixed at 20 000, so supply is perfectly inelastic. If we plot demand and supply, then the result may look like Figure 4.11.

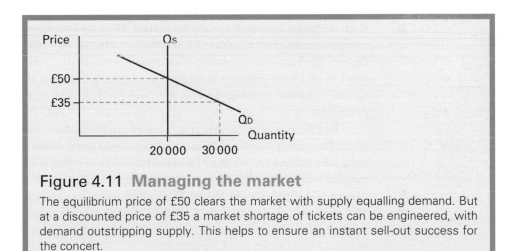

Figure 4.11 Managing the market

The equilibrium price of £50 clears the market with supply equalling demand. But at a discounted price of £35 a market shortage of tickets can be engineered, with demand outstripping supply. This helps to ensure an instant sell-out success for the concert.

In equilibrium, demand equals supply. The task is to sell 20 000 tickets, so your business problem becomes one of finding the price that will generate a demand of 20 000. In this example we have assumed that £50 is the price that will ensure a demand of exactly 20 000.

Unfortunately, £50 as an equilibrium price is not a good outcome for Robbie Williams. Selling all of the 20 000 tickets for £50 is a huge success but, since the price of £50 is the equilibrium price, the concert is only just a sell-out. Robbie Williams is a megastar and, as such, the media and press expect him to sell out in a matter of hours. A price of £50 will *only just* ensure that he sells out.

However, if we set a ticket price of £35 we can engineer a ticket shortage in the market. At £35, 30 000 fans are willing to buy a ticket. With only 20 000 seats the concert will be a sell-out, with an additional 10 000 fans still trying to find a ticket on the black market. The importance of a sell-out concert will be evidenced by the positive media attention. Column inches in the celebrity pages of the UK press confirming Robbie Williams's success will help to reinforce his image as a major celebrity. In this way, Robbie Williams's management company are sacrificing ticket revenue, but they are gaining free advertisements in the press.

The price reduction in the market place also generates positive momentum in the market for Robbie Williams's other products. As a successful recording artist, fans will be more willing to buy Robbie Williams's album, calendars, T-shirts and videos. Furthermore, a sell-out concert this year ensures that Robbie Williams can tour next year. However, if the tickets are mispriced and sales are slow, negative press will follow. This is only likely to slow demand for Robbie Williams's products. His megastar status will come under question and next year's tour will be in doubt.

Clearly, understanding how to manage the market is of crucial importance for individuals such as Robbie Williams. But the case of Robbie Williams is only an example of where it is essential to be perceived as successful in the market place. Launching a new product also requires a perception of success. The first people to try your product will be innovators. If the initial customers like your product, additional customers are more likely to try your product. We know from Chapter 2 and demand theory that one of the easiest ways to increase sales of your product is to discount the product in the market place heavily.

Consider the ongoing fight among rival game consoles Xbox, Cube and PlayStation 2. Each company aims to dominate the market. In order to achieve this it needs to generate momentum among consumers for its product. One way of achieving this is to sell below the equilibrium price, creating a shortage in the market. As more people buy your product and news leaks out that stocks are running low, then the product is obviously a success. Anyone choosing among the rival products will hopefully look on this fact positively.

In Box 4.3 it is clear that Microsoft under priced the Xbox 360 prior to the Christmas sales. The retail price of £210 was an administered price, it was set by Microsoft and had to be adhered to by retailers, or face penalties, such as removal of future supply. The eBay auction price reflected consumers' true willingness to pay and suppliers' true willingness to supply. A difference of £400, or 200 per cent over list price suggests that Microsoft were very keen to engineer a complete sell-out. In so doing they ensured the media's attention, a valuable dose of free advertising and in the eyes of consumers the Xbox 360 appeared a success. More market share should follow.

 Box 4.3 Xbox fans warned that shops have sold out

Adapted from an article by Holden Firth, The Times, 2 December 2005

Frustrated games enthusiasts have been warned that they will struggle to find an Xbox 360 in the shops this weekend after limited stocks of the Microsoft games console were snapped up within minutes of the console's midnight launch.

The online retailer Amazon said that it would not be able to meet the demand from customers who had pre-ordered. 'Due to limited supply from Microsoft, we are unable to guarantee delivery of some Xbox 360 pre-orders for Christmas,' the company said in a statement. 'All pre-orders made on or after November 2nd, 2005, will have expected delivery dates in 2006.'

The online auction site eBay offered a glimmer of hope to shoppers with deep pockets. More than 1600 Xboxes were on sale on the UK site this lunchtime, but the basic version of the console, which retails at £210, was attracting bids of more than £550.

4.7 **Business application: labour markets**

Input markets

Input markets are where factor inputs, such as land, labour, capital or enterprise, are traded.

Firms do not only sell into markets, they also buy inputs, such as labour and raw materials from markets. It is therefore important to understand how these **input markets** will develop as rises in input prices will lead to increases in firms' costs.

For example, consider the market for IT staff. In the late 1990s demand for IT staff by firms was very high. Two reasons drove this high level of demand. First, the impending millennium bug associated with the start of 2000 forced companies to spend vast amounts of money on IT staff to test and rectify computer systems. Second, the rise of virtual and dot.com businesses encouraged firms to develop Internet-based businesses. This combined increase in demand for IT staff increased the wage rate for IT staff and is illustrated in Figure 4.12.

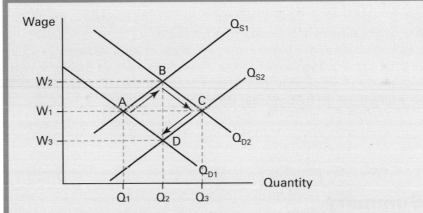

Figure 4.12 Input price changes over time

Beginning at A: demand for IT workers shifts to the right following a rise in demand for Internet-based business and the millennium bug. The equilibrium moves to B and wage rates rise to W_2. Higher wages attract new additional workers into the market and supply shifts from Q_{S1} to Q_{S2}. The equilibrium is now at C and wages fall to W_1. Following overinvestment in IT, a lack of a millennium bug problem and a slow take up of Internet-based business, the demand for IT staff shifts back to the left from Q_{D2} to Q_{D1}. The equilibrium is now at D and wages have fallen to W_3.

Two further influences then occurred. First, the high wage rates being paid to IT staff attracted workers into the IT industry, graduates entered IT employment and new student recruitment moved towards IT-based courses. The supply of IT-capable workers shifted to the right. Second, the millennium bug did not appear and Internet-based business did not increase as rapidly as expected. Firms reduced demand for IT staff and the demand curve shifted back to the left. With an increase in supply and a reduction in demand, IT wages have fallen. Companies now seeking IT support know that the market price has fallen and forcibly negotiate prices down. This is in contrast to the late 1990s when IT workers in a very tight market could forcibly negotiate prices upwards.

Ever thought of becoming a miner? Probably not. Dirty dangerous, poorly paid and poor job security? Think again. With a rising demand for mined commodities such as copper and gold the demand for miners is high. On the supply side for the last 20 years university graduates have avoided mining as a career. Taken together, rising demand and falling supply result in a joint upward pressure on the wages that can be earned by a miner. Even if you do not wish to become a miner, identifying factors which will drive demand for your skills and limit the competing supply will help you to leverage your value in the labour market (see Box 4.4).

 Box 4.4 Thinking of a career change? Mining is the new dotcom

Adapted from an article in the Daily Telegraph, 17 October 2005

Mining, according to Fred Goodyear, the head of the world's largest resources group, BHP Billiton, is the new dot.com. Mostly driven by demand growth in China and the developed world, prices for commodities are at record highs.

Meet a miner and they always look barrel-chested, big forearms, grizzled; and one more thing, old. After years of being in the doldrums the industry is now suffering from a serious staff shortage. 'We've skipped a generation', says a miner. 'Nobody wanted to be a mining engineer in the 1980s and 1990s. They only wanted to do arts subjects at university.' This hits home.

Salaries for graduates have tripled in the past couple of years. Mining superintendents are attracting a salary of $150 000. And if you are a bit more experienced, a project director to work in the jungle in Brazil can ask $500 000 a year package, plus a house, staff, car and education and health care for your family. 'But that is for a tough old bastard,' says the miner.

 Summary

1   The supply curve shows a positive relationship between the market price and the willingness to supply.

2   The industry supply curve is the sum of all the individual firms' supply curves.

3   The market equilibrium occurs where the willingness to supply equals the willingness to demand.

4   The equilibrium is changed whenever demand or supply change. If demand increases, the price will rise and more will be traded. But if supply increases the price will drop while more will be traded. A reduction in demand leads to a reduction in prices and the amount traded, while a reduction in supply leads to higher prices and less being traded.

5   If the current price is above the equilibrium, supply will exceed demand and the market will show a surplus. Suppliers are likely to discount the price to shift excess stock and eventually return to the equilibrium price.

6   When the current price is below the equilibrium, demand will exceed supply and the market will show a shortage. The price will rise in the market as consumers seek out scarce supply and eventually the market will return to its equilibrium.

7   If consumers cannot differentiate between quality differences among competing products, the market is said to exhibit a pooling equilibrium. Providers of good-quality products will strive to create a separating equilibrium by undertaking behaviour that poor-quality providers are unwilling to match.

8   Good businesses can attempt to control or influence the market. Setting a price below the market equilibrium can help to launch a product and gain valuable market share.

9   Understanding how the market will develop in the future requires an understanding of supply and demand. Such an understanding can be used to forecast changes in product prices and input prices, all of which are essential for strategic planning.

 Learning checklist

You should now be able to:

◆ Explain the concept of market equilibrium and use a demand and supply diagram to show the equilibrium

◆ Use demand and supply diagrams to analyse changes to price and quantity following changes in demand and supply

◆ Explain how changes in the equilibrium price and quantity are influenced by the elasticity of demand and supply

◆ Explain the difference between a shortage and a surplus

◆ Explain the difference between a pooling and a separating equilibrium

◆ Explain how firms can benefit from pricing below the equilibrium price

◆ Explain how an understanding of future trends in demand, supply and prices is of use to business

❓ Questions

1   Celebrity status brings riches, but will the increase in the number of boy bands, docusoaps and reality TV programmes, such as *Big Brother*, change the market price of celebrities?

2   If incomes were rising in an economy would you wish to invest in a house-building company?

3   Is studying for a degree a strategy for creating a separating equilibrium in the labour market?

4   Healthcare in the UK is free. Draw a diagram illustrating how waiting lists for hospital treatment in the UK reflect a market shortage at zero price.

Exercises

1   True or false?
    a)   An increase in demand for coffee will lead to a higher price at Starbucks.
    b)   The merger of two firms can lead to higher prices.
    c)   The equilibrium price is always optimal for a firm.
    d)   Demand and supply are said to move separately under a separating equilibrium.
    e)   The adoption of clam phones by celebrities will raise the equilibrium price of clam firms.
    f)   Prices above the equilibrium will create a shortage.

2   Suppose that the data in Table 4.1 represent the market demand and supply for baked beans over a range of prices.

Table 4.1 Demand and supply

Price	Quantity Demanded (million tins per year)	Quantity Supplied (million tins per year)
8	70	10
16	60	30
24	50	50
32	40	70
40	30	90

a)   Plot on a single diagram the demand and supply curve, remembering to label the axis appropriately.
b)   What would be the excess demand or supply if the price were set at 8p?
c)   What would be the excess demand or supply if the price were 32p?
d)   Find the equilibrium price and quantity.
e)   Suppose that, following an increase in consumers' incomes, demand for baked beans rises by 15 million tins per year at all prices. Find the new equilibrium price and quantity.

3   Refer to Box 4.2 when considering the following questions.
a)   'As China sucked in every available tonne, prices soared ... from ... $200 ... to $600 a tonne'. Draw a demand and supply diagram to explain this change.
b)   Will the drive towards merger and consolidation increase or decrease the amount of supply in the industry?
c)   Draw two diagrams: one for China which illustrates a temporary surplus in the Chinese domestic steel market; and one for the global steel market which illustrates how the Chinese surplus impacts world prices for steel.

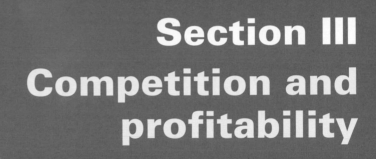

Section III
Competition and profitability

Section contents

Chapter 5
Market structure and firm performance

Chapter contents

Learning outcomes

By the end of this chapter you should understand:

Economic Theory

♦ Why firms maximize profits by producing an output where marginal cost equals marginal revenue

♦ Perfect competition

♦ The difference between normal and supernormal profits

♦ How profit and losses lead to entry and exit

♦ Monopoly

♦ How barriers to entry protect supernormal profits

♦ The key differences in profit, output and prices between perfect competition and monopoly

Business Application

♦ How a firm can organize both its output and input markets to take advantage of the insights offered by monopoly and perfect competition

♦ How markets might be strategically designed to create positions of monopoly

Perfect competition and monopoly at a glance

The issue

An essential business skill is being able to understand why different market structures create differing levels of competition and, therefore, business performance, particularly in terms of profit. On this matter economics offers some interesting insights.

The understanding

The understanding rests on how firms compete with each other. Firms can find themselves with any number of competitors. But instead of modelling every possible scenario, economists have concentrated on three: perfect competition, where there are many competitors; monopoly, where there are no competitors to the firm; and oligopoly, where there are only a very small number of competitors.

The usefulness

This chapter will provide you with an understanding of the important industrial characteristics which in part influence the level of competition and profitability that your business will generate.

5.1 Business problem: where can you make profits?

The simple answer is that you can make profits in any market where consumers are willing to pay a price that exceeds your costs. But an economist and a successful businessperson have a more valuable insight into this problem. They can identify markets that are more likely to make profits. They can do this because they understand the factors that determine whether the market price will be in excess of the firm's costs.

However, before we begin the theory, we will take a semi-empirical approach to this problem. Think about a business that you are familiar with and consider how profitable they are. We will take some common examples. Consider the pizza and kebab shops located near your university or accommodation. Are they profitable? We suspect that they make money. But you rarely see a local outlet growing and operating more than one or two outlets. The interiors of the shops are often basic and the decorations tend to be worn. Refurbishments occur only occasionally. So, given that the owners do not grow the business, or invest in new fixtures and fittings, it might be argued that profits are limited.

Now consider Google, a company so profitable and valuable that its shares are forecast to hit $600. The article in Box 5.1 suggests that Google is hoovering cash into its bank account. Its co-founders are billionaires and wherever it decides to spend its money, companies shake with fear. Such is the enviable position of Google that even Microsoft, the cash-generating king of the corporate world has decided it too wants an improved slice of the search engine market.

So why is it that Google made its owners into billionaires and kebab shops do not? It can be argued that Google has been successful in managing its market and principally its competition. By managing competition effectively, Google has grown into a successful company. In contrast, there are many kebab and pizza shops around your university. They are all competing with each other. Demand is elastic: if one shop drops its prices, students will flock to this shop. So price competition, or the threat of price competition keeps prices low. Google currently faces little competition, its search engine performs better than all of its rivals. It attracts customers/searchers and advertisers at a better rate than any of its competitors. With limited substitutes Google faces relatively inelastic demand.

In this chapter we will present the assumption that firms are in business to maximize profits. After explaining how firms should maximize profits we will examine how the different market structures of perfect competition and monopoly influence the amount of profits earned by a firm in each type of market structure.

 Box 5.1 Google: $600 or Bust?

With at least one analyst saying the shares will skyrocket in 2006, here's a closer look at the risks to the Internet giant's growth trajectory

Adapted from an article by Ben Elgin in BusinessWeek, 4 January 2006

Google at $600? A year ago, it hovered below $200. Despite its glowing successes, Google still gets almost all of its business from a single source of revenue – one that is maturing and slowing in growth. In addition, Google faces deep-pocketed competitors that will likely figure out how to mount a more successful challenge to Google's search stronghold and at least slow its advance across the globe.

This is as good as it gets. To be fair, it is pretty easy to miss the negatives. Google vaulted to more than $6 billion in gross sales last year, according to analyst estimates. In a blink, it has entrenched itself as the biggest player in the online ad market worldwide. However, Google is estimated to have generated 99% of its $6 billion gross sales last year from a single fledgling concept – selling relevant text ads alongside pages of search results and other Internet content. It has been a geyser of a business, going from virtually nothing six years ago to more than $10 billion worldwide in 2005. Google has managed to capture as much as 64% of that. But various analysts predict this market's growth will slow to 20% to 40% a year, beginning in 2006.

So if Google is to maintain its breakneck expansion, it will have to outperform the market. So far, that has been easy for Google, which currently owns more than 55% of the global search market. Not only does Google handle the lion's share of the world's searches, it has figured out how to serve ads that people are more likely to click on. In the past year, for instance, Google tinkered with the way it places ads in such a way that the number of ad clicks per search increased by 33% – enhancements that went unmatched by competitors and straight to Google's bottom line.

But with growth in the search market slowing, are such gains sustainable? Or has Google plucked all of the low-hanging fruit in its efforts to glean nearly two-thirds of all search revenues? Nobody knows. But it is unrealistic to expect Google to go much above that 64% figure – particularly with companies like Microsoft and Yahoo shoveling resources and dollars at halting Google's advance.

Already, competitors have placed some major bets that Google has not attempted to match. Yahoo is investing heavily in its so-called social search platform. It relies on written comments and input from users to determine the value of Web pages. That is in contrast to current search technology that relies on computers to determine the value. Of course, Yahoo's test project could fizzle.

Google's best shot, however, would likely be in expanding into new types of online ads. So-called branded ads, which carry corporate logos or other images, are scattered over most of the Internet. But Google has so far eschewed them for fear of slowing down its site and alienating users. This is about to change, with Google poised to add small images and icons next to its search ads.

5.2 Profit maximization

Economists assume that firms are in business to maximize profits.

This seems reasonable. As an investor you take a risk when investing in a company and so you expect a financial return for taking on the risk. In Chapter 7 we will challenge the assumption of profit maximization, but for now it will suffice as a reasonable assumption for the firm.

The profits of a company are determined by the degree to which revenues are greater than profits. Therefore, in order to understand both (1) the output level at which profits are maximized and (2) the amount of profit generated at the maximum, we need to understand average and marginal revenue, plus average and marginal costs. We discussed average and marginal costs in detail during Chapter 3, but we need to develop your understanding of **marginal** and **average revenues**.

Average revenue is the average price charged by the firm and is equal to total revenue/quantity demanded: $(PQ)/Q$.
Marginal revenue is the change in revenue from selling one more unit.

Average and marginal revenues

Consider the demand data in Table 5.1. In the first two columns we have data from a demand curve, as the price increases in column 1, the quantity demanded, listed in column 2, decreases. Total revenue = price × quantity; for example, at a price of £7 demand is 6 units, therefore total revenue = £7 × 6 = £42. The remaining total revenue values are provided in column 3. Average revenue = (price × quantity)/quantity. Therefore, at a price of £7 we have $(£7 \times 6)/6 = £7$. The average revenue is the same as the price. You can see this clearly by noting that the column for price and the column for average revenue in Table 5.2 are identical. If you were asked to plot the demand curve

Table 5.1 Demand and total, average and marginal revenue

Price £	Quantity demanded	Total revenue PQ	Average revenue PQ/Q	Marginal revenue
12	1	12	12	
11	2	22	11	10
10	3	30	10	8
9	4	36	9	6
8	5	40	8	4
7	6	42	7	2
6	7	42	6	0
5	8	40	5	−2
4	9	36	4	−4
3	10	30	3	−6
2	11	22	2	−8
1	12	12	1	−10

(price against quantity demanded) and then also asked to plot the average revenue line (average revenue against quantity) on the same piece of graph paper, the two lines would lie on top of each. If you are not convinced, take the data from Table 5.1 and use a spreadsheet package such as MS Excel to create an XY scatter plot of the demand and average revenue. You will only see one line on the screen, not two.

The demand line and the average revenue line are therefore the same thing.

Table 5.2 Monopolistic average and total revenues

Price	Quantity	Total revenue PQ	Average revenue PQ/Q	Marginal revenue
12	4	48	12	
11	5	55	11	7
10	6	60	10	5

In the final column we have the values for marginal revenue. Marginal revenue is the revenue received by selling one more unit. Therefore, in moving from 1 unit to 2 units (selling one more unit) our revenues have increased from 12 to 22. Marginal revenue is therefore $22 - 12 = 10$. All the values for marginal revenue are plotted in Figure 5.1.

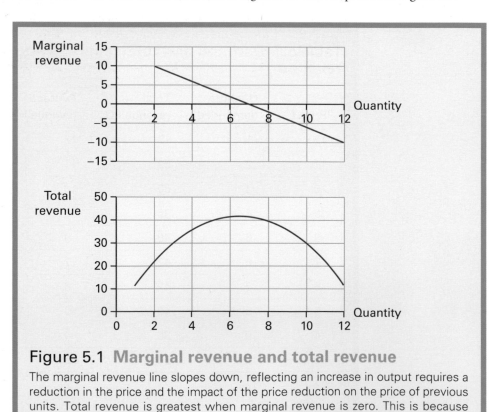

Figure 5.1 Marginal revenue and total revenue

The marginal revenue line slopes down, reflecting an increase in output requires a reduction in the price and the impact of the price reduction on the price of previous units. Total revenue is greatest when marginal revenue is zero. This is because selling one more unit neither adds to or subtracts from the total revenue.

The marginal revenue line slopes down. This is because of two factors. First, marginal revenue is related to the demand curve. In order to sell one more unit, we know from Chapter 2 that we have to reduce the price of the product. Second, in reducing the price we are also reducing the price of all the previous units. Consider the following. We can sell 7 units at a price of 6, or reduce the price to 5 and sell 8 units. In comparing the two situations we gain one more unit at a price of 5, but we are reducing the price from 6 to 5 on the other 7 units. Therefore, the marginal revenue associated with selling one more unit is $+5 - (7 \times 1) = -2$. We can see that in order to sell one more unit we also have to accept a reduction in marginal revenue and not just the price.

Finally, in the bottom half of Figure 5.1 we have the plot of total revenue. You can see that maximum revenue occurs where marginal revenue equals zero in the top diagram. This is because a marginal revenue of 0 lies between positive and negative marginal revenue. When marginal revenue is positive, each unit adds a positive amount to total revenue. Once marginal revenue becomes negative, each additional unit reduces total revenue.

Profit maximization

We can now combine our understanding of revenue and costs to understand how firms maximize profits. Economists have discovered that: Firms will maximize profits, or make the most amount of profit, when the marginal cost of the last unit of output equals the marginal revenue, or $MC = MR$.

In understanding how the economist arrives at the **profit maximization** rule of $MC = MR$, we need to make some assumptions. The firm does not decide to produce 10 or 20 units of output; rather, it decides if it wants to produce one unit of output. Then it decides if it wants to produce the second unit. At some point it will decide not to produce any more. So the economist is assuming that the firm is making stepped decisions.

In Table 5.3 we have added marginal cost data to the marginal revenue data discussed above. In the fourth column we have marginal revenue minus marginal cost.

Profit maximization is the output level at which the firm generates the highest profit.

Table 5.3 Marginal revenue and marginal cost Output Quantity MR MC MR – MC decision Profit

Quantity	MR	MC	MR – MC	Output decision	Profit
1	21	15	6	Raise	6
2	19	11	8	Raise	14
3	17	8	9	Raise	23
4	15	7	8	Raise	31
5	13	8	5	Raise	36
6	11	10	1		37
7	9	12	–3	Lower	34
8	7	14	–7	Lower	27
9	5	16	–11	Lower	16
10	3	18	–15	Lower	1

Marginal profit is the profit made on the last unit and is equal to the marginal revenue minus the marginal cost.

The firm maximizes profits when marginal cost equals marginal revenue, i.e. MC = MR. If MC = MR then MR − MC = 0. The firm maximizes profits when the **marginal profit** = 0. This is similar to revenue maximization in Figure 5.1. When MR > MC, the firm is making a marginal profit – each additional unit generates a positive profit and adds to overall profits. However, once MR < MC the firm is making a marginal loss – each additional unit generates a loss and therefore diminishes total profits. We can, therefore, argue that the firm will increase production if marginal revenue is greater than marginal cost, i.e. MR > MC. But the firm will reduce output if it is incurring a marginal loss, i.e. MR < MC.

Using these insights we can take our stepped approach to discover the profit-maximizing output. From Table 5.3, if the firm produced one unit of output, then, the marginal profit would be 6. Since this is positive the firm will make one unit. The firm now decides whether or not to make unit 2. The additional or marginal profit associated with making the second unit is 8. Again, since this is positive the firm will make the second unit. Likewise, the firm will decide to make units 3, 4, 5 and 6, as the marginal profits are all positive. The firm will not produce beyond unit 6, because the marginal profits are negative. For example, a loss of 3 is associated with making the seventh unit. Profits are, therefore, maximized at 6 units of output. This can be seen in the final column of Table 5.3, with profits peeking at 37 with an output of 6.

Admittedly, we stated that the firm will maximize profits when MC = MR and in our example profits appear to peak at 6 units of output, where marginal revenue is one unit greater than marginal cost. From an examination of the data we might argue that MC = MR somewhere between 6 and 7 units, let us say 6.5. Some products are easy to divide into smaller units of output, for example oil, beer and milk. A firm could decide to produce 6.5 litres of milk. But it would not be sensible to produce 6.5 cars. We can, therefore, say that MC = MR is strictly and mathematically correct, but it is not always the most practical output level for a firm to maximize profits at. If the firm produces whole units, it will stop at the highest level of output with a positive marginal profit. This way the firm chooses a level of output that is nearest to its profit-maximizing level of output.

Changes in costs and revenues

Figure 5.2 provides a diagrammatic illustration of profit maximization where marginal cost equals marginal revenue. Firms will increase output if marginal revenue is greater than marginal cost; and they will reduce output if marginal cost is greater than marginal revenue.

In Figures 5.3 and 5.4 we examine what happens if either marginal revenue or marginal cost changes. If demand increases for a product, then the marginal revenue curve will similarly shift to the right. This is because when the market price increases at all output levels, the firm will receive a higher price for each additional unit of output. In Figure 5.3 we illustrate this idea and see that marginal revenue now meets marginal cost at a much higher level of output. In response the firm can maximize profits at a much higher level of output. Therefore, firms do not increase output because prices rise; rather, they increase output because the marginal revenue has risen above marginal cost. The motive for increasing output is, therefore, one of increased profits, not increased prices. In contrast, if demand for the product fell, then the marginal revenue curve would shift to the left. With lower marginal revenues the profit-maximizing output would be reduced.

In Figure 5.4 we illustrate a reduction in marginal cost. We saw in Chapter 3 that marginal cost is influenced by the price of factor inputs such as labour and factor

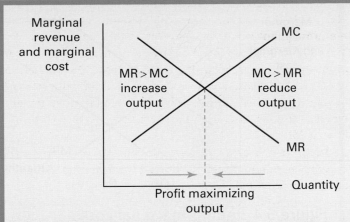

Figure 5.2 Marginal revenue, marginal cost and profit maximization

The firm maximizes profits where MC = MR. Alternatively the firm will produce an additional unit of output if the MR is greater than the MC, because it then makes additional profit. But it will not produce any more output if the marginal revenue is less than the marginal cost, because this will generate a loss on the last unit produced, leading to a reduction in overall profits.

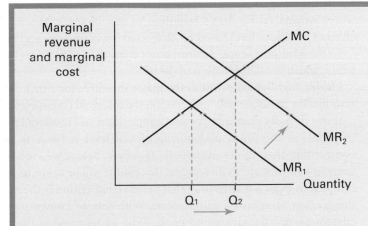

Figure 5.3 Increases in marginal revenue

If demand increases for the firm's product, then the marginal revenue curve will also move out to the right. Marginal revenue now equals marginal cost at a much higher level of output and the firm will therefore produce more output in order to maximize profits. We can now view increased output as a reflection of increasing profits rather than simply increasing prices.

productivity. If labour became more productive it could produce more output and the marginal cost would fall. We see from Figure 5.4 that if this did occur, then the marginal cost would fall below marginal revenue and the firm would increase output in order to maximize profits. Similarly, marginal cost could increase because labour wage rates increase. The marginal cost curve would then shift to the left. With higher marginal costs at all levels of output the profit-maximizing level of output would be reduced.

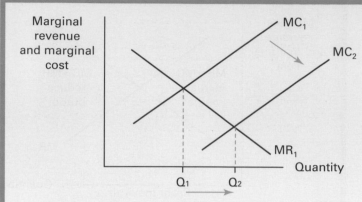

Figure 5.4 Falling marginal costs

If a firm experiences productivity growth, then its marginal costs may fall. With lower marginal costs at all levels of output the firm will be more able to maximize profits at a higher level of output. We can now view increased output as a reflection of increasing profits rather than simply deceasing costs.

We have now brought together the understandings of demand and prices from Chapter 2 and cost theory from Chapter 3. Combining the two enables an understanding of how the firm will maximize its profits. Unlike in Chapter 2, where we discussed a firm's response to changes in the price of the final good or service, and in Chapter 3, where we analysed a firm's responses to cost changes, we can now see how the firm changes its output level based on an interaction of revenue and costs.

In the economic sense, the firm is not concerned with prices or costs per se, but rather profit, which is a combination of the two.

Having highlighted profit as the major incentive for firms, we now need to consider how market structure will impact upon the marginal revenue and perhaps even marginal cost of a firm. By examining perfect competition and monopoly we will see how the level of profits at the profit maximizing output level is likely to be lower under perfect competition than under monopoly. However, before we embark upon the theory it is fairly straightforward to understand that profits will be lower in perfect competition. This can be seen from our definition that perfect competition is the market environment with the greatest amount of competition. With lots of competitors all chasing the same customers, profits have to be small. Now let us provide the theoretical, rather than commonsense framework.

5.3 **The spectrum of market structures**

Briefly, **perfect competition** is a highly competitive market place. **Monopoly** is a market place supplied by only one competitor, so no competition.

We can see in Figure 5.5 that **perfect competition** and **monopoly** are extreme and opposite forms of market structure. In reality it is difficult to find true perfectly competitive markets or even monopolies. Financial markets trading shares in companies are highly competitive, as are commodity markets trading such goods as oil, copper and gold. But, as we will see below, while such markets are *highly* competitive, they are not necessarily *perfectly* competitive.

Perfectly competitive signifies that competition in the market is the greatest possible. No alternative market structure can be more competitive.

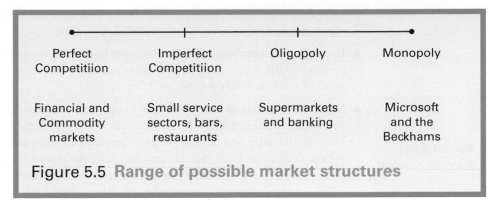

Figure 5.5 **Range of possible market structures**

Similarly, Microsoft is not a perfect example of a monopoly, as its products compete with a number of smaller suppliers, such as Linux. Likewise, the Beckhams have a monopoly on their lifestyle, image and personalities but, in the celebrity market, they still face competition from a range of married celebrity couples.

Other types of market structure are **imperfect competition** and **oligopoly**. Imperfect competition is very competitive, but differs from perfect competition by the recognition of product differentiation. Small service sector industries tend to have the characteristics of imperfect competition. The supermarket industry and the banking industry are oligopolistic. These are clearly more common modes of **market structure** and we will analyse imperfect competition and oligopoly in more detail in Chapter 6.

We will see when we examine the alternative market structures of perfect competition and monopoly that important competitive structures are (1) the number of competitors; (2) the number of buyers; (3) the degree of product differentiation; and (4) the level of entry and exit barriers. Further explanation of these concepts will be provided when we discuss perfect competition in detail, where we will see very clearly how the structure, or characteristics, of a market determines the level of competition and, ultimately, profitability.

5.4 **Perfect competition**

Perfect competition is the most competitive type of market structure. Economists assume that perfect competition is characterized by the following structure:

- Many buyers and sellers

- Firms have no market power

- Homogeneous products

- No barriers to exit or entry

- Perfect information

- **Buyers, sellers and market values**. The first two assumptions are related. The market has many different buyers and sellers. Because of this no firm, or indeed buyer, has any market power. Market power is the ability to set prices. By many buyers and sellers we do not mean 10, 50 or 100 – we mean *many*! Each buyer and seller is a very small part of the market. For example, the market for shares in any FTSE 100 company might be in excess of 10 million traded shares per day. But an individual shareholder may only hold 1000 shares, which is clearly small when compared to the entire market. The

Imperfect competition is a highly competitive market where firms may use product differentiation.
Oligopoly is a market that consists of a small number of large players.
Market structure is the economist's general title for the major competitive structures of a particular market place.

individual shareholder, therefore, has little power over the market price; they simply accept the current price on the stock exchange screens.

- **Homogeneous products**. If all products are homogeneous, all firms provide identical products. Milk is an example; milk from one supermarket is the same as milk from another. Cars are heterogeneous or differentiated.

- **No barriers to exit or entry**. In order to operate a 3G telecommunications network you require a licence from the government and a very large amount of investment. Both restrict entry into the market and, therefore, act as an **entry barrier**. Similarly, if a firm decides to leave the 3G market, then the cost associated with selling the accumulated assets, whether technical network infrastructure or brand name capital, will be costly and act as a restraint on exit. Alternatively, if you wished to start selling flowers from your garden, then you only need some seeds, sunshine and water. The entry barriers into the flower market are limited. Similarly, if you decided to stop producing flowers in your garden, then you would face little if any **exit barriers** or costs. You simply pull up the flowers and lay some additional turf.

  No barriers to exit or entry means that a businessperson can move economic resources into a market in the pursuit of profit and can also move them out. This transfer of resources is assumed to be effortless and relatively inexpensive, if not free.

- **Perfect information** If you have a secret ingredient for your kebabs, then any competitor will be able, to discover what the ingredient is. They can send in a customer and then have the kebab analysed by a scientist or master kebab chef. So any informational advantage will be short-lived. Similarly, if a firm decided to sell at a higher price than their competitors, everyone in the market place would know that the price was expensive. In the stock market all offers to sell and buy are published on the brokers' screens, hence there is **perfect information** regarding prices.

> **Barriers** make entry into a market by new competitors difficult.
> **Exit barriers** make exit from a market by existing competitors difficult.

> **Perfect information** assumes that every buyer and every seller knows everything.

Perfect competition and the firm's demand curve

We will now see how the assumptions of perfect competition drive the outcomes of a perfectly competitive market. For example, the assumption regarding a lack of market power is illustrated in Figure 5.6.

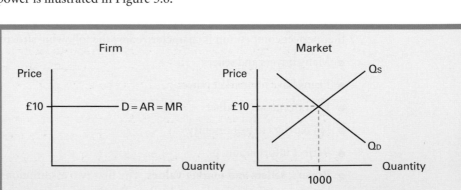

Figure 5.6 Perfect competition and the firm's average and marginal revenues

Buyers and sellers in the market place set the price of £10. Each firm, as a price taker, then accepts the market price and can sell any amount of output at the market price. Therefore, the firm's average revenue, AR, is £10, and so is marginal revenue.

In the market place many buyers and sellers come together and the market price of £10 is set. This is illustrated in the right-hand side of Figure 5.6. As the firm has no market power it simply accepts the market price.

As a **price taker**, the demand curve for a perfectly competitive firm is perfectly elastic. The firm can sell whatever quantity it likes at £10. This is illustrated on the left-hand side of Figure 5.6. While a perfectly competitive firm can sell whatever quantity it likes at the market price, this does not mean that the firm produces everything the market can bear. Rather, all firms can reasonably expect to sell their profit-maximizing level of output at the market price.

Since the firm faces many competitors, its market share will be extremely small. When this competition is coupled with perfect information, if the firm raised its prices above the equilibrium level it would sell nothing, with customers quickly swapping to the cheaper suppliers. In contrast, because the firm can sell all that it likes at the current market price, there is no reason to sell below the market price. Taking these points together, the firm faces a perfectly elastic demand curve, because demand reacts instantly, fully and perfectly to an increase or decrease in the firm's price.

Average and marginal revenue

In our discussion of average revenue in Section 5.2 we said that the demand curve is also the average revenue curve. We can therefore say that, since our perfectly competitive firm faces a perfectly elastic demand curve, it will also face a perfectly elastic average revenue line. At the market price of £10 the firm can sell any amount of output at £10. Since the price at all outputs is £10, the average revenue at all output levels is also £10. The average revenue line is horizontal, just like the demand line.

Marginal revenue is the revenue received by selling one more unit. In perfect competition the firm faces a perfectly elastic, or horizontal demand line. If it decides to sell one more unit, then it does not have to reduce its price. Therefore, if the market price is £10 the firm can sell one more unit and receive an additional £10. Unlike in our discussion of Table 5.1 and Figure 5.2, the perfectly competitive firm does have to suffer a reduction in revenue on its previous units. Therefore, the marginal revenue line is also horizontal and equal to the average revenue line, but only in the special case of perfect competition.

Adding in costs

We can now take Figure 5.6 and add in the short-run average cost curves developed in Chapter 3 to produce Figure 5.7. In so doing we will have average revenue and costs on the same figure as well as marginal revenue and marginal cost. We can then examine the profitability of the firm.

The diagram is fairly straightforward. Remember, we are assuming the firm is a profit maximizer and we would simply like to know how much profit the firm would make. So:

- **Step 1:** The firm maximizes profits by producing the profit maximizing level of output associated with MC = MR.

- **Step 2:** What does it cost to produce the profit-maximizing output? Simply draw the line up from the profit-maximizing output until it touches the short-run average total cost curve, SRATC. So in this case £8 per unit.

- **Step 3:** What revenue will the firm earn by selling the profit-maximizing output? Simply draw the line up from the profit-maximizing output until it touches the average revenue line, AR. So in this case £10.

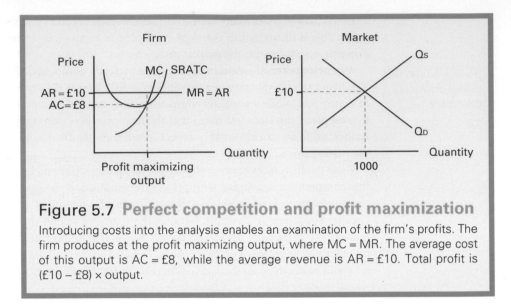

Figure 5.7 Perfect competition and profit maximization

Introducing costs into the analysis enables an examination of the firm's profits. The firm produces at the profit maximizing output, where MC = MR. The average cost of this output is AC = £8, while the average revenue is AR = £10. Total profit is (£10 − £8) × output.

- **Step 4:** Profit per unit is AR minus AC, so £10–£8 or £2 per unit.

- **Step 5:** Total profit is profit per unit times the number of units produced. Or in our figure the rectangle defined by AR − AC and the profit-maximizing output.

So we can see that this particular firm is making a profit. In economic terms it is making a **supernormal profit**.

Economic profits are revenues minus costs. However, unlike accounting costs that simply include raw materials, wages and payments for buildings and machinery, the economist also includes a return to investors. This return is a **normal level of profits**. If the bank is paying 5 per cent on savings deposits then, given firms are more risky investments, a return of 10 per cent might be considered normal. That is, the investor receives the base return of 5 per cent plus an additional 5 per cent for the increased risk.

We can also consider the situation where a firm is making a loss, and this is depicted in Figure 5.8. In comparison to Figure 5.7 we have simply reduced the market price from

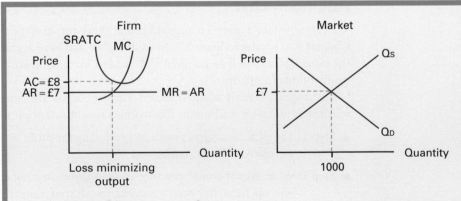

Figure 5.8 Short-term loss

With the average revenue of £7 less than the average cost of £8 the firm will seek to minimize its losses. It will do this by selecting the output level where MC = MR. The overall loss will therefore be (AR − AC) × loss-minimizing output, or (7 − 8) × loss-minimizing output.

£10 to £7, and therefore the AR and MR to £7. At this market price the firm's average revenue is below even the lowest point on the firm's average cost curve, so the firm cannot make a profit at any output level. The firm will now seek to minimize its losses rather than maximize its profits. It will achieve this in the same way as it maximizes its profits – that is, by selecting the output level where MR = MC. The loss generated by the firm will be equal to (AR − AC) × loss-minimizing output.

Long-run equilibrium

Having seen supernormal profits and losses in the short run it is now time to recall the remaining assumptions regarding perfect competition. Perfect information implies that all business people outside the industry are aware of the profits to be made inside this industry. No barriers to entry imply that entry into this market is easy. Therefore, businesses know about the profitable opportunities in this market and can enter the market with ease. The consequences of increased market entry for profits is illustrated in Figure 5.9.

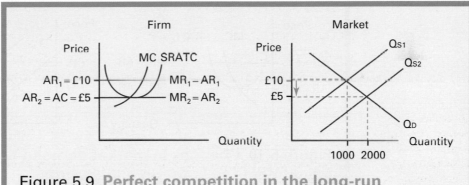

Figure 5.9 Perfect competition in the long-run

At a price of £10 firms are making supernormal profits, with average revenues greater than average costs. These high profits attract new entrants into the market and the supply curve moves out to the right. The price falls until it reaches £5. At this price the average revenue and average cost are equal, the firm earns normal profits, and firms are no longer attracted into the market.

As more firms enter the market, supply will increase. In the market diagram we illustrate this with the supply curve moving out to the right. The equilibrium price falls and total output increases. As the market price falls from £10, then the revenue received by the firm moves nearer to its costs. In the firm diagram at a market price of £5, average revenue equals average cost. Firms now break even and in the economic jargon firms earn normal economic profits. There is no longer any reason to enter the market as similar risk-adjusted profits can be earned by putting money in the bank.

We can also consider the situation where firms are making a loss. In such a scenario firms will have an incentive to leave the industry and place their money in the bank. As they do this the industry supply reduces. The market price increases and eventually the firms remaining in the industry will earn normal profits.

Clearly entry and exit are not the only factors that will influence the market equilibrium. We can envisage a number of short-term scenarios leading to a long equilibrium.

Scenario 1: the good is a normal good. Income increases and, therefore, the market demand shifts to the right. The market price increases and the firm's marginal revenue and average revenue rises relative to costs. Increased profits then attract new entry into the market. The market supply curve shifts to the right and the market equilibrium price drops until average revenues equal average costs and only normal profits are earned. These points are highlighted in Figure 5.10.

Scenario 2: following wage negotiations the cost of labour increases. The firms' marginal cost curves shift to the left and average costs rise upwards. Firms' profits decrease. Exit occurs and the market supply curve shifts to the left. As a result the market equilibrium price increases until the average revenues earned by the firms match the higher cost level brought about by increased labour costs. Normal profits are earned and exit stops. These points are illustrated in Figure 5.11.

The review questions contain an additional scenario to test your understanding and use of the diagrams.

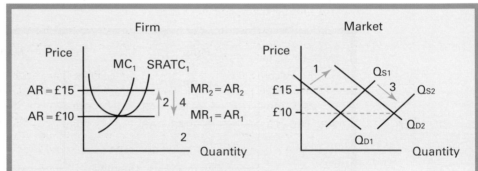

Figure 5.10 Changes in market demand and adjustments to long-run equilibrium

The market is in equilibrium where Q_{D1} equals Q_{S1}. The market price is £10. At this price the firm earns a normal profit, with average revenue equal to average cost at the profit-maximizing output, where $MR_1 = MC$. Then:

1 Income levels in the economy increase. The good is income normal and therefore the demand curve shifts to the right to QD_2 (consumers use the increased income to buy more of the good). The equilibrium price rises to £15.

2 The average revenue for the firm rises to £15 reflecting the increased market price. The marginal revenue also increases to £15 and the profit-maximizing output increases. Since average revenues exceed average cost, the firm is making a supernormal profit.

3 The supernormal profits attract new entrants into the market and supply shifts from Q_{S1} to Q_{S2} and the market equilibrium price falls to £10.

4 The average and marginal revenues fall to £10. The profit-maximizing output returns to its original level and the firm generates normal profits.

Productive efficiency means that the firm is operating at the minimum point on its long-run average cost curve.

It is important to remember that, whether we begin with a supernormal profit or a supernormal loss, firms in perfect competition will always end up earning only normal profits in the long run. That is, firms in a perfectly competitive long-run equilibrium will be indifferent between being in business and placing their money in the bank.

In the long-run equilibrium, the perfectly competitive firm is operating at the minimum point of their average cost curve. This means that the firm is **productively efficient** as it is producing at least cost.

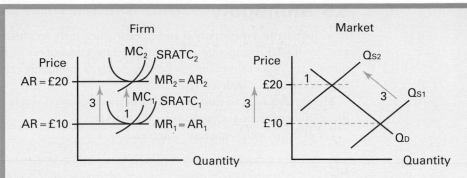

Figure 5.11 An increase in firms' costs and adjustment to long-run equilibrium

The market is in equilibrium where Q_D equals Q_{S1}. The market price is £10. At this price the firm earns a normal profit, with average revenue equal to average cost at the profit-maximizing output. Then:

1 Negotiations lead to a rise in the wages paid to the firms' labour forces. This leads to an increase in the individual firm's costs. The average and marginal cost rise to MC_2 and $SRATC_2$.
2 The firm's costs are now greater than the average revenue of £10, leading to losses. Some firms exit the industry and the industry supply curve shifts to the left, to Q_{S2}.
3 The equilibrium market price rises to £20, also raising average revenue to £20. This is just enough to cover the increase in the firms' costs. Firms again generate normal profits at the profit-maximizing output.

Moreover, in the long-run equilibrium the firm is charging a price that is equal to the marginal cost. This means that the firm is also **allocatively efficient**.

Recall that the marginal cost is the cost of using scarce factor resources to produce one more unit of output; and the price paid by consumers reflects the value placed on the final good. If the marginal cost is £10, but the price paid is £5, consumers do not value the final product by the same amount as the cost of using the resources to make the final product. The resources should have been allocated to the production of a final product with a higher value among consumers. That is, resources need to be allocated efficiently, and this occurs when price = marginal cost. We will return to these points when we compare perfect competition with monopoly.

> **Allocative efficiency** occurs when price equals marginal cost, or $P = MC$.

A quick consideration of kebab shops

Now let's consider kebab shops. There are many students. There are many kebab shops. A kebab is a fairly homogeneous product. Kebabs from different shops are fairly similar. Prices are listed on boards inside the shop and are usually visible from the street, so information regarding prices is near perfect. Barriers to entry are fairly limited. You need a shop, a food licence, some pitta bread and some cheap meat. All are easily available. The market is not perfectly competitive, but its characteristics are nearly so. Therefore, we now know or can predict that the kebab market is not a fantastic business proposition. Let us now consider monopoly.

5.5 **Monopoly**

In a strict sense a monopoly is said to exist when only one firm supplies the market. In practice the UK competition authorities define a monopoly to exist if one firm controls more than 25 per cent of the market. So, clearly, a monopoly exists if there is a dominant firm in the market with few rivals.

Monopolies tend to exist because of barriers to entry; where barriers to entry restrict the ability of potential rivals to enter the market.

Let us begin with some easy examples.

Licences

The National Lottery is a monopoly. Only one firm, currently Camelot, is licensed by the government to operate a national lottery in the UK. Licences also act as a barrier to entry on the railways. Only GNER is allowed to operate high-speed trains between Leeds and London King's Cross.

Patents

When a pharmaceutical company develops a new drug it can apply for a patent. This provides it with up to 20 years of protection from its rivals. While everyone can discover the ingredients within Viagra, only the patent owner Pfizers is able to exploit this knowledge in the market. So patents also act as a barrier to entry.

Natural monopoly

A **natural monopoly** exists if scale economies lead to only one firm in the market.

Consider long-run average costs introduced in Chapter 3. The minimum efficient scale, MES, is the size the firm has to attain in order to operate with minimum costs. If the MES is a plant capable of producing 1 million units per year and consumers demand around 10 million units per year, then the market can support about 10 firms. However, if the MES is a plant producing around 10 million units, then the market can only support one firm.

Natural monopolies were thought to exist in the utility markets such as water, gas and telecommunications, where the infrastructure required to operate in these markets was so large that it restricted entry. For example, the scale needed to operate an effective telecommunications network in the UK was thought to be so large, because of all the cables, switches and exchanges that were required, that only one firm was capable of investing and generating a return. Two firms would double the amount of investment, but at best share the market and, therefore, the financial returns. However, when telecommunications began to move from copper wire to mobile communications, other firms could build networks much more cheaply. The barriers to entry fell and more firms now operate in the telecommunications market.

What does one firm and significant entry barriers mean for firm-level profitability?

Revenues and costs in monopoly

Just like perfect competition we need to think about the revenues and costs generated by a monopoly. In perfect competition MR and AR are the same. As a price taker, if the firm sells more output it does not cause the market price to fall, so its MR and AR stay constant. In monopoly the situation is different. As the only supplier in the market, the monopoly faces the downward sloping market demand curve. Therefore, if it sells more output, the price must fall. This has implications for the monopoly's AR and MR.

Consider Figure 5.12. The average revenue line, AR, is downward sloping and this follows from above. If the firm sells more output then, under the law of demand, consumers will only demand more output at lower prices. So as the price drops, the average price per unit must drop.

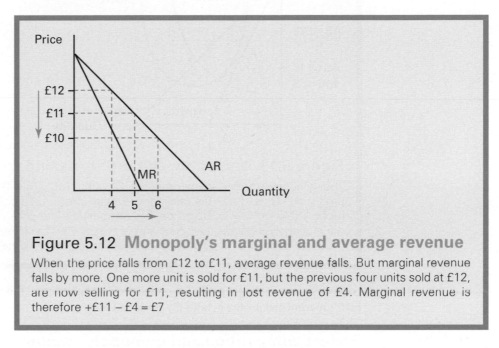

Figure 5.12 Monopoly's marginal and average revenue

When the price falls from £12 to £11, average revenue falls. But marginal revenue falls by more. One more unit is sold for £11, but the previous four units sold at £12, are now selling for £11, resulting in lost revenue of £4. Marginal revenue is therefore +£11 − £4 = £7

Marginal revenue is more difficult to understand. Again consider Figure 5.12 and Table 5.3. Initially we are selling 4 units at £12. Total revenue is £48 and average revenue is the price, £12. To sell one more unit we need to drop the price to £11. This generates total revenue of £11 × 5 = £55 and the average revenue is now £11. But what has happened to marginal revenue? Two things have occurred. First, we are selling one more unit for £11 but, second, we are losing £1 per unit on the previous four units. So marginal revenue = +£11 − (4 × £1) = £7. So MR = £7, while AR = £11. Now let us drop the price to sell one more unit. Selling 6 units at £10 generates a total revenue of £10 × 6 = £60. The marginal revenue from selling the sixth unit is £60 − £55. So MR = £5, while AR = £10. Going from the fifth to sixth unit changed the price from £11 to £10; in effect we reduced the average revenue by £1. However, the marginal revenue changed from £7 to £5, a change of £2. We can therefore see that in selling more units we have to accept a bigger reduction in marginal revenue than in average revenue. Reflecting this point, in monopoly, the marginal revenue line will always be steeper and below the average revenue line.

As with perfect competition, we now need to add in the firm's cost curves (see Figure 5.13).

The monopoly will also maximize profits where MC = MR. This point defines the profit-maximizing output. If we then draw the line up from Q until in touches the short-run average total cost curve, SRATC, then we see that the average cost equals £10. Drawing the line further until it touches the average revenue line, we see that the output can be sold for £20 per unit, making a profit per unit of £20 − £10 = £10. Total profit is £10 per unit multiplied by the profit-maximizing output Q. This is the short-term profit-maximizing position and because of significant entry barriers this profit will not be

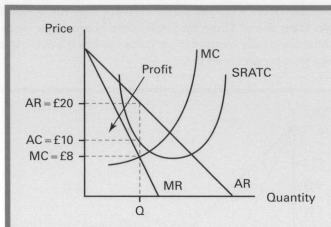

Figure 5.13 Monopoly and profit maximization

The monopoly's profits are maximized at Q, where MC = MR. The average cost of producing Q is £10, the average revenue from selling Q is £20. Total profit = (£20 − £10) × Q. Unlike perfect competition, the price of £20 charged by the monopoly is greater than the marginal cost of £8. This difference between the price and the cost of making the last unit are an indication of market power.

competed away in the long run. So: unlike perfect competition, monopolies can expect to earn supernormal profits in both the short and long run.

Perfect competition and monopoly compared

The long-term profit position of monopoly is not the only difference and so it is worth comparing perfect competition and monopoly in more detail. In order to do this we will assume that we have a perfectly competitive industry with 1000 firms supplying the market. Overnight a businessperson buys out all the firms and begins to act as a monopoly.

As a consequence of this transfer of ownership from 1000 people to one person the cost structure will not change; the monopoly will simply have a cost curve that is the sum of all the 1000 individual cost curves under perfect competition. The same will apply to the marginal cost curve and this is illustrated in Figure 5.14. The customers in the market have not changed, so the demand curves or AR lines faced by the perfectly competitive industry and the monopoly are identical. The marginal revenue lines are different. Remember, in perfect competition, marginal and average revenue are the same, but in monopoly they are different. We can now use Figure 5.14 to assess the differences between perfect competition and monopoly.

In order to maximize profit, the perfectly competitive industry will set $MC_{pc} = MR_{pc}$. Its profit maximizing output is Q_{pc} and the price it sells for is Price PC. The monopoly sets $MC_{mp} = MR_{mp}$ and its profit-maximizing output is Q_{mp} and the price it sells this output for is Price MP. It is now clear to see that in moving from perfect competition to monopoly the industry output drops and the price increases. Furthermore, in perfect competition the price equals the industry's marginal cost, but in monopoly the price is higher than the industry's marginal cost.

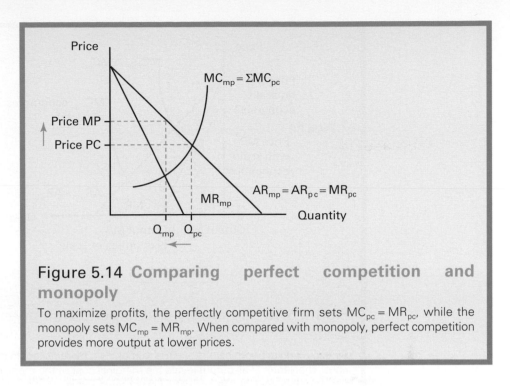

Figure 5.14 Comparing perfect competition and monopoly

To maximize profits, the perfectly competitive firm sets $MC_{pc} = MR_{pc}$, while the monopoly sets $MC_{mp} = MR_{mp}$. When compared with monopoly, perfect competition provides more output at lower prices.

This difference between price and marginal cost in monopoly is known as 'market power', which is the ability to price above the cost of the last unit made.

Monopoly and economies of scale

However, the arguments put forward are weak. The idea that a monopoly would have the same cost curves as a perfectly competitive industry neglects the points made in Chapter 3 relating to economies of scale. A monopoly may be capable of reducing costs. A single company is unlikely to operate 1000 separate plants. Instead, they are more likely to rationalize the 1000 plants into a smaller number of very large plants, which can exploit economies of scale. If this is true, then the cost reduction would lead to the monopoly's marginal cost curve moving out to the right. This is shown in Figure 5.15, with the marginal cost for the monopoly shifting to the right. At all output levels the marginal cost of the monopoly is now lower than the marginal cost of the perfectly competitive industry. The monopoly is now more cost efficient than perfect competition. The profit maximizing output for the monopoly now occurs where marginal revenue intersects the new marginal cost curve under economies of scale. Output is higher than in perfect competition and the market price is lower than in perfect competition.

Of course it also needs to be recognized that a monopoly has no incentive to improve efficiency, as it has no competition. So why should it try to exploit economies of scale? Moreover, it is also possible that the monopoly may be too large and displays diseconomies of scale. Its costs would then be greater than the perfectly competitive industry, with the marginal cost curve shifting to the left. This would lead to even higher prices and a greater reduction in output under monopoly.

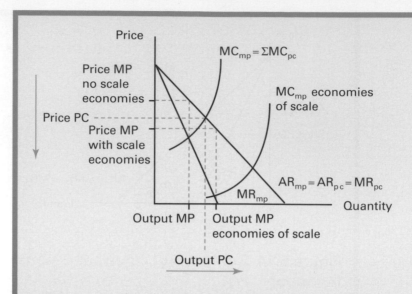

Figure 5.15 Monopoly and exploitation of economies of scale

By exploiting economies of scale the monopoly's marginal costs curve shifts to the right. Therefore, at all output levels the marginal cost of the monopoly is lower than the marginal cost of the perfectly competitive industry, illustrating the improved cost efficiencies of the monopoly.

   The profit-maximizing output for the monopoly is now greater than the output of the perfectly competitive industry and the monopoly price is also lower.

Creative destruction occurs when a new entrant out competes an incumbent monopoly by virtue of being innovative.

Rent-seeking behaviour is the pursuit of supernormal profits. An economic rent is a payment in excess of the minimum price at which the good or service will be supplied.

Creative destruction

An alternative argument in favour of monopoly is that of creative destruction. Under this approach, monopolies are generally accepted as raising prices, restricting output and earning supernormal profits, which are potentially all bad. However, what should also be recognized is the benefits which stem from the supernormal profits, especially when they act as an incentive to innovate. Firms which are not monopolies can be motivated to be innovative and creative. Developing new products for the market, or new production techniques which provide them with a competitive advantage and destroy the entry barriers of the incumbent monopoly. The innovating firm, through creative destruction, then becomes the monopoly. The firm benefits from higher profits; and society benefits from the supply of new innovative goods and services. One potential drawback with this approach is that firms have to undertake expensive **rent-seeking behaviour** and they may not always be successful. Some inventions, work, others do not. So for every monopoly brought about by innovation, there can be many failures which have used the scarce resources of the economy. Box 5.2 mentions the fall in sales of a number of blockbuster drugs following the arrival of new competition. For example, the rise of Viagra through scientific innovation revolutionized the treatment of impotence. But while its financial success was huge, it was soon deflated by the arrival of competitive drugs in the form of Cialis and Levitra. Rent-seeking behaviour led to the creative destruction of Viagra's monopoly.

Box 5.2 Pfizer suffers big profits slump amid growing drug competition

Adapted from an article by David Teather, The Guardian, 21 October 2005

Pfizer, the world's biggest drug company, which is struggling with the loss of patents on key treatments and a health scare linked to the arthritis drug Celebrex, has reported a 52% slump in quarterly profits.

Celebrex sales crashed by 44% to $446m after being linked with heart attacks and strokes. Sales of Neurontin, Pfizer's epilepsy drug, fell 80% as it faced generic competition for the first time. Another key Pfizer drug, Zithromax, its best-selling antibiotic, will find itself in competition against generic versions as early as next month. In the US, sales of branded prescription drugs fell 3% in the third quarter, under pressure from the cheaper copycat drugs produced when patents expire.

Sales of the cholesterol treatment Lipitor, the world's best-selling drug, rose 6% during the quarter to $2.9bn. However, the rate of growth has 'declined significantly', the company said. Pfizer also gave warning that the market for impotence treatments was getting more competitive. Pfizer's pioneering treatment, Viagra, suffered a 4% decline in sales, partly due to competition.

5.6 Business application: how to design a market – the cases of Microsoft and Premiership football TV rights

From a business perspective monopoly is preferable to perfect competition. In monopoly there is no competition, the price is higher and barriers to entry ensure that supernormal profits are long term. So a businessperson would clearly like to be in a monopoly or be capable of deriving a business strategy that takes them from a perfectly competitive market to a monopoly.

The creation and maintenance of a monopoly are the reasons why Microsoft has been so successful. Microsoft's initial success was based on its operating system, the product that has been developed into Windows Vista. As the operating system is the base package that all computer programs run on, Microsoft allows any potential software developer free access to training and technical advice on how the Windows program works. This makes the development of Windows-based programs very easy. As a consequence Windows remains the main operating system because software companies are willing to design programs for it. If a new operating system came along, then software producers would have to learn about the new system and its programming code. This creates huge costs known as **switching costs**.

Switching costs are the costs of moving between products.

It is these switching costs that help to create an effective entry barrier. It is of no surprise that Microsoft is using the same strategy with software producers for the Xbox.

The organization for the live broadcast of Premiership football games has been another good example of how a market has been designed by clever business people. With 20 sides in the UK Premiership there are 380 games in a season. Without offending too many of you, some games are not worth watching, particularly near the bottom of the Premiership. So we might not expect to see all 380 games on TV, but the fact that the owner of the TV rights since 1993, a company named BSkyB, has only shown around 60 games is intriguing.

When comparing monopoly with perfect competition we discovered that monopolies produce less output. So, given that BSkyB has only shown 60 out of 380 games, can the theory be used to explain this commercial strategy?

The first starting point would be to ask whether BSkyB has been a monopoly supplier of televised Premiership football. With exclusive television rights to the games, clearly it is a monopoly, especially with live games. This suspicion has been around for a while and has been the subject of a long-standing challenge by the UK and EU competition authorities (see Box 5.2). If BSkyB was acting as a monopoly, was there any commercial incentive to restrict the number of televised live games? In this chapter and in Chapter 4, when examining markets, we have seen that restricting supply leads to a price rise. In effect, it could be argued that BSkyB restricts supply in order to make Premiership games scarce, thereby pushing up the market price of Premiership games to viewers of the Sky Sports channel.

Is there though a perfectly competitive alternative to BSkyB? Alternatives exist but they may not be what we consider perfectly competitive. At present the Football Association sells TV rights on behalf of all Premiership teams, thus creating single supply. The more competitive approach would be for each club to sell its rights on an individual basis to various TV companies. With 20 clubs competing against each other for TV contracts, as opposed to the Football Association acting as sole agent, competition increases. The output of games will rise and the price in the market will fall. A better deal all round for football fans. An alternative approach would be for Sky to retain a significant share of live games, but also provide the BBC and ITV with greater access to the live games. As discussed in Box 5.3, this appears to have been one of the options considered by the competition authorities.

 ### Box 5.3 Premier League and EC near the endgame in broadcasting deal

Adapted from an article by Jane Martinson and Cosima Marriner, the Guardian, 17 November 2005

A deal which could signal the end of the long-running dispute between the Premier league and the European commission competition authorities will spell out the auction process for the lucrative live broadcast rights that have been owned exclusively by the TV broadcaster BSkyB since the league was formed 13 years ago. In 2003 it paid £1bn to secure rights for 3 years.

The league is understood to have guaranteed it will create six 'balanced' packages of games. At least two broadcasters will be able to televise live Premiership games, so Sky will be banned from bidding for the sixth package if it has succeeded in securing the other five. Each bidder will also have to make a standalone bid for each package and will not be able to offer a premium for winning two or more.

NTL, a rival cable supplier of TV, has complained saying that the deal should ensure that the second bidder is guaranteed half of the games.

While BSkyB's days as a monopoly supplier of live games appear to be at an end, it is reasonable to expect it to continue to dominate the market and achieve ownership of five packages. The important point for students of business is to appreciate and understand the success of the business strategy entered into by the Premiership and BSkyB since 1993. Clearly at some point someone within football and within BSkyB thought about what would be an ideal business solution to selling and broadcasting

Premiership football games. They put economics into action and with this strategy created a successful business model that excluded competition. It is to their credit as businesspeople how skilfully they achieved this and it is for the rest of us to watch and learn.

However, there should be a word of warning. In order to exploit a monopoly position you need customers who are willing to pay a price which will cover your costs. The auction for the right to be a monopoly is likely to be very competitive, because the future potential profits can be huge. But if you over-bid, your costs could rise above your revenues and you will be left making a loss. Take Figure 5.16 as an example. The average cost curve is higher than the average revenue line. Since profits are revenues minus costs, the firm can only make a loss. In the case of ITV Digital, the high price paid for the television rights pushed the average cost curve above the average revenue line, where the average revenue line represents the level of demand for Division 1 games.

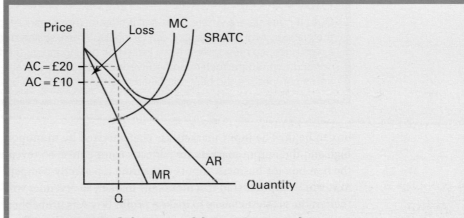

Figure 5.16 A loss-making monopoly

If the average cost curve is above the average revenue line it is impossible for the firm to make a profit. In the case of monopoly this is no different. At the profit-maximizing output where MC = MR, the average revenue = £10 and the average cost = £20. The firm is making a loss per unit of £10. Total losses are the loss per unit times the number of units, (−£10 × Q).

5.7 Business application: 'Oops, we are in the wrong box' – the case of the airline industry

Financial performance is essential or, in other words, profits count. The firm's revenues and costs determine profits. If we look closely at revenues and costs they are both influenced by prices. A firm's revenues are determined by the price it sells its output for and a firm's costs are determined by the price it has to pay for its labour, capital and raw materials. Price is determined by market structure – it is higher in monopoly and lower in perfect competition. We can use this to think about business structures that are optimal for business by considering the input–output matrix in Figure 5.17.

Across the top we have the market structure of the firm's output market, where it sells its product. Down the side we have the market structure for the firm's input markets, where the firm purchases its labour, capital and raw materials. Box C could be the worst

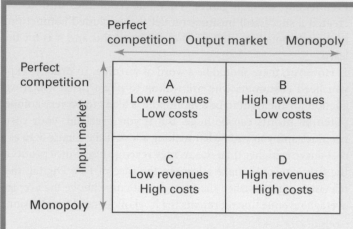

Figure 5.17 Optimal mix input and output markets
Output markets are where firms sell products. Input markets are where firms buy their labour, raw materials and capital inputs. When selling output the firm desires a high price, so monopoly is best. But when buying inputs the firm likes to keep its costs down, so perfectly competitive markets are preferable. Therefore, from a firm's perspective the best combination is associated with box B.

box to be in. The input markets are characterized by monopoly supply, so cost will be high and the output markets are perfectly competitive, so revenues will be low. Box B is the best box for business. Inputs come from a perfectly competitive market, so costs are low, while output is sold in a monopoly market, so revenues will be high. Box B is where there is the greatest chance to make a profit. Box A is probably preferable to box D. In A both markets are perfectly competitive so supernormal profits are unlikely. But how do you think box D compares with box C? In C and D both firms face a monopoly input supplier. But firms in C have a perfectly competitive output market. This could actually make it more attractive than D. With a perfectly competitive output market the firm will make only normal profits, so the monopoly input supplier cannot afford to squeeze the perfectly competitive firms. In fact there are no profits to squeeze; but in D the monopoly output will create profits that the monopoly supplier can try to expropriate for itself by charging higher input prices. So D may be less attractive than C.

Rarely will a firm find itself comfortably inside box B, but it might be expected to try to move towards box B over time. For example, in box D the obvious solution is to purchase the monopoly input supplier and make it part of your company. This is known as vertical integration, and it will be discussed at length in Chapter 7. While in box A you would try to buy up your competitors or force them out of the market. This way competition is reduced and the market moves towards monopoly.

But for a more illuminating example let us look at the airline industry. First, examine its key inputs: aircraft, landing rights at international airports and pilots. There are only two major aircraft manufacturers in the world, Airbus and Boeing. The market is not perfectly competitive. Most major cities have one airport, a monopoly. Pilots are expensive and unionized. Unions are effectively a monopoly supplier of labour. So, on the input side airlines are not in a good position. In terms of output, tickets for airlines are sold via travel agents or via the Internet. Most travellers say, 'I would like to go on this date between these two cities: who is offering the cheapest fare?' Ten options appear up on the screen and the cheapest option is generally selected. This would suggest that the market is highly competitive. This is clearly not good for the airline industry.

Solutions

With monopoly suppliers and competitive output markets, airlines are firmly located in box C. How can they deal with this situation? Airline alliances are a likely solution. In such alliances airlines come together and in the first instance they agree to share passengers – so-called code sharing. This reduces competition in the output market and moves airlines towards box B. In addition, airlines may also swap landing rights at various airports and share the training of pilots. On the aircraft front they can place joint orders for aircraft and, as with many products, a bulk order usually generates a substantial discount. This provides some control over input prices and again moves airlines towards box B.

A more intriguing idea is the exploitation of natural monopolies. As discussed earlier a natural monopoly exists where scale economies lead to one supplier in the market. Often these are associated with industries which require enormous levels of infrastructure such as utilities, gas, water and electricity, but they are equally applicable in much smaller markets. Consider the level of demand for flights between two regional airports, say Leeds in the UK and Nice in France. It is a two-hour flight and around 80 people a day wish to fly direct between the two airports. A small commercial jet might carry 120 passengers. So this route will only be supplied by one airline. A monopoly.

Now consider flying from Leeds to Singapore. Here are a couple of suggested routings. Leeds, Heathrow, and then either direct to Singapore, or via Dubai, Bangkok, or Kuala Lumpur. Or Leeds, Amsterdam and then either direct, or via Dubai, Bangkok, or Kuala Lumpur. There are many other options. Therefore, because international airlines utilize hub-and-spoke operations, the market for flights from Leeds to Singapore is a combination of many sub-markets. There is no natural monopoly on these routes. Airlines can fill planes with passengers who are travelling to multiple destinations.

What can we learn from this? Discount airlines tend to fly point-to-point between small regional airports. International carriers operate hub-and-spoke operations. Discount airlines make huge profits, international airlines do not. So are discount airlines natural monopolies? If they are, the very intriguing thought is that they could charge a lot less than they currently do.

✎ Summary

1   The profitability of a market is determined by the competitive structure of the market.

2   Perfect competition is highly competitive. It has no entry barriers, perfect information, homogeneous products and buyers and sellers.

3   In the short run firms in perfect competition can earn supernormal profits. But in the long run rivals will enter the market and compete away any excess profits.

4   Monopoly is a market supplied by only one firm.

5   Entry barriers such as licences, patents, economies of scale or switching costs make it difficult for competitors to enter the market.

6   Supernormal profits can exist in the short run and, because of high entry barriers, can also persist into the long run.

7   In monopoly output is lower and prices are higher than in perfect competition.

8   Monopolies are seen as desirable by business but usually undesirable by governments.

9   Many successful business ventures occur because managers are capable of steering a strategic path from competitive environments to low competitive environments.

Learning checklist

You should now be able to:

◆ Explain why firms maximize profits when marginal cost equals marginal revenue

◆ Recall the main assumptions behind perfect competition

◆ Explain why the demand curve faced by a perfectly competitive firm is perfectly elastic

◆ Explain the level of profits in the short and long run in a perfectly competitive industry

◆ List the potential barriers to entry used by a monopoly

◆ Explain why the marginal revenue line is steeper than the average revenue line in monopoly

◆ Draw a diagram to illustrate the amount of profit earned by a monopoly

◆ Explain the key differences between perfect competition and monopoly

◆ Explain when perfect competition and monopoly are good for a firm

◆ Provide examples of how firms have created monopolies

Questions

1   List markets that you think are (i) perfectly competitive and (ii) monopolies.

2   If the demand for wheat increased: (i) What would happen to wheat farmers' profits? (ii) What would happen to wheat farmers' profits next year?

3   Draw a diagram for a perfectly competitive industry with firms earning normal profits. All firms in the industry use oil as a key input. Using your diagram illustrate a reduction in the price of oil. Will firm level profits increase or decrease and will market supply increase or decrease?

4   Will the lack of competition in monopoly result in the company making losses?

Exercises

1   True or false?
   a)   Price is equal to marginal revenue for a firm under perfect competition.
   b)   A firm making normal profits is said to be breaking even by an accountant.
   c)   A monopoly makes supernormal profits because it is more efficient than a perfectly competitive firm.

d) A perfectly competitive firm will sell at a price equal to marginal cost. A monopoly may sell at a price above marginal cost.

e) A patent protects a monopoly by not enabling perfect information.

f) In perfect competition, if price is above short-run average cost, firms will exit the market.

2 Figure 5.18 shows the short-run cost curves for a perfectly competitive firm.

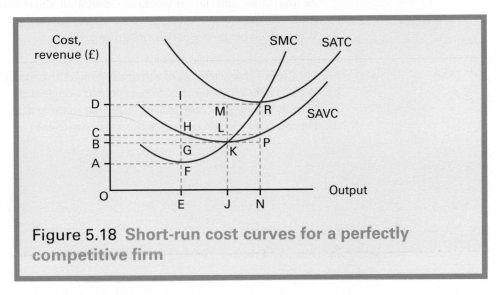

Figure 5.18 Short-run cost curves for a perfectly competitive firm

a) What is the shutdown price for the firm?

b) At what price would the firm just make normal profits?

c) What area would represent total fixed cost at this price?

d) Within what range of prices would the firm choose to operate at a loss in the short run?

e) Identify the firm's short-run supply curve.

f) Within what range of prices would the firm be able to make short-run supernormal profits?

A perfectly competitive industry is taken over by a monopolist who intends to run it as a multi-plant concern. Consequently, the long-run supply curve of the competitive

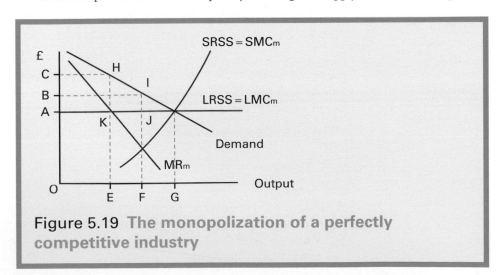

Figure 5.19 The monopolization of a perfectly competitive industry

industry (LRSS) becomes the monopolist's long-run marginal cost curve (LMCm); in the short run the SRSS curve becomes the monopolist's SMCm. The position is shown in Figure 5.19.

a) What was the equilibrium price and industry output under perfect competition?

b) At what price and output would the monopolist choose to operate in the short run?

c) At what price and output would the monopolist maximize profits in the long run?

d) What would be the size of these long-run profits?

3 Consider the case of Google in Box 5.1

a) List the key characteristics of a perfectly competitive market.

b) Which of the characteristics do not apply to Google and why?

c) Identify examples of rent-seeking behaviour in the article.

d) Do you think Google will suffer creative destruction?

Chapter 6
Strategic rivalry

Chapter contents

Learning outcomes

By the end of this chapter you should understand:

Economic Theory

- Monopolistic competition
- Oligopoly and interdependence
- Natural and strategic entry barriers
- The kinked demand curve model
- Game theory and strategic behaviour
- Auction theory

Business Application

- Why it maybe better for leading technology firms to co-operate on standards, rather than compete.
- Why supermarkets use blind auctions to prevent co-operation between suppliers

Strategic rivalry at a glance

The issue

Firms in perfect competition earn normal economic profits. But can firms avoid direct price competition, say by product differentiation; and, if so, what are the consequences for pricing and profits? In addition, in markets where there are only a small number of large players, should firms compete or try to co-operate with each other? Co-operation leads to increased profits, competition does not.

The understanding

Many firms in highly competitive markets, such as bars, restaurants and hairdressing, differentiate themselves by location, style and the range of products, or services. Prices then often vary across differentiated providers, but this may not necessarily lead to supernormal profits. We will address these issues using the model of monopolistic competition.

In terms of co-operation, or competition, we will examine the concept of strategic interdependence. For example, while co-operation is likely to lead to increased profits, it is not necessarily the correct option. If you decide to be friendly and your rival is aggressive, then they will win. So, given that your rival is aggressive, it is best if you are also aggressive. This is an essential part of the understanding; optimal strategies are developed from an understanding of what your rival is going to do, not from what you would like to do. This is known as strategic interdependence. The strategy of one firm is dependent upon the likely strategy of its rivals. We will explore these ideas more fully by examining game theory.

The usefulness

An understanding of monopolistic competition provides insights into the consequences for prices and profits resulting from product positioning and differentiation, especially in services sector markets characterized by numerous small-scale providers.

An understanding of strategic interaction from the perspective of game theory is extremely powerful. Government uses game theory when designing auctions for telecommunications licences. Sporting associations and team owners use game theory and auctions when selling television rights. Car dealerships use game theory when selling second-hand cars, and so should you. Finally, supermarkets use it to reduce the price that they have to pay for own-label products by applying game theory to auctions.

6.1 Business problem: will rivals always compete?

A good competitor can control their rivals. In sport Formula One drivers try to achieve this from pole position and in war armed forces try to gain control through air supremacy. In fact any successful competitor, whether it be in sport, war, politics or business, will ordinarily have a good strategy.

An important recognition is that competition is expensive. War is hugely expensive, particularly in terms of lost lives. Ferrari's annual racing budget exceeds $200 million. Competition in business is also expensive. In monopoly, with no competition, profits are higher and more sustainable than in the highly competitive environment of perfect competition.

So, if competition is expensive, should rivals always compete? The answer depends on the expected response of your rival. Consider this old, but illuminating true story. When the Spanish arrived in Central America in the seventeenth century they were greeted by fearsome-looking locals, sporting warpaint and shaking menacing spears in the air – a clear declaration that they were willing to compete with the Spanish invaders. In response most of us would sensibly pull up the anchor and sail away. The Spanish burnt their boats and walked on to the beach. If a fight between the Spanish and the Incas started, the Spanish had to fight or die: no boats, no escape plan. The local Incas quickly understood the Spanish soldiers' need and desire to win and retreated inland. So, by committing to a fight, the Spanish influenced the behaviour of their rivals. This is a significant point for business.

In perfect competition the behaviour of one firm will not influence its rivals. Each firm is a price taker and it can sell any amount of output at the market price. If the market price is £10 there is no point starting a price war and selling at £5 because you can sell everything at £10. There is said to be no **strategic interdependence**. We will also assume that there is no strategic interdependence when we discuss monopolistic competition. However, under **oligopoly**, if one firm begins a competitive move, such as starting a price war, then it will have immediate implications for its rivals. The actions of one firm are linked to the actions of its rivals. Strategic interdependence exists.

> **Strategic interdependence** exists when the actions of one firm will have implications for its rivals.
> **Oligopoly** is a market place with a small number of large players, such as banking, supermarkets and the media.

In developing your understanding we will begin by introducing the model of monopolistic competition. While not directly addressing the issue of strategic interdependence, it does examine the profitability of many small firms under product differentiation. As such it provides an insight into how firms in near-perfect competition try to deal with competitive rivalry. We then develop the analysis through an examination of the characteristics of an oligopolistic market. In discussing why oligopolies exist we will consider both natural and strategic entry barriers. Finally, we will turn our discussion to strategic responses and in so doing develop your understanding of game theory. We will then utilize the insights from game theory to understand the operation and optimal design of auctions.

6.2 **Monopolistic competition**

> **Monopolistic competition** is a highly competitive market where firms may use product differentiation.

We begin with an examination of **monopolistic competition**, which for the most part is an industry much like perfect competition except for the existence of product differentiation. So, we are still assuming a large number of competitors, freedom of entry and exit, but not homogeneous products. Rather, firms produce similar goods or services which are differentiated in some way. For example, bars can be differentiated by location, the beers or other drinks offered for sale, the type of food offered; or the bar's theme, such as a cocktail or a sports bar. Because each supplier offers a similar but not identical product, each supplier does not face a perfectly elastic (horizontal) demand line, as they would in perfect competition. Instead, the element of differentiation lowers the degree of substitutability between rival offerings; and results in each firm facing a downward sloping demand line.

Each monopolistic firm can influence its market share to some extent by changing its price relative to its rival. By lowering drink prices a bar may attract some customers from its rivals, but it will not attract all the rival's customers. Differentiation will lock in some customers to the more expensive provider. For example, if one bar provides beers, while another specializes in fruit and alcoholic cocktails. Cheap prices in the beer bar will not attract drinkers who have a strong taste and preference for cocktails.

Monopolistic competition also requires an absence of economies of scale. Without the ability, or need to exploit size and scale, a monopolistic industry will be characterized by a large number of small firms. We will see that when we discuss oligopoly in the next section, the existence of economies of scale can lead to a small number of large players.

The demand curve for the firm depends upon the industry demand curve, the number of firms and the prices charged by these firms. A bigger industry demand, with a fixed number of firms will result in a higher demand for each firm. An increase in the number of firms will lead to a reduced share of the market for each firm. While finally the price of a firm, relative to its rivals, will also determine its level of demand.

In Figure 6.1 we have drawn a diagram depicting a firm's supply decision under monopolistic competition. Initially the firm faces an average revenue line of AR_1 and marginal revenue line MR of MR_1. Under profit maximization the firm will produce Q_1 units and sell at price of P_1. With an average cost per unit of AC_1, the firm will make $(P_1 - AC_1) \times Q_1$ profit. These supernormal profits will attract entry into the market. As more firms enter this market the firm will lose market share and the demand curve for the firm will move back towards the origin. Entry stops when each firm is breaking even. This is when the new demand line, AR_2, just touches the average cost line at a tangent. The firm now makes Q_2 units at a price of P_2. Economic profits are now zero since $P_2 - AC_2 = 0$; and therefore entry into the industry stops.

Tangency equilibrium occurs when the firm's average revenue line just touches the firm's average total cost line.

The monopolistic long-run equilibrium has some important features. First, the **tangency equilibrium** results in average costs being above minimum average costs. The firm has excess capacity and could produce a higher level of output at a lower cost per unit. Second, the monopolistic firm has some monopoly power because its price exceeds marginal costs. This reflects the point that each firm differentiates itself from its rivals.

The characteristics of monopolistic competition: product differentiation, few opportunities for economies of scale, zero economic profits, but yet some power over pricing, are the characteristics we often associate with service sector businesses, such as, bars, restaurants, local grocery stores, hairdressers, estate agents, fast food/take away outlets. As such, the model of monopolistic competition has some merit in being able to explain the characteristics of many service sector industries. However, apart from a simple consideration of product differentiation, the model does not provide much of an

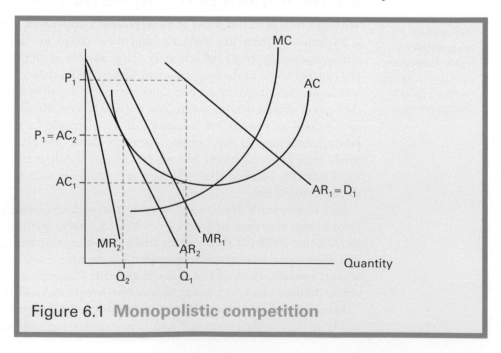

Figure 6.1 **Monopolistic competition**

insight into strategic interdependency. This is principally because monopolistic competition still assumes a large number of small players. As such each firm is small relative to the market; and its competitive actions have only limited consequences for all of its rivals. This negligible impact results in strategic interdependence being almost entirely ignored. We will address this concern in the next section by examining oligopoly theory.

6.3 Oligopoly theory – competition among the big ones

An oligopoly is a market with a small number of large players. Unlike perfect competition, each firm has a significant share of the total market and therefore faces a downward sloping demand curve for its product. Firms in oligopoly are price setters as opposed to price takers.

Optimally all firms in an oligopoly should agree to co-operate and act as one monopolist, as this generates the highest level of profits. This is known as a cartel and is illustrated in Figure 6.2. For simplicity assume each firm faces constant marginal and average costs. These are shown as a horizontal line in Figure 6.2. As output increases costs remain constant. The profit-maximizing output occurs where MR = MC. This output maximizes the joint profits of all the firms in the cartel acting as a monopoly. However,

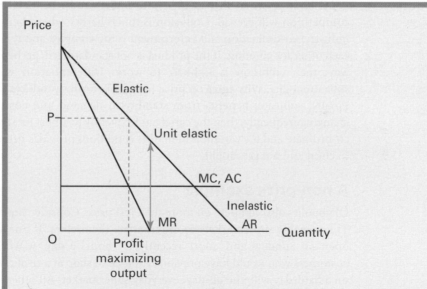

Figure 6.2 **Collusion versus competition**

Marginal cost has to be positive. It is not possible to produce one more unit of output for a negative amount of money. Resources such as labour will have to be paid for. Under profit maximization MR = MC, therefore if MC has to be positive, MR also has to be positive in order for the two to be equal. From the above, positive marginal revenue is only associated with output levels where demand is price elastic. With price-elastic demand, reducing the price and expanding output will lead to higher total revenues. Since costs are constant, revenues will grow more quickly than costs and profits will increase for the individual firm. With constant cost levels the individual firm can expand output, raise revenues and therefore boost profits.

each firm will quickly recognize that it can undercut the market price and raise its own profits at the expense of its rivals. Why?

The answer rests in an understanding that a profit-maximizing monopoly will only operate in the price-elastic region of its demand curve. Marginal cost has to be positive, because it is impossible to produce an additional unit of output without incurring additional costs. Therefore, if profits are maximized when MC = MR then, because MC is positive, MR must also be positive. If marginal revenue is positive, reducing the price to sell one more unit has made a positive contribution to total revenue. We saw in Chapter 2 that cutting prices and raising total revenue only occurs when demand is price elastic.

Therefore, a single firm within the cartel illustrated in Figure 6.2 can see that its marginal and average costs are constant. However, reducing prices will generate greater revenues, because demand is price elastic. The individual firm can, therefore, earn more profit by cheating on its cartel colleagues and expanding output. Unfortunately, any member of the cartel could recognize that, being on the elastic part of the demand curve, it could also drop its own prices and raise revenues. Therefore, all rivals would respond by dropping their prices, leaving the cartel and effectively competing with each other. This is the strategic interdependence in action. Should firms in oligopoly co-operate with each other and act as a monopoly, or compete with each other and start a price war?

When a cartel might work

Some basic points at this stage help to understand when a cartel can work and when competition will prevail. Collusion is much harder when there are many firms in the industry: co-ordination and enforcement is too complex and it is easy for firms to blame each other for cheating. If the product is not standardized, perhaps differentiated in some way, then collusion is unlikely to work. Differentiation is a means of reducing substitutability. Why agree on price fixing, when your products are not near-substitutes? Finally, collusion benefits from stability in demand and costs. If the equilibrium is changing frequently, then the cartel has frequently to adjust its agreed prices. It is costly to co-ordinate and the variation in market conditions provides firms with the cover needed to cheat and not get caught.

A non-price example

Oligopolies also compete on more than just price. Consider supermarket opening times. These enable supermarkets to differentiate themselves. If one supermarket decides to open on Sundays and, more recently, 24 hours a day, it will gain market share, as customers who would have previously waited to shop at a rival can now shop at 2.00 a.m. on a Saturday with the all-day, everyday supermarket. All other supermarkets recognize this, so they too open on Sundays and 24 hours a day. Market shares stay constant, but all supermarkets now have higher costs with no additional revenues. This is the strategic interdependence in action. Should supermarkets agree to stay closed on a Sunday, or compete with each other and open?

6.4 **Natural and strategic entry barriers**

Competition with rivals begins before a firm enters a market. Potential competition can exist between firms in the industry, so-called 'incumbents', and firms outside the industry, so-called 'potential rivals'. A major feature of oligopolies is the existence of barriers to entry. These barriers can exist for natural or strategic reasons.

Natural entry barriers

The costs for a firm can be exogenously or endogenously determined. Our natural entry barriers are concerned with **exogenous costs**, so let us concentrate on them first.

> Exogenous means external, outside. The **exogenous costs** of the firm are outside its control.

The fact that exogenous costs are outside the firm's control does not mean that these costs are uncontrollable; rather, the firm does not influence the price of labour, machines, raw materials and the production technology used. For example, the price of labour is a market price determined outside the firm's control. The level of costs associated with a particular industry, as we saw with monopolies, can create an entry barrier.

In Figure 6.3 we have the long-run average cost curve LRAC. At the minimum efficient scale, MES, the average cost is £10. But with a much smaller plant, Q_1 the cost per unit rises to £20. In order to enter and compete in the industry it is essential to build a plant that is at least as big as the MES. In oligopolies the MES is large when compared to the overall market. For example, if we have 50 million customers and the MES is 10 million units per year, then we might reasonably expect 50m/10m = 5 firms in the market.

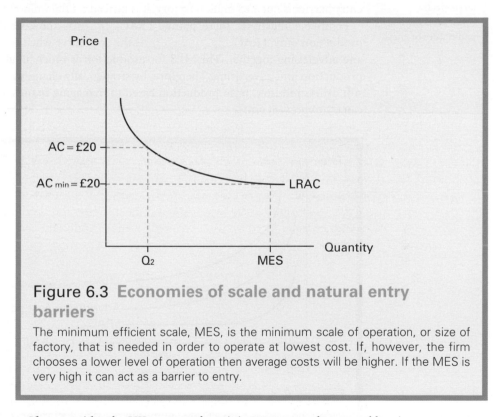

Figure 6.3 Economies of scale and natural entry barriers

The minimum efficient scale, MES, is the minimum scale of operation, or size of factory, that is needed in order to operate at lowest cost. If, however, the firm chooses a lower level of operation then average costs will be higher. If the MES is very high it can act as a barrier to entry.

If we consider the UK supermarkets, it is easy to see why natural barriers to entry may exist. In the case of supermarkets the big players have in excess of 500 stores each. So the MES must be around 500 stores. This level of scale is probably essential when trying to negotiate discount from product suppliers, optimizing marketing spend and building efficient distribution systems to move stock from suppliers to the stores. Given that the UK is a small island with around 60 million inhabitants, it is sensible that we should only see a small number of large supermarket chains. Five large players operating at 500 stores plus is all that the UK market is capable of supporting. So, it is the natural, or exogenous cost characteristics, coupled with the market size that leads to a natural entry barrier and the creation of an oligopoly.

Strategic entry barriers

What happens if the MES is not very big when compared with the market size? Entry is easier and aids competition. Consider the case of soft drink manufacturers. If you wish to enter the soft drinks market, then you need to buy a bottling plant and a big steel factory to house it in and a warehouse; and a couple of trucks for deliveries will also help. The cost will not exceed £5 million. (Amazing what you can learn when taking summer jobs as a student.) For many businesses £5 million is not a huge sum of money. The MES is not big and, therefore, the entry barrier into the market is limited. So, as a firm inside the market, how do you prevent entry?

Easy – you change the cost characteristics of the industry and make the MES bigger or, as the economist would say, you **endogenize** the cost function.

Coca-Cola and Pepsi are clear examples of how to achieve this. The core assets for these companies are not production facilities; rather, they are brand names. A successful brand may cost £100 million or more to buy, or develop through advertising. Therefore, the entry barrier is not a £5 million factory, it is instead a £100 million brand.

Figure 6.4 illustrates these points. $LRAC_{Production}$ is the cost curve that relates to production only. $LRAC_{Production + Advertising}$ is the cost curve when we consider production and advertising together. The MES for production is much smaller than the MES for production and advertising. Therefore, by strategically changing the cost nature of the soft drinks industry, from production based to managing brands, the dominant players can try to prevent entry.

> If costs are **endogenized** then the firms inside the industry have strategically influenced the level and nature of costs.

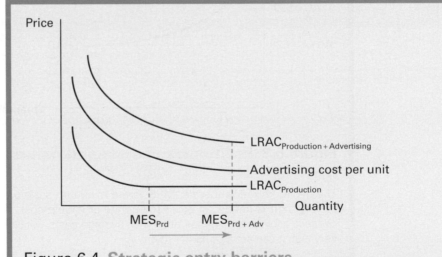

Figure 6.4 Strategic entry barriers

When the MES is naturally low, entry can be easy. Incumbents can change this by altering the cost characteristics of the industry. One suggestion is to move away from production and build in large investments in intangible assets such as brand names. This can substantially increase the MES and reduce entry.

> A **sunk cost** is an expenditure that cannot be regained when exiting the market.

Perhaps more important, the £100 million brand development fee is a **sunk cost**. This means that if the entrant decided to exit the market after spending £100 million on brand development then it would be unlikely to sell the asset on. The asset has no value to any other business and so the cost is sunk. In contrast, the production facility could be sold on. A soft drinks manufacturer may not buy the plant, but some other food processing company could be interested in the facility. This asset can be sold on, so its costs are not sunk. As a consequence, the need for a brand simultaneously increases the size of entry into the market and it makes it more risky as the asset cannot be sold on. The investment is lost.

The existence of sunk costs is important because without them markets are **contestable**.

With freedom to enter and exit, contestable markets proxy perfectly competitive markets. So, even if the market has only a small number of large players, the absence of sunk costs enables potential rivals to threaten future entry. The only way to prevent entry is to make it look unattractive with low levels of profit. So, contestable markets, even with oligopolistic structures, only produce normal economic profits.

> A **contestable** market is one where firms can enter or exit a market freely.

Examples of contestable markets

The airline industry is commonly used as an example of contestability. An aircraft does not represent a sunk cost. A jumbo jet can be used on a route between London Heathrow and New York. It can equally be used on a route between Heathrow and Hong Kong. There are no costs in moving the asset (aircraft) between the two routes, or any other route. Therefore, the airline can quickly and easily move the aircraft to the most profitable route. This ability should keep profits low on all possible routes, as the threat of entry by rivals is very real with no entry barriers.

As a further example, in the UK, banks and insurance companies have competed against each other for over a decade. Banks sell insurance and some insurance companies now operate as banks. In the US, banks, until recently, were restricted to banking activities and insurance companies were restricted to insurance activities. Following a change in the law that enabled banks to enter the insurance industry, the banking stock prices remained unchanged, but insurance stock prices fell. The explanation for this is simple. By enabling banks to enter the insurance market, the insurance market became more contestable. Insurance companies had to reduce prices and profits in order to reduce the threat of entry by the banks. Therefore, insurance stock prices fell. Banks are unlikely to enter the market because in the future the market will look unattractive because it is now contestable; therefore, bank stock prices remain unchanged. In order to increase profitability the insurance companies need to develop new entry barriers and reduce the contestability of the insurance market.

6.5 Competition among rivals

Firms inside an oligopolistic market have two options – compete or co-operate. Cartels are seen as collusive attempts to co-operate and are now illegal in many countries. Economists' earliest attempts to model oligopolies involved the **kinked demand curve**, shown in Figure 6.5.

At the price of £10 there is no point in a firm changing its prices. If it increases prices, all rivals will hold their prices; but if the firm drops prices, all rivals will also reduce their prices. Therefore, above the price of £10 demand is price elastic, below demand is inelastic, thus leading to the kinked demand curve.

> The idea behind the **kinked demand curve** is that price rises will not be matched by rivals, but price reductions will be matched.

The marginal revenue line is vertical at the profit-maximizing output. This is because the demand curve changes slope at this output level. The difference between the elastic and inelastic demand curves leads to a stepped change in the marginal revenue.

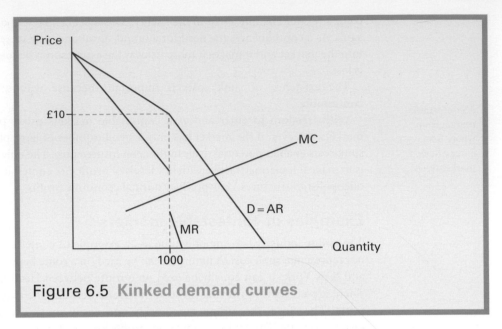

Figure 6.5 Kinked demand curves

As a result the demand curve has a different shape above and below the current market price:

1 If the firm raises its price, rivals will keep their prices constant. The firm will, therefore, lose customers when it raises prices. As a result, demand above the current market price is elastic.

2 In contrast, if the firm reduces its prices, all rivals will match the price reduction. The firm will not gain more demand by reducing prices. Demand below the current market price is therefore inelastic.

We will see below that economists question the theoretical merits of the kinked demand curve, but it provides a reasonable starting point for understanding some real-world examples. The pricing of petrol, or at least the reduction in petrol prices, can be explained using the kinked demand curve. See Box 6.1 for a common discussion of price

 Box 6.1 Pump wars

Asda and Tesco cut petrol prices

Adapted from the BBC News Online, 15 September 2005

Both Asda and Tesco are cutting up to four pence off a litre of petrol. Prices are coming down as global oil and petrol prices retreat from post-Hurricane Katrina highs. On Thursday, oil prices reversed early gains with US light crude down 34 cents to $64.75, while London Brent fell 21 cents to settle at $63.91 a barrel.

Asda said it would cut the cost of petrol to a maximum of 89.9p a litre at its 158 petrol stations and diesel to 92.9p a litre. 'Drivers have been ripped off in the past 10 days as drivers rushed to fill up,' said Tony Page, general merchandise director at Asda. Meanwhile, Tesco said it was cutting prices from 0600 BST on Friday at all its 380 petrol stations by up to 4p a litre.

'The price of petrol has fallen and we are passing those savings back to shoppers as soon as we can,' a Tesco spokeswoman said.

changes at the pump. Once one firm announces a price reduction, all other firms respond with similar price reductions in order to protect their market shares. We might therefore argue that demand is inelastic for price reductions. Similarly, no firm would increase prices without full knowledge that other firms would follow. This occurs in the petrol market because of the cost of oil. So price rises only occur when all firms face increased input costs and are therefore willing to increase prices together. But no firm would make a decision to be more expensive than its rivals.

Problems with the kinked demand curve

The kinked demand model has a number of positive features. First, the demand curves for the firm are based on potential or expected responses from the firm's rivals. Hence, strategic interdependence is a feature of the model. Second, the model predicts stability in pricing. This occurs because of strategic interdependence; rivals will react to price changes in a way that makes them ineffective. Also, price stability occurs because, even when the firm's costs increase, because of the vertical portion of the firm's MR line the profit-maximizing output and price is unlikely to change. Only when costs change by a large amount will the intersection of marginal cost and marginal revenue move from the vertical portion of the marginal revenue line.

The major drawback associated with the kinked demand curve is that it does not explain how the stable price is arrived at in the first place. There must be a prior process that determines the price. The kinked demand curve merely explains the stability once the price is set. We therefore need an approach that understands strategic inter-dependence more fully.

6.6 Game theory

> **Game theory** seeks to understand whether strategic interaction will lead to competition or co-operation between rivals.

In response to this challenge economists have now turned to **game theory** as a means of understanding strategic interdependence. In economic jargon a game has players who have different pay-offs associated with different strategic options. In the business sense we could have two firms (players): they could start a price war and compete against each other or they could try to co-operate with each other (strategic options). Each combination has different profit outcomes (pay-offs) for the two firms.

The pay-off matrix in Figure 6.6 illustrates these points.

Each firm has two options: co-operate or begin a price war. In the boxes are the profits to each firm, the value on the left is always the pay-off to firm B and the value on the right is always the pay-off to firm A. If firm A and B both co-operate, then they both receive £50m profit. However, if A decides to start a price war and B still holds out for co-operation, then A receives £60m and B only receives £20m. The obvious question to ask is, which pay-off box will the firms end up in?

John Nash, the person on whom the film *A Beautiful Mind* was based, provided the answer to this question. Each firm will make an optimal choice given the potential response of its rivals. This is now known as the 'Nash equilibrium'.

> **Nash equilibrium** occurs when each player does what is best for themselves, given what their rivals may do in response.

The important point to note from the **Nash equilibrium** is that each firm considers what its rivals can do before deciding on its own strategy. The firm does not simply decide what it wants to do. For example, Chelsea or Barcelona do not decide to run on the pitch and kick the ball in the back of the opposition's net. Clearly this is what they want to do. Instead, they think about what their rivals will do, how they play, what formation they might use and who are their opponent's key players. Chelsea or Barcelona can then develop a football strategy based on what their rivals are going to do. The Nash

		Firm A	
		Co-operate	Price war
Firm B	Co-operate	50:50	20:60
	Price war	60:20	30:30

Figure 6.6 Game theory, pay-off matrix

The numbers in each box are the pay-offs to each firm (firm B is always on the left and firm A on the right). The Nash equilibrium is where both firms choose to start a price war, earning £30m each. This is because when choosing its strategy A examines B's options: if B tries to co-operate, A's best response is to start a price war; and if B starts a price war, A's best response is again to start a price war. B will come to the same conclusion when examining its response to A.

equilibrium is just formalizing this obvious decision-making process by saying, 'Consider your rival's likely behaviour before you decide what you are going to do'.

Now let us examine our own game in Figure 6.6, using Nash's argument. Firm A looks at firm B and sees that B can do one of two things: co-operate or start a price war. We can begin by examining what happens if B decides to co-operate. If A then also co-operates, it will earn £50 million, but if A begins a price war, then it will earn £60 million. Firm A now thinks about B's other option, which is to start a price war. If A tries to co-operate it will only earn £20 million, but if A also takes up the option of a price war, then it will earn £30 million. Firm A now knows that whatever B does it is always optimal for A to start a price war. Firm B will go through a similar decision-making process and come to the same conclusion – that whatever A does, B will start a price war. The Nash equilibrium has both firms embarking on a price war earning £30 million each.

Even though each firm is starting a price war, this is the best option, given what their rivals can do. Clearly if both firms co-operate, then they will both earn higher profits, £50 million each. But if A chooses to co-operate, then B will choose a price war, as B can then earn £60 million. If B chooses to co-operate, then A will choose a price war and earn £60 million. Hence, both choose a price war.

Repeated games

In a **single period game**, the game is only played once. In a repeated game, the game is played a number of rounds.

Starting a price war or displaying 'non-cooperative' behaviour is a general response in a **single period game**. Therefore, as a rule, whenever you play a game once, as our rivals did in Figure 6.6, or strategically interact with someone once, then cheat. For example, consider buying a second-hand car from the classified ads. You see a car and go to meet the owner. You will say the car is not perfect and the owner will tell you that the car is fantastic. It does not matter whether the car is good or not; you are both displaying non-cooperative behaviour. You both do this because you do not expect to meet again to buy or sell cars in the future. It is a one-period game, so you both cheat. You would like the price to fall; they would like the price to rise.

The way of moving from a non-cooperative equilibrium to a co-operative one is to play the game repeatedly and use a strategy known as 'tit-for-tat'.

Under tit-for-tat, you will co-operate with your rival in the next round if they co-operated with you in the last round. If they cheated on you in the last round, you will never co-operate with them again.

In the game above, if A and B co-operate they both receive £50 million. If in the next round A decides to cheat and start a price war it will earn £60 million, or £10 million more than from co-operation. But in the next rounds B will always commit to a price war, so the most A can earn is £30 million. Firm A has the choice of gaining £10 million in the next round and then losing £50m − 30m = £20 million for every round afterwards. Therefore, short-term gains from cheating are outweighed by the long-term losses of a repeated game.

However, in order for tit-for-tat to work, the threat to always display non-cooperative behaviour, if your rival cheated in the last round, has to be a **credible commitment**.

A **credible commitment** or threat has to be one that is optimal to carry out.

Recall the Spanish invaders who burnt their boats – their threat to fight the local Incas, rather than sail off to a safer shore, was very credible when they no longer had any boats!

For a business illustration, let us go back to the car example. This time consider buying a car from a dealer of one of the major manufacturers. With a second-hand car they usually provide a warranty. They do this because they value your repeat business. The dealer does not want to sell you a bad car. Instead, they would like you to feel secure in the fact that the car is good and they will fix any problems. They are not cheating; they are trying to co-operate. In fact, by offering extended warranties they are making a credible and contractual commitment to provide you with a trouble-free motor car. They are willing to do this because the potential revenue streams from your repeat business outweigh any gains from selling you a bad car at an expensive price.

Finally, we can consider the market for love. Marriage is a repeated game. If one partner cheats by seeing someone else, then divorce is a fairly robust method of never agreeing to co-operate with the cheating partner ever again. While in the singles market, seeking co-operation for fun with someone you find attractive could be a one-period game if you only expect to see them once. If they ask what you do, it is better to cheat. Claiming to be a catwalk model or a professional footballer are better options than admitting to being an indebted student.

In summary, strategic decisions require an understanding of the potential responses. If a firm, or individual, plays a game once they should cheat. If they play repeatedly then they should try to co-operate for as long as their rivals co-operate.

6.7 Auction theory

Auctions have become a popular pastime. The online auction site eBay offers for sale everything from the mundane to the bizarre. If you are trying to find something, eBay is generally worth a search, even for those of us who are not addicted to bidding online. Amazingly, if all the transactions across the world on eBay were added together, eBay would be the world's fourth largest economy; and auction fever does not stop with eBay. Where home makeover programs once dominated television programme making, auction format television programs now lead the schedules. With the likes of Flog It, individuals are invited to bring along heirlooms and see what they can make in an auction.

While clearly an attraction of auctions is the risky, almost gambling-based adrenalin of seeing what you have to pay to gain an item, or what you can gain by selling an item. The uncertainty is a very important part of the experience.

However, while eBay and Flog It might be a bit of fun, for firms auctions are serious commercial activities and, just as with eBay and the like, auctions for commercial services have grown in popularity. Supermarkets use auctions to place orders for own-label items. Sporting associations use auctions to license live television rights and governments use them to license railway operators, mobile telecommunications and even the right to run lotteries. Fortunately game theory can provide an understanding of optimal behaviour in auctions. Under a Nash equilibrium each player will make an optimal bid based on what they believe their rivals will do in response.

The purpose of this section is to provide you with this understanding of auctions. It will begin by explaining the four main types of auction format and introduce the important concepts of private versus common values. With these basic blocks of knowledge in place the discussion assesses auctions from both a buyer's and a seller's perspective. Understanding optimal bidding strategies under each auction format will enable a seller to assess the auction format which will deliver the greatest revenue, while recognizing the problem of the winner's curse will provide a cautionary note to bidders.

Auction formats

There are seen to be four auction formats: the English auction, the Dutch auction, the first-price, sealed-bid auction and the second-price, sealed-bid auction. Each will be discussed in turn.

In an English auction bids begin low and are increased incrementally until no other bidder is willing to raise the bid. Bids can either be cried out by the auctioneer, with bidders nodding, or waving their papers in acceptance, or they can be inputted electronically, as is the case with eBay. In a Dutch auction prices start high and are gradually reduced until a bidder accepts the price and wins the auction. This type of auction is commonly used in Holland to sell flowers and agricultural produce. Under the first-price sealed auction, bidders must submit a single bid, usually in writing. Bidders have little idea what anyone else has bid; and the highest bidder wins. The second-price sealed bid is a variation on the first-price auction. Again bids are submitted in writing, but the highest bidder pays the price of the second highest bid.

Common versus private values

Private values each bidder has a private subjective value of an item's worth.

Auctions can also differ in the values held by bidders. With **private values** each bidder forms a private, probably subjective, view of the item for sale. This would be especially true with items on eBay such as a watch, a suit, an antique. Some individuals will like the item, but others will love it! Each bidder knows their own value of the item, but they do not know the valuation of the item to the other bidders. Furthermore, each bidder is unlikely to change their assessment of the item's value, even when they become informed of other bidders' valuations.

Common values – the value of the item is identical for all bidders, but each bidder may form a different assessment of the item's worth.

Under common values, an item is worth exactly the same to all bidders, but no bidder is sure what the item is truly worth. For example, as part of a game you might be shown a jar filled with coins. Along with your friends you are asked to bid for the jar, the highest bid wins the jar. Clearly in this example the jar is worth the same to each bidder, but no one is sure how much the jar is worth (without opening it and counting the coins). Real-life commercial auctions tend to be characterized by **common values**. The rights to an oil field, the rights to show live football games, the rights to run a national lottery. The commercial value of the rights are common to all bidders, but what they are truly worth is presently unknown. Significantly, under common values a bidder might be willing to change their bid once they know all the bids. For example, a comparison of bids will help to inform bidders about the accuracy of their own valuation of the item for sale. If other bidders are bidding high, then a bidder might be led to believe that they have undervalued the item.

With this basic understanding of auction formats we can now consider which is the best auction format for a seller. If we assume that a seller wishes to maximize their revenue, we need to find the auction format which results in the highest bid. We will therefore analyse bidding behaviour in each auction format under which bidders have private values.

English auction with private values

A second-hand Swiss watch is offered for sale. You value the watch at £1000, a rival bidder values the watch at £900. What is your optimal bidding strategy? Under a Nash equilibrium you should consider what your rival will do in response. So, if your rival bids £500 offer £501. Your rival may back out of the auction and you win at £501, saving yourself £499. Or your rival may top your bid and you are no worse off, since it cost you nothing to bid and you gained nothing. This strategy of raising the bid should continue until either your rival quits, or you reach your maximum willingness to pay. Significantly, in English auctions the winning bid will always be a fraction higher than the second highest valuation. For this example, you will win the auction with a bid of £901.

Second-price sealed bid auction with private values

Under this auction format each bidder's dominant strategy is to submit a bid equal to their maximum willingness to pay. So, in the case of the Swiss watch you will bid £1000 and your rival will bid £900. Since the highest bidder pays the second highest price, you will win the auction for £900, which is almost identical to the outcome from the English auction.

To see why submitting a bid equal to your maximum willingness to pay is optimal consider the following:

1　**Lowering the bid**. If you lower your bid below your maximum willingness to pay, this will only alter the outcome if your new lower bid is less than your rival's. For example, a bid of £950 will still ensure you win the auction and pay £900. But a bid of £850 will result in you losing the auction (and your rival gaining the item for £50 less then they were willing to pay). So in simple terms you cannot win by lowering your bid, you can only lose.

2　**Raising your bid**. If you bid £1050, this will not help you if your rival is going to bid less than £1000, your maximum willingness to pay. You will still win the auction and still pay the second price. If your rival is going to bid more than £1050, then again raising your bid has no impact. However, if your rival was to bid in between £1000 and £1050, say £1030, you would now win the auction, but at a penalty. You would now have to pay £30 more than your maximum value. So, raising your bid above your maximum willingness to pay can only harm you.

So you should not raise or lower your bid, simply submit your maximum willingness to pay.

First-price sealed auction and private values

Again we are bidding for the Swiss watch and you value it at £1000. Should you submit a bid equal to your maximum willingness to pay as in the second-price sealed auction? To answer this question consider Figure 6.7. The line S has a positive slope indicating that an increase in your bid raises the probability of winning the auction. If you bid your maximum willingness to pay £1000, the expected payment on winning the auction will be equal to the areas A + B + C + D + E + F. If you lowered your bid to, say, £900 your expected payment upon winning the auction will be E + F.

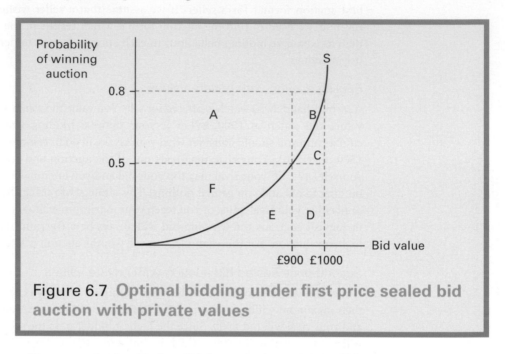

Figure 6.7 Optimal bidding under first price sealed bid auction with private values

The expected value (the benefit) from winning at £1000 will be A + B + C + D + E + F; exactly equal to the expected payment. The expected value (the benefit) of winning at £900 will be made up of the expected value of £900, plus the expected value of saving £100. So the expected value will be E + F + D.

In the case of bidding £1000, the expected value equals the expected cost, so you break even. But when reducing your bid to £900, the expected value exceeds your expected payment by the area D. It is therefore always optimal to bid below your maximum willingness to pay. You reduce your chances of winning, but you raise your potential gains.

The question now becomes by how much should you reduce your bid below your maximum willingness to pay. The answer rests on understanding the likely behaviour of your rival bidders and recognizing the interdependence of your bids. While beyond the scope of this discussion, it can be shown in Nash equilibrium that the optimal bid is $(N-1)/N$ multiplied by the bidder's maximum willingness to pay, where N is the number of bidders. So, with two bidders, the bid should be a half of your maximum willingness to pay. The winning bid will turn out to be the expected value of the second highest willingness to pay.

Dutch auction and private values

Under this type of auction prices are called out and you bid when they have fallen to a level which is optimal for you to make a bid. In the case of our Swiss watch you will not bid when prices are above your valuation of £1000. You will also not bid when the watch reaches the price of £1000, because you would not save yourself anything. Rather you will let the price fall and try to maximize the difference between the price you pay and the price at which you value the item. In essence, you would be trying to maximize area D in Figure 6.7. But how far should you allow the price to fall? The answer to this question is the same as for the first-price sealed bid auction. You would consider the likely bidding behaviour of your rivals and as long as your rival had not accepted a higher price, you would bid $(N-1)/N$ multiplied by your maximum willingness to pay. In Nash equilibrium, the price received by the seller would again be the expected value of the second highest willingness to pay.

The revenue equivalence theorem

This brings us to an important result. Under all auction formats the bidder with the highest willingness to pay wins, but they always pay a price roughly equal to the second highest valuation. So, since the auction format does not alter the amount of revenue received by the bidder, we observe revenue equivalence across competing auction formats.

> **The revenue equivalence theorem** states that under private values each auction format will generate the same level of revenue for the seller.

> **The winner's curse** is where a winning bid exceeds the true value of the sale item.

Auctions and common values – the problem of the winner's curse

Let us return to our jar filled with coins. The auction will be a first-price sealed bid auction. No bidder is better or worse at estimating the value of the jar of coins. Some will overestimate, others will underestimate, but on average (if the auction was repeated) all bidders would form an unbiased estimate of the jar's value. Each bidder also submits a bid which is increasing in their estimation of the jar's worth. So, the bidder with the highest valuation submits the highest bid and wins.

The problem with this type of auction for bidders is that the winner must by definition have formed an overly optimistic valuation of the jar of coins. They will therefore end up paying more for the jar than it is actually worth. So the winner's curse is that the winner actually loses.

Knowing that the winner's curse exists will alter bidders' behaviour. If you think the jar is worth £100, then you might then adjust your bid down to compensate for the risk of overestimating its worth and bid say £50. If all bidders are rational, they will all reduce their bids for this reason. In addition, bidders might reduce their bids further in order to maximize area D in Figure 6.7. Therefore, the problem for the seller in auctions with common values is that bidders will behave conservatively in order to avoid the winner's curse, leading to a lower sale price.

Unlike the case with private values and first-price auctions where the optimal bid increases with the number of bidders, e.g. when $N = 2$, $(N-1)/N = \frac{1}{2}$; and when $N = 3$, $(N-1)/N = 2/3$; under common values and a first-price sealed bid auction, optimal bids will decrease with an increase in the number of bidders. For example, if there are three bidders and you win, you have outbid only two other people. However, if there are 101 bidders then you have outbid 100 other bidders and your estimate must have been very wrong. So, with an increase in the number of bidders, individual bidders will behave more conservatively and reduce their bids by more to avoid the winner's curse.

What can sellers do to avoid this problem? Simple, the winner's curse and conservative pricing occur because of a lack of information. If bidders had more information regarding other bidders' valuations then they could more appropriately gauge the accuracy of their own willingness to pay. English auctions offer a solution. As bids are called out, each bidder can observe the valuation and willingness to pay by other bidders.

If bids rise quickly, pessimistic bidders can revise their valuation of the item and enter the bidding. Therefore, within an English auction and common values, the incentive to be conservative is removed and the final price is higher. This perhaps helps explain why the English auction is the most commonly observed format.

6.8 Business application: compete or co-operate?

If we return to our game theory illustration in Figure 6.6 the most desirable box for firm A is top right, where it earns 60. However, from our discussion we know that A will never find itself in this box. In a one-period game its rival will also compete and the two firms will earn 30 each, while in a repeated game both firms will try to co-operate and earn 50 each. Earning 60 in the top right is a situation where firm A competes and B decides to be friendly. A, therefore, dominates its rival B and in so doing controls the market. So, how do you convince your rival not to compete?

Box 6.2 describes the fight between Sony and its Blu-ray DVD format and Toshiba's HD DVD. Both formats are designed to meet the next generation of video entertainment which rests on high-definition technology. A DVD is not capable of storing all of the information from each frame of film that makes up a movie – it would simply take up too much memory. Computers, therefore, sample and compress the information from each image. High-definition technology will enable more information to be stored on a disc, and hence more information from each frame of film can be stored, creating a picture with a higher definition and a better viewing experience.

The race to win this market can be viewed as a game. If Toshiba and Sony agreed to co-operate and develop the same format, then movie makers and consumers would be very happy. Movie makers would feel assured that they could sell high-definition DVDs of their films; and consumers would be happy to purchase a high-definition DVD player and television to view the films. The market would grow and Sony and Toshiba would share a higher level of overall profits.

In contrast, if Sony and Toshiba continue competing, then movie makers do not know which format to support and consumers run the risk of buying a machine that can only play one format of disks. Worse still, their chosen format might be the least popular and their machines become obsolete. The overall market shrinks and both firms earn reduced profits.

Finally, if Sony is able to convince Toshiba to pull out of the race and stop developing its own HD DVD format, then Sony is left with the entire market. Movie makers adopt the Sony format, consumers buy machines which can read the Sony format. The market grows and Sony captures it all and earns the largest amount of profits possible.

To make this happen Sony appears to need to achieve a few things. First, it must offer a good technical solution. Second, it must gain the majority of support from key players; which means adopting some of the features from the Toshiba system. Therefore, rather interestingly, through an element of co-operation Sony can win the entire market. Game theory highlights the scenarios that Sony faces. Sony has to develop the strategy to attain market dominance.

This is nothing unique to Sony. Box 6.3 discusses how leading software companies are utilizing open source software to stifle competition.

Box 6.2 Blu-ray to win format war?

Adapted from an article in BusinessWeek, 21 October 2005

Independent technology and market research company Forrester Research has predicted victory for Blu-ray in the next-generation DVD format wars. Unfortunately for consumers, however, the firm believes that the battle will not end that quickly. After a long and tedious run-up to the launch, it is now clear to Forrester that the Sony-led Blu-ray format will win. But unless the HD DVD group, led by Toshiba, abandons the field, it will be another two years before consumers are confident enough of the winner to think about buying a new-format DVD player.

Forrester feels that Blu-ray's multi-use functionality for movies, computers and games gives it the edge over the Toshiba-led HD DVD camp. Indeed, the inclusion of Blu-ray in Sony's PlayStation 3 could be a big factor, and it is largely for that reason that Paramount recently decided to endorse Blu-ray when the movie studio had formerly only backed HD DVD. In addition, the Blu-ray format offers greater storage capacity and uses the familiar Java for its interactive features. And although manufacturing costs for Blu-ray will be slightly greater than HD DVD initially, the industry is working on ways to bring down those costs quickly.

Although a tedious format war seems almost inevitable, companies backing the respective groups would like to avoid such a scenario. PC maker Hewlett-Packard, a Blu-ray supporter, offered an olive branch of sorts yesterday, when it urged the Blu-ray group to be more consumer friendly by loosening its copy protection. Maureen Weber, HP's general manager of personal storage, said that consumers want to be able to store copies of their movies on their PCs to make them accessible over a home network. This 'mandatory Managed Copy' feature is standard on the competing HD DVD. 'It's critical that we have the ability to move content around the home', Weber told Reuters.

The idea behind this is that if the Blu-ray camp compromises and includes a feature heavily touted by HD DVD, then it should be able to attract further studio support and eventually convince Toshiba to drop out of the race. That being said, movie studios naturally prefer stronger copy protection of their content.

The longer the format war drags on, the longer consumers are likely to wait before even trying out a high-definition DVD. They do not want to get involved in a battle similar to the Betamax/VHS days. 'Consumers will postpone a decision until the winner is obvious. The war between Betamax and VHS trained a generation of consumers to be wary of competing formats. Many consumers were caught with an expensive device that couldn't play the movies available at the video store', said Schadler.

 ## Box 6.3 An open secret

Adapted from The Economist, 20 October 2005

Sharing intellectual property can be more profitable than keeping it to yourself.

IBM recently pledged 500 of its existing software patents to the open-source community, to be used without infringement. Since then, some other companies have taken similar initiatives. Nokia and Red Hat have all contributed Linux software. Even Sun Microsystems, for years the epitome of a proprietary company, made its Solaris operating system open-source.

The trend towards open software code is an example of a bigger development in the technology industry: a new approach towards collaboration and 'open innovation'. This is about how to kill your competitor and you kill your competitor these days by sharing IP.

Opening a company's R&D efforts translates into more development from external companies, more add-ons, less lock-in for potential adopters and therefore greater sales.

6.9 Business application: managing supply costs – anonymous auctions for supermarket contracts

We have seen that in repeated games, firms are likely to behave co-operatively. This presents a substantial risk to supermarkets who repeatedly run auctions to provide them with products. In particular, because supermarkets are retailers, they do not ordinarily manufacture their 'own-labelled' products. Instead they ask competing manufacturers to bid for contracts. Today it might be next month's lemonade contract; tomorrow it might be fish fingers or soap powder. The firm that can produce the product most cheaply wins the contract. With supermarkets coming to the market repeatedly, it is in the interest of competing manufacturers to co-operate with each other. For example, rival manufacturers of fish fingers could agree to split the market. When bidding for supermarket X's contract, company A would never undercut company B. In return, when bidding for supermarket Y's contract, B would never undercut A.

For a supermarket this is a serious problem. The way to stop it is to prevent co-operation. Supermarkets try to achieve this by organizing blind auctions over the Internet. The fish finger contract opens for bidding at 2.00 p.m. on Wednesday and companies make bids. The web page shows the amount of the bid, but it does not say who made the bid. The bidders now find it difficult to co-operate. In fact, it is now very easy to cheat because only the supermarket knows who you are. In this example, supermarkets can see the problem of co-operation and take steps to prevent its occurrence.

There is, however, a problem with the supermarket's strategy. In generating competition among its suppliers, it runs the risk of pushing some of them out of business. Therefore, in the long run the supermarkets could end up with monopoly suppliers in their key product markets rather than competitive industries, and we saw in Chapter 5 that such a situation could be dangerous.

 Summary

1 Under monopolistic competition there are a large number of small firms, freedom of entry and exit, few opportunities for economies of scale and the use of product differentiation.

2 Long-run equilibrium in monopolistic competition is a tangency equilibrium, which results in zero economic profits, excess capacity, above minimum average costs and price in excess of marginal costs.

3 Oligopolies are market places with a small number of large firms, typically four or five big ones. UK banking, supermarkets and even the media industry are good examples.

4 An important feature of oligopolistic markets is strategic interaction. If one firm makes a strategic change, all other firms react. When one UK supermarket decided to open on Sundays, all other supermarkets followed.

5 Two interesting questions occur when examining oligopolies: (i) Why do oligopolies exist? (ii) How will firms compete with each other?

6 Oligopolies can exist because of exogenous economies of scale. The natural cost structure of the industry results in only a small number of large firms meeting the minimum efficient scale.

7   Alternatively, natural scale economies might be limited and so, in order to create entry barriers, existing firms might manipulate the cost characteristics of the industry by perhaps making advertising a large component of operating costs. This creates high levels of endogenous costs and reduces entry.

8   Sunk costs cannot be recovered when exiting a market. If large costs are associated with brand development, then these will be sunk. This increases the risk of entry and so can also lead to the creation of entry barriers.

9   Without sunk costs markets are contestable. Potential rivals can threaten to enter a market. In order to limit entry, firms within the market will reduce prices and profits to make entry less attractive. As a result, even with a small number of large firms, contestable markets will approximate to perfect competition.

10   Game theory can be used to understand strategic interaction. Games consist of players, pay-offs and decision rules.

11   A Nash equilibrium is where players make an optimal decision based on what their rivals might do. In single-period games the Nash equilibrium requires each player to cheat or display non-cooperative behaviour. In a multi-period game with no known end, the optimal strategy is tit for tat, where if you co-operated last round, your rival should co-operate with you in the next round. If not, you should never co-operate with them again.

12   There are four auction formats, English auction, first-price sealed bid auction, second price sealed bid auction and a Dutch auction.

13   Under private values, the value of an item differs across bidders. Under common values, the item has the same intrinsic value to each bidder, but bidders are unsure of the true value of the item.

14   Under private values all four auction formats enable the bidder with the highest willingness to pay to win the auction. But they only pay the second highest price. This is known as the 'revenue equivalence theorem'.

15   Under common values bidders face the problem of the winner's curse, where the highest willingness to pay vastly exceeds the intrinsic value of the item.

16   To avoid conservative bidding under the winner's curse an English auction format provides bidders with clearer information on the item's true value.

17   In the repeated environment of firms bidding for supermarkets' own-label contracts it is likely that co-operation will occur where rivals agree not to undercut each other on price. In order to prevent this and generate competition in the auction, supermarkets run blind auctions, where it becomes difficult for rivals to co-ordinate their bids. It even enables rivals to cheat on each other behind a cloak of secrecy.

Learning checklist

You should now be able to:

♦ Explain monopolistic competition

♦ Provide examples of oligopolies

♦ Explain the concept of strategic interdependence

♦ Explain the difference between natural and strategic entry barriers

♦ Explain the kinked demand curve model of oligopoly and provide a critical review

♦ Explain game theory, the concept of a Nash equilibrium and optimal strategies in single period and repeated games. Explain how game theory can be used to control the behaviour of rivals in auctions

♦ Explain the main types of auctions and discuss the difference between common and private values. You should be able to explain the revenue equivalence theorem and the winner's curse

❓ Questions

1 Think of five adverts on television. Is their function primarily informative, or the erection of entry barriers to the industry?

2 Your economics lecturer offers to take bribes: £50 for 60 per cent in the exam; £100 for 70 per cent. Should you take him up on the offer?

3 Electrical retailers promise to match each other's prices: is this co-operation or competition?

4 Assume your company is operating in a tacit cartel, agreeing to raise prices and reduce output. If the cartel is ongoing then the game is effectively repeated. Under what circumstances would your company cheat?

Exercises

1 True or false?
   a) A key aspect of an oligopolistic market is that firms cannot operate independently of each other.
   b) Cartels may be workable if members enter into binding pre-commitments.
   c) Under a kinked demand curve, demand is assumed to be price inelastic under a rise in prices.
   d) In a one-period game the strategy of tit for tat is optimal.
   e) In a repeated game with no known end, it is always optimal to cheat.
   f) With private values an English auction format will raise the highest revenue for an item.

2 Suppose that there are two firms (X and Y) operating in a market, each of which can choose to produce either 'high' or 'low' output. Table 6.1 summarizes the range of possible outcomes of the firms' decisions in a single time period. Imagine that you are taking the decisions for firm X.
   a) If firm Y produces 'low', what level of output would maximize your profit in this time period?

b) If you (X) produce 'high', what level of output would maximize profits for firm Y?

c) If firm Y produces 'high', what level of output would maximize your profit in this time period?

d) Under what circumstances would you decide to produce 'low'?

e) Suppose you enter into an agreement with firm Y that you both will produce 'low': what measures could you adopt to ensure that Y keeps to the agreement?

f) What measures could you adopt to convince Y that you will keep to the agreement?

g) Suppose that the profit combinations are the same as in Table 6.1 except that if both firms produce 'high' each firm makes a loss of 8. Does this affect the analysis?

Table 6.1 Firms' decisions

Profits	Firm Y chooses:	High output			
	Low output	X	Y	X	Y
Firm X chooses:	Low output	15	15	2	20
	High output	20	2	8	8

3   Consider the case of Sony in Box 6.2.

a) Draw a game theory diagram that illustrates each of the possible scenarios from its competition with Toshiba.

b) Arguably, Sony and Toshiba have both tried to compete; but may now wish to move to a position of co-operation. In a repeated game will this be possible?

Chapter 7
Growth strategies

Chapter contents

Learning outcomes

By the end of this chapter you should understand:

Economic Theory

- The difference between horizontal, vertical and diversified growth

- Learning curves

- Transaction costs

- The hold-up problem

- Economies of scope

Business Application

- Why a small company within an oligopoly wished to merge with a rival

- Why the media company Sky has vertically integrated its entire value chain

- Why Google is branching out beyond search technology

Growth strategies at a glance

The issue

If firms are profit maximizers, then it seems reasonable to assume that, in the longer term, increasing profits will be associated with increased size. Admittedly, in the near term some profits may have to be sacrificed in order to grow the business. Managerial time might be diverted to finding and selecting growth opportunities, rather than concentrating on generating profits from the current operations. It therefore becomes important to understand how a firm can grow, benefit from and manage the problems associated with different modes of growth.

The understanding

A firm can grow in three main ways. First it can 'do more of the same'. A car-maker might decide to make more cars. Second, a firm might reduce its trading relationships by providing its own inputs, or by organizing its own distribution and retailing. Third, a firm might begin to operate in a completely different market. These three options are respectively known as horizontal, vertical and diversified growth. The reasons behind each type of growth are varied, but essentially they relate to the ability to increase revenues and reduce costs. This chapter will provide an understanding of these issues.

The usefulness

An understanding of growth options is essential for understanding how a business can exploit profitable opportunities. Moreover, an understanding of growth options provides an insight into strategic behaviour and, therefore, how the firm can gain greater control over its markets and its competitors.

7.1 Business problem: when should companies buy or sell other companies?

Examine the discussion in Box 7.1 and ask yourself how are Canal Plus and TPS attempting to grow their business?

 ### Box 7.1 French pay-TV giants agree merger

Adapted from an article on Asiamedia, 12 December 2005

A 5 billion euro ($5.9bn; £3.4bn) tie-up will unite Vivendi's Canal Plus and its rival TPS, which is jointly owned by French TV channels TF1 and M6.

The companies said their alliance would support the French film industry and give wider coverage to sport. It would also bring an end to the current price war between TPS and Canal Plus, and enable them to share the costs of acquiring expensive football broadcasting rights. Last year, Canal Plus outbid TPS for the rights to broadcast France's top football league, paying 600mn euros a season.

There will be enormous economies of scale from combining the two operations and they would have much more negotiating power when bidding for things like football rights.

Horizontal growth occurs when a company develops or grows its activities at the same stage of the production process.

Vertical chain of production encapsulates the various stages of production from the extraction of a raw material input, through the production of the product or service, to the final retailing of the product.

A company is said to be **vertically integrated** if it owns consecutive stages of the vertical chain.

Diversification is the growth of the business in a related or an unrelated market.

Acquisition involves one firm purchasing another firm. This might occur by mutual consent or, in the case of a hostile takeover, the managers of the acquired firm might try to resist the takeover. **Merger** generally involves two companies agreeing by mutual consent to merge their existing operations.

Economists would point to important differences in how the companies are attempting to grow. Merging the two companies is the obvious point to grasp and the article mentions the potential to gain enormous economies of scale. Economists would refer to this as **horizontal growth**.

The article also mentions the need to gain some control over the costs of bidding for sporting rights. Football games and TV broadcasting are generally separate activities and constitute what economists refer to as separate aspects of the **vertical chain of production**.

The vertical chain is composed of all the separate commercial activities that add value to a product. If we take sporting programmes, the value chain is composed of players, teams, stadiums, clubs, camera crews, satellites, presenters, broadcasters, set-top boxes and TVs. Canal and TPS are positioned roughly in the middle of this long value chain. By coming together they are seeking to gain greater control over this vertical chain. If they were to go one step further and own a football club then they would be described as being **vertically integrated**.

Finally, the merger of the companies is said to strengthen their interests in film production. This would be considered diversification by an economist. The definition of **diversification** is not as helpful as the previous ones, as it is not particularly clear what related and unrelated markets are. For example, Virgin is an oft-cited example of diversification, operating in music, airlines, drinks, trains, weddings, flowers, mobile phones and banking. All are unrelated markets, but they are also all related by successful management of the Virgin brand. Aside from these concerns we can see that programme making and films are similar, but not identical and so for these companies represents a related diversification.

In order to understand why a company might wish to grow, horizontally, vertically, or in a diversified manner we need to understand the benefits and problems associated with horizontal, vertical and diversified expansion.

7.2 Reasons for growth

If we begin by accepting the general proposition that firms are in business to maximize profits, then it seems reasonable to suggest that firms grow in order to improve profitability. If this is true then, examining Figure 7.1, a firm seeking horizontal, vertical or diversified growth must be expecting to gain from increases in total revenues and/or decreases in total costs. In this way the two curves in Figure 7.1 will move further apart from each other. As the curves move apart, both the profit-maximizing level of output and the amount of profit-maximizing profit will increase.

We will examine horizontal, vertical and diversified growth in turn.

7.3 Horizontal growth

Horizontal growth, or expansion at a singular point on the vertical chain, can occur in a number of ways.

Organic growth is associated with firms growing through internal expansion.

For example, a manufacturer might build additional production facilities, such as assembly lines, or a new factory. A retailer, such as a supermarket, might build more outlets. An airline would buy more aircraft. Crucially, the firm is growing by investing in new assets, which add to its current stock of capital. As an alternative, a firm might consider growth by **acquisition** and **merger**.

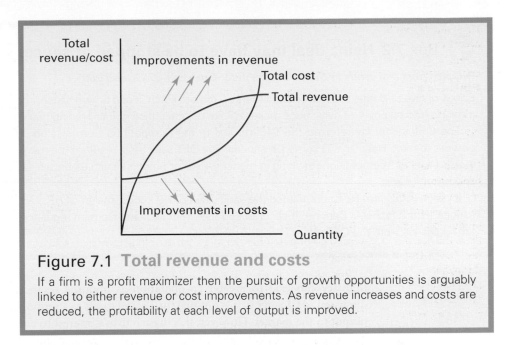

Figure 7.1 Total revenue and costs

If a firm is a profit maximizer then the pursuit of growth opportunities is arguably linked to either revenue or cost improvements. As revenue increases and costs are reduced, the profitability at each level of output is improved.

In either case the company grows by merging its activities with those of an existing operator. By going back through the theory established in previous chapters we can now begin to analyse the benefits of horizontal growth.

Horizontal growth and revenue

In Chapter 2 we examined the elasticity, or responsiveness of demand to a change in price. The greater the number of substitutes, or rival products, the greater the price elasticity of demand. If demand is elastic, then a small change in the price results in a huge change in the quantity demanded. Therefore, in price-elastic markets, with lots of substitute products, we argued that there is a clear incentive for firms to engage in a price war. If one firm reduces its prices, it quickly attracts market share from its rivals. However, in response, rivals may also drop their prices and each firm will retain the same market share, but be selling at a lower price. If demand is price inelastic, or not responsive to a change in price, then a price reduction will not have a significant impact on demand. Moreover, total revenues will decline. Therefore, the optimal response under price-inelastic demand is to raise prices in order to boost total revenues.

Reducing competition

If we now think about merger and acquisition, by definition the number of competitors in the market is reduced by one. Therefore, because merger and acquisition lead to a reduction in the number of substitutes, it is likely that the elasticity of demand is reduced. When competition is reduced, price wars are less likely and firms have more scope for increasing, rather than decreasing, prices. See Box 7.2 and the case of tomato ketchup and brown sauce.

If we also think about perfect competition, oligopoly and monopoly, as discussed in Chapters 5 and 6, we can reinforce the arguments made above. Under perfect competition with a large number of competitors, prices and profits are lowest. Under monopoly, prices and profits will be highest. In the case of oligopoly, consolidation in the

Box 7.2 Heinz deal may have to be stopped at sauce, says OFT

Adapted from and article by Simon Bowers in the Guardian, 27 October 2005

Prices of two of Britain's favourite condiments – tomato ketchup and brown sauce – could increase unfairly after Heinz's takeover of rival sauce maker HP Foods, the Office of Fair Trading has warned.

The OFT yesterday referred the £460m deal to the Competition Commission. The commission has powers to force Heinz to sell some UK sauces. The OFT said: 'As a result of the merger, consumers could suffer from less competition resulting in higher prices for products such as brown sauce, tomato ketchup and baked beans.'

In August, US firm Heinz completed the acquisition of HP Foods, maker of HP, Lea & Perrins and Amoy sauces – from France's Danone. It secured approval from Irish and German regulators but did not wait for firm guidance from the OFT.

industry can lead to greater co-operation as opposed to increased competition. As discussed in Chapter 6, it is optimal for a cartel to act as a monopoly supplier and reduce output to the market. However, it is in each firm's interest to cheat and increase output. It is easier to monitor and enforce the tacit or explicit agreement made among the members of a small cartel, than of a large one. In a small cartel you only need to gain agreement among, say, two or three companies. In a large cartel you need to gain agreement among a much larger number of companies, which is difficult. Therefore, mergers and acquisitions can lead to increased co-operation and the success of cartels.

Exploiting market growth

Aside from any changes in the price elasticity of demand, horizontal growth may be undertaken in order to exploit revenue growth. Growing demand could stimulate organic growth. As more customers move into a market, the firm can exploit increased revenue opportunities by investing in more productive assets. As more passengers have been willing to fly on low cost airlines, easyJet and Ryanair have purchased more aircraft. In recent years, coffee bars have suddenly appeared on many high streets, seeking to meet and exploit the rapid increase in customers.

In summary, the incentives from revenue and horizontal growth emanate from two main sources: first, a reduction in the number of competitors and, therefore, a fall in the price elasticity of demand, making price rises easier and price wars less likely; second, to take advantage of customer growth opportunities in the market.

Horizontal growth and costs

The obvious reason for horizontal growth relates to costs. In Chapter 3 we discussed economies of scale at length. However, in summary, as a firm increases its scale of operation, by increasing its capital input, it generally experiences a reduction in long-run average costs. Therefore, we can argue that a firm will try to grow in order to exploit economies of scale. This is often used as a rationale for merger. When bringing two companies together, managers often talk up the potential for cost reductions by reducing and sharing managerial functions. Two companies need two chief executives, one company only needs one chief executive. Two companies need two finance, legal, marketing and HRM departments, one company needs only one of each. These single departments will generally be capable of operating at a size which is less than the sum of the two separate departments, achieving this through greater staff utilization. This is often referred to as **rationalization**.

However, it is also possible that a firm can become too big. We saw in Chapter 3 that a very large firm can experience diseconomies of scale, where problems of control and co-ordination make the productivity of a large firm decrease, leading to a rise in long-run average costs. Therefore, it is sometimes the case that large firms decrease the scale of their operations in order to bring about cost improvements.

An alternative cost reason for horizontal expansion is the benefit to be had from the **learning curve**.

This is depicted in Figure 7.2 and shows that as the firm produces successive units, or adds to its cumulative output, average costs fall. The reason is that as a firm produces additional output, it learns how to improve productivity. The classic example is the production of a jumbo jet. This is a massive project and requires careful planning and learning. In what order should the plane be assembled? When are the wings attached, when is the wiring completed, when can the seats be added? If wings are added too early, then there is the risk of having to remove them at a later date in order to finish another task, such as adding the fuel tanks. However, once the mistake is made and learnt, it will not be made again. So, when the next plane is built, fewer assembly mistakes will occur. The plane will be built more quickly and at a lower cost. As more planes are built, the assembly teams will learn how to carry out each assembly task more quickly and develop new operating techniques. Eventually, at high levels of cumulative output, all learning opportunities are exploited and the reduction in costs diminishes to zero. At this point the learning curve becomes flat.

Rationalization is associated with cutbacks in excess resources in the pursuit of increased operational efficiencies.

The **learning curve** suggests that as cumulative output increases, average costs fall.

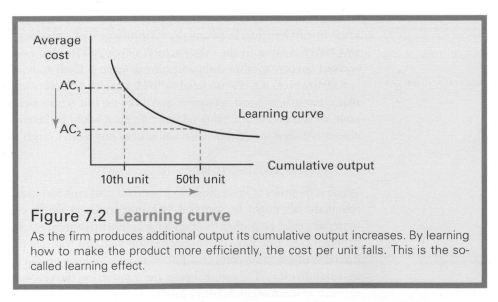

Figure 7.2 Learning curve
As the firm produces additional output its cumulative output increases. By learning how to make the product more efficiently, the cost per unit falls. This is the so-called learning effect.

A firm producing 100 units a day learns faster than a firm producing 10 units a day. In recognizing this point a firm could grow organically in order to be in a position to exploit the learning effect sooner than its rivals. Alternatively, a competitor may have already produced many units and acquired the relevant cumulative experience through learning. An attractive strategy is to merge, or acquire the existing firm in an attempt to gain the acquired experience. However, it is debatable how easy it is to transfer experience between organizations. The experience of one company is likely to be related to the systems, producers and cultures of that company. The learning effect stems from the experiences of a group of individuals with shared memories, values and understanding. How to transfer such intangible understandings and benefits effectively to another organization is more than likely to be problematic.

7.4 Vertical growth

Cost reasons

When a firm grows vertically, either moving up or down its vertical chain, it is attempting to integrate additional value-adding activities into its existing activities. There can be a number of reasons for doing this.

Location benefits

Integrating consecutive activities from the vertical chain can reduce production costs. For example, steel smelting plants are often located next to steel rolling plants. This reduces transport and heating costs. Extremely high temperatures are needed to produce steel. Similarly, in order to roll the steel into usable sheets, the steel has to be hot. With the plants co-owned and located next to each other, the hot steel can be transferred easily to the rolling plant. If the two activities were separate, the new hot steel would have to be cooled, transferred by road to the rolling plant, re-heated and then rolled – resulting in much higher production costs.

Economies of scale

In contrast, when economies of scale are important, vertical disintegration may also result in cost benefits. For example, a manufacture of a product may require a particular raw material input. If the manufacturer developed its own raw material division then, without supplying other companies, the division is likely to be operating at a very small scale. However, if a raw material supplier is able to operate independently and supply many manufacturers, it is possible that it can exploit economies of scale. If economies of scale are important in a value-adding activity, it could be better for the manufacturer to abandon its raw material division and instead buy from a larger independent company.

Problems from monopoly

While economies of scale might be important cost considerations, it is also possible that raw materials might be supplied by a monopoly, in which case the price of the raw material could be higher than under a competitive market. A simple solution to this problem is to purchase the monopoly supplier and transfer the raw material between divisions of the same company. But what price will the production division pay the raw material division? The optimal price for transferring the raw material to the production division is the marginal cost of production in the raw material division. Under such a price, allocative efficiency would hold with the price being equal to marginal cost. As an explanation, the price paid and, therefore, the value of the last unit will be exactly equal to the cost of producing the last unit. This enables the combined profits of the raw material division and the production division to be maximized. More important, if we return to an argument made in Chapter 5, the monopoly price is always greater than the marginal cost. Therefore, buying the raw material supplier and charging an internal price equal to the marginal cost has to be cheaper than the price charged by a monopoly supplier.

Box 7.3 Steelmakers on a roll, until the next glut

Adapted from an article in The Economist, 28 November 2005

China's appetite for steel has provided the rest of the world's big producers with a rare period of boom and helped to finance a buying spree, of which the past week's bids for Dofasco are just the latest example.

As recently as six years ago, while investors were still in thrall to a dot.com bubble, steel was derided as one of the last bastions of the 'old' economy. Many firms in the industry were state-owned or heavily protected by governments keen to preserve assets deemed vital to national interests. It is a measure of the changes that have swept the business that last week Arcelor, a company created through a 2001 merger of the top French, Spanish and Luxembourg steelmakers, made a hostile bid of C$4.4 billion ($3.8 billion), in cash, for Dofasco, Canada's leading steel firm. This week, Arcelor's offer was trumped by a friendly bid of €3.5 billion ($4.1 billion) by Germany's ThyssenKrupp.

This wave of mergers, acquisitions and asset sales has helped to revive the fortunes of the world's steelmakers by reducing the chronic overcapacity that had troubled the industry for decades. By far the most important factor behind steel's revival, however, is China's booming economy. China's soaring demand for steel sent prices spiralling upwards until recently: benchmark hot-rolled coil, which sold for as little as $200 a tonne in 2001, broke the $600 barrier in 2004. But problems still confront steelmakers.

The first is that their improving lot has not gone unnoticed by those who sell the raw materials that feed the world's steel mills. Suppliers of iron ore grouped together to demand hefty price rises of 72% for their products in March this year, even after obtaining a 19% rise last year. Suppliers of coking coal, also vital to the steelmaking process, insisted on even greater hikes. Early forecasts suggest that iron-ore suppliers could want another big price rise – perhaps as much as 20% – next year. This year's rise is likely to add $40–60 to the price of producing a tonne of steel, just as prices for end users are falling.

The world's big steelmakers are hoping that, by getting bigger, they can reap the rewards in the good times and insulate themselves if things turn nasty. Lakshmi Mittal, head of the eponymous steelmaker, and Guy Dollé, the boss of Arcelor, both agree that the industry will be dominated by a few big firms, each producing over 100m tonnes annually, in the coming years.

More consolidation would certainly give steel firms extra clout when negotiating ore and coke prices. The world's top five steelmakers still command only around one-fifth of the global market, whereas the three leading ore firms control 70% of supplies. The level of consolidation that would confer significant market power on the largest mills still seems a long way off.

One way to shift the balance of power is to encroach on the suppliers' turf, and a few big steel firms have been doing just that, buying into ore and coke operations. Dofasco is a tempting target partly because it has its own ore business.

The big steelmakers hope that further consolidation will help to shift the balance of power in their favour, and they appear convinced that sheer bulk will help them to ride out any future slackening of demand. But size in the steel business does not, in itself, bring great rewards in terms of economies of scale – especially if, as many suspect, predators are overpaying for assets.

Transaction costs

Transaction costs are the costs associated with organizing the transaction of goods or services.

In order to fully develop your understanding of the various cost reasons for vertical growth we need to introduce a new cost concept. In Chapter 3, when examining costs, we only focused on production costs. These are the costs of the factor resources – land, labour, capital and enterprise – used by the firm in the production of the good or service. In addition to production costs, we also need to consider what are known as **transaction costs**.

When goods or services are traded, the costs of organizing the transaction can range from low to very high. At the most simplistic level, if a contract or agreement is entered into for the supply of goods or services, the time of managers negotiating the contract and the cost of lawyers hired to write the contract all represent transaction costs. Economists highlight a number of factors that are likely to lead to higher transaction costs. These factors are all related to the degree to which the contract or agreement can be declared 'complete'.

> Under a **complete** contract, all aspects of the contractual arrangement are fully specified.

For example, the nature of the product, including the characteristics of the product, the materials used to make the product and the size of the product, will all be described within the contract terms. The price and time of delivery will also be covered by the contract. Finally, the contract will also set out how the performance of the product supplier will be measured and how the contract will be enforced through the legal system, should the terms of the contract be breached.

Clearly, given the conditions detailed above, no contract is ever complete. However, for some products it is much easier to write a nearly complete contract, while for others it is almost impossible. As examples, it is much easier to write a complete contract for a bag of sand than it is for lecturing services. Sand comes in standard bag sizes, a limited number of ranges, such as river sand or building sand, and if a company agreed to deliver a bag you would be able to verify its arrival. Now consider writing a contract for lecturing services. For a complete contract it would be necessary to define many things including: during which hours the lectures would be given; what textbooks should be used; what topics should be covered each week; how the module should be examined; what topics and questions should be used during the tutorials; how difficult the examination should be; how marks should be awarded; how many students are expected to pass; how tutorial staff should be managed; and much more. It is clearly very difficult to define in full all the actions a lecturer should take during the running of a module. As a consequence, universities, like many employers, use incomplete contracts. Instead of defining all possible actions, contracts resort to simple statements such as 'a lecturer will be expected to communicate and expand knowledge'.

Rather than being complete, the contract is extremely vague. A sensible interpretation of the statement is that a lecturer is expected to communicate knowledge through teaching and expand knowledge through research. But of course there are many other interpretations. For example, answering the telephone and handling student enquiries is communicating and expanding knowledge. If the university expected the lecturer to teach and research, but the lecturer decided to simply answer telephone enquiries, then the university would experience substantial transaction costs. This is because the lecturer is choosing to undertake activities that the university did not intend. Aside from the ability to reinterpret the meaning of the contract, it is also very difficult for the university to measure the lecturer's performance. For example, let us assume many students fail the module. There could be many explanations, but let us concentrate on two. First, the lecturer did not perform well and the students did not benefit from the lectures. Second, even if this is true, the lecturer could blame the poor performance on the students' lack of effort during tutorials and revision. Because the effort of the lecturer and the students is not monitored by anyone from the university, it is difficult to support either argument. This therefore creates an environment within which the lecturer could act less than professionally. Lower performance by the lecturer represents a transaction cost.

We will shortly see how firms, and in our case universities, try to deal with these problems. But, first, it is useful to provide an understanding of the general factors which lead to greater transactional costs.

Complexity

Complexity is an obvious factor. Sand is an uncomplicated product; lecturing is a very complicated product. As the product or service becomes more complex (simple), the more incomplete (complete) the contract becomes. As the contract becomes more incomplete (complete), the higher (lower) are the costs of transacting.

Uncertainty

Uncertainty also affects the ability to write a complete contract. In the case of a bag of sand, uncertainty is less of an issue. You are not going to request a different bag of sand depending upon the nature of the weather. By contrast, in the case of lecturing services a university will expect the lecturer to be adaptable in the face of future changes. New theories may enter the subject, new ways of teaching might emerge, or the quality of the students each year could change. The university cannot write a contract detailing how the lecturer should deal with these changes, but a good lecturer will be expected to deal with these problems and opportunities using their professional discretion.

So, as uncertainty increases, the ability to write a complete contract diminishes and the costs of transacting increases.

Monitoring

While complexity and uncertainty are problems associated with writing a contract, monitoring and enforcement are problems associated with managing a contractual arrangement. The more simple and certain the environment, the easier it is to monitor a contract. Again, let us compare a bag of sand with the lecturer. It is very easy to monitor whether or not a bag of sand is delivered. You can see it, you can feel it and you can weigh it. But how do you know if a lecturer has communicated and expanded knowledge? How do you measure effective communication, or teaching? A high pass rate for the module could indicate good teaching. But it could equally indicate good students, or an easy examination.

In general when the good or service is more complex and the environment is more uncertain, the ability to monitor the incomplete contract is more difficult and costly.

Enforcement

When the contract is incomplete, the enforcement of the contract, by use of the legal process, is much more difficult.

If a company does not deliver your sand, it is fairly easy to prove breach of contract and ask a court to enforce delivery. However, if you cannot effectively define or measure the activities of a lecturer, then it is almost impossible to prove breach of contract. For example, if the university says that the lecturer has not communicated knowledge effectively, it will have to find a way of measuring the lecturer's level of effective communication. Since measuring communication is very difficult, it will be almost impossible to ask a judge to enforce the contract on a lecturer. The legal system cannot be used to enforce the contract. In knowledge of the fact that a university will find it difficult to measure and enforce performance, the lecturer can use the discretion provided within the contract to teach what they like, in a fashion that they prefer and examine the topics that they would like. Some do it well, others less well. The difference is transaction costs.

Make or buy?

In the case of production costs, we argued that firms are cost efficient when they operate with minimum average costs at the lowest point on the average cost curve. It therefore also seems sensible to argue that firms will try to minimize transaction costs. In fact, the reduction or control of transaction costs is of fundamental importance for economists, because transaction costs are the very driving force behind firms. Without transaction costs firms would not exist.

Transaction costs can be managed through competing systems. These are the market and the hierarchy, or managerial structure, of a firm. Theoretically the system with the lowest transaction cost will be chosen.

The hierarchy, or managerial structure, of a firm is composed of the various managerial layers, beginning with directors, then moving down to senior managers, and eventually ordinary workers.

Transaction costs and markets

For market-based transactions to have a low transaction cost, the contract has to be as complete as possible. This requires low complexity and low uncertainty. In addition, monitoring must be easy and enforcement feasible. In such situations the ability to write a contract is easy and, therefore, low cost. Furthermore, the scope of the provider to perform below expectation in the delivery of the good or service is constrained by the easy monitoring and legal enforcement of the contract. The transaction costs of operating through the market are low.

In contrast, when the product is complex and uncertainty is high, it becomes more difficult and, therefore, more costly to write a contract. In addition, as the contract becomes more incomplete, greater discretion is handed to the provider of the good or service. Monitoring of the output becomes difficult, as the output is not clearly defined by the contract. As a result, enforcement becomes impossible. Recall the lecturer communicating and expanding knowledge. The output of the lecturer is not defined. It is left to the lecturer to use their discretion when designing the syllabus and delivery of the module. The potential for very high transaction costs by operating through the market becomes very high.

Transaction costs and hierarchies

The alternative is to organize the transaction within the firm and use the hierarchy or managerial structure to organize the transaction. The problem with incomplete contractual relationships is that they provide the producer of the good or service with too much discretion. To economize on writing a complete contract the university uses the phrase 'communicate and expand knowledge'. But by using the managerial structure of the university, it is possible to minimize the resulting transaction costs. For example, when a lecturer begins employment they will ordinarily be placed on probation for perhaps three years. Removal from probation and the confirmation of employment will only follow a set of successful lectures. Before a module begins the lecturer will not generally be allowed to choose any set of topics. Rather, they will be required to work to a module descriptor, which details the topics to be taught, the nature of the assessment and the key learning outcomes of the module for the students. At the end of the module, students are asked to evaluate the module on various criteria. This is monitoring and over a number of years and across a range of taught modules the university can develop an understanding of how well the lecturer performs. Through annual appraisals, annual training programmes and departmental discussions, the lecturer can begin to understand peer expectations regarding the acceptable level of lecturing performance and the nature of acceptable teaching styles. Management and colleagues have the potential to condition the lecturer's discretion, by advising on what is acceptable behaviour at work. Finally, with a shared understanding of acceptable performance the university can attempt to enforce acceptable delivery of lecturing services through pay awards and promotions. Lecturers who continually provide superior services, develop new teaching methods and lead research will generally be promoted. In contrast, over time, management will also be able to see who is not performing optimally and their cases for promotion might be declined.

Essentially, in the market place the legal process and competition among the various suppliers are used to enforce contractual commitments and keep transaction costs low. Within firms, contractual commitments are enforced through long-term monitoring by the managerial hierarchy and the periodic pay awards and promotion associated with good performance. In this way transaction costs are reduced.

Firms therefore exist in order to reduce transaction costs. In fact, economists often refer to firms as a **nexus of contracts**.

Nexus of contracts is a collection of interrelated contractual relationships, where the firm represents a nexus or central point, where all these interrelated contractual relationships are managed in the pursuit of profit.

Transaction costs and vertical growth

How can we use these insights in order to understand how and when a firm will grow or shrink along its vertical axis?

If we consider the vertical chain, the answer is simple. The firm as a nexus of contracts will grow up or down its vertical chain when it needs to reduce its transaction costs by making use of its hierarchy or managerial structure to control its transactions. Similarly, a firm will shrink, or reduce in size as a nexus of contracts, when it believes it is possible to use the market to control its transactions. Consider the following examples.

Hospitals produce healthcare, but we need to recognize that healthcare is a combination of various value-adding activities: medical treatment from doctors and nurses, plus catering and cleaning services. Traditionally, all three services were performed by employees of the hospital. More recently, catering and cleaning services have been subcontracted to independent private companies. In doing so, the hospital has not grown vertically; rather, it has reduced its vertical boundaries. This is illustrated in Figure 7.3. The dotted lines represent the boundaries of the hospital's activities. In the top half of Figure 7.3 cleaning, catering and medical treatment are all inside the dotted lines. This is how hospitals traditionally organized themselves. Staff of the hospital carried out all three activities. In the lower part of Figure 7.3 we see that only medical treatment is within the dotted lines of the overall healthcare provided by a hospital. Catering and cleaning are within their own dotted lines. This signifies that private companies provide catering and cleaning. Cleaning and catering are now being provided, or transacted through the market. Periodically, the hospital will hold a tendering process, where it effectively holds an auction for its catering or cleaning contracts. The firm willing to offer its services at the lowest cost may win the contract.

Why have cleaning and catering been moved into the market, while medical treatment has been retained inside the hospital? The answer is that, from a transactional perspective, it is cheaper to buy catering and cleaning services from the market, but it is cheaper to provide medical treatment in-house. Consider trying to write a contract for cleaning services. It is reasonably easy to write a near complete contract: each hospital ward must be cleaned twice a day, each waiting room once; and operating theatres after each operation. Now consider trying to write a complete contract for a heart surgeon. For each possible heart problem the contract would have to stipulate how the surgeon would treat the patient. This is very complex and therefore, just as in the case of the university

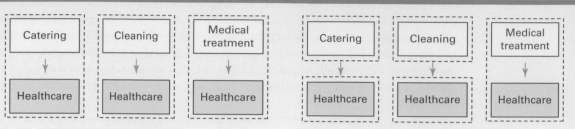

Traditional healthcare integration
The dotted lines represent the boundary of the firm's or hospital's activities. Traditionally catering, cleaning and medical services were all carried out by hospital employees. Therefore, the scope of the hospital's activities covered all three areas. The modern structure, opposite, has seen significant changes.

Modern healthcare integration
Hospitals have begun to recognize that it is more expensive to have catering and cleaning done by in-house departments. The cheaper option is to have such services provided by private companies. The vertical boundary of the hospital, or the scope of its activities, is now concentrated on medical treatment.

Figure 7.3 **Vertical integration**

lecturer, it is better to leave treatment to the surgeon's discretion using an incomplete contract, where the contract might simply state that the 'surgeon will provide medical expertise in the cardiovascular department'. The hospital needs to measure the surgeon's performance against the contract. However, the performance of the surgeon can only be monitored over time by the hospital's management team. Good surgeons are promoted; poor ones are advised to move on. This long-term monitoring is best done inside the hospital's management systems, where other medical consultants can periodically provide a review of the surgeon's efforts and expertise. Such a process is very difficult if the hospital decided to contract surgeons on a short-term basis through the market.

Vertical growth: strategic considerations

> The **hold-up problem** is the renegotiation of contracts and is linked to asset specificity.

> A **specific asset** has a specific use; a general asset has many uses.

An important transactional problem, not discussed above, is associated with asset specificity and the **hold-up problem**.

An aircraft can be used on a number of routes. Its use is more general than specific. A production line designed to make bumpers for a Ford Focus is a very **specific asset**, as it is very difficult to use the production line to make bumpers for any other car.

Consider the vertical chain for airlines. A new aircraft is purchased and used to fly between cities A and B. Additional value adding inputs are landing slots at each city's airport. If the route between A and B is highly profitable, one of the airports, say B, might try to gain some of the airline's profit by increasing its landing charges. However, since the aircraft is a general asset, the airline has the option of moving the aircraft to a route between A and C (assuming this route is also profitable). The airline can use the general nature of aircraft to discipline airport B and prevent an increase in landing charges.

Now consider the producer of bumpers for a particular car. Each car model is unique and the shape of the car's bumper will be very specific. The production plant will be dedicated to producing bumpers for this one type of car. The car manufacturer could approach the bumper manufacturer and ask for a new production facility to be built for its bumpers. In return the car manufacturer agrees a price for each bumper. We might assume that the agreed price is £100 per bumper. This price per bumper will make the investment in the new plant profitable for the bumper manufacturer. However, once the plant is up and running, the car manufacturer has a substantial incentive to renegotiate a discount price for the bumpers. Why? Because, unlike the airline company, the bumper manufacturer has a specific asset; it only makes one type of bumper. The plant cannot be used to produce bumpers for another car manufacturer, so it is dependent upon the one car maker. This is the hold-up problem.

The car manufacturer can take advantage of the bumper producer's investment in a specific asset. In fact, so obvious is this type of hold-up problem that the bumper producer would not invest in the production facility. The car producer, therefore, has to build its own bumper-producing plant. The car manufacturer grows vertically and begins to produce one of its key inputs. For many car parts this is very common. Take a look at a car and find the most obvious component on the car that has not been made by the car maker itself. It will probably be the tyres. This is because tyres are round and will fit on many different types of cars. Tyres, or more correctly the plant making tyres, is a general asset. The production of tyres for Ford can easily be switched to the production of tyres for Toyota. A producer of tyres, therefore, does not face a hold-up problem, because they are not dependent upon one buying relationship. A bumper manufacturer would be.

The hold-up problem can also represent a strategic opportunity when one firm is able to gain a monopoly position in the vertical chain. Consider Figure 7.4. For simplicity, assume an industry has three firms, all manufacturing a similar product, beer. In the top half of Figure 7.4, each firm is a producer of beer, buying hops from farmers and selling the beer on to independent pubs. In the bottom half of Figure 7.4, firm 1 has gained ownership of the pubs. As a monopoly supplier of beer retailing, firm 1 can promote its own brands and negotiate cheap beer supplies from the remaining brewers. An equally effective growth strategy would have been to gain control of the hop supply and gain a monopoly position at the top of the vertical chain. It could then sell hops to itself cheaply, but charge brewing rivals a very high price.

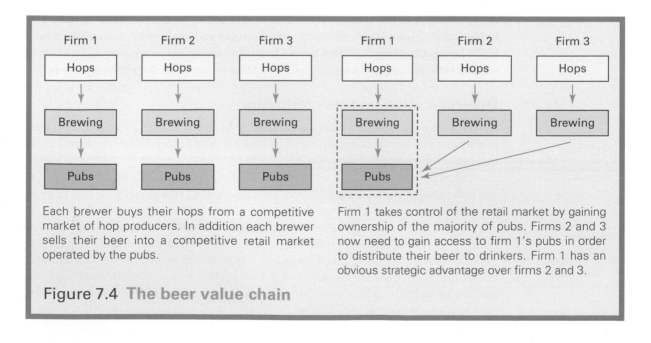

Each brewer buys their hops from a competitive market of hop producers. In addition each brewer sells their beer into a competitive retail market operated by the pubs.

Firm 1 takes control of the retail market by gaining ownership of the majority of pubs. Firms 2 and 3 now need to gain access to firm 1's pubs in order to distribute their beer to drinkers. Firm 1 has an obvious strategic advantage over firms 2 and 3.

Figure 7.4 **The beer value chain**

In summary, firms will grow vertically up or down the vertical chain if the transaction costs of operating through the market are too high. By internalizing transactions, or making the value-adding product or service inside the company, the firm will attempt to control its transaction costs more effectively. Similarly, when the transaction costs of the market are very low, a firm will seek to reduce its vertical integration and begin to seek subcontractors for some of its inputs. Buying in, rather than making the product or service, has lower transaction costs. In addition to the costs of organizing the transaction, we also need to consider the transaction costs generated by the hold-up problem. The firm will grow vertically along the vertical chain whenever it can gain strategic advantage over its rivals and whenever the market refuses to supply products for fear of the hold-up problem. We will return to these issues in the business application of the BBC and BSkyB.

7.5 Diversified growth

Diversification involves a company expanding its operations into related or unrelated markets. This can occur for a variety of reasons, but a strong cost reason centres on the concept of **economies of scope**.

> **Economies of scope** are said to exist if the cost of producing two or more outputs jointly is less than the cost of producing the outputs separately.

If two products A and B are being produced, then economies of scope are sometimes expressed as:

Cost (A) + Cost (B) > Cost (A + B)

This suggests that the costs of producing A on its own, Cost (A), plus the cost of making B on its own, Cost (B), is greater than making A and B together, Cost (A + B).

An obvious example can be found in the news-gathering services of the BBC. News on politics, business, world affairs and crime can be collected centrally. This is then drawn on by BBC News 24, BBC Evening News, Radio One, Two etc., and by BBC News Online. If each division operated separately, then the news would be collected many times. By centralizing news gathering, the BBC cuts down on duplication and exploits economies of scope. An alternative example can be found in the business activities of Virgin. The brand name of Virgin is very important, but just like the news gathering of the BBC, it can reduce duplication. As Virgin initially invested many millions developing its brand name for the music industry, the brand could then also be used to launch products in other markets. This has included airlines, mobile phones, financial services and much more. Admittedly, money has to be spent building the Virgin Airlines brand, but the expense is arguably much less than starting with no brand and launching all these different commercial activities separately.

Diversification and risk reduction

Diversification can reduce a company's exposure to risk. Consider a company operating in only one market. The company could be making good profits. However, there is a risk that in the future profits will change. Profits will fall if new competition enters the market, a recession occurs and sales fall, or a raw material becomes expensive. Equally, profits will rise if the level of competition falls, sales increase during a recession, or the cost of a raw material decreases.

Profits can, therefore, go up or down. But they can go up or down for any firm, or industry. More importantly, profits at any particular point in time might go up for one firm or industry, but come down for another. It is, therefore, possible to have multiple operations and reduce the variability in overall profits. By operating in more than one market, or industry, falling profits in one operation can hopefully be offset by rising profits in another part of the business.

Tesco, the leading UK supermarket chain, is a reasonable example. Operating across grocery, as well as non-foods such as CDs, magazines, and home electricals; and financial services, including insurance and banking enables Tesco to reduce its operating risks. If grocery and non-food profits fall, it is possible that financial services profits could rise. In order for this to be true the various operations must form a **diversified portfolio** of business activities.

A **diversified portfolio** of activities contains a mix of uncorrelated business operations.

If two business activities are correlated, then the profit levels of each activity will move together. As such, the combined profits will still show large swings over time. For a diversified portfolio business activities must be uncorrelated. This means the level of profits from one business activity are not related to the level of profits from another activity. The combined profits from diversified activities will now be less variable; as one operation incurs losses, another is likely to rise into profitability.

While diversification can reduce the financial risks of a company, it does not add value to the company. The problem lies in the fact that variability in profits is the risk of shareholders. If an individual shareholder wishes to diversify their risks, then they can do so at low cost. They achieve this by simply buying small amounts of shares in various different uncorrelated companies. If a Tesco shareholder is worried about future losses in the grocery business, they can buy shares in any high street bank. They do not need Tesco to create its own bank. Furthermore, the investor may already have shares in a bank. As a result of Tesco moving into the personal financial services sector the investor's risk or exposure to the financial services sector has increased, not diminished. Therefore, diversification by a company does not add value for shareholders. So, why do companies diversify?

As we will see in Chapter 8, we need to make a distinction between shareholders and managers. On a day-to-day basis it is managers who run and control companies. Managers have a great deal of asset tied up in the company they work for. The company pays their salary and funds their pension. If the company closed, due to substantial losses, how likely is it that the manager would gain employment elsewhere? Managers, therefore, face substantial non-diversified risk from employment. Diversification is arguably more in the interests of managers than shareholders.

7.6 Business application: horizontal growth by merger

The UK supermarket sector is a classic oligopoly, a small number of large players. The three biggest players are Tesco, Sainsbury's and Asda. Of these three, Tesco is clearly the dominant leader with 26 per cent of the market (see Table 7.1). Until recently the

Table 7.1 Supermarket fact file

Supermarket	Market share %	Turnover (£bn)
Tesco	23.7	27
Sainsbury	12.5	18
Asda	11.7	Unknown
Morrisons	9	6

market also had a number of minor competitors, Safeway, Wm Morrison and Waitrose. Recently Morrison's acquired Safeway and almost doubled its market share.

Using our understanding of horizontal growth strategies we can understand why Morrison's was keen to acquire Safeway. As the smallest of the UK supermarkets, Wm Morrison needed increased size. It operated predominately in the north of England and viewed Safeway's stores in the south of the UK as highly desirable. Acquisition of Safeway would provide easy access to growth opportunities in the south of the country and through a doubling of Morrison's size the merger would provide much-needed economies of scale in distribution, marketing and price negotiations with product providers. All helping to boost growth and profits.

Moreover, it was essential for Morrison's to prevent the likes of Asda and Sainsbury's from buying Safeway since the additional market share would have helped these companies to catch up with Tesco and create a second dominant competitor. Finally, Tesco had to be prevented from gaining control of Safeway as a means of accelerating its growing market share. Therefore, Safeway offered economic opportunities to Morrison's, while denying its rivals strategic opportunities.

However, the journey has not been easy. With the removal of a competitor from the market place the competition authorities intervened. In Morrison's favour the UK Competition Commission blocked Tesco, Sainsbury's and Asda from making bids for Safeway. At the same time, however, they also insisted that Morrison's would have to sell off Safeway stores in locations where it already had a Morrison's store. The Commission was clearly keen not to manage market share at the level of the economy, but it was also very keen to place competition at the heart of Morrison's existing business. The consequences of this are reported in Box 7.4 where Morrison's has reported three profits warnings in a row. With Morrison's ultimately selling off over half of the Safeway stores, the spoils have been spread around all the key players.

A crucial part of Morrison's growth strategy was to reduce costs through rationalization. Two supermarkets need two teams of senior managers, one big supermarket only needs one team of managers. Two supermarkets need two distribution systems. One merged supermarket can push more volume through its existing supply chain. Morrison's has suffered under the burden of what is referred to as 'dual running' – that is, running a

---

 Box 7.4 **Last Safeways make the switch**

Adapted from an article by Russell Hotten, the Daily Telegraph, 24 November 2005

The Safeway supermarket brand will be erased from the high street when Morrison's finally converts the remainder of the 479 stores bought in the £3bn acquisition of its rival. The passing will be marked not with a fanfare, but with a sigh of relief.

The purchase of Safeway was disastrous, bringing into question the future of one of the most admired managements in retailing and destroying an earnings record that was the envy of the sector.

It brings to an end what is believed to be the UK's biggest store conversion. But along the way the company issued three profits warnings and last month made the first loss in its 106-year history.

The costs of running dual distribution, administration and IT operations proved far higher than expected. The company underestimated the hurdles of expanding its brand outside its northern heartland to southern England and Scotland. Although Morrisons got rid of a lot of management dead wood, some talented people were also eased out.

merged business as two separate enterprises. The future challenge is to push through cost cutting and gain efficiency, but expertise and senior management experience have been lost and the company has also been threatened with strike action by its workers fearful of change. However attractive a merger looks on paper, it is the execution which is often most important.

7.7 Business application: vertical growth – gaining control of the value chain

Sky, the UK's satellite broadcaster and owner of television rights to Premiership football, provides an interesting example of how to control the vertical chain.

A representation of Sky's vertical chain in the market for Premiership football programmes is shown in Figure 7.5. Whether you are a football fan or not, you will rapidly appreciate the benefits of what Sky has managed to do.

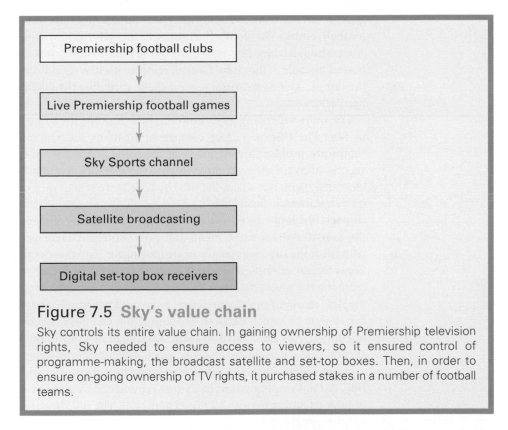

Figure 7.5 Sky's value chain

Sky controls its entire value chain. In gaining ownership of Premiership television rights, Sky needed to ensure access to viewers, so it ensured control of programme-making, the broadcast satellite and set-top boxes. Then, in order to ensure on-going ownership of TV rights, it purchased stakes in a number of football teams.

At the top of the vertical chain are Premiership football clubs, which create value by buying players, forming sides and playing football. Football games form the next stage in the value chain, with sides coming together to play for the Premiership title. Sky Sports, as a programme maker, creates a team of presenters, a studio, a camera crew and provides a television programme based on the live games. This programme is beamed to a satellite, which then beams the programme back to viewers' homes. Set-top boxes, or decoders, pick up the signal from the satellite and feed a picture into the viewer's television. While this is an example of a vertical chain, the important point is that Sky owns all of it. Sky owns the set-top boxes, it owns the satellite, it owns the TV channel Sky Sports, it owns the rights to live Premiership games and it has had significant shareholdings in a number of UK football clubs, including Manchester United, Leeds, Chelsea and Sunderland. Why?

The vertical integration displayed by Sky is simply a reflection of transaction costs. In gaining ownership of live rights to Premiership football, Sky has to outbid many competitors and often pays in excess of £1 billion. In order to maintain the exclusivity of the product and in order to ensure delivery of live games to paying viewers, Sky has to ensure it has access to a distribution channel. For Sky, it makes sense to own a satellite and to provide set-top boxes to its viewers. If it relied on an external supplier of broadcasting, then it would be vulnerable to the hold-up problem. Ownership of the rights to live games is a fairly specific asset. You can only do one thing with it: sell football games to viewers. If this is profitable, an independent broadcaster might try to squeeze profits out of Sky by raising the price for broadcasting the games. In the longer term, given that Sky has invested in a satellite, set-top boxes and the development of its football programmes, it has to ensure that it will not lose control of rights to the live football games. Sky, therefore, vertically integrates further and buys stakes in some of the leading football clubs. The football clubs sell the television rights through the Football Association. Because Sky owns parts of the football clubs, it is effectively in a position to oversee the sale of the clubs' football rights to itself. A significant step towards protecting the rest of Sky's downstream vertical chain, including the satellite and set-top boxes, has been achieved.

The more interesting issue, however, is to examine the strategic value of set-top boxes to Sky. The BBC is a clear competitor in many areas of programming for Sky. A significant problem for the BBC was the rising dominance of digital television and the success of Sky's policy of providing its viewers with free digital set-top boxes. As Sky increased its market share, the BBC became more reliant on Sky for the broadcasting of its programmes. Since Sky owns a satellite and the set-top boxes, it can behave strategically. It has the potential to place one of its main competitors in an obscure part of the available programme menu and gain strategic advantage. For example, consider yourself at the supermarket: if you are looking for soap powder you do not look in the fish finger freezer cabinet. Similarly, if you wish to watch BBC One you will not expect to find it among the music channels. By owning the set-top boxes, Sky has the potential to hide the BBC channels away from its own popular Sky channels, and, therefore, make it harder for viewers to switch between the competing channels. Therefore, by being vertically integrated, Sky has gained strategic advantage by controlling an essential part of the vertical chain, namely distribution, which its main competitors need to use.

As we saw in Chapter 5, when examining how firms deal with competitive issues, the BBC did not waste any time in trying to counter Sky's strategic objective. The popularity of cable television has also increased in the UK. The BBC began offering its news channels to cable television companies for free. In response, the cable providers stopped using Sky News, which they had to pay for. With fewer viewers for Sky News, advertisers were less willing to place business with Sky. The BBC had gained some leverage over Sky.

Eventually the BBC and Sky became involved in the launch of Freeview, providing digital television via the traditional transmitter network. Consequently, through Freeview the BBC now has its own access to digital distribution. Sky can also deliver its products to viewers who have not adopted satellite dishes. With the launch of Freeview, a long and complicated business problem, driven in the main by transaction costs in the value chain, was resolved.

Sky's strategy rests on owning as much of the value chain as possible. Seeking to control the hold-up problem and extract as much profit as possible for itself. Of course, every business strategy has risks and Sky's stems from the willingness of customers to use its value chain. There is little point in owning the entire railway track if customers wish to travel by road.

Broadband is now a proven technology and adopted by many households. The ability to download movies and TV programmes is now a realistic possibility. Coupled with the ability to access the Internet and provide voice telephony, a broadband connection to each home looks preferable to a satellite link providing only TV services.

It is therefore very easy to understand why Sky raised £1 billion in debt and then promptly began to use it to buy a leading broadband service provider, as described in Box 7.5. Without access to customers, a vertically integrated value chain is reduced in value; especially, when new technology enables new entrants to attack your customer base.

 ## Box 7.5 BSkyB deal to enter the Internet market

Adapted from an article by Philip Aldrick in the Daily Telegraph, 22 October 2005

BSkyB, the satellite TV broadcaster, has launched itself into the home internet market with an agreed £211m bid for Easynet Group, the first company in the UK to have offered super-fast, eight megabyte broadband.

The purchase will allow BSkyB to offer broadband Internet and home telephone services alongside its satellite television. Chief executive James Murdoch said: 'The whole rationale is being driven by the consumer. They want the whole home solution with the best and easiest to use technology. Once the right technology is in place, they could download movies and music straight to their Sky+ box. It will be entertainment without compromise'.

Analysts described the move as a 'defensive' reaction to the combined packages offered by cable operators, such as NTL and Telewest – which are merging – and BT Group. Mr Murdoch countered: 'We will have a whole home solution on which you won't have to compromise on quality'.

Lessons from Sky

Companies should not always seek to control the entire value chain in the same way as Sky. Rather, it is crucial to understand how each asset within the Sky value chain will tend to exhibit high transaction costs when traded in the open market. Therefore, in order to reduce transaction costs Sky have vertically integrated the entire chain. In contrast, when we discussed the case of NHS hospitals, catering and cleaning have been subcontracted to independent companies, indicating that the transaction costs associated with buying catering and cleaning services in the market are limited. This is because the UK catering market has a large number of competing suppliers. Therefore, in contracting with one catering supplier, a hospital can threaten to move to an alternative supplier if it experiences opportunistic behaviour from its catering supplier. This threat to move business to a competing supplier reduces transaction costs. In contrast, because there are few suppliers of satellites, football rights and set-top boxes, Sky needs to own these assets in order to ensure access. A lack of competing suppliers prevents Sky from relying on the market in the same way as a hospital does for catering. Recognizing the key differences between the business cases of Sky and the hospitals helps business to develop optimal trading relationships with upstream and downstream aspects of their value chain.

7.8 **Business application: economies of scope**

As described in Box 7.6 Google is everywhere and offering everything. Why? The range of services now offered by Google simply reflect economies of scope. The ability to provide services jointly at a lower cost than offering each separately. But where do these economies of scope stem from?

At the core of Google's success is a search engine which is arguably unsurpassed by any competitor. The technology advantage rests on clever computer programming and a vast bank of computers, some estimate as much as a 100 000 machine server farm. Such an asset base means it becomes technically feasible and economically low cost to launch related services, such as Gmail, movie download, desktop search software. The more Google can exploit its massive technical advantage across products, the greater the economies of scope it can realize. As revenues and, ultimately, profits grow from its scope advantages, Google has more finance to pour back in to boost its technological advantage and remain dominant.

The example of Google illustrates what is perhaps related diversification. However, the economies of scope arguments can also be used to explain some examples of unrelated diversification. Tesco, a UK supermarket chain, developed its business from grocery into non-food electricals, and prior to this into financial services. It simply capitalized on its huge existing customer base. With details about its customers gained from loyalty cards and online shopping, Tesco can use this marketing research data not only to sell groceries, but also other products such as financial services, including personal loans and insurance. Therefore, by operating as a supermarket and as a personal financial services company, Tesco is able to reduce its costs by exploiting the customer information base across multiple activities.

 Box 7.6 **Bubbling over**

Adapted from an article by Dominic White, the Daily Telegraph, 6 January 2006

Just as Microsoft ate Netscape for lunch in the 1990s, so Google has sped from the outer edges of the search engine universe and landed on the home page of half the planet's web users. Now it is unleashing a tidal wave of new products and services upon that vast captive audience, treading on the patch of its bigger rivals and threatening Microsoft's imperial position.

There is Google Local, Google Picasa, Google, GMail, Google Talk and Google Earth. And that's just for starters. Google's video search service to buy television shows is happening; and Google's icon will appear on the screen of *millions of Motorola mobiles* when users turn them on.

The Google brand is starting to look like it may become as all purpose as the Virgin brand.

'There are even rumours it will move into computing hardware and set up a music download service to challenge Apple's iTunes. Google's aim is to own the 'webtop' – the things you see on your screen when you first access the web – in the same way that Microsoft owns the desktop with Windows. At the moment it's not an unrealistic prospect that they'll do it.

While grocery and financial services are very different activities, one of the core underlying assets that ensures success in both markets is an informative customer database. This database includes information on customers' ages, marital status, income levels, home address, and products generally purchased within the Tesco stores. This data can be analysed and used to target particular customer groups with specific products.

Economies of scope and control

An important issue when considering economies of scope is control. If we extend the economies of scope condition to Tesco then we would have:

Cost (Grocery) + Cost (Financial Services) > Cost (Grocery + Financial Services)

An obvious reason for these economies of scope is lower production costs associated with the joint use of the Tesco customer base. But in addition we also need to consider transaction costs. Tesco does not have to enter the financial services market in order to exploit its customer base. Rather, it could sell its customer information to a number of third parties, including existing financial services companies. The obvious problem with such an approach is that valuable information could then find its way into the hands of Tesco's rivals in the supermarket sector. Lowering the transaction costs associated with the information's additional use, therefore, protects the value of the customer base. Tesco cannot risk selling the information in the market place; instead, in order to exploit the asset beyond grocery, it has to enter into the financial services sector. In this particular instance Tesco has achieved this through an exclusive arrangement with Direct Line, a leading insurance provider.

We can also use the case of Tesco to address the issue of managerial motives for merger, as discussed in Section 7.5. Managers may pursue diversification to protect their own employment, as opposed to adding value for shareholders. We even argued that if a shareholder of Tesco was concerned about risks in the supermarket sector they could easily diversify this risk by buying shares in a financial services company. However, we can now see that diversification will add value for shareholders if the control of the economies of scope reduces transaction costs. Tesco is a clear example of this. So too is the Virgin brand. Licensing the brand to other users would run the risk of a third party damaging the brand. (This of course does not prevent Virgin from damaging the brand via its rail operations.) However, when Virgin takes the brand into many different markets the integrity of the brand is the sole responsibility of Virgin. It retains control over the use of the brand and reduces its transaction costs.

 ## Summary

1   Horizontal growth is the expansion of a firm's activities at the same stage of the production process.

2   Vertical growth is expansion of the firm up or down the value chain, incorporating more than one stage of production.

3   Diversified growth is an expansion of the firm's activities into related and unrelated markets.

4   Growth in its various forms can be organic, where the firm grows internally by developing ties to existing operations; alternatively, growth can occur externally, where the firm either acquires, or agrees to merge with, another firm.

5   Firms can grow for a variety of reasons, but if we accept that a firm is a profit maximizer, then growth must be linked to long-term, profit-maximizing objectives. Growth opportunities must, therefore, offer revenue enhancements or potential cost savings.

6 Horizontal growth can promote revenue enhancements by exploiting growth in the market. As the market size grows, the firm can seek to expand its operations. Moreover, the firm can seek to grow its share of the market. Greater control of the market improves the potential to set prices. If greater market share stems from merger, or acquisition of a rival, then the elasticity of demand must fall and the potential to raise prices increases.

7 Economies of scale are important motives for horizontal growth. As a company increases its scale of operation, its average costs fall. In addition, the positive effects of learning can motivate horizontal growth. As cumulative production increases, the firm begins to learn how to produce the product more efficiently. The firm learns how to reduce its costs. However, if the size of the firm is bigger, the potential to erase cumulative output more quickly also exists.

8 Vertical growth can also be motivated by considerations of production costs. Consecutive stages of the value chain could be merged if production and transaction costs have the potential to be reduced.

9 In addition to production costs, transaction costs are also a potential reason for vertical growth.

10 Transaction costs are associated with organizing the transaction of goods and services. These include the costs associated with writing, monitoring and enforcing contractual relationships. Transactions are seen to increase when complexity and uncertainty are greater, monitoring is difficult and enforcement limited. If the transaction costs associated with buying the good or service through the market increase, then a firm will attempt to minimize its transaction costs by vertically integrating and making the good or service within the firm.

11 A specific asset is designed for one use only. Without the flexibility to deploy the asset to an alternative use, a firm can be subject to the hold-up problem. Contract prices can be renegotiated and the financial value of the specific asset can fall. In order to avoid such problems firms will tend to vertically integrate and thereby avoid market negotiations.

12 Economies of scope exist if the production of two goods jointly is less than producing the two goods separately. Diversification can sometimes be understood as a process of exploiting economies of scope, i.e. where a firm uses an asset that it has developed in its current operations to exploit opportunities in another market.

13 If diversification is pursued in an attempt to create a portfolio of activities, then the firm's overall financial risk might be reduced. However, it is questionable whether such strategies add value for shareholders who may already hold a diversified portfolio of shares in many different companies. Diversification is more likely to reduce the non-diversified employment risks faced by managers.

✔ Learning checklist

You should now be able to:

♦ Explain the difference between horizontal, vertical and diversified growth

♦ Provide arguments for why firms may grow in a horizontal, vertical or diversified manner

♦ Explain how the learning curve links cumulative output with falling unit costs

♦ Understand and explain transaction costs

♦ Recognize the hold-up problem and explain why firms try to avoid this problem

♦ Explain economies of scope, provide examples and argue why firms might exploit scope economies

❓ Questions

1   What are the main reasons for horizontal growth?

2   What are the main reasons for vertical growth?

3   What are the main reasons for diversified growth?

4   How can a firm use horizontal, vertical or diversified growth to gain a strategic advantage over its rivals?

Exercises

1   True or false?
   a)   Following a merger the price elasticity of demand should fall.
   b)   Economies of scale can be a rationale for merger.
   c)   Late delivery of supplies due to heavy traffic are an example of the hold-up problem.
   d)   An organization's total costs are production costs plus transaction costs.
   e)   Diversification reduces a firm's level of risk.
   f)   Free cash flow is cash in excess of funds required to invest in all projects with a positive net present value.

2   a)   Draw a long-run average cost curve and use it to explain the gains in scale achieved by two small firms merging.
   b)   Diversification is not about moving the firm's total cost and total revenue lines further apart, it is more concerned with reducing the volatility of earnings. Discuss.

3   Consider the following questions by referring to Box 7.3.
   a)   Identify all of the possible motives behind the spate of consolidation in the steel industry.
   b)   'Suppliers of iron ore grouped together to demand hefty price rises of 72% for their products'. Explain why this occurred and is it an example of the hold-up problem?
   c)   'Size in the steel business does not, in itself, bring great rewards in terms of economies of scale – especially if, as many suspect, predators are overpaying for assets.' Explain this statement.

Chapter 8
Governing business

Chapter contents

Learning outcomes

By the end of this chapter you should understand:

Economic Theory

- Principal–agent problems

- The separation of ownership from control

- Alternative theories of the firm

- The concept of positive and negative externalities

- The notion of market failures

- The use of tax and subsidies to correct market failures

- The regulation of monopoly

Business Application

- Why companies use stock options to reward chief executives

- Why governments have introduced trading in carbon emission permits

Governing business at a glance

The issue

Actions taken by managers and workers are often not in the interests of their shareholders. Similarly, actions taken by firms, such as polluting the atmosphere, are often not in the interests of other stakeholders, such as wider society. Can these conflicts be resolved?

The understanding

Conflicts exist because of a misalignment of interests. Without government control, firms can pollute the environment without cost to themselves. The cost of pollution is instead picked up by society. By making the firm bear the responsibility and costs of pollution, both the firm's and society's interests are aligned. The way to achieve this is to tax the firm if it pollutes; and perhaps even provide it with subsidies if it tries to operate without pollution. More generally, one solution to the misalignment of interests is the use of financial incentives to change the behaviour of one of the parties.

The usefulness

Why do company executives receive huge bonuses via stock options? The answer is because stock options provide financial incentives for managers to act in the interests of shareholders. Can the government reduce carbon emissions by creating a market for pollution permits? We will now explore each of these issues.

8.1 Business problem: managing managers

Within all of us there is an element of Homer Simpson. The similarities at work are particularly acute where we often have a willingness to do little but appear to be doing a great deal. Colleagues and perhaps even ourselves display a need to frequent the coffee room, the toilets or even the local pub during work hours. Such behaviour is a deviation from what our employers might consider best practice. They might consider we are employed to sit at our desks and pursue profit maximization. When such behaviour occurs we might label it 'lazy', 'cheeky' or 'taking the Michael'. You will not be surprised to learn that economists prefer the more complicated label of 'the **principal–agent** problem'.

Principals can suffer two confounding problems when hiring agents to work for them. First, the interests of the agent and the principal may differ. For example, the principal may value hard work, while the agent may dislike hard work. Second, principals can often find it difficult to monitor the work and effort of their agents. Given the potential difference in interests and the difficulty associated with monitoring the agent, there is little reason why the agent should expend effort on the principal's behalf.

We can compare examples of a taxi driver and a manager to illuminate these arguments. In the case of the taxi driver, you may wish to be driven between two points using the shortest route. In contrast, the taxi driver may wish to take you via a much longer route, hoping to generate a higher fare. Hence, there is a difference in interest between you as the principal and the taxi driver as the agent. However, since you are sitting in the taxi, you can monitor with ease the route taken by the driver. Therefore, if you know the area, and are not a tourist in a foreign land, the taxi driver will generally take you by the shortest route.

A **principal** is a person who hires an **agent** to undertake work on their behalf.

A manager of a company, the agent, may be tasked with improving the profitability of a company by the shareholders of that company, the principals. However, if the shareholders are buying and selling shares in many companies on the London stock market, they will find it difficult to monitor the manager on a daily basis. Unlike the passenger in a taxi, the shareholders cannot directly observe the behaviour of their manager. The manager could decide to sit in the office surfing the Internet, or practising their golf putting. When the profits of the company fail to increase, the shareholders will not be aware that the agent has been lazy. In fact because of the lack of monitoring the manager could blame the poor performance on external factors such as a lazy workforce, a bad sales manager, or a fall in demand for the product.

Economists describe the manager as displaying **moral hazard**-type behaviour.

The manager offers to increase the profits of the company but, once hired by the shareholders, he or she exploits the monitoring problems of shareholders and behaves in their own best interests. In contrast, the taxi driver, actively monitored by the hiring passenger, does not display moral hazard-type behaviour because the passenger will contest the higher fare.

The costs of moral hazard-type behaviour, such as inferior performance by the agent, coupled with monitoring costs, result in what are more generally termed **agency costs**.

In the case of the taxi driver agency costs are very low. Monitoring is easy and, therefore, moral hazard-type behaviour is unlikely. In the case of the manager, agency costs are very high, because monitoring is difficult and costly, and therefore this behaviour is likely.

A natural question arises as to how principals might seek to reduce agency costs. In particular, how can shareholders motivate managers to provide higher levels of output or, as the economist would say, how can we align the interests of firms and managers so that managers act in the interest of shareholders?

The answer will be developed throughout the first part of this chapter; but in the case of managers, modes of corporate governance are placed on the firm that provide incentives for managers to work in the interests of shareholders. At a very simple level managers can be turned into shareholders by providing them with shares in the company. As shareholders, managers then have an interest in working hard in order to improve the performance of the company. In order to consider these ideas further we will extend our analysis of how firms are owned and managed and examine why managers may not wish to follow the interests of shareholders. Only then can we return to the issue of how shareholders can try to motivate managers to act in their interests.

> **Moral hazard** occurs when someone agrees to undertake a certain set of actions but then, once a contractual arrangement has been agreed, behaves in a different manner.

> **Agency costs** reflect reductions in value to principals from using agents to undertake work on their behalf.

8.2 Profit maximization and the separation of ownership from control

Throughout this book we have assumed that firms are profit maximizers. In fact, when we first introduced the idea in Chapter 5, we suggested that this was a sensible argument. We would now like to question this assumption.

In order to maximize profits firms are required to set marginal cost, MC, equal to marginal revenue, MR. Even though professional accountants are also schooled in this central idea, many are incapable of calculating MC or MR from a company's cost and revenue data. Accountants are not fools, it is just that the task of measuring and collating data on MR and MC is extremely complex, especially when the firm makes and sells multiple products. Furthermore, the firm's costs and revenues may not be very stable. Changes in raw material prices or output prices will lead to repeated changes in MC and

MR. Therefore, if anything, firms can at best only approximate profit maximization. They may seek to maximize profits, but they will never be sure what is the optimal level of output and profits.

Aside from these practical problems of trying to equate MC and MR, there are strong reasons why a firm might pursue objectives other than profit maximization. Crucially, it is often the case that the individuals who manage a firm are different from the individuals who own a firm. Table 8.1 provides data on the size of shareholdings within the telecommunications company BT. With 1.5 million shareholders it is reasonable to say that many people and investment companies own BT. BT employed just in excess of 100 000 individuals in 2005. Therefore, with 1.5 million shareholders and only 100 000 workers, it is clear that shareholders and the people who work for BT are, in the main, different individuals. Among the largest shareholders, 2213 holdings are greater than 0.5 million shares. Of these 225 holdings only one relates to share options held for the benefit of employees. We can see, therefore, that the vast majority of shareholders, small and large, are not the same people who manage BT. While BT is a popular share among many individuals in the UK, the pattern of disperse shareholdings is common among large companies and is known as the separation of ownership from control.

Table 8.1 Analysis of BT shareholdings 2005

Range	Number of holdings	Percentage of total	Number of shares held (millions)	Percentage of total
1–399	603 955	40.1	129	1.5
400–799	441 583	29.4	245	2.8
800–1599	275 372	18.3	307	3.5
1600–9999	175 825	11.7	506	5.9
10 000–99 999	5539	0.4	108	1.3
100 000–999 999	940	0.1	346	4
1 000 000–4 999 999	428	0	961	11.1
5 000 000 and above	213	0	6032	69.9
Total	1 503 855	100	8634	100

Separation of ownership from control exists where the shareholders, who own the company, are a different set of individuals from the managers that control the business on a day-to-day basis.

The **separation of ownership from control** becomes more acute when shareholders become more disperse. With 1.5 million shareholders it is difficult for all BT shareholders to co-ordinate themselves and try to remove a poorly performing management team. Moreover, in the UK it is common for the largest shareholder to own less than 3 per cent of a company's shares. This is important because if the largest shareholder wanted to remove a team of underperforming managers, then they would bear the full costs of this activity. This might include meetings with the managers, meetings with other large shareholders, meetings with legal advisers and recruitment of a new management team. While bearing all these costs, the benefits of better company performance would be shared among all shareholders. Therefore, if the major shareholder has only 3 per cent, then it will only gain a 3 per cent share of the benefits of employing a new management team. All other shareholders can **free ride** on the back of the dominant shareholder.

Given the unattractive financial terms brought about by free riding and small shareholdings, even the dominant shareholder is unlikely to act against the incumbent management team.

Dispersed shareholdings, therefore, leave management teams, even bad ones, in a position where they do not have to react to shareholders' interests. So, while it might be reasonable to argue that shareholders are profit maximizers, managers have the scope to pursue their own objectives. But what might these objectives be?

> **Free riders** are individuals, or firms, who can benefit from the actions of others, without contributing to the effort made by others. They gain benefits from the actions of others for free.

Managerial objectives

Economists have proposed a number of alternative theories relating to the objectives that managers might pursue. The first relates to what is known as 'expense preference behaviour'. If shareholders are interested in maximizing profits, then managers are interested in maximizing their own satisfaction.

Consumption of perquisites

So, rather than work hard for the company's owners, managers would rather indulge themselves in the purchase of expensive cars, jets, lavish expensive accounts that can be used to dine clients (and friends) at the most fashionable restaurants, and, of course, lots of personal assistants. A clear reason for doing this is a positive recognition provided by society for success, dominance and status. In trying to meet these requirements managers use the company's funds to finance a prestigious image make-over and lifestyle.

Managers may even spend the company's money on business projects that have little value to the shareholder but have personal value to the company's managers. Diversification, as discussed in Chapter 7, is a case in point. Companies that specialize in one product line are vulnerable to competition, or a downturn in demand. In order to protect themselves, managers may diversify and use the company's money to buy unrelated businesses. Statements of strategic change along the lines of 'yes, I know we are in waste handling, but I think we should move into leisure and purchase a cruise ship' are extreme, but sadly evident among some senior managers. However, the essential problem is that managers are using the company's and, therefore shareholders' money, to diversify a risk that only managers face. If shareholders are concerned about risk in one market, they can buy shares in other companies. Hence, diversification within firms does not protect shareholders; rather, it protects managers.

Sales maximization

An alternative hypothesis is that managers will seek to maximize a tangible measure of performance, such as sales. A common misunderstanding follows the reasoning that if sales are increasing, then so are profits. But, as we have seen, this is not true – the law of diminishing returns and diseconomies of scale point to increases in costs as output increases. Sales maximization may, therefore, indicate that sales managers are doing a good job but, without an additional consideration of costs and ultimately profits, sales growth may not be a good indicator of overall performance.

Growth maximization

The final hypothesis is that managers will seek to maximize growth, rather than profits. It is of no surprise that the pay of top directors is linked to the size of a company. The bigger the company, the greater the responsibility. What is of surprise is that chief executive (the leading director of a company) pay is linked more closely to company size, than it is to financial performance, such as profitability. This suggests that managers have a financial, or salary incentive, to pursue growth maximization over profit maximization. However, while seeing this rather obvious argument, there are some subtleties. If a company grows at a faster rate now, will it be in a stronger position to outperform its rivals in the future? Economies of scale can be attained more quickly, leading to a reduction in costs. In addition, as we saw in Chapters 5 and 7, increased market share brings increased power over pricing. If this is true, growth maximization now is simply a strategy for profit maximization over the long term.

Behavioural theories

Behavioural theories of the firm are based on how individuals actually behave inside firms. This is in contrast to theories such as profit maximization, which predict how individuals should behave. Important behavioural points are what goals will be set for the organization and how will the targets be set?

Goal setting

Cyert and March recognized that organizations are complex environments represented by a mixture of interest groups including shareholders, managers, workers, consumers and trade unions. Even within managers there are various sub groups including marketing, accounting and production. The goals of the organization, or firm, are more a reflection of these competing interests than a theoretical prediction such as profit maximization. If a marketing manager rises to the top of the organization, it is likely that marketing issues will rise to the top of the managerial decision-making agenda. Resources may flow into the marketing department and the goals of the organization may reflect marketing issues, such as the most recognized global brand or growing customer reach and market share. In contrast, if an accountant led the organization, then goals relating to sales growth, cost reduction and profitability might be set. Decision-making, the development of targets and the focus of the organization are, therefore, a reflection of the coalition of interests within the organization. Whichever group has greater power, or enhanced negotiation skills, will have a greater say over the targets of the organization.

Target setting

Regardless of which goals or objectives predominate, the complexity of the environment will mean that measures and targets are difficult to set. Should sales growth be 10 per cent or 20 per cent? How do managers accommodate failure in meeting the target? In recognizing these points Herbert Simon developed the concept of **satisficing**.

> **Satisficing** is the attainment of acceptable levels of performance. Maximizing is the attainment of maximum levels of performance.

For example, 20 per cent annual growth in sales could be the maximum possible. But a 10 per cent growth in sales would be acceptable, especially if other firms or organizations were achieving similar results; 10 per cent represents a satisfactory level of performance. If managers negotiate a 10 per cent target growth rate, rather than a 20 per cent target, they are displaying satisficing rather than maximizing behaviour. Why might they do this? First, the maximum growth rate is unknown; it could be 15, 20, 25, even 50 per cent. Second, failure to meet a target creates tension between the group setting the target and the individuals pursuing the target. Therefore, in order to avoid failure in a complex world, where the maximum is unknown, it is perhaps better to set a realistic and satisfactory target. Behavioural considerations, therefore, lead to firms and organizations setting minimum levels of performance, rather than maximum ones.

We do not have to decide which of the above alternative hypotheses are correct. Instead, we simply have to recognize that the separation of ownership from control provides managers with the incentive to pursue any of the above objectives. The problem for shareholders is in the absence of direct control over managers: how might they motivate managers to behave in the interests of shareholders? The straightforward answer is to make managers shareholders. But the complex answer is to understand how difficult this might be. To understand the problem more fully we will examine principal–agent theory.

8.3 Principal–agent theory

Agency costs between managers and shareholders

A **principal** hires another person, the agent, to carry out work on their behalf.

Shareholders are **principals** when they employ managers, the **agents**, to run their companies.

When a business is small the owner is also likely to be the manager. In this case there is no agency relationship because the owner and the manager are the same person. Therefore, there can be no misalignments of interests. The owner-manager is likely to work very hard to ensure the success of the business. Furthermore, even if the owner-manager decides to pursue expense preference behaviour and spend the company's money on a top-of-the-range BMW, he is only robbing himself as the shareholder. An important consideration is that the value of the company to the owner does not change with the behaviour of the manager; simply, the financial benefits are being paid to the same person in different ways. For example, if the company generated £100 000 in profits, but the owner-manager decided to use £30 000 to buy the BMW and only receive a dividend of (£100 000 − £30 000 = £70 000, then the owner-manager has still received £100 000 from the company.

We can now consider what happens when the company grows and the owner wishes to sell half their stake in the company. The original owner will still manage the company, but the new shareholder will just be an owner, not a manager. Before buying the stake any potential buyer will attempt to value the company. Crucially, the value of the company now depends upon the expense preference behaviour of the owner-manager. When the owner-manager buys a top-of-the-range BMW with the company's money, the other shareholder is paying for half of the car, but gaining no benefit. For example, if the company again generates £100 000 in profits, then each shareholder should receive £50 000. But if the shareholder who also manages the company uses £30 000 of the profits to buy the BMW, then the remaining profits are only £70 000. Split two ways, each shareholder receives £35 000. The owner-manager has received a £30 000 car plus £35 000 in dividends = £65 000. The shareholder who does not run the company has only received £35 000 in dividends. Therefore, the value of a share in the company is not £50 000, but rather £35 000. Indeed, the more a manager displays expense preference behaviour, the lower the potential buyer will value the company.

This reduction in company value from employing an agent to manage the company is an example of an agency cost. Agency costs are not the wages associated with employing an agent; rather, they reflect reductions in value to principals from using agents to undertake work on their behalf.

The agency cost in our example is £50 000 − £35 000 = £15 000. It arises because the interests of the owner-manager are different from those of the other shareholder; and because the owner-manager is not monitored on a daily basis. It is, therefore, possible to use the company's money to fund benefits for the owner-manager at the expense of the remaining owner.

Agency costs between workers and managers

Agency costs do not just occur between owners and managers of companies. They can also occur when managers employ workers to do work for them. For example, let us consider two employment relationships. First, a supermarket employs a shelf stacker on **piece rates**. For each tray of tinned food put on the shelf, the shelf stacker receives £0.20. Second, a supermarket employs a shelf stacker on an hourly rate of £5.

> **Piece rates** occur when a worker is paid according to the output produced. Under hourly wage rates, workers are paid for time at work.

If agency problems exist because principals find it difficult to monitor the effort of their agents, then piece rates will reduce agency costs. With an hourly wage rate of £5, the shelf stacker will earn £5 for one hour's work if they fill the shelf, or if they sit in the staff restaurant drinking coffee and reading the paper. However, under piece rates the worker has to provide sufficient effort to place 25 trays of tinned food on the shelf in order to earn the same £5. Under piece rates the employer does not have to continually monitor the effort of the agent; instead, they can merely add up all the output at the end of the shift. If the agent works hard, then greater output will lead to greater pay. If they are lazy and read the newspaper, then their pay will decrease. By linking pay more directly to the effort provided, the agency costs are reduced.

We tend to see piece rates used when the output is easy to verify. For example, car salespersons are paid a commission for selling cars. It is fairly easy to verify that a car has been sold. Packers are often paid by the number of boxes that have been filled; and bricklayers are paid by the square metre of laid bricks and not by the hour.

However, when it comes to managers and many other occupations, output is more difficult to verify. How do you measure if a manager has managed? The many activities undertaken by managers, including monitoring workers, communicating and implementing business plans, reviewing operations and making investment decisions, make it difficult to measure the total output of the manager. The outputs are numerous, varied and difficult to quantify. For example, how do you measure effective communication? However, given that we have shown that company value is reduced by increased agency costs, we need to develop a means of aligning managers' interests with those of shareholders, thereby reducing agency costs and boosting company value. How might this be achieved? We need an alternative way of reducing agency costs. In the following business application, stock options will highlight how agency costs associated with employing managers might be reduced.

> **Stock options** provide individuals with the *option* to buy shares in the future at a price agreed in the past.

8.4 Business application: stock options and the reduction of agency costs

In order to reduce agency costs, principals have to develop contracts that align agents' interests with their own. Piece rates lower agency costs by forcing the agent to work hard to receive greater pay. A more complicated example is the use of **stock options** in the financial packages offered to senior managers of leading companies.

For example, assume the share price today for company X is £10. A manager at X may be offered the option to purchase 1 million shares at £10 in three years' time. Assume the manager works hard, the company makes profits and over the three years the shares rise to £12. The stock option has moved into the money. The manager can take up the option and buy at £10 and then sell instantly for £12, making £2 million profit. Stock options, therefore, link managers' and shareholders' interests via the share price. But how effective are stock options as a solution to agency problems?

An examination of the key points associated with stock options will help:

1   Stock options transfer an element of shareholder risk to the manager. Under a fixed salary contract a manager will earn perhaps £30 000 per annum. The manager will earn this salary if the company performs well or not. Under a stock option, part of the fixed contract is swapped for the stock options. The manager may now be offered a basic salary of £20 000, plus stock options. When the company performs well, the manager's stock options move into the money. The manager's pay increases whenever the stock option moves into the money and the manager executes the option, that is, uses the option to buy the shares cheaply and make a profit. But when the company underperforms, the share price drops and the stock options are worthless. Therefore, performance contracts, such as stock options, swap part of the certain salary for a chance of earning a higher overall amount. This increase in risk may not be attractive to the manager and they could decide to reject the contract or work somewhere else.

2   Stock options make a manager's pay contingent upon the share price. The share price is being used as a measure of the manager's hard work. The harder the manager works, the higher the share price climbs. But what if the share price is influenced by industry factors, such as the degree of competition, or by domestic government policy on interest rates? A manager may work very hard but, due to government policy, the share price may fall. This increases the risk being transferred to the manager. For this reason, the measure of performance should be linked closely to managerial, or worker effort. In some cases the measures can be very specific. Workers in telephone sales are paid a commission every time they secure a sale, while car salespersons are paid every time they sell a car. In contrast, the output measures for managers tend to be very general, based on overall profitability, or simply linked to the share price.

3   The stronger the link between worker effort and the performance measure, the stronger the incentive. This merely reflects risk again. If you work hard, but the output measure does not reflect high effort, then you receive no pay. Managers are measured by share prices and car salespersons by number of sales. We might argue that there is a stronger link between worker effort and car sales than between worker effort and share price. At a simple level, if a salesperson works hard to sell a car, then a sale may materialize. But if a manager works hard, other managers may not and, therefore, due to a lack of team work, the share price is unaffected. As a reflection of these arguments, what tends to be observed is that, as a percentage of their overall pay, car salespersons receive a low fixed salary component and a high performance bonus. In contrast, managers tend to receive a high fixed salary component and a lower performance bonus. Therefore, as in the case of car salespersons, when the performance measure is a more accurate measure of worker effort, the more likely it is that pay will move to performance-based, rather than fixed, salary.

4   Incentive contracts can promote a single type of behaviour. Managers with stock options face incentives to raise the company's share price. But what if shareholders are interested in more than this? Box 8.1 provides Vodafone's strategic statement.

5   Finally, a manager's behaviour and effort must be verifiable. It should not be possible for the worker or manager to influence the performance measure inappropriately. This was clearly not the case with Enron and Worldcom. With Enron, managers were able to keep liabilities off the company's balance sheet, thereby inflating its share price. Even though the company was performing badly, the managers were able to

Box 8.1 Company missions

Vodafone's strategic direction

Source: Vodafone website

Vodafone is uniquely positioned to succeed through our scale and scope and the customer focus of all our employees. To achieve this success, we are focused on the execution of the six strategic goals that we outlined last year; delighting our customers, leveraging our scale and scope, expanding market boundaries, building the best global team, being a responsible business and providing superior shareholder returns.

Vodafone's strategic vision is based on six approaches, of which one is shareholder returns. While each of the six approaches may seem sensible, it is difficult to envisage a performance contract which is able to reward managers for such a complexity of targets. Recently companies have recognized this and some have moved to multiple measures of performance, splitting performance bonus between the short term and the long term. Performance is not necessarily measured by reference to the share price – it might include sales growth compared with the firm's three leading competitors, or profit growth compared to the top 25 per cent of the FTSE 100, or profitability compared with other leading global players in the sector.

make it appear that it was highly successful. The share price rose and stock options were cashed in. In the case of Worldcom, expenses on stationery were capitalized and moved to the balance sheet as an asset, rather than sent to the profit and loss statement as an expense. This is common practice for substantial assets such as buildings and cars, but not for stationery, which you may no longer own as you have sent it out in letters! But again profits were seen to rise, assets increased and the share price rose. Once again managers cashed in on stock options.

Therefore, performance contracts can help to resolve the principal–agent problem. But only if:

- Workers accept the contracts, receiving greater rewards for higher risks
- There is a link between worker effort and the performance measure
- The performance can be co-ordinated across a number of objectives
- Workers cannot unduly influence the measure

We can use these points to understand some of the concerns relating to the excessive rewards provided to managers through stock options. One of the potential reasons why executive compensation has increased so markedly is to do with risk. A guaranteed payment of £100 is better than a 50 : 50 chance of receiving £100 or £0. But how much money would you require in order to accept the 50 : 50 gamble and give up the guaranteed £100? Would you require £200, £300, or perhaps even £1000? If you asked for £1000 then you would be described as not liking risk, or **risk averse**, and, therefore, requiring a large reward for accepting the risk of the 50 : 50 gamble.

Individuals can be **risk averse**, risk neutral or risk seeking.

Assume an executive is equally risk averse. For every £100 that is taken from their guaranteed salary, a potential reward of £1000 has to be offered through the stock option. So, executives can receive large financial rewards, but they receive such rewards for (it is hoped) improving shareholder value and taking personal financial risk. We can even suggest where the executive's risk stems from. Linking a large amount of executive wealth to one company's share price does not provide the executive with a diversified portfolio of investments. The bulk of the executive's wealth is linked to one asset. We saw in Chapter 7 that diversification reduces risk. Therefore, reduced diversification must increase risk and, in order to accept greater risk, executives require a higher potential reward. As a consequence, the size of executive stock options and executive remuneration contracts increase.

The alternative view of managers using stock options to camouflage large financial rewards also has some merit. Raising the executive's salary by 100 per cent is likely to attract the wrong type of attention from shareholders and the media. By contrast, raising total financial remuneration through stock market performance provides a tangible link between pay and performance that is more publicly palatable.

However, all of our discussion has been linked to shareholders offering managers contracts that are designed to align the interests of shareholders and managers. In reality managers propose contracts to shareholders. It is then shareholders who reject or accept the proposed financial terms for the executive(s). This is generally discussed at the company's annual general meeting. Why is this a problem?

First, managers are defining pay and performance. Admittedly this is achieved through the company's remuneration committee that supposedly consists of independent remuneration experts and non-executive directors of the company.

Non-executives are directors from other companies who provide independent advice to the boards where they are non-executives. For example, Mr X may be an executive director of company Y, his main employer. But Mr X may also be a non-executive director of company Z, the company where he provides independent advice to the board.

From our discussion of behavioural theories of the firm, we might suspect that the targets set by remuneration committees will be satisficing targets, not maximizing targets. From the behavioural perspective there is a fear that executives can negotiate the proposed financial rewards, arguing with the members of the remuneration committee what are reasonable targets and performance rewards given what is occurring in other companies. Second, due to the separation of ownership from control, once the executive(s) package is proposed, the dispersed nature of the shareholdings may lead to free riding among the shareholders, making a majority vote against the executive(s) financial terms difficult.

 ## Box 8.2 BT boss could get 300% bonus as staff accept 0.3% real rise

Adapted from an article by Richard Wray, the Guardian, 2 June 2005

Ben Verwaayen, the chief executive of BT, has been given £1.8m worth of shares merely for sticking with the business for the past three years. News that Mr Verwaayen, who joined BT in February 2002, could receive £2.8m in pay and bonuses next year emerged as unions representing many of the 100 000 staff agreed on a 3.5% pay rise, averting industrial action.

While Mr Verwaayen's salary has been pegged at £700 000 since he joined, from this year BT will increase the maximum bonus available to him from 195% of his salary to 300%.

Meanwhile, it emerged yesterday that Mr Verwaayen's predecessor, Sir Peter Bonfield, whose grandiose expansion plans saddled BT with almost £30bn of debt and forced it to sell its mobile phone business for nothing, is still pocketing cash from the business he left in January 2002.

We can, therefore, understand how to develop pay packages for managers and executives in attempting to reduce agency costs. However, crucially, and in practice, it appears debatable whether or not agency problems are solved by remuneration packages, or whether remuneration packages are an overt example of increasing agency costs.

8.5 **Regulation of business**

We have examined the governance of managers by shareholders. We would now like to examine the governance of firms within their market places. We have already seen in Chapter 5 that monopolies are an example of market places that are not in consumers' interests, with higher prices and lower output than under perfect competition. We will now also show that in other ways markets can act against the interest of consumers, or even the public more generally. In representing the interests of society, governments can intervene in such markets in an attempt to improve the benefits society receive from the market. We will begin by providing an overview of the issues and some further examples.

How many times have you sat at a set of traffic lights having 'to keep it real' by listening to the loud bass tunes from the car parked next to you? The person playing the loud music obviously likes the artist. The unfortunate problem is that everyone within earshot of the car also has to listen. The driver sets the volume of the car stereo without considering the interests of the people they may be driving past. Effectively the interests of the driver and those of a wider group of individuals are not aligned.

Not surprisingly the private interests of firms and wider society also differ. Polluting the environment, rather than cleaning factory emissions, is a cheap alternative for a profit-maximizing firm. Unfortunately society as a whole has to bear the costs of a polluted environment. This is again because the interests of society and the private firm are not aligned. The firm will choose to produce more pollutants than society finds desirable.

An important but underlying issue within this book, and many other texts on economics, is that markets are an optimal means of allocating society's scarce resources. That is why we have spent so much time looking at supply, demand, perfect competition and monopoly. How do markets work and how do firms operate within markets?

At the heart of most economists' understanding is that an economy characterized by perfectly competitive markets is **Pareto efficient**. In perfect competition firms operate at the minimum point on their long-run costs curves. Hence, they are productively efficient. Firms make the highest level of output for the lowest amount of cost. Also in perfect competition price equals marginal cost. So, the price paid by consumers for the last unit also equals the cost of the resources used in making the last unit. Therefore, input resources are also allocated efficiently. So, in perfect competition the goods that consumers desire are the ones that are made and, moreover, they are made at lowest cost. Intuitively we can accept this as a good outcome and economists can go one step further and prove that it is Pareto efficient.

However, perfect competition is rarely achieved in reality and in some cases monopoly might exist. Under monopoly, products are not necessarily produced at lowest cost and they are not priced at marginal cost. So, Pareto efficiency will not hold.

Monopoly is an example of a **market failure**, with perfect competition providing a more efficient market equilibrium. But there can be other reasons for market failures. As we will discuss in detail below, so-called 'externalities' can lead to a difference between the interests of private individuals and society and an inefficient production or

> **Pareto efficient** means that no one within an economy can be made better off without making some people worse off. Therefore, the wellbeing of society is at a maximum.

> Economists use the term **market failure** to cover all circumstances in which the market equilibrium is not efficient.

consumption of goods and services from the perspective of society. For example, the production and consumption of loud music by our car driver is not an efficient (desirable) allocation of resources from the perspective of society (passers-by). We will now discuss externalities, monopoly and the problems relating to market failures. Following this we can begin to assess various government intervention strategies for making markets potentially more Pareto efficient – that is, strategies that make people better off without making others worse off, thereby improving the wellbeing of society.

8.6 **Externalities**

Externalities occur when the production, or consumption, of a good or service results in costs, or benefits, being passed on to individuals not involved in the production, or consumption. Negative externalities occur when costs are passed on to society, or benefits are reduced. Positive externalities occur when costs to society are reduced, or benefits are enhanced.

A number of examples will help to explain the concepts of **positive** and **negative externalities**.

The cost to the private firm of producing a particular output is the **marginal private cost**, MPC. We have previously referred to this as the marginal cost. MPC measures the costs to the firm from producing one more unit and includes the cost of raw materials, labour and machinery. We now wish to also include in the analysis the **marginal social cost**, MSC. This is the cost to society of producing one more unit. As the private firm or individual is a member of society, then the MSC must include the MPC. However, in addition it will also include the costs associated with using or exploiting public assets such as the environment. So, the MSC could include costs of pollution. In such cases, the costs to society will always be bigger than the costs to the private firm. These points are summarized in Table 8.2.

> **Externalities** are the effects of consumption, or production, on third parties. If production, or consumption, by one group improves the wellbeing of third parties, then a **positive externality** has occurred. If production, or consumption, by one group reduces the wellbeing of third parties, then a **negative externality** has occurred.
>
> **Marginal private cost** is the cost to the individual of producing one more unit of output.
> **Marginal social cost** is the cost to society of producing one or more unit of output.

Table 8.2 **Marginal private and social costs**

Marginal private cost	Marginal social cost
Raw materials	Raw materials
Labour costs	Labour costs
Machinery	Machinery + Environmental costs of production

MSC is greater than MPC

The consequences of this can be seen in Figure 8.1. The optimal level of output for society and the private firm will occur where marginal revenue equals marginal cost. If the firm is a price taker, then equilibrium for the private firm occurs at point B, where MPC equals demand and, therefore, marginal revenue. The output level is 2000 units. However, for society, MSC equals demand and, therefore, marginal revenue at point A, with an output of 1000 units. Therefore, when the private firm creates negative cost externalities for the rest of society, the private firm will choose a level of output that is greater than that

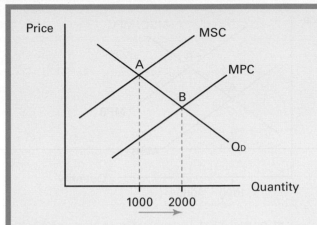

Figure 8.1 Negative cost externalities

The marginal private cost, MPC, is much lower than the marginal social cost, MSC. As a result, when choosing the optimal level of output, the private individual will choose a level of output that is higher than the socially optimal level of output. Pollution is a good example.

deemed desirable by society. In its simplest terms, the firm does not recognize the costs of pollution; society does. Therefore, society has a desire to reduce output and pollution; the firm does not.

MSC is less than MPC

If we reversed the arguments and the marginal social cost was lower than the marginal private cost, then society would find it desirable to produce more output than the private firm or individual deem optimal. For example, society might decide that it is optimal for all individuals to gain a degree. But this requires your input in terms of time, effort and tuition fees. The costs to you are greater than to society. Hence, when deciding whether to go to university, you did not take into account society's views.

MPB is greater than MSB

Marginal private benefit is the benefit to the individual from consuming one more unit of output.
Marginal social benefit is the benefit to society from the consumption of one more unit of output.

The excessive car music example is a clear case of negative consumption externalities. The driver receives **marginal private benefit**, MPB, from consuming loud music. The benefits for surrounding individuals are captured by the **marginal social benefit**, MSB. For simplicity we will assume that the marginal social costs and the marginal private costs are equal. Figure 8.2 captures these points.

The optimal output of loud music for society occurs where MSC equals MSB at A, with 1000 units of output. The optimal amount of output for private individuals is where MPB equals MPC at B, with 2000 units of output. Therefore, we have 1000 too many drivers playing their music too loud. This figure would also capture the negative externalities associated with passive smoking. Private smokers gain a higher satisfaction from smoking than non-smokers do. As a result, if society is dominated by non-smokers, then smokers exhale pollutants at a level beyond what society deems desirable.

What are the business implications? If you consider advertising, the private benefits for firms are (they hope) increased sales. The benefits for consumers in society are improved

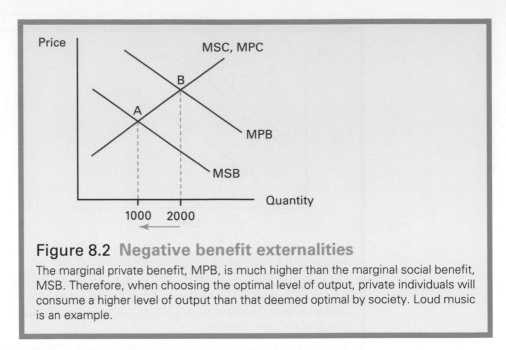

Figure 8.2 Negative benefit externalities

The marginal private benefit, MPB, is much higher than the marginal social benefit, MSB. Therefore, when choosing the optimal level of output, private individuals will consume a higher level of output than that deemed optimal by society. Loud music is an example.

information about what products are available, where they can be sourced and at what prices. If firms value higher sales more than consumers value information, firms will advertise at levels that are greater than that deemed desirable by society. If you have ever hated the adverts appearing on TV, become irritated by pop-up adverts on the Internet, or been plagued by junk (e)mail, then you now understand why you were angry.

8.7 Dealing with externalities

Clearly, if the private actions of individuals, or firms, are at variance with those of wider society, there is a case for at least questioning if anything can be done to solve the problem. We will see that some solutions are fairly straightforward to describe, but they may be difficult to implement.

Taxation and subsidy

The central problem with an externality is that the pricing mechanism does not impose the costs, or benefits, on the correct individuals. If a person smokes, or a firm pollutes the river, society bears the cost of living with a polluted environment. Therefore, a means has to be found where the private firm or individual internalizes, or pays all costs associated with their behaviour. In Figure 8.3 we revisit the situation where the marginal social cost is greater than the marginal private cost, the case of river pollution by a firm. Society views 1000 units of output as efficient; the firm would rather produce 2000 units of output. The problem is that marginal private costs, MPC, are different from marginal social costs, MSC. So, the obvious solution is to make MPC and MPS equal. This is achieved by taxing the firm for polluting the river, or environment. This adds to the firm's costs and, optimally, the tax will be equal to the difference between the MPC and the MSC. The imposition of the pollution tax provides firms with an incentive to cut output and move from point B to point A, thus lowering output to the socially optimum level.

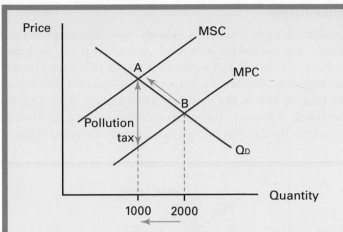

Figure 8.3 Dealing with externalities through taxation
The MPC is lower than the MSC, leading to overconsumption of the good from society's point of view. In order to encourage individuals to consume less the government can impose a tax. If the tax is set correctly, the MPC will become equal to the MSC, and result in private individuals choosing the same level of output as society.

In 2002, company car tax changed from a tax linked to the value of the car and mileage driven to a tax based on value and the emissions of the car. As the emissions of the car increase, so does the amount of car tax that has to be paid by the owner. Company car drivers are therefore faced with a rising marginal private cost of driving as emissions increase. This provides drivers with an incentive to buy cars that are more environmentally friendly.

In Box 8.4, the fact that aviation fuel is not taxed raises the issue that, as massive users of fuel, airlines are not being made to face up to the pollution that they create. As a result demand for air travel is cheaper and demand is higher. Governments are even thinking of expanding runway capacity to further increase the growth in air travel. But should they do this?

 Box 8.3 **Headwinds**

Adapted from The Economist, 14 December 2005

Plans to expand airports are causing headaches for the government. Passengers through Britain's airports are expected to rise from 215m a year today to 500m by 2030. Bigger airports are clearly needed, but the subject is viciously controversial. And pressure is building for the sort of sensible tax and emissions policy that could reduce the increase in air passengers.

The broadest criticism comes from green groups. Compared with most other forms of transport, they maintain, aviation is under-taxed. Airlines pay no fuel duty, and passengers pay no VAT. These tax breaks inflate demand. Under pressure, the government re-ran its computer models, assuming that aviation fuel was taxed at the same rate as petrol and that the VAT exemption was removed. Passenger numbers predicted for 2030 fell to 315m, 37% below the government's estimate. So much of the planned new capacity would go unused.

Subsidies

Subsidy is a payment made to producers, by government, which leads to a reduction in the market price of the product.

An alternative to taxation is **subsidy**. Subsidies make consumption, or production, cheaper for the private individual. At present if you wish to buy an energy-efficient washing machine, or fridge, often the Energy Efficiency Council will provide you with a substantial subsidy. So, if a fridge costs £300, the subsidy might amount to £50, making the price to you as the customer £250. Clearly, with a subsidy more fridges will be purchased, as they are cheaper. So, subsidies will be used when the private level of output is less than the socially optimal level of output. Consider Figure 8.4. The marginal private

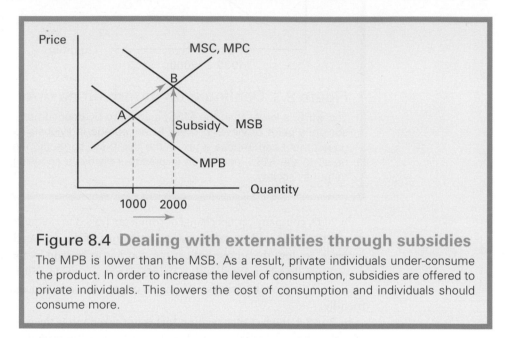

Figure 8.4 Dealing with externalities through subsidies

The MPB is lower than the MSB. As a result, private individuals under-consume the product. In order to increase the level of consumption, subsidies are offered to private individuals. This lowers the cost of consumption and individuals should consume more.

benefit, MPB, of an energy-efficient washing machine is associated with lower water and electricity bills. The marginal social benefit, MSB, also includes the wider social benefits of a cleaner environment resulting from lower electricity generation and better use of our water resources. Hence, the MSB is greater than the MPB. In order to persuade consumers to buy the energy-efficient washing machines at the socially optimal level, a subsidy has to be offered that is equal to the difference between MPB and MSB. This effectively reduces the price of energy-efficient washing machines and consumers buy in greater quantities.

8.8 Market power and competition policy

In Chapter 5 we compared perfect competition with monopoly and argued that under monopoly the price is higher and output is lower than under perfect competition. With the introduction of Pareto efficiency, we can now move on to show how monopoly, from the perspective of society, is not necessarily a desirable form of market structure.

In the left-hand side of Figure 8.5 we have perfect competition. The profit-maximizing level of output, Q_{pc}, is sold at a price of P_{pc}. Consumer surplus is the difference between the price a consumer is willing to pay and the price charged. In this case the consumer surplus is the light blue shaded area above the market price and below the demand curve. Consumer surplus is an important measure of welfare or wellbeing. If you are willing to pay £50 for a product and you can buy it for £30, then you are £20 better off. Producers also have a surplus. This is the difference between the price they would be willing to sell at and the price that they do sell at. This is the darker blue area below the market price and above the marginal cost curve for the industry.

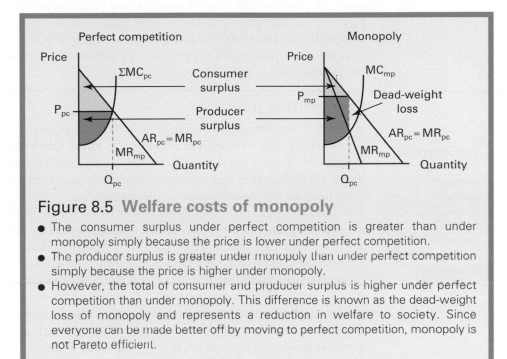

Figure 8.5 Welfare costs of monopoly

- The consumer surplus under perfect competition is greater than under monopoly simply because the price is lower under perfect competition.
- The producer surplus is greater under monopoly than under perfect competition simply because the price is higher under monopoly.
- However, the total of consumer and producer surplus is higher under perfect competition than under monopoly. This difference is known as the dead-weight loss of monopoly and represents a reduction in welfare to society. Since everyone can be made better off by moving to perfect competition, monopoly is not Pareto efficient.

Dead-weight loss of monopoly is the loss of welfare to society resulting from the existence of the monopoly.

Seeking out a **monopoly status** is known as undertaking '**rent-seeking activities**'.

Innovation can enable a firm to overcome the entry barriers of an existing monopoly. This is **creative destruction**, with the creative innovation destroying the existing monopoly position.

The case of monopoly is shown in the right-hand side of Figure 8.5. Under monopoly the price increases and the output shrinks. Therefore, the consumer surplus must reduce. In contrast, because the monopoly sells at a higher price, producer surplus must increase. In essence, part of the consumer surplus is being transferred to the monopoly. However, and this is the important part, if we compare the total of consumer and producer surplus under perfect competition and monopoly, we can see that the total surplus is lower under monopoly. This difference is known as the **dead-weight loss** from monopoly. It is a loss of welfare from society. Under Pareto efficiency no one can be made better off without making someone worse off. Monopoly is clearly not Pareto efficient, because if we change the market into a perfectly competitive one then the dead-weight loss will vanish. People can be made better off without making anyone worse off. Essentially, more products are sold and, moreover, sold at a lower price.

Dead-weight loss may not be the only detrimental aspect of monopoly. Many companies will spend resources trying to attain **monopoly status**.

Rent-seeking activities are the allocation of resources to non-socially optimal ends and they also need to be added on to the dead-weight losses. However, following the ideas of an economist called Schumpeter, monopolies have enjoyed the academic protection of a concept known as '**creative destruction**'.

For example, Microsoft is a global monopoly supplier of operating systems. If one innovator manages to invent a new and commercially successful way of operating computers, however, then Microsoft's position could be under threat. The potential to take over Microsoft's dominant position acts as a huge incentive for innovators to develop new products and approaches.

In terms of prices, output and dead-weight losses, monopolies are not good, but they do create incentives for other firms to try to become monopolies. In order to become monopolies, firms invest in research and development. Innovation brings about the destruction of existing monopolies. So, rent-seeking behaviour, or the pursuit of monopoly, may actually create innovation, new products, new production process and, hence, better economic efficiency. While these debates can be left to the academic economist, it is reasonably clear that monopolies can be suspected of being detrimental to economic performance, and it is with this view in mind that governments have developed competition policy.

Competition policy

The **Competition Commission** investigates whether a monopoly, or a potential monopoly, significantly affects competition.

In the UK the Director General of Fair Trading supervises company behaviour and, where fit, can refer individual companies to the **Competition Commission** for investigation. A company can be referred for investigation if it supplies more than 25 per cent of the total market, or if a complex monopoly is seen to exist where a small number of big firms are seen to collude and restrict competition.

Within the definition lies the approach taken by the UK competition authorities. There is no presumption, as in economic theory, that monopolies are bad. Rather, a decision is based on each case and whether the case seriously undermines competition. The Competition Commission has wide powers to make and enforce remedies.

A potential problem with the UK Competition Commission is that it simply looks at the UK market. Many mergers are now rationalized on the basis of building a company which is large enough to be an effective competitor across Europe.

The Restrictive Practices Court deals more directly with collusive oligopolies and examines agreements between UK firms, such as price fixing.

Any agreement needs to be notified to the Director General of Fair Trading. If the agreements are abandoned or seen to be insignificant, they will not be sent to court. However, at court, agreements will be found unlawful if they are not in the public interest. Unlike competition investigations, the defending firms have to prove that they are acting in the public interest. Gateways allow for this where a firm can argue that the removal of a restrictive practice will lead to serious unemployment among the firm's workers. A cute solution is for colluding firms to merge and take the chance of being investigated by the Competition Commission.

8.9 Business application: carbon trading

Carbon dioxide, a greenhouse gas, is a by-product of burning fossil fuels such as oil and coal. Modern industrial economies consume vast amounts of energy on a daily basis. Energy which is provided by burning fossil fuels. Oil and coal are used to generate electricity and are used to propel cars, trucks and aircraft. As a greenhouse gas, carbon dioxide is a pollutant. Unfortunately, the creation of carbon dioxide is an example of a negative externality. The marginal private cost of producing electricity does not reflect the full marginal social cost which also includes the effects of pollution on the environment.

In seeking to reduce carbon emissions European governments have resorted to a system of tradable carbon permits. Each firm has a yearly carbon pollution allowance. If it does not use all of its allowance, then it can sell its surplus to a company which is short of credits. In essence, there is a market in pollution permits. If you wish to pollute more, then you have to pay for extra permits. And paying for it is the crucial thing. Through the market, paying for the right to pollute increases the marginal private cost faced by polluting firms. As such it should reduce the equilibrium level of pollution. Box 8.4 describes some of the issues developing around the market, but in essence the requirement to pay for the right to pollute is nothing more than a tax on excessive polluters. While at the same time, clean producers are effectively subsidized by being able to sell their surplus permits at a profit: concepts which we discussed in section 8.7.

 ## Box 8.4 Revving up

Adapted from an article in The Economist, 7 July 2005

The Kyoto treaty, which came into effect in February, saw an international emissions-trading system as one weapon against greenhouse gases. The idea is that a market-based system which gives countries and companies flexibility to meet their targets will produce the greatest emission reductions at the lowest cost.

Europe's energy and industrial plants are being issued tradable annual allowances for emissions. Polluters that cannot squeeze under their caps buy the surplus of light polluters. The right wrists are slapped, and emissions overall are reduced at a lower cost than if each installation had had to meet an individual target.

Though the markets stuttered into life, they have grown surprisingly quickly. Volumes traded recently topped 2.2m tonnes a day. What has made headlines, however, is the recent surge in the price of carbon allowances. On 4 July, it touched €29.35 ($34.90), a record. The cost of the allowances to produce one kilowatt-hour of coal-fired power is now greater than the cost of the coal itself. Many reckon that the rise in emissions prices simply mirrors the rise in gas prices. When gas is dear, as it is now, utilities use more coal; because coal is dirtier, they have to buy more pollution permits in penance, and a heatwave in Europe since late June has dried up hydro power in the Iberian Peninsula and in Scandinavia.

Others, however, see a structural imbalance between supply and demand that may be harder to resolve. One reason why demand is outstripping supply is that a lot of firms that might have permits to sell are not yet participating, especially in new EU member states where allocation registries have not yet been set up.

The shortage, if there is one, may be eased by credits from projects outside Europe. Under Kyoto's Clean Development Mechanism (CDM), rich-country companies can earn certified emission reductions (CERs) by cleaning up emissions in developing countries. The EU allows them to be used to comply with caps. There is a rush to do just that, especially since CERs are changing hands for €7 or €8 and European allowances are heading for €30.

An important feature of this solution is that it generates an opportunity cost. Polluters are faced with a trade-off. They can either buy more credits to meet their level of pollution, or they can they decide to invest in new technology which is more environmentally friendly. The market for carbon permits provides firms with an alternative option and price. As permit prices rise, then it is hoped the attractiveness of investment in cleaner technology should increase, helping to reduce long-term pollution levels. This is discussed in Box 8.5. If you are thinking that prices might just as easily fall, governments have this under control. Each year the supply of permits will be reduced. Our understanding of markets assures us that a reduction in supply will lead to an increase in the equilibrium price.

Box 8.5 What price pollution?

Adapted from an article in BusinessWeek, 28 February 2005

One of the most active players in the forward market so far has been Royal Dutch/Shell Group, which in the past two years has made much of its commitment to a cleaner environment. The energy behemoth, which has 46 installations covered under the EU plan, says emissions trading will help with its investment in pollution control. 'It tells us whether it's more efficient [right now] for us to invest in new technologies, practices, or fuels,' says Garth Edward, Shell's trading manager for environmental products, 'or whether it's more efficient for us to buy or sell allowances in the external marketplace.'

 Summary

1 It is debatable whether firms are profit maximizers. Measuring marginal revenue and marginal cost can be difficult in practice.

2 The owners of modern corporations are often very different from the managers. This is known as separation of ownership from control.

3 If shareholders are unable to control managers, the potential exists for managers to pursue their own objectives. Various objectives have been put forward by economists, including the consumption of perquisites, growth maximization and sales maximization.

4 Managers can be incentivized to work in the interests of shareholders by also making them shareholders. This is commonly achieved through the use of stock options.

5 Financial incentives such as stock options are only useful if four criteria are met: (i) managers are not overly risk averse; (ii) there is a link between manager effort and measured performance; (iii) performance is not focused on single activities to the detriment of other key activities or tasks; (iv) managers are not capable of falsely manipulating the performance measure, such as the share price.

6 Pareto efficiency occurs when no one can be made better off without making someone worse off.

7 Externalities exist when the cost or benefits from consumption or production are not borne entirely by the person undertaking the production or consumption.

8 The existence of externalities leads to a difference between the socially optimal level of output and the private optimal level of output.

9 The optimal level of output can be targeted by the introduction of taxes and subsidies.

10 Monopoly can result in a dead-weight loss, or lower welfare for society, when compared with perfect competition.

11 Competition policy in the UK provides a pragmatic solution to the problems presented by monopolies.

Learning checklist

You should now be able to:

- Explain the difference between a principal and an agent
- Highlight the nature of the principal–agent problem
- Explain what is meant by the separation of ownership from control
- Provide a discussion of alternative theories to profit maximization
- Explain the concepts of positive and negative externalities, and provide examples
- Explain what is meant by the term 'market failure'
- Provide an explanation and evaluation of how tax and subsidies can be used to correct market failures
- Discuss how competition legislation functions in the UK
- Explain how stock options align the interest of managers and shareholders
- Provide an economic evaluation of carbon pollution permits

❓ Questions

1 Assess whether, or not, firms are profit maximizers.

2 Will a management buyout of a company increase, or decrease, agency costs?

3 List four negative externalities and four positive externalities.

4 Draw a diagram of MSB and MPB of train travel in rural and semi-rural areas. Illustrate how a subsidy might improve usage of train travel.

5 Fill in the blanks:
   To deal with externalities it is common to use _____ to reduce output when private output is higher than the socially optimal level, whereas _____ are used to increase supply when the socially optimal level of output is higher than the private level of output.

Exercises

1 True or false?
   a) Worker absence is highest on Mondays. This is an example of agency costs.
   b) Risk-averse workers need to be compensated with higher rates of contingent pay.
   c) Managers are said to suffer from shareholders' free riding on their hard work.
   d) The marginal social benefit of education is likely to exceed the marginal private benefit.
   e) A negative externality can occur when the marginal private cost is less than the marginal social cost.
   f) Subsidizing the marginal private cost of polluters will help to reduce the amount of pollution.

2   Figure 8.6 shows the market for a good in which there is a negative production externality such that marginal social cost (MSC) is above marginal private cost (MPC). MSB represents the marginal social benefit derived from consumption of the good.

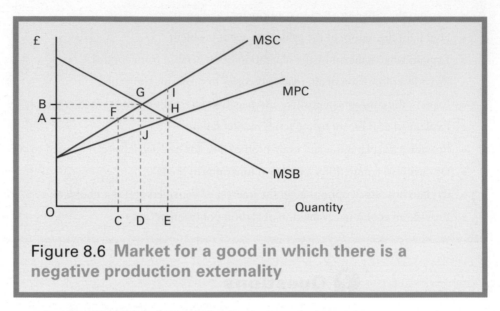

Figure 8.6 Market for a good in which there is a negative production externality

a)   If this market is unregulated, what quantity of this good will be produced?
b)   What is the socially efficient quantity?
c)   What is the amount of the deadweight loss to society if the free market quantity is produced?
d)   What level of tax on the good would ensure that the socially efficient quantity is produced?
e)   Suggest an example of a situation in which this analysis might be relevant.

3   When considering these questions refer to Box 8.4
a)   Assuming that the higher demand for coal is increased demand for permits, draw a demand and supply diagram which illustrates the increase in price of permits.
b)   Draw a demand-and-supply diagram which illustrates the argument that the higher price of permits reflects a shortage of supply.
c)   Nuclear power has been re-positioned as the energy source for the future. Why do you think this is; and do you think it is a good idea?

Section IV
Domestic macroeconomics

Section contents

Chapter 9
Introduction to the macroeconomy

Chapter contents

 Learning outcomes

By the end of this chapter you should understand:

Economic Theory

- The key concepts of GDP, inflation, unemployment and the balance of payments

- The concept of the business cycle

- The circular flow of income

- Leakages and injections

- Aggregate demand and aggregate supply

- How changes in aggregate demand and supply lead to changes in equilibrium GDP and inflation

Business Application

- How to optimize investment decisions by understanding the business cycle

- How to use income elasticities to profit during a recession

Macroeconomics at a glance

The issue

The business cycle, consisting of economic booms and recessions, drives changes in the consumption levels of consumers and firms. Predicting the business cycle and positioning the firm for changes in economic activity are crucial for financial success.

The understanding

In basic terms we can understand changes in macroeconomic activity as resulting from changes in overall demand and supply in the economy. In an economic boom, overall demand or supply in the economy can be rising, while in a recession, overall demand or supply can be falling. Therefore, predicting the business cycle rests on predicting economy level demand and supply.

The usefulness

In order to survive firms have to be financially successful in booms as well as busts. By anticipating when the economy is likely to peak, or bottom out, firms can plan their investments in new products, new production facilities or new retail outlets. They can also change their product offerings to reflect different consumer preferences during booms and busts.

9.1 Business problem: business cycles and economic uncertainty

Understanding the macroeconomic environment is of crucial importance to business. Just like private individuals, business also needs to take financial decisions. An individual might decide to buy a house, while a firm might decide to buy a new production facility.

Consider buying a house: two significant issues need addressing. How much should you offer for the house and how much can you afford to borrow?

When valuing the house you will need to consider whether the market price will fall in the near future, perhaps during a recession. Similarly, when thinking about how much you can borrow, you need to think about how much you will earn in the future. Will you be made unemployed during a recession? Furthermore, will an increase in interest rates make mortgage repayments impossible for you to meet?

A business deciding whether to spend many millions of pounds on a new production facility will go through the same process. What is the plant worth? How much can the business afford to borrow? Will a new facility be needed if consumer demand falls during a recession? Will changes in interest rates make the investment unprofitable?

Therefore, just like individuals, firms need to think very carefully when committing themselves to investment projects, because the **business cycle** will affect the success of the investment. These points are highlighted in Box 9.1, with the German economy, on one level, appearing to grow hand-in-hand with business confidence and investment. It also suggests a dynamic link, where a prolonged period of economic recession may force firms to develop international operations and thereby lowering their dependence on the domestic economy.

The background to the business investment decision is a recognition of the **business cycle**, where, over time, an economy can grow at a faster rate, a so-called 'economic boom', and then move into a period of slower growth, an economic recession.

Box 9.1 Germany flexes some new muscle

Adapted from an article by Jack Ewing, BusinessWeek, 4 January 2006

Is the German economy getting its mojo back? It certainly seems that way. The positive indicators keep coming, most recently a report from the Federal Labor Office that the normal December rise in unemployment was unusually low. And it comes after a series of unexpectedly positive reports on business confidence, industrial orders, and investment that prompted the German Institute for Economic Research in Berlin, a leading think tank, to boost its prognosis for 2006 growth to 1.7% from 1.2%. The European economy is also looking better, with forecasters such as Dresdner Bank predicting growth of 2% for the year, with unemployment falling to 8.1% from 8.5% in 2005.

As if to underline the nation's growing economic confidence, German companies are also getting expansionary. Chemical giant BASF made a $4.9 billion unsolicited takeover offer for Engelhard. And Dusseldorf steelmaker ThyssenKrupp raised its bid for Canada's steel maker Dofasco.

In fact, German corporate aggressiveness and German economic performance are only tenuously linked. BASF, like most of the country's other big companies, has for years been reducing its dependence on the slow-growth domestic economy, which currently provides about 40% of sales. The Engelhard bid is part of a continuing effort to build market share in the U.S. 'BASF is a global company. There is a low correlation with the German economy.'

A common thread does link corporate and macroeconomic performance, though: years of restructuring, often painful, are paying off. In BASF's case, the company has cut $570 million in costs from its German operations. Job reductions and divestments led to a net 5% decrease in global employment, to 80 695. The leaner operations helped third-quarter profit more than double, to $970 million, on sales of $12.4 billion – and gave BASF the reserves it needs to offer all cash for Engelhard.

'Dampening effect.' The question is whether Germany can continue to gain momentum – or will the growth peter out after a year or so? Unfortunately, based on current trends, growth will probably slow in 2006 as corporate investment in equipment peaks and the government raises the value-added tax to bring the national budget into accord with European Union guidelines. Dresdner Bank expects growth in 2007 to slide to an unimpressive 1% as the higher sales tax drains some $30 million from consumption. 'The dampening effect is coming from government policy,' says Dresdner economist Wolfgang Leim.

Clearly an understanding of how the economy works and how it is likely to develop in the short, medium and long term is of crucial importance. Firms that make bad decisions will suffer financially. Firms that understand the macroeconomy and plan expansion and consolidation of the business at the right times are more likely to prosper.

In this chapter we will provide an overview of recent macroeconomic activity. In addition, we will provide a basic understanding of how the business cycle occurs, introducing the circular flow of income and then developing our application of the demand and supply framework used in the microeconomic section of this book. This will then provide the basis for an assessment of government economic policy in later chapters.

9.2 **Macroeconomic issues**

Key macroeconomic outputs

Macroeconomics studies the workings of the entire economy. In Figure 9.1 we have charted four key macroeconomic issues: **GDP**, **inflation**, **unemployment** and the **current account**.

GDP, gross domestic product, is a measure of the total output produced by an economy in a given year.

Inflation is the rate of change in the average price level. Inflation of 2 per cent indicates that prices have risen by 2 per cent during the previous 12 months.

Unemployment is the number of individuals seeking work, but do not currently have a job.

The **current account** is the difference between exported and imported goods and services.

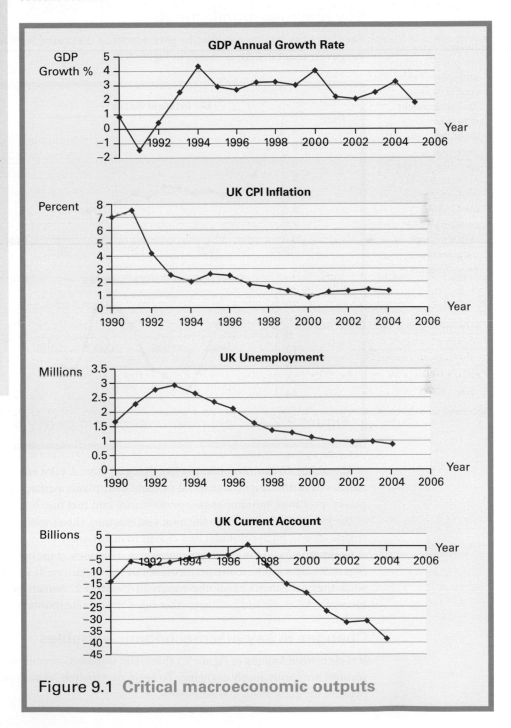

Figure 9.1 Critical macroeconomic outputs

It can be argued that Figure 9.1 represents the key measures of an economy: growth in GDP, or the improvement in economic activity; price stability via inflation; unemployment and success in trade overseas. For an economy to be functioning well, each of these outputs needs to be controlled and managed, with governments targeting higher economic growth, improved price stability, low unemployment and growing, but balanced, international trade.

Key macroeconomic inputs

Interest rates are the price of money and are set by the central bank.
The **government deficit** is the difference between government spending and tax receipts. Just as students run up overdrafts, spending more than they earn, so too does the government.

The key policy inputs controlled by government or the central bank are **interest rates** and the **government deficit**, as shown in Figure 9.2.

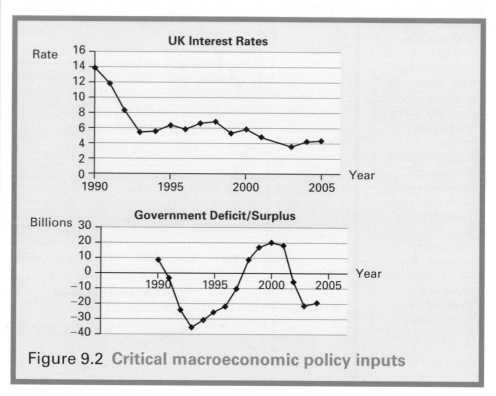

Figure 9.2 **Critical macroeconomic policy inputs**

Managing the macroeconomy is like flying a plane. A pilot will look at the instrument panel, check the height and speed of their own plane, perhaps take account of other planes' positions, monitor engine performance and fuel use. If any of the characteristics of the plane's flight are not to the pilot's satisfaction, then inputs will be changed – faster engine speeds, higher altitudes or a change in direction.

Governments do the same with economies. They look at the outputs of the economy in Figure 9.1 and examine the performance of the economy. If governments do not like what they see, they change the inputs in Figure 9.2. Sometimes governments make successful take-offs and landings; other times they create monumental crashes.

Changes in key macroeconomic variables

It is clear from looking at Figure 9.1 that GDP, inflation, unemployment and the current account are continuously changing. To begin our analysis let us concentrate on two time periods: the early 1990s and mid-2000s.

In the early 1990s:

(i)   inflation was high;

(ii)   the government raised interest rates (see Figure 9.2) to try to control inflation;

(iii) high interest rates led to a reduction in economic activity, fewer goods and services were produced and GDP growth fell;

(iv)   with lower production of goods and services, fewer workers were needed and unemployment increased;

(v)   a reduction in tax receipts, due to falling GDP, and an increase in social security payments to the unemployed led to an increase in the government deficit;

(vi)   the high interest rate led to an increase in the value of the UK pound, exports became very expensive and the current account went into a large deficit, with imports exceeding exports.

In the mid-2000s:

(i)   inflation was low;

(ii)   interest rates were low because inflation was low and under control;

(iii) GDP growth was rising steadily in an environment of low inflation and interest rates;

(iv)   unemployment was steadily falling as GDP grew and firms looked to hire additional workers;

(v)   the government was running a surplus in some years and a deficit in others.

(vi)   the current account was still in deficit.

Observations and comments

1   The economic conditions of the mid-2000s, with rising GDP, low unemployment and inflation, were preferable to the conditions of 1990, with high inflation, falling GDP and rising unemployment. In a similar way the rising employment, increasing business confidence and rising economic growth are all preferable to recession, falling investment and rising unemployment which have been the recent characteristics of the German economy, discussed in Box 9.1.

2   Following on from this, how does a government set and prioritize its objectives? Is low inflation more important than high GDP? Is unemployment acceptable? Should the government manage its deficit and should the current account be in surplus?

     In Chapter 10 we will return to this question and provide a review of how each key macroeconomic variable is measured, provide a review of the issues associated with each variable and, more important, the objectives generally set by government for each key macroeconomic variable.

3   Why are GDP, inflation, unemployment, the current account, interest rates and government deficits all linked?

In the remainder of this chapter we will introduce the circular flow of income as a means of describing some of the linkages between the macroeconomic variables. We will then develop this analysis by adapting our supply and demand framework utilized in the microeconomic section of this book. By the end of this chapter you will be able to answer question 3. As we progress through Chapters 11 and 12 you will develop your understanding of how governments can use different policies to manage the links within the macroeconomy.

9.3 **The circular flow of income**

In contrast to microeconomics, which examined product-specific markets such as the market for pizzas, or the market for cars, macroeconomics focuses upon the workings of the whole economy. In order to begin our understanding of the macroeconomy we will introduce the **circular flow of income** as a descriptive framework of macroeconomic activity. Figure 9.3 provides an illustration of the circular flow of income.

Within the framework of the circular flow of income households are assumed to own the factors of production – land, labour, capital and enterprise. As producers of goods and services, firms need to use the factors of production owned by the households. Firms will clearly provide households with a financial reward for using the factors of production. In the case of labour the financial reward is wages. Households will then use the money they have earned from firms to buy the finished goods and services, thus returning cash to the firms. A virtuous circle or, in our terminology, a circular flow of income is seen to exist.

> The **circular flow of income** shows the flow of inputs, output and payments between households and firms within an economy.

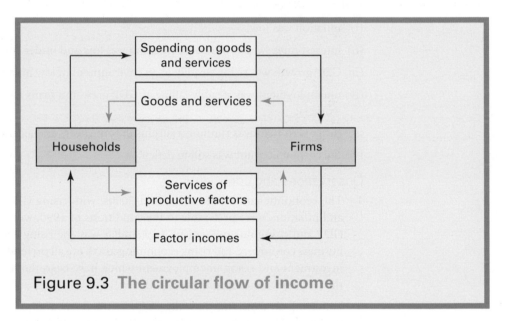

Figure 9.3 **The circular flow of income**

The inner loop captures the flow of resources between the two sectors. For example, resources such as labour flow to firms from households, and then goods and services flow from firms back to households. The outer loop captures the corresponding financial flows between the two sectors. Firms pay households wages for supplying labour resources. In return, households use their income to purchase the goods and services sold by the firms.

The circular flow of income captures the essential essence of macroeconomic activity. The economy is seen as nothing more than a revolving flow of goods, production resources and financial payments. The faster the flow, the higher the level of economic output.

The level of income activity within an economy is measured as Gross Domestic Product.

Leakages and injections

The economy described in Figure 9.3 contains only firms and households, which produce goods and spend income on goods and services. We can begin to broaden the circular flow to take account of saving by households, investment by firms, government spending and taxation, and international trade.

In order to account for these additional items we need to understand how **leakages** and **injections** fit into the circular flow of income.

Savings and investments

Rather than spend all income on goods and services, households could save a proportion of their income. Because income is being taken from the circular flow of income and saved, it represents a leakage. But an important question relates to where these savings go. If the money is placed on deposit at the bank, then the bank will try to lend the money for profit. Borrowers are likely to be firms seeking to invest in equipment, or needing to fund overdrafts. If firms invest in capital equipment, then they are buying goods and services from other firms. As a result, investment is spending in the economy that does not come from the income earned by households. As such, investments represent an injection of financial resource and spending, by firms, into the circular flow. In equilibrium, savings will equal investments. This is because banks will set an interest rate where the supply of funds from savers equals the demand for funds by investing firms.

Taxes and government spending

Government taxes the earnings of individuals and companies. Tax payments represent a leakage from the circular flow of income as they reduce the ability of households to spend on goods and services. However, the government also undertakes a number of activities that inject financial resources back into the economy. Governments buy hospitals and schools. They employ nurses and teachers. They also pay social benefits to the needy. All of which are injections.

Exports and imports

Finally, some consumption by households will be on goods made in other economies. If you buy a German car, then this represents a leakage from the UK circular flow of income, as it is income spent in another economy. However, an injection will occur if a German spends money on a British car, as this represents an export.

The various leakages and injections are illustrated in Figure 9.4, which simply extends the circular flow of income. On the left of Figure 9.4, savings, taxation and imports leak from the income households could spend on consumption. On the right of Figure 9.4, investments, government spending and exports inject spending into the circular flow of income.

Total expenditure

Total expenditure is simply all the separate sources of spending within the economy. That is, consumption by households, investment by firms and public spending by government. Net exports adjusts for expenditure on exports and imports by consumers, firms and government. Being able to identify the individual components of total expenditure is particularly important because it provides an understanding of which expenditures lead to an increase (or decrease) in economic activity. If consumption, investment, government spending, or net exports increase, then total expenditure increases, and potentially the flow of goods and services in the inner loop also increases to match the increased demand in the economy. Similarly, if total expenditure is reduced,

A **leakage** from the circular flow is income not spent on goods and services within the economy. Leakages can be savings, taxation and imports.

An **injection** into the circular flow is additional spending on goods and services that does not come from the income earned by households in the inner loop. Injections can be investment, government spending and exports.

Total expenditure is equal to consumption, plus investment, plus government spending, plus net exports (exports minus imports).

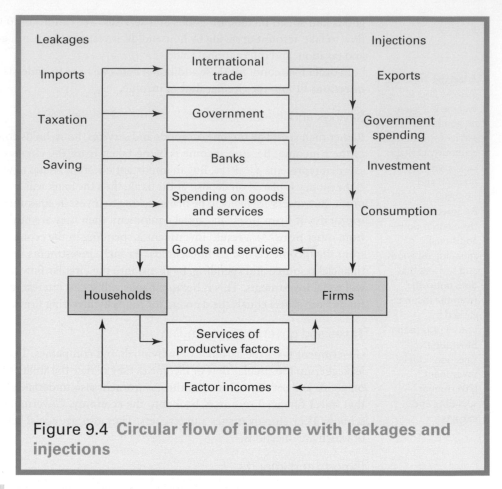

Figure 9.4 **Circular flow of income with leakages and injections**

Aggregate demand is the total demand in an economy. **Aggregate supply** is the total supply in an economy.	the flow of goods and services in the inner loop falls due to decreasing demand. We will now use these ideas to develop our understanding of changes in economic activity over time and the idea of a macroeconomic equilibrium.

9.4 **National income determination and business cycles**

When examining individual markets in the microeconomic section of this book we focused on the demand and supply curve for the product. Since in macroeconomics we are examining the whole economy, we need a demand and supply curve for the whole economy.

The **average price level** is the average price of goods and services in an economy. The *change* in the average price level is a measure of inflation, where 5 per cent inflation means that prices on average have changed, i.e. increased by 5 per cent.

Total expenditure representing consumption, plus investment, plus government spending, plus net exports is in fact **aggregate demand**. In microeconomics we argued that the demand for a product is negatively related to its price. As prices increase, less is demanded. We could also draw an aggregate demand curve showing a negative relationship between the average level of prices in the economy and the level of aggregate demand. However, we are going to make a subtle, but important change. We will analyse the relationship between aggregate demand and the *change* in the **average price level**.

The benefit of looking at the relationship between aggregate demand and inflation is that control of inflation has become a key aspect of modern macroeconomic policy.

Therefore, by using inflation, rather than the level of prices, we are bringing inflation to the centre of our economic models.

Aggregate demand and inflation

Fortunately, the relationship between aggregate demand and inflation is also negative. If we assume that the central bank is tasked with keeping inflation at 2.5 per cent, as it is in the UK, then we know from experience that the higher the rate of inflation, the higher the central bank has to raise interest rates in order to stem inflation. As interest rates increase, consumers and firms are less willing to borrow in order to fund the purchase of goods and services. Therefore, aggregate demand falls. These points are picked up in Figure 9.5.

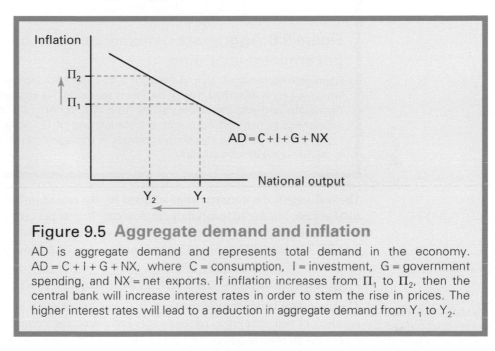

Figure 9.5 Aggregate demand and inflation

AD is aggregate demand and represents total demand in the economy. $AD = C + I + G + NX$, where C = consumption, I = investment, G = government spending, and NX = net exports. If inflation increases from Π_1 to Π_2, then the central bank will increase interest rates in order to stem the rise in prices. The higher interest rates will lead to a reduction in aggregate demand from Y_1 to Y_2.

From the circular flow of income we have argued that aggregate demand is composed of consumption, investment, government spending and net exports. Therefore, an increase in any of these types of expenditure will lead to an increase in aggregate demand. In Figure 9.6 we illustrate this idea by assuming that government spending has increased from G_1 to G_2. We could equally have assumed that consumption, investment or net exports had increased. The consequences of the increase in government spending are for the aggregate demand curve to shift from AD_1 to AD_2, with higher levels of economic output being demanded at all inflation levels.

Aggregate supply and inflation

Nominal prices and wages are not adjusted for inflation. **Real** prices and wages are adjusted for inflation.

In Chapters 3 and 5 we saw that, as profit maximizers, firms will supply output if the market price is equal to, or greater than, marginal cost. Therefore, an increase in the price will bring about an increase in supply from an individual firm. But at the macro level, how will **aggregate supply** react to a change in inflation?

We need to make a distinction between **real** and **nominal** values.

Assume you are earning £100 a day and inflation is 2 per cent per year. At the end of one year your *nominal* wage will still be £100 per day. But your *real* wage will only be £98.

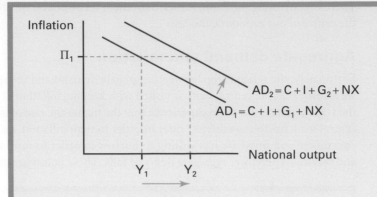

Figure 9.6 Aggregate demand, inflation and increased government spending

Aggregate demand will shift to the right if, C, I, G, or NX increase. As an example, we have simply assumed that government spending has increased from G_1 to G_2. Aggregate demand, therefore, shifts from AD_1 to AD_2. As this happens, the willingness to demand output at an inflation rate of Π_1 rises from Y_1 to Y_2. In Figure 9.10 (p. 205) we show how changes in aggregate demand lead to changes in equilibrium GDP and inflation.

The real wage is the nominal wage adjusted for the rate of inflation. You are receiving £100 in cash, but due to inflation it can now only buy 98 per cent of what you could buy last year with £100. In order to keep your real wage constant you need to ask for a 2 per cent pay rise, because you now need £102 to buy what £100 could purchase last year.

Aggregate supply and full wage adjustment to inflation

The important issue for aggregate supply is whether or not a bout of inflation leads to nominal, or real, changes in relative wages and prices. For example, if inflation leads to a 3 per cent increase in prices for final products and workers also ask for a 3 per cent pay rise to compensate for the rise in prices, then the real wage and the real price of goods and services has stayed the same. Because real prices and wages are the same, the real costs and revenues faced by the firm have not changed. Aggregate supply will therefore remain unchanged as firms are faced with no reason to increase (or decrease) their willingness to supply. We can, therefore, argue that when wages fully adjust to inflation, aggregate supply remains constant. This is illustrated in Figure 9.7 with a vertical aggregate supply curve. As inflation increases, supply stays constant.

Aggregate supply without full wage adjustment to price increases

We can now consider what happens if prices and wages do not adjust to keep real values constant. Assume again the price of goods and services is increasing by 3 per cent, but workers only manage to negotiate a 2 per cent increase in wages. The real cost of employing labour has now reduced by 1 per cent. Firms are experiencing a reduction in their real costs of production. If firms are profit maximizers then, as we saw in Chapter 5, a reduction in marginal cost leads to an increase in the profit maximizing output by the firm (see Section 5.2). Therefore, with a reduction in the real wage rate, firms will now be

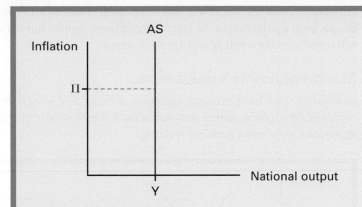

Figure 9.7 Aggregate supply and full wage adjustment to inflation

AS is aggregate supply and represents total supply in the economy. If prices and wages adjust to keep real prices and wages constant, then aggregate supply will remain constant.

willing to increase supply and overall aggregate supply increases as inflation increases. Therefore, when wages do not fully adjust to price changes, a positive relationship between inflation and aggregate supply can exist. This is shown in Figure 9.8.

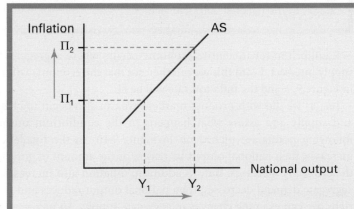

Figure 9.8 Aggregate supply without full wage adjustment to price increases

If prices increase faster than wages, then the real wage decreases. This represents a real cost reduction for firms. If firms are profit maximizers, then a reduction in the real marginal cost will motivate firms to increase output. Therefore, a reduction in the real wage leads to an increase in aggregate supply.

At this stage we can perhaps go one step further and suggest that Figure 9.8 represents the short run, while Figure 9.7 represents the long run. In the short run workers may not accurately guess the inflation rate. In our example workers agreed a 2 per cent rise in wages, when inflation turned out to be 3 per cent. In the long run, workers will try to rectify this reduction in real wages and so, over time, real wages will fully adjust to the inflation rate and real wages will remain constant. Therefore, in the short run firms might benefit from a reduction in the real wage and boost supply. But in the long run, real wages will remain constant and so will aggregate supply.

Macroeconomic equilibrium

In Figure 9.9 we have brought aggregate demand and supply together for the whole economy. We have assumed that wages do not fully adjust to inflation and, therefore, aggregate supply is not perfectly inelastic.

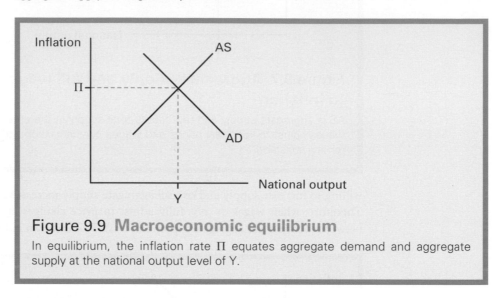

Figure 9.9 Macroeconomic equilibrium

In equilibrium, the inflation rate Π equates aggregate demand and aggregate supply at the national output level of Y.

Equilibrium for the entire economy occurs where aggregate demand and aggregate supply intersect. From this we can then see that the economy will produce an output of Y in Figure 9.9; and the inflation rate will be Π.

Just as we did with product markets, we can also begin to change aggregate demand and supply and assess what happens to the equilibrium output and inflation. The following points are picked up in Figure 9.10. In the top left, if aggregate demand increases, then national output increases, or the amount of goods and services traded in the economy increases. But, in addition, inflation also increases. In the bottom left, if aggregate demand decreases, then national output reduces and inflation falls. In the top right, we can examine changes in aggregate supply. An increase in aggregate supply will lead to an increase in economic activity, but a reduction in the inflation rate. The bottom right of Figure 9.10 shows that a reduction in aggregate supply will lead to a reduction in national output and an increase in the rate of inflation.

We can now say that an increase in aggregate demand leads to an **inflationary** boom. But a reduction in aggregate demand leads to a **deflationary** recession. An increase in aggregate supply leads to a deflationary boom, while a reduction in aggregate supply leads to an inflationary recession.

In Section 9.5 we use these ideas to show how a firm might try to predict the business cycle.

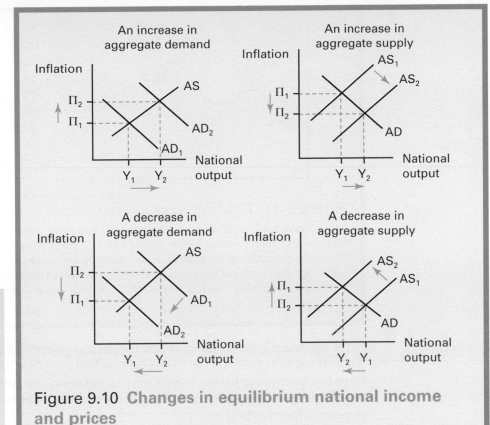

An increase in national output is a sign of economic growth or economic **boom**. A reduction in national output is known as a **recession**. **Inflation** is a rise in the price level. A decrease in the price level is **deflation**.

Figure 9.10 Changes in equilibrium national income and prices

Top left: an increase in aggregate demand leads to an inflationary **boom**. Bottom left: a reduction in aggregate demand leads to a **deflationary** recession. Top right: an increase in supply leads to a deflationary boom. Bottom right: a decrease in supply leads to an inflationary **recession**.

9.5 Business application: predicting the business cycle

While the business cycle is outside the control of individual firms, strategies for dealing with the cycle are not. An important step for firms is to predict the business cycle and this is no easy task. Even skilled economists sitting on the Bank of England's monetary panel disagree about how fast the economy is growing and how high interest rates should be set. Alongside predicting the growth of the economy, firms also need to time their strategies to perfection. Examine Figure 9.11.

There is no commercial value in being told that the economy is at point A in an economic boom because by the time the firm has made investments in new products, production facilities and distribution, or retail outlets, the economy will have moved into recession at point B. Take the example of the airline industry in Box 9.2. The industry has been in recession for five years, generating $43 billion in losses. Airlines are now forecasting that the dip in fortunes is over and the world economies are turning towards boom. Ploughing huge financial resources into additional capacity is important if the peak boom period is to be exploited.

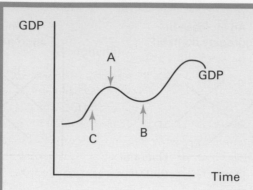

Figure 9.11 The business cycle

As the economy moves through the business cycle firms need to plan and manage their capital investments. There is little point in beginning to invest when the economy is booming, as at point A, because by the time the extra capital is in place, the economy will have moved on to B, a period of recession. Therefore, the smart businessperson has to judge when the economy is at C and likely to move to A in the future.

The business skill lies in making an educated guess at point C that in the near future the economy will be at point A. Then investments can be put in place to exploit the economic boom in a more timely fashion. Indeed, when the economy is at point A, the firm should begin to plan for the recession at point B. But how do you spot an economic boom, or recession before they happen?

 Box 9.2 After losing $43 billion in five years, airlines are at the beginning of a massive boom

Adapted from an article in The Economist, 10 November 2005

Airlines are loss-making, inefficient, prone to extreme cycles and vulnerable to fickle consumers. Only an idiot would buy shares in an airline. The trouble with truisms is that they can obscure big changes as they start to happen. In fact, the airline industry is poised for an almost unprecedented boom.

Driven by economic growth international traffic has risen by 8.3% so far this year, compared with 2004. In America, total traffic is up by 5.4%; in Europe the rise is 6%. In Asia, annual growth of 6.8% through to 2009 is forecast; then we have China at 10%.

Not surprisingly, Airbus is scouring Europe and farther afield for 1000 engineers to help with design. Boeing is booming even more. Some observers think Boeing could finish this year with almost 1000 orders, while Airbus will net nearly 900. In a good year the two manufacturers usually share 800 orders between them.

Economic insights

The aggregate demand and supply framework suggests that, in order to understand the business cycle, it is useful to be able to address how much demand and supply are changing in the economy. For example, in order to understand aggregate demand it is essential to have a grasp of how fast consumption, investment, government spending and net exports are changing. In particular, it is important to know if any of these expenditures are increasing, or decreasing. If aggregate demand is increasing, the economy is likely to grow; however, if aggregate demand is falling, the economy is likely to move towards recession.

Aggregate supply, is in part, influenced by the costs faced by firms. When important input prices such as oil increase, firms will be less willing to supply and aggregate supply will fall. In contrast, when new technologies become available, which lower the costs of supplying goods and services, firms will be more willing to supply and aggregate supply will increase. The Internet was seen as a technology capable of improving firms' costs and helping to develop the supply of goods and services. When aggregate supply is rising, the economy is likely to grow. However, when aggregate supply is falling, the economy is likely to move into recession.

Government agencies, statistical offices, central banks and trade bodies all provide commentary and opinion on the likely development of the economy over the short and medium term. In the main these reports are based on projections for aggregate demand and supply. However, you do not have to be a skilled economist to understand the development of the economy.

Business experience

Experience probably counts for a great deal. If you know how the market works and have experience of working in the market for a number of years, you will have seen it move through its cycles. You will have a feeling for when it is going to boom and also a feeling for when it is time to cut back and await the recession. This experience, or 'feelings', are likely to come from an assessment of the more measurable lead indicators. Markets do not generally switch from boom to bust. Rather, they gradually grow into a boom and then slowly decline into a recession. During the growth phase enquiries from customers will increase; and then these will begin to materialize into orders and sales. You may also find that customers switch to you, not because of price, but because you can promise to deliver on time. This would indicate that rivals are also becoming busy. So, as sales and profit margins begin to improve, plans for expansion should follow.

Once expansion across the industry begins, you need to have an eye on when the market begins to soften, with falling prices and excess supply of goods and services. If demand in the economy either shrinks or grows at a slower rate than supply, then prices will fall and margins will shrink. So, if you think the expansion by your own company, and also that of your rivals is too great for the likely growth rate in demand by consumers, then you need to think about readdressing your growth options for the future. Cutting costs and reining in excess output become key in order to compete.

9.6 Business application: profiting from recession

Economies do not stop during recessions. In fact, when compared with previous years, GDP during a recession often falls by only 1–2 per cent. So, even during a recession there are still many goods and services being supplied and demanded. However, many firms do struggle during recessions and eventually either cutback on workers and generate unemployment, or close down altogether, with even greater consequences for unemployment.

The point that needs to be addressed is that while the economy may only shrink by 1–2 per cent, this is only the net effect. For example, demand for some goods and services may have reduced by 20 per cent, while for others it could have increased by 18–19 per cent. But how can demand increase during a recession? To answer this question you need to recall the concept of income elasticities covered in Chapter 2. For normal goods, when incomes rise, demand also rises, but when incomes fall, demand also falls. In the case of inferior goods, however, when income rises, demand falls. Similarly, when incomes fall, demand increases. So, during a recession demand for normal goods decreases, but demand for inferior goods increases. Therefore, the way to profit in a recession is to have product lines that are income inferior, products that customers like to buy more of when they have reduced incomes, or are trying to be careful when spending money.

As discussed in Box 9.3, Whitbread, a supplier of leisure services, including hotels, pubs and restaurant chains, is insulating itself from the downturn in consumer expenditure in the UK. As recessionary pressures increase, consumers switch their spending to companies offering value propositions. The no-frills hotel chain, Premier Inn, supplies this product offering and with high occupancy rates and high sales growth, income-constrained consumers are finding it an attractive proposition. In contrast, the restaurant arm of Whitbread, catering towards lunchtime treats for employees, or weekend treats for families is struggling to halt a decline in sales. The hotel chain is arguably income inferior, while the restaurants can be described as income normal.

Moreover, a lack of fixed costs is essential for profitable performances during a recession. From Chapter 3 we know that high fixed costs require high volumes. Unfortunately, high volumes are difficult to find during a recession. It is therefore essential to have a cost base which is driven by variable costs, not fixed ones. Luxury hotels, with many frills, including swimming pools, bars, restaurants, tennis courts and concierge services, often located in expensive city centres, are nothing but a huge collection of fixed costs. Not surprisingly, luxury hotel chains do not perform well during recessions.

 Box 9.3 Why on earth would you invest in leisure business when consumers are tightening their belts?

Adapted from an article in Investors' Chronicle, 6 January 2006

At present, most people seem more interested in paying off credit cards than joining an expensive gym or eating out. Nevertheless Whitbread's budget hotel chain Premier Inn is still achieving growth. Like-for-like sales are up 7.3% and occupancy is averaging 82%. Demand should continue to grow robustly as people embrace the fixed-price, no-frills room for the night, which coupled with Premier's low fixed cost should boost profits.

Admittedly, the situation is not as bright elsewhere in the Whitbread empire. Of particular concern is the sluggish performance of its restaurants: Pizza Hut and TGI Fridays have suffered a 3.4 per cent decline in sales. Whitbread's pubs are coping no better. Its Brewers Fayre and Beefeater outlets reported a drop in sales of 2.1 per cent

However, it is clearly not a good idea to be solely dependent upon demand for inferior goods, as demand will fall during a boom. Instead, a portfolio approach as developed by Whitbread is advised. This was discussed in Chapter 7 under diversification. Car manufacturers such as Ford are renowned for this. In addition to the Ford cars, they also make Jaguars, Land Rovers, Mazdas and Aston Martins. A more extreme example is the fact that Fiat Unos are made by the same firm that makes Ferraris! The reason is that throughout the business cycle demand for one product in the portfolio will rise. Ferraris and Jaguars sell well during a boom, Fiat Unos and Fords sell better during a recession. Supermarkets are even more skilled at mixing the portfolio. Stores in the affluent districts of Chelsea and Mayfair will stock different products from stores located in inner-city Manchester. But during a recession and boom, each store will fine-tune its product offering. In a boom, the Manchester store will allocate more shelf space to branded items and reduce its offering of value own-label products. Then, during a recession, the store will switch back to more-value items.

Clearly, firms operating within a changing macroeconomic environment need to be able to prosper during both boom and recession. Success is critically dependent upon being able to sell products during booms and recessions and being able to read the business cycle. Plan ahead and be better placed than rivals to exploit the ever-changing environment.

 # Summary

1   Macroeconomics is the study of economic activity at the aggregate level, examining the entire economy rather than just single markets.

2   The circular flow of income is a representation of how an economy works. Households own all factors of production and firms hire these factors to produce goods and services. Firms pay households for using input resources and households in return purchase the goods and services.

3   The level of demand for goods and services is conditioned by the level of injections into and leakages from the circular flow of income. Savings, taxation and imports all represent leakages, while investment, government spending and exports all represent injections.

4   The whole economy can be viewed as a collection of the many small markets that go into making an economy. Therefore, rather than thinking about demand we now talk about aggregate demand and similarly aggregate supply as opposed to simply supply.

5   Aggregate demand has a negative relationship with inflation. As inflation increases, the central bank increases interest rates, resulting in a reduction in aggregate demand.

6   Aggregate supply will have a positive relationship with inflation, if real wages do not adjust fully to rises in prices. However, if real wages adjust fully to inflation, then aggregate supply will be perfectly inelastic.

7   Gross domestic product, or GDP, is a measure of economic output of an economy.

8   Inflation is a measure of price changes. The quicker prices rise, the higher the rate of inflation.

9   In part, the business cycle can be explained by changes in aggregate demand and aggregate supply. As demand increases the economy grows and inflation increases. As the demand falls, the economy slows and inflation falls. If, in contrast, supply increases, then the economy grows and inflation decreases. However, if supply shrinks, the economy shrinks and inflation increases.

10 The business cycle is a description of the tendency for economies to move from economic boom into economic recession and vice versa.

11 The rate of inflation tends to change throughout the business cycle, but this is a reflection of changes in aggregate demand and supply. An increase in aggregate demand will tend to generate an inflationary boom, while an increase in aggregate supply will tend to generate a deflationary boom. Conversely, a reduction in aggregate demand will generate a deflationary recession, while a reduction in aggregate supply will generate an inflationary recession.

12 Predicting the business cycle is not an exact science. Economists and businesspeople will only ever know when an economy has hit its peak after the event, perhaps up to 12 months after. And the same is true of recessions. It is, therefore, crucial to plan and implement investment decisions in advance of any detrimental macroeconomic changes. How to achieve this is challenging. Some people use their experience – how did the economy behave in the past? What can I learn from other economies? What are the experts saying? And do I believe them?

13 An interesting question, or fallacy, surrounds the fact that GDP only falls by a small amount (1–2%), during a recession and yet many businesses suffer severe financial hardship. Why is that? In part, recessions have different impacts in different product markets. Falling consumer incomes will cut demand for normal goods, but raise demand for inferior goods. This provides an opportunity to create a mixed portfolio of products for the business cycle. Supermarkets do this through greater use of own-brand items during recessions, while many car manufacturers produce both high- and low-value cars.

 Learning checklist

You should now be able to:

♦ Discuss the key topics of GDP, inflation, unemployment and the balance of payments

♦ Explain what is meant by the term business cycle

♦ Provide a discussion of the circular flow of income, highlighting the various relationships between firms, households, government and international economies

♦ Explain the difference between leakages and injections

♦ Explain the determinants of aggregate demand

♦ Discuss whether or not aggregate supply will be perfectly inelastic

♦ Explain how changes in aggregate demand and supply can explain the business cycle

❓ Questions

1   In an economy, if aggregate demand increases while aggregate supply stays constant, what happens to GDP and inflation?

2   An economy benefits from an influx of additional workers. Using the circular flow of income, assess how these additional workers will impact upon the output of the economy. How will the extra workers influence aggregate supply?

3   Explain why producing income normal and income inferior goods can help a firm deal with the business cycle. Will such a strategy confuse consumers' understanding of the company's brand?

4   The economy has been growing for 12 months and sales are increasing, but margins, the difference between revenues and costs, are beginning to fall. Is now a good time to invest in additional production capacity?

Exercises

1   True or false?
   a)   Savings provide an injection into the circular flow of income.
   b)   Total expenditure in an economy is equal to consumption, investment, government spending and exports.
   c)   Under complete wage adjustment aggregate supply is unresponsive to a change in inflation.
   d)   Higher inflation will lead central banks to increase interest rates. This explains a negative relationship between inflation and aggregate demand
   e)   The main injections into the circular flow of income are investment and government spending.
   f)   Diversifying macroeconomic risk through normal and inferior products is beneficial for shareholders.

2   Table 9.1 presents consumer price indices (CPIs) for the UK, USA and Spain.
   a)   Calculate the annual inflation rate for each of the countries.
   b)   Plot your three inflation series on a diagram against time.
   c)   By what percentage did prices increase in each country over the whole period – i.e. between 1996 and 2006?
   d)   Which economy has experienced most stability of the inflation rate?
   e)   Which economy saw the greatest deceleration in the rate of inflation between 1998 and 2001?

   Table 9.2 presents some data relating to national output (real GDP) of the same three economies over a similar period, expressed as index numbers.
   f)   Calculate the annual growth rate for each of the countries.
   g)   Plot your three growth series on a diagram against time.
   h)   By what percentage did output increase in each country over the whole period?
   i)   To what extent did growth follow a similar pattern over time in these three countries?

Table 9.1 Consumer prices

	United Kingdom		USA		Spain	
	Consumer price index	Inflation rate (%)	Consumer price index	Inflation rate (%)	Consumer price index	Inflation rate (%)
1996	71.7		77.6		68.2	
1997	77.3		81.4		72.9	
1998	84.6		85.7		77.7	
1999	89.6		89.4		82.4	
2000	92.9		92.1		87.2	
2001	94.4		94.8		91.2	
2002	96.7		97.3		95.5	
2003	100.0		100.0		100.0	
2004	102.4		102.9		103.6	
2005	105.7		105.3		105.6	
2006	109.3		107.0		107.5	

Table 9.2 National production

	United Kingdom		USA		Spain	
	GDP index	Growth rate (%)	GDP index	Growth rate (%)	GDP index	Growth rate (%)
1996	91.4		86.7		86.0	
1997	93.4		89.7		90.2	
1998	93.7		90.8		93.6	
1999	91.9		89.9		95.7	
2000	91.4		92.3		96.3	
2001	93.3		94.5		95.2	
2002	97.3		97.8		97.4	
2003	100.0		100.0		100.0	
2004	102.6		103.4		102.4	
2005	106.2		107.5		106.0	
2006	108.5		111.7		110.1	

3   Refer to Box 9.1 when considering the following questions.
    a) Identify the reasons behind the expected higher rate of economic growth in
        Germany. Support your answer using an aggregate demand and aggregate supply
        diagram.
    b) In terms of total expenditure in the German economy, will the acquisition of
        international rivals boost investment or exports.
    c) Use an aggregate demand and supply diagram to illustrate how leaner German
        companies will help to drive higher rates of economic growth.
    d) On the same diagram used for c) show how an increase in tax will dampen
        economic growth.

Chapter 10
Measuring macroeconomic variables and policy issues

Chapter contents

Learning outcomes

By the end of this chapter you should understand:

Economic Theory

- How to measure GDP using the income, expenditure and value added approaches
- How to measure inflation using index numbers
- The potential causes of inflation
- The costs of inflation
- The reasons behind inflation targeting
- Frictional, structural, demand deficient and classical as various types of unemployment
- The Phillips curve
- Balance of payments problems

Business Application

- The importance of manufacturing competitiveness to the economy; and equally the importance of economic policy for manufacturing competitiveness.
- How might inflation targeting impact the business environment?

Measurement and policy issues at a glance

The issue

How are various macroeconomic variables measured? In addition, why is managing GDP, inflation, unemployment and the balance of payments important? What are the issues and trade-offs associated with targeting each aspect of the macroeconomy?

The understanding

Higher and stable GDP is associated with economic prosperity and enhanced economic growth. Higher GDP may lead to higher incomes for consumers and could facilitate investment by firms and government. High inflation may lead to economic instability and increased costs for the economy. Lower inflation might facilitate economic stability and investment planning by firms, leading to higher rates of economic growth. Unemployment reflects an underutilized resource, but labour market concerns are now switching towards productivity. The balance of payments reflects a country's trading position with the rest of the world. Just like individuals, an economy has to be concerned about running a long-term deficit. It is important to recognize that a government may not be capable of targeting all macroeconomic variables. For example, higher GDP may lead to higher inflation.

The usefulness

As businesses operate within macroeconomic environments it is essential that businesspeople are capable of deciphering the policy messages and changes instituted by governments. How will decisions regarding the management of inflation and long term growth impact upon the economy and the firm?

10.1 Business problem: what are the macroeconomic policy issues?

It is evident from Box 10.1 that macroeconomic risks are wide ranging and vary across different parts of the global economy. Since companies operate within macroeconomic environments, managers need to be capable of understanding the key macroeconomic policy issues pursued by governments. Government policies not only influence the macroeconomic environment, but they may also have direct implications for business, where policy responses are targeted at business. We can begin by analysing the following case.

Interest rate policy and the Bank of England

The Bank of England has the task of keeping inflation in the UK at 2.5 per cent on average. In pursuing this target the Bank of England is empowered to alter interest rates. What does this mean for business?

1   If firms borrow money to invest in capital, will interest rates be higher or lower when controlled by the central bank?

2   Will the central bank be capable of meeting the 2.5 per cent target?

3   Moreover, will targeting inflation have any implications for the business cycle, the growth of GDP and perhaps even the exchange rate?

4   Will central bank management of interest rates and inflation aid entry into the Euro?

Box 10.1 **Scaremongers likely to be disappointed again**

Adapted from an article by Ashley Seager, the Guardian 3 January 2006

Despite the US deficit, oil prices and sluggish growth, 2006 should be a good year. The global economy surprised most people yet again in 2005 and grew nearly as fast as 2004's 30-year high of 5% in spite of surging oil prices and a sharp tightening of monetary policy in the United States.

This year is likely to be dominated by what happens to oil prices, a further recovery in parts of the world economy, such as Japan and Germany, which have been weak up to now, and rising interest rates in many major economies as central banks seek to mop up the ultra-cheap money that has fuelled a global housing boom for the past three years.

The Doha round of world trade talks looks set to limp on during 2006, although after the aborted summit in Hong Kong last month, there has to be the real chance of failure this year, at a cost of hundreds of billions of dollars to the world economy.

A real positive this year is likely to be the recovery, at last, in both the Japanese and German economies, the world's second and third-largest economies respectively. This is a real positive because the US and China have had to provide the main impetus for world growth in recent years while Japan and Germany stagnated.

Both seem to be on a firmer footing, although the European Central Bank has already started to raise interest rates and is likely to do so again this year. Let us hope that does not prevent the strength in the export sector from spilling over into the domestic economy.

The implications for business are significant but, in the main, potentially beneficial. Economists would argue that the central bank can commit more credibly than politicians to an inflation target of 2.5 per cent. The problem for politicians is that in the run-up to an election, they may sacrifice inflation for a quick spurt of economic growth. Since the central bank need not worry about re-election, it will be less inclined to sacrifice inflation for greater economic growth. As a consequence, individuals view the central bank's willingness to control inflation as being more credible than the government's. The government may have to use higher interest rates to prove that it is equally tough on inflation. Therefore, the central bank can fight inflation with much lower rates than the government. Lower interest rates could be good for business. Moreover, stable inflation may aid stability in GDP and, in particular, stability in the economy may help the development of expenditure on investment, training and innovation, all of which are seen as essential for economic growth.

Entry into the Euro may be aided by central bank's management of inflation. We will see in Chapter 13 on exchange rates that low and stable inflation may be required for entry into the Euro. However, if the Bank of England is better than the European Central Bank at controlling inflation and the stability of economy, then why enter the Euro? The potential problem is whether the central bank will help business during a recession. In particular, will the central bank cut rates and allow inflation to rise above 2.5 per cent until the economy begins to grow?

With a modicum of economic knowledge it is possible to evaluate the implications of policy for business. Often during shifts in policy, debates and commentary will take place in the media, including TV interviews and newspaper columns. Businesspeople need to be capable of not only following the debate, but also evaluating the debate and eventually assessing the implications for their businesses. These skills become even more important for large multinational organizations seeking to expand operations into new international markets. In choosing between setting up facilities in the UK or the Euro Zone, the company has to be capable of understanding how the different policy issues will influence each economic region and businesses inside those regions.

This chapter will develop your understanding of key macroeconomic variables, namely, GDP, inflation, unemployment and the balance of payments. You will discover how each variable is measured and the concerns and policy issues associated with each variable. The importance of priorities and trade-offs between each macroeconomic variable will be highlighted.

10.2 **GDP: measurement and policy**

The aggregate demand and supply framework developed in Chapter 9 highlighted the importance of GDP and inflation. As aggregate demand or supply changed, the equilibrium level of GDP and inflation changed accordingly. We will begin by analysing GDP.

GDP

Variations in GDP over time

Figure 10.1 is a plot GDP growth for the UK over the period 1990 to 2005. GDP is an estimate of the amount of economic activity in an economy and is produced by the Office for National Statistics. Since 1990, UK GDP has grown at various rates between −1.5 per cent and 4.25 per cent per annum. In 2005 GDP topped $9 trillion. Trend growth in the UK is around 2.5 per cent per annum. Whenever growth is below 2.5 per cent then the economy is experiencing slowing economic growth. Persistent slow growth, can constitute a recession. Whenever GDP growth is above 2.5 per cent the economy is heading towards economic boom. The variation between recession and boom is known as the **business cycle**. In fact, Figure 10.1 is a picture of the business cycle, where the economy moves through a series of booms and recessions.

The **business cycle** describes the tendency of an economy to move from economic boom to economic recession and then back into boom to repeat the cycle.

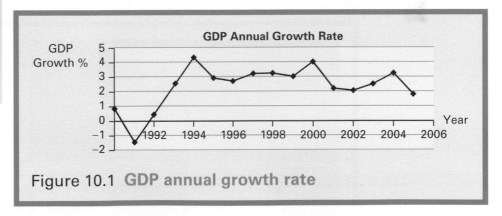

Figure 10.1 **GDP annual growth rate**

Measuring economic output

By examining the circular flow of income, in Chapter 9, we can see three potential ways of measuring output. We can either measure (i) the net value of goods and services produced by firms, (ii) the value of household earnings, or (iii) the value of spending on goods and services. We are simply measuring the flow at different points; each is equally applicable and will provide a similar figure to the rest.

However, the net value of goods and services approach needs to avoid the problem of double counting.

We can examine the manufacture of a car as an example. A car contains many different parts to be assembled and then sold to a customer through a dealership. Consider paint as one component. Assume the raw materials for car paint are £100; the car paint producer mixes the materials, packages them and sends them to the car maker at a price of £200. This mixing, packaging and distribution represent, £200 − £100 = £100 of value added. The car maker uses many different inputs, including paint, exhausts and engines. All the inputs cost £10 000. But the car is sold to the dealership for £12 000, so the value added from designing and assembling a car is £12 000 − £10 000 = £2000. The dealer polishes the car, shows it in a clean showroom environment, provides test drives and sells the car for £13 000. So, the **value added** of the dealership is £13 000 − £12 000 = £1000. If we add up all the value added in the economy, or we use statisticians to estimate total value added, then we have an estimate of total economic activity, or GDP.

Unfortunately, there are two more complications which need be considered when measuring economic output. The first recognizes that not all factors of production are domestically owned and profits from the use of these resources will flow to another country. For example, Toyota the Japanese car manufacturer owns production facilities in Turkey and the UK. Until recently, the UK telecommunications company Vodafone owned a Japanese telecommunications company. The flows of profits, interest and dividends from these assets are known as property incomes; and the balance of flows for any particular country is known as net property income.

The (i) output and (iii) expenditure methods will not add to the (ii) incomes measure of output without making a correction for net property income. We therefore make a distinction between Gross Domestic Product, GDP, and Gross National Product, GNP, which is GDP adjusted for net property income from abroad.

The second issue is to recognize that the creation of economic output results from the use of productive capital. This is such items as plant, machinery, buildings and shops. All of which need to be maintained, repaired or replaced as they wear out. These

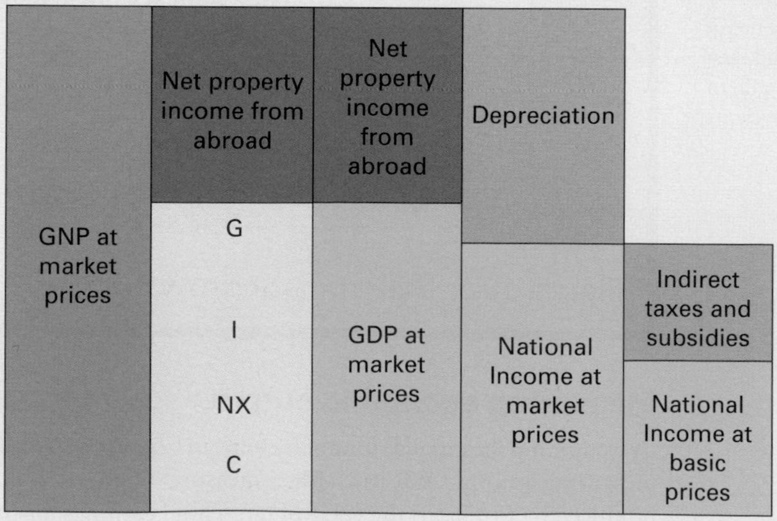

> **Value added** is net output, after deducting goods and services used up during the production process.

Figure 10.2 National Income accounting

expenditures come under the heading of depreciation. Subtracting depreciation from GDP leads to National Income.

Finally, all prices are quoted as market price, which can be distorted by indirect taxes and subsidies. In order to measure economic output we would prefer price measures which are not distorted by taxes and subsidies: these are known as basic prices. Adjusting National Income at market prices for the distortion of taxes and subsidies leaves us with the figure of National Income at basic prices. Figure 10.2 provides an illustration of all of these adjustments.

GDP policy issues

> **GDP per capita** is the GDP for the economy divided by the population of the economy. GDP per capita provides a measure of average income per person.

Is higher GDP preferable? Broadly speaking, yes. Higher GDP means more goods and services are being produced. Households' economic resources are being used more fully by firms and, as a result, financial payments to households rise. The level of income within an economy is often measured as **GDP per capita**.

We can see in Table 10.1 the level of GDP per capita for 30 leading countries in the world. All values have been converted into US dollars. These figures suggest that average income per person in the UK is around $14 000 lower than in the US.

However, higher GDP per capita can mask an unequal distribution of GDP among individuals within an economy (see Box 10.2).

Table 10.1 GDP per capita

Country	GDP per capita $	Rank	Country	GDP per capita $	Rank
Luxembourg	36 400	1	Iceland	24 800	16
United States	36 200	2	Jersey	24 800	17
Bermuda	33 000	3	Cayman Islands	24 500	18
San Marino	32 000	4	France	24 400	19
Switzerland	28 600	5	Netherlands	24 400	20
Aruba	28 000	6	Germany	23 400	21
Norway	27 700	7	Australia	23 200	22
Monaco	27 000	8	Liechtenstein	23 000	23
Singapore	26 500	9	Finland	22 900	24
Denmark	25 500	10	UAE	22 800	25
Hong Kong	25 400	11	United Kingdom	22 800	26
Belgium	25 300	12	Sweden	22 200	27
Austria	25 000	13	Italy	22 100	28
Japan	24 900	14	Ireland	21 600	29
Canada	24 800	15	Guam	21 000	30

Source: CIA Factbook

Box 10.2 **Gaps in income and wealth still remain large**

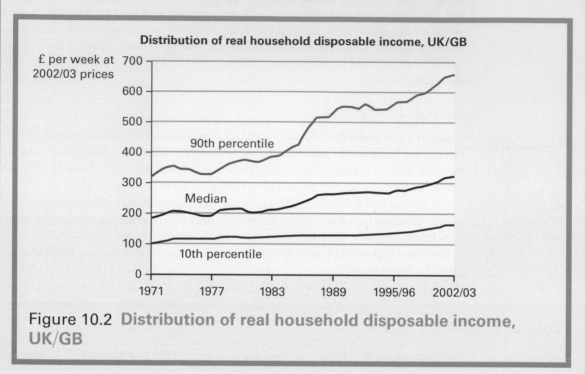

Figure 10.2 **Distribution of real household disposable income, UK/GB**

The extent of inequality in the income distribution has changed considerably over the last three decades. Between 1994/95 and 2002/03 the income distribution was broadly stable. Disposable income (adjusted for inflation) grew by over a fifth for both those on incomes at the top of the distribution (90th percentile) and those at the lower end (10th percentile).

However, between 1981 and 1989 disposable income in real terms grew by 38 per cent for those at the 90th percentile. This was more than five times the rate of growth of 7 per cent for those at the 10th percentile.

The distribution of wealth is even more unequal than that of income. Half the population of the UK owned just 5 per cent of the wealth in 2001. This compares with 8 per cent in 1976. However, wealth became more evenly distributed over the 20th century as a whole. It is estimated that the richest 1 per cent held around 70 per cent of the UK's wealth in 1911, compared with 23 per cent in 2001.

Source: Office for National Statistics

Sustainable economic growth

These distributional elements aside, a broad consensus is that high levels of GDP and growth in GDP are desirable. Indeed, the UK government has made 'sustainable economic growth' a central element of its economic policy. A common reason for promoting economic growth is employment. If households are buying firms' products, then firms will be using households' labour. However, when a recession occurs, households buy less, firms produce less and, as a consequence, firms employ fewer workers. As we will see later, unemployment and employment are, therefore, linked to the business cycle and economic growth.

Economies with higher levels of GDP are better able to invest in the economy's infrastructure, such as schools, hospitals and roads. This is because higher levels of GDP are likely to lead to higher incomes for workers. This in turn will result in increased taxes being paid to the government. Higher tax receipts enable the government to invest in important assets, such as schools, teachers, nurses, motorways and rail networks. Road and rail improvements help business to move products around, while better education and health services enable individuals to be more productive over their lifetime.

A combination of rising profits and better educational systems in a growing economy can facilitate improved levels of, and success in, research and development. Innovation can aid the development of new products that improve the lifestyle of individuals in the economy. Or innovation can bring about new and cheaper ways of making products. The Internet is a good example of both. It has changed how people can access many types of information and it has reduced the cost of providing consumers with banking and retail services.

Trade-off between GDP and inflation

However, a cautionary note regarding higher GDP has to be made. If higher GDP stems from an increase in aggregate demand, then higher inflation will follow. This is depicted on the left-hand side of Figure 10.3. However, if higher GDP stems from an increase in aggregate supply, then lower inflation will follow; see the right-hand side of Figure 10.3. Therefore, if economic growth is important, a crucial and basic question to ask is, how are higher levels of GDP attained and what are the implications for inflation? We will now explore these issues further by considering inflation and, more important, the targeting of inflation.

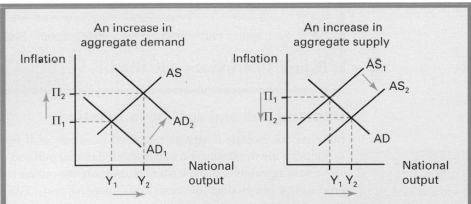

Figure 10.3 Trade-offs between GDP and inflation

Left-hand side: an increase in aggregate demand from AD_1 to AD_2 results in the equilibrium levels of GDP increasing from Y_1 to Y_2. But inflation also rises from Π_1 to Π_2.

Right-hand side: an increase in aggregate supply from AS_1 to AS_2 results in the equilibrium levels of GDP increasing from Y_1 to Y_2, while inflation falls from Π_1 to Π_2.

10.3 **Inflation: measurement and policy**

Variations in inflation over time

In Figure 10.4 we have a graph of inflation in the UK. Prices are currently rising at around 2 per cent and the government has a target rate of 2.0 per cent. But we can see that in our recent history inflation has been much greater, even approaching 25 per cent. But, more important, look at Figure 10.3 around the mid 1970s, 1980 and 1990, the same years that were associated with recessions in Figure 10.1. In the mid 1970s inflation was very high. So, the UK experienced an inflationary recession. But in 1980 and 1990 **the rate of inflation** dropped, so we then experienced deflationary recessions. Finally, note that in Figure 10.1 we pointed out the economic boom of the late 1980s; if you examine inflation around the same time, it was rising, so the UK experienced an inflationary boom.

> The **rate of inflation** is a measure of how fast prices are rising.

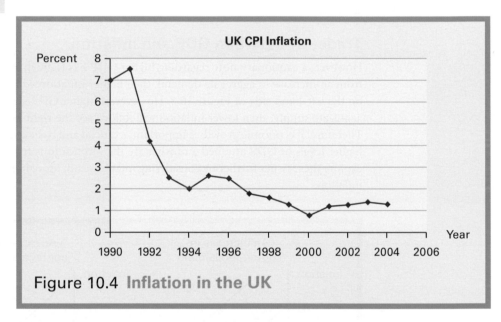

Figure 10.4 Inflation in the UK

Demand pull and cost push inflation

Inflation can increase if aggregate demand increases, or if aggregate supply decreases. Economists use this distinction to talk about **demand pull** and **cost push inflation**.

A rise in aggregate demand leads to many more consumers trying to buy products. But producing more products increases firms' marginal costs. This leads to firms increasing prices in order to recoup the higher costs of production. Demand pull inflation is depicted in Figure 10.5. An increase in aggregate demand moves the macroeconomic equilibrium along the aggregate supply curve, to a point where output and inflation are both higher.

In the case of cost push inflation, firms' costs of producing products increases. Wage rates might increase or, as in 1973, the cost of oil might increase, making fuel, plastics and distribution more expensive. As costs rise, firms find it difficult to make a profit and some may even exit the market. In Figure 10.6 aggregate supply reduces and the macroeconomic equilibrium changes, with national output falling and inflation increasing.

> **Demand pull inflation** occurs when a rise in aggregate demand leads to an increase in overall prices.
> **Cost push inflation** occurs when a reduction in supply leads to an increase in overall prices.

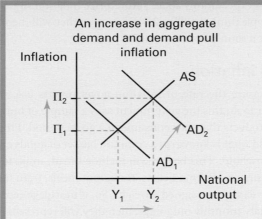

Figure 10.5 Demand pull inflation

An increase in aggregate demand shifts the AD curve from AD_1 to AD_2. This results in a new equilibrium where inflation rises to Π_2 and output to Y_2. Inflation has been pulled up by an increase in aggregate demand.

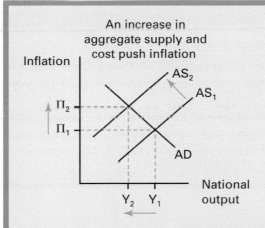

Figure 10.6 Cost push inflation

An increase in input prices, such as a rise in wage rates or the cost of raw materials, increases firms' costs. With higher costs, firms are less able to make profit. Some firms exit the market and, as a result, aggregate supply is less and shifts to the left. The macroeconomic equilibrium changes, with national output falling and inflation increasing. Increasing input prices push up inflation across the economy.

Inflationary expectations

Expectations are beliefs held by firms, workers and consumers about the future level of prices.

Expectations are also seen as an important determinant of inflationary pressures.

For example, if workers think prices in general will rise by 2.0 per cent, they will ask for a 2.0 per cent pay rise in order to keep their level of earnings constant. Because they ask for 2.0 per cent, the cost of making goods goes up by 2.0 per cent, so final prices rise by 2.0 per cent. As a result, expectations become self-fulfilling prophecies. Now it should be clear why the government explicitly targets 2.5 per cent for inflation. It is trying to manage society's expectations about future price inflation. By saying inflation should be 2.5 per cent, people think it will be 2.5 per cent, so they will then demand 2.5 per cent pay rises and inflation should converge on 2.5 per cent.

Measuring inflation

In order to measure the rate of inflation governments use what are known as price indices. In order to do this the government asks a sample of households across the UK to record all the products that they consume in a given period. From this data, government statisticians build what is known as a common basket of goods and services bought by the average UK household. This basket will include bread, milk, tobacco, petrol, mortgage repayments, insurance, cinema tickets, restaurant meals, train fares and so on.

Each good or service is assigned a weight. So, if mortgage repayments represent 50 per cent of individuals' monthly outgoings, then they will represent 50 per cent of the basket. If bread only represents 2 per cent of monthly outgoings then bread will only fill 2 per cent of the basket. The price of all these goods and services are then monitored on a monthly basis. A report of price changes within the basket is provided in Box 10.3 from the Office for National Statistics.

 Box 10.3 Condoms used to measure inflation

Adapted from Office for National Statistics, March 2006

The UK's Office for National Statistics (ONS) updates its list every March and this year corned beef and cycle helmets were two of the products removed to make way for chicken nuggets, champagne and fizzy drinks.

In Cyprus the anti-impotency drug Viagra might be joining the shopping basket of items used by the Cypriot government to measure inflation. The Cypriots are also looking into the inclusion of hair wax, contact lenses, hair gel, hands-free mobile phone accessories, pay-TV subscriptions, blank CDs and a visit to the osteopath.

Index and base years

The price index has a base year, where the value of the index, or the basket of goods and services, is set at 100 (see Chapter 1 for a reminder). Inflation is a measure of how quickly prices are rising and it measures the difference between the price level last year and the price level this year. As such, inflation is measured as:

Inflation = (Index in current year – Index in previous year)/Index in previous year

In Table 10.2 the **price index** has been set at 100 for the year 2002, and it rises to 113 by the year 2006. Using the formula above, the inflation rate in 2003 was 2 per cent, while in 2005 it was 4.8 per cent.

The **price index** can be used to deflate current prices into constant prices, where constant prices are prices expressed in the base year.

Box 10.4 **Price changes within the common basket of goods and services**

Inflation falls to 2.1%

Adapted from the Office for National Statistics, 13 December 2005

CPI annual inflation – the Government's target measure – fell to 2.1% in November. The largest downward effect on the CPI annual rate came from transport. Petrol and diesel prices fell for the second successive month, with the average price of ultra-low sulphur petrol down by 3.6p per litre, compared with a rise of 1.1p a year ago. There was also a large downward effect from air travel, with fares on international routes falling by more than a year ago, particularly to European destinations.

A small downward contribution came from restaurants and hotels, with the cost of accommodation services falling this year, particularly for overnight stays in UK hotels, but rising a year ago. A small upward contribution to the CPI annual rate came from alcoholic beverages and tobacco, with retailers continuing to pass on price increases which started in October affecting all tobacco items. Upward pressure also came from food and non-alcoholic beverages, mainly due to meat prices rising by more than last year, particularly for beef products.

Table 10.2 Price index and inflation

Year	Price index	Inflation	Nominal salary	Real salary
2002	100		£20 000	£20 000
2003	102	(102 − 100)/100 = 2.0%	£20 000	£19 608
2004	105	(105 − 102)/102 = 2.9%	£20 000	£19 048
2005	110	(110 − 105)/105 = 4.8%	£20 000	£18 182
2006	113	(113 − 110)/110 = 2.7%	£20 000	£17 699

Price deflators

For example, suppose in 2002 you earned £20 000 and that by 2006 your boss had refused to give you a pay rise and you still only earned £20 000. We can calculate your real wage in each year by using the price index to convert your salary into year 2000 prices as follows.

Real salary = (Nominal salary) × (100/Price index)

So, a nominal salary of £20 000 in 2006 is a real salary of only £20 000 × (100/113) = £17 699. In other words, £20 000 has lost £2301 in value since 2002. This has wider implications: whenever prices are compared over time, whether it be house prices, car prices, wages or wine, they need to be adjusted for inflation and converted into constant prices. Price indices provide a means of achieving this.

Costs of inflation

In recent decades governments around the world, including the UK, have begun to set inflation targets. This is because inflation can be costly. But this cost should not be confused with goods and services becoming more expensive.

For example: 'When I was a lad, a bag of chips cost 5p; now they cost £1.' But chips are not 20 times more expensive now than they were 25 years ago. This is because incomes have also risen by the same amount. So, we will only think inflation makes things more expensive if we suffer from **inflation illusion**. However, if we do suffer from inflation illusion, then we may cut back on consumption, believing the product to be too expensive. If enough people reduce consumption, then a recession may occur.

Even without inflation illusion, inflation can still be costly. If prices are rising quickly, retailers will be constantly changing their prices. Shelf labels will have to be changed at supermarkets and price lists will have to be changed by other types of sellers. These are known as **menu costs** and the more rapidly prices rise, the more often prices have to be changed. So, inflation can create additional costs.

> People suffer **inflation illusion** if they confuse nominal and real changes.

> **Menu costs** are associated with the activity and cost of changing prices in shops, price lists and, of course, menus.

Fiscal drag

Let us assume inflation is fully expected and full adjustment occurs. Price rises of 10 per cent are matched by wage increases of 10 per cent. There are no initial cutbacks in consumption by buyers and, therefore, no recessionary consequences. But what if the government does not adjust its tax policy?

In 2006/07 the UK government allowed individuals to earn £5035 before having to pay tax. If incomes rose by 10 per cent and the government did not lift the tax allowance by 10 per cent, then individuals would start paying more real tax. Therefore, this time, even with fully anticipated inflation, inflexibility by the government creates an inflationary cost known as **fiscal drag**.

Assets and liabilities

If mortgage interest rates are 5 per cent and inflation is 2.5 per cent, then the real interest rate is $5 - 2.5 = 2.5$ per cent. Viewed this way the lender is not making 5 per cent profits out of its customers. Rather, it is gaining 2.5 per cent to cover the rise in inflation and then it is gaining 2.5 per cent as its profit. If lenders and borrowers expect 2.5 per cent inflation, then the real cost of funds is 2.5 per cent. But what happens if expectations are wrong and inflation suddenly rises to 10 per cent? The real interest rate would become $5 - 10 = -5$ per cent. Lenders are now losing 5 per cent a year and borrowers are gaining 5 per cent a year. There is a transfer of wealth from lenders to borrowers.

> **Fiscal drag** occurs when tax-free income allowances grow at a slower rate than earnings. This reduces the real value of tax-free allowances, leading to high real tax receipts.

Borrowers tend to be young people starting out in life, buying a home and raising a family. Lenders tend to be older people who have raised their family and paid off the mortgage and are now saving with banks and building societies. Therefore, a surprise rise in the inflation rate transfers wealth from old people to young people. This influences the spending patterns of old people in a negative way and young people in a positive way. An obvious cost is the need for product suppliers to react to these consumption changes and develop different product lines to meet the main spenders in the economy. Therefore, inflation can create costs through structural change.

Why target inflation?

The answer to this question is very simple. If aggregate supply is perfectly inelastic and aggregate demand increases, there will be no increase in output; the only impact will be higher inflation. This is illustrated in Figure 10.7. Whenever aggregate demand shifts to the right, the government, or central bank, will pursue policies to shift aggregate demand back to the left and, therefore, keep inflation constant. The economy can now only grow if the aggregate supply curve shifts to the left.

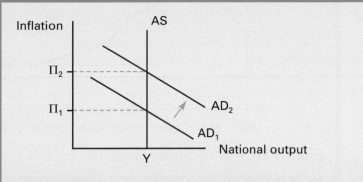

Figure 10.7 Aggregate demand and inelastic aggregate supply

AS is aggregate supply and represents total supply in the economy. As aggregate demand increases from AD_1 to AD_2, national output remains constant at Y, but inflation rises from Π_1 to Π_2.

Frictional unemployment refers to individuals who have quit one job and are currently searching for another job. As such, frictional unemployment is temporary.
Cyclical unemployment is related to the business cycle and is sometimes also referred to as demand deficient unemployment. Cyclical unemployment reflects workers who have lost jobs due to the adversities of the business cycle.

The crucial issue is whether price stability from inflation targeting enables aggregate supply to expand and shift to the right. The belief is that inflation targeting reduces uncertainty in the economy, making investment decisions easier for firms. Volatile inflation rates lead to booms and busts within the economy, as governments try to bring inflation under control. The variations of the business cycle can make investment unprofitable. Therefore, if investment in capital increases the productive capacity of the economy and ultimately the level of aggregate supply, inflation targeting could be highly desirable. We will revisit these arguments during our discussion of fiscal, monetary and supply side policies in Chapters 11 and 12.

10.4 Unemployment

While managing GDP and inflation have moved to the fore of economic policy, unemployment has retreated into the background. There are, perhaps, two reasons for this. First, as illustrated in Figure 10.8, unemployment has fallen sharply in recent times and is now around 1 million individuals, which is markedly below the level of 3 million which was reached in the early 1990s. Compared with Germany, unemployment has not been an important political issue in the UK. Second, the emphasis of government policy has shifted from the number of workers in employment to the productivity and skills base of existing workers. The productivity of UK workers, when compared with workers from our European partners, is seen as a central determinant of UK competitiveness, with more productive workers leading to lower production costs.

Economists identify four categories of unemployment: **frictional**, **cyclical**, **structural** and **classical**.

Structural unemployment occurs when an industry moves into decline. The structurally unemployed find it difficult to gain employment in new industries because of what is known as a mismatch of skills. Shipbuilders know how to build ships; they are less skilled at building houses, or working in a call centre.

Classical unemployment refers to workers who have priced themselves out of a job.

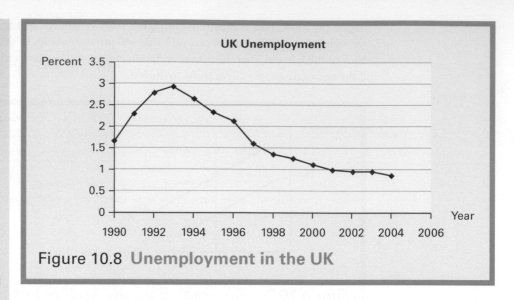

Figure 10.8 Unemployment in the UK

If workers, or their unions, manage to negotiate wages that are higher than the equilibrium wage then, as we saw in Chapter 4, demand will be less than supply. A surplus in the labour market is illustrated in Figure 10.9. When the wage rate rises above the equilibrium rate, two things happen. First, at the higher wage more workers are willing to supply themselves for work. Second, at the higher wage, firms are less willing to demand workers. These two changes create a surplus in the market, with firms being unwilling to demand all workers who are willing to supply themselves for work. Those individuals who are willing to supply themselves for work, but are not demanded by firms are unemployed.

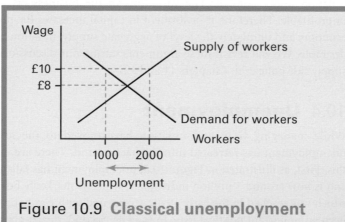

Figure 10.9 Classical unemployment

At the equilibrium wage rate of £8 per hour, the supply of workers is equal to the demand for workers. The market clears with all workers who want to work finding employment. Unemployment is zero. If workers, or unions, are successful in raising the wage rate to £10 per hour, then the supply of workers increases, as more individuals are willing to work once the wage rate increases. But, in contrast, firms are less willing to demand the more expensive workers. So, with the wage rate above the equilibrium a surplus exists with 1000 workers unemployed.

Measuring unemployment

The government measures unemployment on a monthly basis. Over time the measure, or definition, of unemployment has changed many times. However, the UK government has used the International Labour Organisation's definition of unemployment for a number of years.

The ILO definition of unemployment is a count of jobless people who want to work, are available to work, and are actively seeking employment.

The ILO measure is used internationally, so a benefit of the measure is that it enables comparisons between countries to be made and it is also consistent over time.

An alternative measure used in the UK is the **claimant count**.

The claimant count is generally lower than the ILO measure of unemployment because some individuals may be willing to work, but are unable to register for the job seekers' allowance.

Reflecting the separate categories of unemployment, such as frictional and structural, the measures are generally broken down into region, age and time in unemployment. This provides an assessment of where unemployment is highest, which perhaps relates to industries, thereby identifying structural unemployment. Unemployment in high age groups could reflect skill mismatch between older workers and newer industries, while time in unemployment may reflect the difference between frictional unemployment and other types of unemployment.

The **claimant count** simply measures the number of people who are eligible and receiving the job seekers' allowance.

Policies issues

Should unemployment be reduced? Unemployment represents a wasted resource. Unemployed workers would like to work but cannot. If unemployed workers were employed, then GDP could increase. Furthermore, unemployment might be linked to increased stress and illness and, therefore, it places increased strains on individuals, families and the health sector. So, we can see that reducing unemployment is perhaps a good idea. However, such arguments need to be tempered by the insights offered by the **Phillips curve**.

Figure 10.10 illustrates the Phillips curve, indicating a negative relationship between inflation and unemployment. Lower unemployment is gained at the expense of higher inflation.

The Phillips curve was developed by Professor Phillips from the London School of Economics in 1958 after observing inflation and unemployment in the UK. 'Observe' is the crucial word, because the theoretical reasons for a Phillips curve relationship between unemployment and inflation are weak.

Initially, the Phillips curve looked very attractive, showing a clear trade-off between unemployment and inflation. The government merely had to decide which of inflation and unemployment it disliked the most. If the government disliked unemployment, then it had to suffer higher inflation. The problem of the Phillips curve being simply an observation became a serious consideration in the 1970s when the relationship broke down. As unemployment increased, so did inflation. The government no longer witnessed a trade-off between inflation and unemployment.

We can explain the breakdown in the Phillips curve relationship by returning to our discussion of aggregate supply and inflation with full, or partial, real wage adjustments to inflation. If real wages do not increase by as much as inflation, then workers, in real terms, become cheaper to employ and firms will demand more workers. Therefore, higher inflation can lead to a reduction in unemployment. However, if real wages adjust

The **Phillips curve** shows that lower unemployment is associated with higher inflation. Simply, lower unemployment has to be traded for higher inflation.

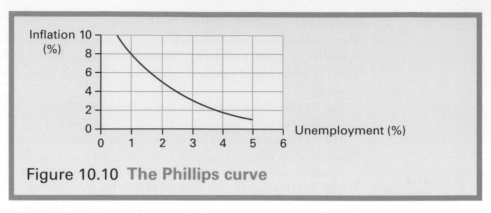

Figure 10.10 The Phillips curve

fully to higher inflation, the real cost of workers remains constant. Firms will not demand any more workers and, as a result, unemployment remains constant. There will be no trade-off between inflation and unemployment. What we will observe instead is a short- and a long-run Phillips curve, as in Figure 10.11. In the long run unemployment will be constant at what is referred to as the **natural rate of unemployment**. The natural rate of unemployment should be essentially composed of the frictionally unemployed.

The **natural rate of unemployment** is the unemployment rate when the economy is operating at full employment.

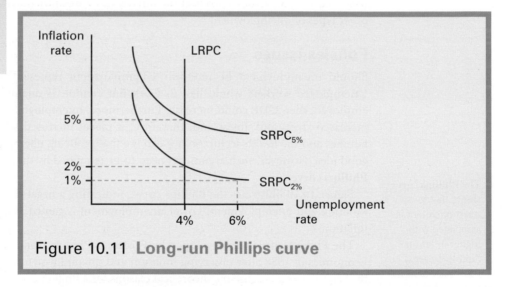

Figure 10.11 Long-run Phillips curve

In Figure 10.11 the long-run Phillips curve, LRPC, is vertical and suggests a 4 per cent natural rate of unemployment at all inflation rates. Each short-run curve is associated with an expected inflation rate. So for the short-run Phillips Curve SRPC$_{2 \text{ per cent}}$ there is an expectation that inflation will be 2 per cent. If it turns out that inflation is lower, at say 1 per cent, then unemployment in the short run will increase to 6 per cent. This is because firms will have expected prices to rise faster in order to meet the expected wage inflation of 2 per cent. Firms therefore cut back on employment.

If the government changed the target inflation rate to 5 per cent, then expectations would change and the new short-run Phillips curve would be SRPC$_{5 \text{ per cent}}$. In the long run unemployment will be at the natural rate, but inflation will be at the higher rate of 5 per cent. A trade-off can still occur between inflation and unemployment in the short run as long as the actual rate of inflation differs from the expected rate.

These ideas are important because rising inflation, or nominal values, do not lead to an increase in aggregate supply or an increase in GDP and, therefore, no increase in employment. The only way to make the economy grow is to improve real values. The most obvious means of improving the real value of labour is to improve labour's productivity. If, for example, a worker is paid £10 per hour and extra training results in the worker producing 5 rather than 2 units of output, then the worker has become more productive. The cost per unit of output has fallen and firms will be more willing to produce output and hire increased numbers of productive workers. Hence, government's focus on productivity and not unemployment.

10.5 Balance of payments

We will cover the balance of payments in detail in Chapter 13 but, essentially, the balance of payments represents a country's net position with the rest of the world. Consider your own position. You might provide a service to a company and receive a wage in return. You may then buy products and pay cash in return. If the value of the goods that you buy is greater than the value of work you provide to an employer, then your wage will be less than your spending. On a net basis, the cash flows into your bank account will be less than the cash flows out, and you may need an overdraft. In reverse, if you spend less than you receive as a wage, then the cash into your account will be greater than the cash out, and you will begin to save.

The balance of payments measures these flows for an economy, rather than for a person. For example, if the UK is buying, or importing, more goods and services than it is exporting to overseas, then the UK will have to transfer financial resource from the UK to overseas. In contrast, if the UK is exporting more than it is importing, then financial resource to pay for the exports will flow into the UK. Reflecting these points, the balance of payments measures the flow of goods and services between the UK and its trading partners; and the financial flows between the UK and its trading partners. The Office for National Statistics measures these flows for the government.

Policy issues

Is it bad to run a balance of payments deficit with the rest of the world?

In the short run, a one-off deficit is unlikely to be a problem, much as a temporary overdraft is unlikely to be a problem for you. At some point in the future you may expect to run a surplus by working extra hours and earning money to pay off your debts. Similarly, a country may expect to run a deficit this year and a surplus next year. More important, why has the deficit occurred? In your case, as a student you may have an overdraft, or student loan, because you are investing in your future productivity as a worker. Similarly, a country may be running an external deficit with its overseas partners because it is purchasing high-productivity capital items, which will improve the country's productivity in the future.

In the long run, the real concern arises when the deficit represents a structural, as opposed to a temporary, problem. For example, you may not be a highly valuable worker and you may be earning a low wage, but you do have very expensive tastes. As a result, you will run a deficit, spending more on goods and services than you earn in income. Similarly, if a country produces low-quality output but demands high-quality and expensive products from overseas, then it will run a deficit. The way for you to solve your debt problems is for you to either stop spending or improve your value as a worker and gain a higher wage. Similarly, a country has to improve the type, quality and cost of the products that it sells to the rest of the world. In essence, by becoming more internationally competitive a country may be able to generate the finances that it requires to fund its expenditure on expensive imports.

How a country improves its international competitiveness may present another trade-off for the government. Reducing aggregate demand will result in lower inflation and more internationally competitive prices. But lowering aggregate demand may also lead to a recession. Perhaps the best option is to once again return to managing aggregate supply, introducing policies that lead to an increase in aggregate supply and a reduction in the rate of inflation, coupled with an expansion of GDP.

10.6 Macroeconomic policies

The discussion has highlighted how changes in aggregate demand and aggregate supply lead to changes in the GDP and inflation. Changes in these variables may ultimately lead to changes in unemployment and the balance of payments. We have also discussed the policy issues associated with GDP, inflation, unemployment and the balance of payments, arguing why governments are interested in managing each of these macroeconomic variables. Higher GDP can improve income levels across the economy, while low and stable inflation may provide a preferable investment environment for firms. The clear question is, how do governments control aggregate demand and aggregate supply and thereby manage the economy?

The answer to these questions will be discussed at length in Chapters 11 and 12. However, as an introduction we can identify demand and supply side policies:

- Demand side policies influence aggregate demand.

- Fiscal policy is the use of government spending and taxation to influence the level of aggregate demand in the economy.

- Monetary policy is the use of interest rates to influence the level of demand in the economy.

In Chapter 11 we will see how the government can use fiscal and monetary policies to control the economy.

Given that we have seen that aggregate supply can be vertical, or perfectly price inelastic, then aggregate supply defines the equilibrium level of GDP for the economy. In the long run, growth in GDP and lower inflation can only occur with an increase in aggregate supply. Therefore, sustainable economic growth, low inflation and even international competitiveness are crucially linked to developments in aggregate supply. How aggregate supply can be managed by government and the implications of **supply side policies** for business will be discussed in Chapter 12.

Supply side policies influence aggregate supply.

10.7 Business application: international competitiveness and the macroeconomy

Box 10.5 details the economic decline of Italy. Highlighting the bi-directional relationship between industrial competitiveness and macroeconomic performance. Competitiveness matters for the entire economy. It matters for a number of basic reasons: competitiveness in manufacturing is a source of economic growth, it can deliver export growth; it can help to stem a balance of payments problem. It funds investment in infrastructure and education; and it raises living standards.

Box 10.5 **For all its attractions, Italy is caught in a long, slow decline**

Adapted from an article in The Economist, 24 November 2005

The economic miracle after the Second World War, culminating when Italy's GDP surpassed that of the UK, has faltered. Italy's average economic growth over the past 15 years has been the slowest in the European Union. Its economy is now only about 80% the size of Britain's.

Italian family-owned firms, which have been the backbone of the economy, are under ever-increasing pressure. Costs have risen, but productivity has declined. Italy's competitiveness is deteriorating fast, and its shares of world exports and foreign direct investment is very low. Also, because so many small Italian firms specialize in such areas as textiles, shoes, furniture and white goods, they are bearing the brunt of South-East Asian competition.

Italians' living standards are falling. The cost of living is widely believed to have risen sharply under the Euro. Many Italians are cutting back on their annual holidays, new cars and even suits. Supermarkets report that spending now falls in the fourth week of every month before the next pay cheque arrives.

A lacklustre economy is causing broader problems too. Roads, railways and airports are falling below the standards of the rest of Europe. Educational standards have slipped and no Italian university now makes it into the world's top 90. Spending on research and development is low by international standards.

Manufacturing competitiveness, GDP growth and inflation

Manufacturing can be a source of economic growth. Manufacturers of products often compete in global markets. By competing overseas, manufacturers can face increased competition from international rivals. In order to compete and survive, manufacturers can face enormous incentives to improve productivity and the quality of their products.

Investing in workers' skills and new capital technology can improve productivity. Investing in product innovation can improve the quality of the product to end-users. Spillover effects into the rest of the economy may occur if high-skilled workers move to alternative employers, taking their enhanced skills with them. Moreover, workers' experience of using advanced capital equipment may enable other firms to consider purchasing such equipment. Finally, if manufacturers make machines for other companies to use, product innovation may result in improved productivity for end-users. Therefore, manufacturing competitiveness may not only drive economic growth but, through productivity gains and cost improvements, manufacturing competitiveness may also enhance aggregate supply and aid the management of inflation.

Manufacturing competitiveness and the balance of payments

The balance of payments records trading position with the rest of the world. As manufacturing declines, consumers have to import goods, which previously they would have previously purchased from domestic producers. Relying on imports is not a major problem. The issue is, how do we finance the purchase of imports?

In the case of the UK the rise of the service-based economy and service-based exports, such as insurance and banking, has helped to fund the importation of goods. But since manufacturing exports are worth around five times more than exported services, the UK will have to export more services than it would have to export goods. A significant problem is that services do not export easily. Leisure centres, restaurants, cinemas, legal and accounting services and even hairdressing are not easy to export.

Manufacturing competitiveness and employment

Skills required for the manufacture of steel, cars, industrial equipment, domestic appliances, chemicals and even jet fighter aircraft are fairly specific to the industry. If one of these manufacturing sectors declines, then the potential for structural unemployment is immense. Even if service sector employers were to consider locating in areas of high unemployment, the mismatch of skills between unemployed manufacturing workers and the needs of service sector providers are likely to be significant. Manufacturing competitiveness may, therefore, be important to the economy, if only to prevent costly structural change.

Not all economists would agree with the points listed above. Some may think that the points made above are valid, but that they overstate the case for manufacturing competitiveness. If manufacturing has declined, then there must be something inherently wrong about the location of manufacturing sectors in economies such as Italy or the UK. It could be that there are resources in South-East Asia which are more appropriate for a manufacturing base – more abundant labour, better logistics networks, better financing options. It could be that European firms need to migrate to alternative parts of the value chain where they retain a competitive advantage. For example, Italians may have lost competitiveness in shoe manufacture, but they are still perhaps the best shoe designers. The critical success factor for the macroeconomy is adaptation, flexibility and migration to the next commercial opportunity. But this requires modern, up-to-date infrastructure in communications, work space and skills set. Unfortunately, in the case of Italy, the worry is that a lack of economic success has led to a crumbly infrastructure and decay in educational development These are not the vital signs of a healthy, adaptive macroeconomic environment.

Understanding policy

Regardless of how important manufacturing competitiveness is to the economy, it is clear that a case can be built for manufacturing having beneficial consequences for GDP, inflation, employment and the balance of payments or, more important, all of the macroeconomic objectives. But how will policy impact on manufacturing?

If manufacturing is a catalyst for economic growth through innovation and investment, low inflation and economic stability are essential for aiding manufacturers to invest. By keeping inflation low and stable, a government is endeavouring to create a stable environment within which firms feel the risk associated with investing are lower. With stable growth in GDP, the risk of an investment in new machinery being devalued by a recession is reduced.

In terms of aiding skill development, the government can invest heavily in higher education, channelling increasing numbers of students into undergraduate programmes. But, this does not always alleviate skills shortages. For every university graduate, the economy loses one important, but less skilled worker, such as lorry drivers, plumbers, builders and mechanics.

Will it work?

In the short run, business has to recognize that things can become worse before they get better. Low inflation and moderate stable economic growth have provided the UK with sound economic foundations. In the case of Italy, the Euro should help to keep inflation under control. However, under the Euro, prices across the Eurozone are extremely transparent and so without productivity growth, Italian competitiveness will continue to lag behind its Euro partners. If productivity is reasonably seen to reside within the quality of an economy's infrastructure and its labour skill set, then Italy may have a long period of adjustment.

10.8 Business policy: inflation targeting?

The European Central Bank and the Bank of England follow inflation-targeting policies, as do Australia, Brazil, Canada and Sweden. The US does not. What are the implications for business of a policy environment characterized by inflation targeting? Some of the basic issues are highlighted in Box 10.6.

The central issue is one of macroeconomic stability. This is a more general concern than simply one with low inflation fanaticism. Rather, macroeconomic stability can encompass stability in prices and in economic activity, namely GDP. Under inflation targeting, stability in pricing is seen as essential for stability in economic activity. While in contrast, a lack of inflation targeting, such as in the US, is associated with the direct management of economic activity.

The implications for business can be subtle but important. Within a regime of inflation targeting, there is little variation in the inflation rate. As a result interest rate changes to control inflation are small and infrequent, leading to minimal changes to GDP. The head

 ## Box 10.6 **What's the fuss over inflation targeting?**

Adapted from BusinessWeek, 7 November 2005

What is inflation targeting?

The central bank publicizes a target goal for the inflation rate – say, 2% a year. It then steers monetary policy to try to hit the target inflation rate. Raising rates to curb inflation and lowering rates to juice up growth and raise inflation.

Does it work?

Research indicates that countries which implement inflation-targeting policies tend to stabilize their inflation rates while keeping economic growth on an even keel.

Why does Bernanke favour inflation targeting in the US?

A more 'transparent' Federal Reserve policy would promote stable, non-inflationary economic growth by giving businesses and consumers more certainty about the future course of interest rates and inflation.

Why was Greenspan against it?

He thought the Fed could control inflation without announcing a target rate. In addition, he worries that an announced rate would make it harder to respond flexibly and intuitively to a financial crisis or changing economic conditions.

of the Bank of England has suggested that his role is to be as boring as possible (indicating that if inflation is kept under control, then there will be little need for large or even unexpected changes in interest rates to bring about stability in inflation). Such boring stability will shape the decisions and behaviour of consumers and firms. Wage bargaining and investment decisions will be carried out within a context of reasonable certainty of future price levels. With reduced risk and improved decision making a greater willingness to spend and invest should occur. As such, stability in economic activity is assured by a background of stable prices. Therefore, the implications for business are that tomorrow should be very much like today. In effect, no surprises and therefore boring. But boring has its virtues. When investing a huge sum of money in a project which may reach fruition in three to five years time, then a lack of surprises can be very comforting. Macroeconomic stability now can lead to greater and more valuable productive capacity in the future.

Unfortunately, the world is rarely boring. In Chapter 9, Figure 9.10, we saw that an increase in aggregate demand will lead to an inflationary expansion of the economy. An increase in interest rates would then help to reduce demand, leading to a falling inflation and cooling of the economy. If a rise in oil prices occurred, aggregate supply would be reduced, (as firms' costs increase) leading to an inflationary contraction. An increase in interest rates would now cut aggregate demand, reduce inflation and push the economy into an even larger recession. The link between inflation stability and economic stability is not necessarily assured. It maybe better to target GDP directly and place a lesser focus on inflation. In the case of rising oil prices a cut in interest rates might be more accommodating for an increase in GDP while costing an extra 1 or 2 per cent in inflation. The implications for business are important. Interest rates, wages, inflation and international competitiveness could all be more variable in the short run, while GDP should be more stable. On one level this policy is only beneficial to business if stability in GDP is of greater value than stability in inflation and interest rates. On another level, the acceptance of economic surprises and non-boring economic policy may represent a more realistic view of the macroeconomic environment within which a company operates.

 Summary

1 GDP is a measure of economic output.

2 The circular flow of income indicates that GDP can be measured using the income, expenditure and value-added approaches.

3 To avoid double counting, the value-added approach measures the incremental amount of value added at each stage of the production process.

4 GDP is compared across economies using GDP per capita. However, such a measure may hide an unequal distribution of income among the population.

5 Higher and stable levels of GDP are desirable policy objectives. Economic stability enables firms to invest in new capital equipment, leading to improved productivity and economic growth. Higher levels of GDP can, through tax receipts, enable governments to invest in important economic infrastructure, such as education and transport. However, higher GDP might lead to higher inflation.

6 A trade-off may exist between higher GDP and higher inflation.

7 Inflation measures the rate of change of prices. Faster price rises result in higher inflation.

8 A basket of goods and services, representing commonly purchased products, is used in the measurement of inflation. A price index is developed from the basket of goods and services and changes in the price index are used to measure inflation.

9 Demand pull inflation occurs when aggregate demand increases relative to aggregate supply.

10 Cost-push inflation occurs when aggregate supply increases relative to aggregate demand.

11 Inflationary expectations may also drive inflation. If workers expect prices to rise by 2 per cent, then they will ask for 2 per cent pay rises in order to maintain constant real wages. The 2 per cent pay rise may then be passed on in higher product prices and, as a result, the expectation of 2 per cent inflation becomes reality.

12 Inflation can create many costs, including the erosion of debt and increasing menu costs.

13 Inflation targeting may improve economic stability and business investment confidence. Increased investment in productive capital may improve the economy's aggregate supply, boosting GDP and reducing inflation.

14 Targeting increases in aggregate supply avoids the trade-off associated with aggregate demand, with higher demand increasing GDP and inflation.

15 Unemployment is categorized as frictional, structural, cyclical or classical.

16 The Phillips curve suggests a negative trade-off between inflation and unemployment. However, this relationship may only exist in the short run. When real wages fully adjust to inflationary changes, then unemployment will not vary with the inflation rate.

17 Following the shift towards improving aggregate supply, government policy has moved away from unemployment and more towards labour productivity.

18 A balance of payments deficit is problematic if it is persistent and reflects a country's lack of international competitiveness.

 Learning checklist

You should now be able to:

◆ Explain how to measure GDP using the income, expenditure and value-added approaches

◆ Explain how inflation is measured using a basket of goods and services and index numbers

◆ Explain the main drivers of inflation

◆ Provide a discussion of the main costs of inflation and reasons behind inflation targeting

◆ List and explain the main types of unemployment

◆ Explain the potential trade-off between inflation and unemployment

◆ Explain whether a balance of payments deficit is a problem

◆ Explain the relevance of economic policy considerations for business

❓ Questions

1 In Table 10.1 Luxembourg has the highest GDP per capita in the world. Is Luxembourg a good place to start a business?

2 The inflation forecast for next year is 3 per cent. Workers are asking for a 5 per cent pay rise. Should the firm agree to the 5 per cent rise?

3 Unemployment represents a pool of underutilized resource. Should firms relocate to areas of high unemployment?

4 Should a firm be concerned about an economy with a chronic balance of payments problem?

Exercises

1 True or false?
   a) GDP per capita is a measure of economic prosperity.
   b) High growth rates in GDP per capita can be accompanied by high inflation.
   c) Nominal wages are adjusted for inflation, real wages are not.
   d) A mismatch of skills generally results from cyclical unemployment.
   e) The Phillips curve suggests negative relationship between inflation and GDP
   f) A trade deficit is acceptable in the short run, but is troublesome in the long run.

2 Plot the data in Table 10.3 placing inflation on the Y axis and unemployment on the X axis.

Table 10.3

	Inflation Rate	Unemployment Rate
1994	2	8.8
1995	2.6	7.8
1996	2.5	7.1
1997	1.8	5.3
1998	1.6	4.5
1999	1.3	4.2
2000	0.8	3.7
2001	1.2	3.3
2002	1.3	3.2
2003	1.4	3.2
2004	1.3	2.9

   a) Is there evidence in support of a Phillips curve relationship?
   b) What is the long-run Phillips curve?
   c) At what level of unemployment would you propose drawing the long-run Phillips curve?

3   Consider Box 10.5 when considering the following questions:
   a)   'Italy's average economic growth over the past 15 years has been the slowest in the European Union.' Explain why this is a problem.
   b)   'Italy's competitiveness is deteriorating fast, and its shares of world exports and foreign direct investment are very low.' How would you measure competitiveness and why is competitiveness important for macroeconomic success?
   c)   Using evidence from within the case of Italy, identify how commercial fortunes are dependent upon macroeconomic factors; and also identify how the macroeconomic environment is conditioned by commercial success.

Chapter 11
Economic stability and demand side policies

Chapter contents

Learning outcomes

By the end of this chapter you should understand:

Economic Theory

- The Keynesian Cross approach to modelling equilibrium output
- The fiscal multiplier
- The balanced budget
- Problems associated with using fiscal policy
- The key features of money
- The credit creation process
- Broad and narrow measures of money
- The transaction, precautionary and speculative motives for holding money
- Money market equilibrium issues relating to fiscal versus monetary policy

Business Application

- Why business is interested in the size of government spending
- The extent to which low inflation and low interest rates might influence the level of investment by business

Economic stability and demand side policies at a glance

The issue

Both the current level of economic activity and future growth in economic activity are important for business. The government has a number of policies that it can use to control current economic activity. Understanding how these policies influence the economy and business is of enormous importance to firms operating both within their domestic markets and overseas.

The understanding

Economic activity rises and falls with the business cycle. During recessions the government may try to raise economic activity, while during economic booms the government may try to reduce economic activity. Acting through the demand side of the economy, the government can influence economic activity through fiscal and monetary policy. These will be discussed at length but, essentially, by altering interest rates, government spending or taxation, the government can try to influence the level of demand in an economy. For example, raising demand during a recession and lowering demand during a boom.

The usefulness

As the government alters domestic macroeconomic policy, it is essential for business to understand how the economy will react. Some policies, if implemented incorrectly, can have a destabilizing effect on the economy. For planning purposes it may be important to understand what type of policies will be deployed in the future. In recent times, interest rates have been very important policy tools. But as interest rates fall to historic lows, the scope for further cuts becomes limited. Therefore, what might replace interest rate policy and how will firms need to react?

11.1 Business problem: who's spending and where?

Rising GDP should be associated with increased expenditure by consumers. More jobs and higher wages facilitate consumption. In turn greater consumption drives sales and fuels profits. If only it were so simple. We know from the circular flow of income in Chapter 9 that consumption is only one element of total expenditure. In addition, we have spending by firms, which is classified as investment. We have government spending on education, health and public infrastructure; and we have international trade, where exports represent expenditure in the UK and imports represent expenditure overseas by UK residents. In Box 11.1 each of these components has changed not only over time, but also across economies. Different firms and industrial sectors will have differing exposures to consumers, investment, government spending and international trade. Therefore, the manner in which the economy grows has varying implications across industrial sectors. For example, retailers will benefit from an increase in consumption expenditure. In contrast, construction companies are more likely to benefit directly from growth in GDP which is fuelled by firms investing in offices and factories, as well as government wishing to build hospitals and schools. Companies and even economies such as Germany's, which are heavily reliant on external demand will be more likely to benefit from increased consumption in other countries, with for example British consumers increasing their demand for BMWs.

While the drivers of aggregate demand appear to be multifaceted they are still related. Again returning to the circular flow of income: total expenditure occurs with firms, which then pay wages to workers. These wages can then fuel consumption, or leak from the circular flow of income, in savings (to meet investments), in taxes (to meet government spending) and in imports. Therefore a rise in investment can lead to a future rise in employment, wages and eventually consumption. Or an increase in investment expenditure can facilitate more investment, or more government spending. It is clear that there is a complexity of intertwined relationships at the macroeconomic level which the firm needs to appreciate.

It is essential that business people are able to disentangle the macroeconomic environment in order to understand the business opportunities and commercial threats that it poses. When will demand increase in the economy and will it impact your sector?

 ## Box 11.1 The euro area's economies are in better shape than they look

Adapted from an article in The Economist, 17 November 2005

The European Central Bank (ECB) seems to be itching for an excuse to raise interest rates and strangle the euro area's feeble economic growth. For sceptics, nothing has changed: the single currency zone's economies are a miserable sight and will remain so. But if they took a careful look from another angle, they might see an altogether happier picture.

At the very least, European economies are picking up speed. Figures published this week showed that the euro area's GDP grew 2.6% per annum, the fastest for a year and a half. By American standards this looks sluggish: America's GDP grew at an annual rate of 3.8%. Even so, euro-area growth is now above its supposed potential rate of around 1.8%. This is below the American trend of perhaps 3% partly because of Europe's slower productivity growth.

The composition of the whole zone's third-quarter growth is not yet known, but Germany's official statisticians have ascribed almost all of their country's GDP growth to net exports and investment. Economists at HVB, a big German bank, reckon that private consumption probably shrank for the third quarter running, for the first time on record.

Elsewhere, the pattern is reversed, with consumer spending contributing far more and exports far less. The idea that growth in the euro zone depends almost entirely on external demand, while domestic demand stagnates, is a myth. Morgan Stanley calculates that for the zone as a whole, net exports have contributed only 0.1% of the 1.9% average growth in GDP since 1999.

Even in Germany there are now signs that domestic demand is stirring. Bank lending to firms and households has started to rise after falling for most of the past three years. The latest survey of business confidence by Ifo, a Munich research institute, showed a strong uptick in retailing, suggesting that consumers are opening their wallets; and throughout the euro area, surveys of business and consumer confidence continued to rise in October, which bodes well for the current quarter.

Whether the recovery lasts depends on the labour market. In Germany intensive corporate restructuring has depressed jobs and wages for several years. Only if more jobs are created will consumers spend more. There are some hopeful signs. Indeed, the unemployment figures may understate the overall gains: employment has risen by far more than unemployment has fallen as reforms have dragged previously discouraged workers back into the labour market.

This is not to say that everything is rosy in euroland. Europe has to cope with a shrinking workforce and an ageing population, as well as fiercer global competition. Europe's markets will have to become more flexible, its people will need to work for longer and its productivity growth must improve.

Moreover, what factors will help to drive the various categories of expenditure? Box 11.1 alludes to the role of business and consumer confidence in determining consumption and investment levels. But then it can be asked what determines consumer and business confidence? Employment prospects and sales might be two key drivers, which are clearly linked back to the level of economic activity, or the ever-revolving circular flow of income.

What governments have come to recognize is that stability is preferable. Volatility leads to uncertainty, and uncertainty reduces both consumer and business confidence. An increased probability of losing your job in the next 12 months will reduce your willingness to borrow and/or spend. Equally, governments have come to recognize that they can make a meaningful attempt at managing the economy. Interest rate policies would be one example as would the fiscal position of the government, the difference between expenditure and tax receipts. Business people need to be aware of how such policies feed into the circular flow of income and activate changes in consumption, investment, government spending and net exports. This chapter seeks to achieve this by developing your understanding of fiscal and monetary policy.

11.2 Consumption, investment expenditure and the business cycle

In Chapter 9 we introduced the aggregate demand and aggregate supply approach to understanding the **equilibrium** output of an economy and the price level. The approach enables a clear and insightful link to be made between micro- and macroeconomic theory.

It is unfortunate that the aggregate demand and aggregate supply approach ensures that the economy is always in equilibrium. As such, there can be no unemployment. All workers that desire a job will be employed.

This is not ideal given that we observe unemployment most of the time. We can adapt the aggregate demand and supply framework, but a useful approach is to instead introduce the Keynesian Cross as a model of equilibrium output.

Under the Keynesian Cross approach there is an assumption that prices are constant; as a result, inflation is not considered within the approach.

Put simply, what firms produce is exactly equal to what consumers are planning to buy. Figure 11.1 illustrates this idea with the 45° line.

We use the 45° line because it cuts the angle 90° in half. Therefore, when we draw across a planned level of expenditure equal to 100, the actual level of output will also be 100. As a consequence, the 45° line shows all the possible equilibrium points. However, the essential question is, what will be the level of planned expenditure?

Planned expenditure

For simplicity we will assume that we have a **closed economy** with no government sector.

The only groups spending within the economy under such a scenario are consumers and firms (we have no government and no exports). Planned expenditure of aggregate demand can be expressed as:

$$PE = AD = C + I$$

where PE = planned expenditure; C = consumption; and I = investment.

> The **equilibrium** is generally defined as the situation where **planned aggregate expenditure** is equal to the actual output of firms. **Planned aggregate expenditure** is the total amount of spending on goods and services within the economy that is planned by purchasers.

> A **closed economy** does not trade with the rest of the world. An open economy does trade with the rest of the world.

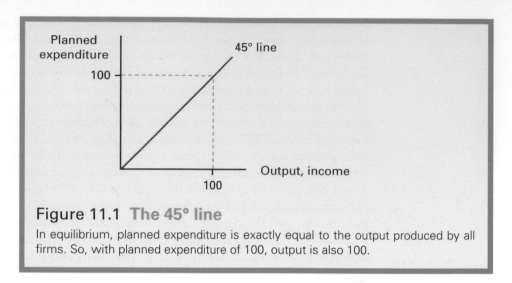

Figure 11.1 The 45° line

In equilibrium, planned expenditure is exactly equal to the output produced by all firms. So, with planned expenditure of 100, output is also 100.

Consumption

The level of consumption undertaken by private individuals is assumed by economists to be related to two factors: (i) a basic need to consume and (ii) the level of personal income. The basic need to consume is the level of consumption undertaken by an individual when their income is zero. It is the basic level of consumption that is required in order to survive. It is more often referred to as **autonomous consumption**, which is linked to **autonomous expenditure**.

> An expenditure is described as **autonomous** if it is not influenced by the level of income. Therefore, **autonomous consumption** does not change if income changes.

As income increases, individuals will begin to consume more goods and services. But they may not spend all of their income on consumption. A small portion could be saved: 100 of income could result in 80 of consumption and 20 of saving.

In our example, the **MPC** = 0.8 and the **MPS** = 0.2. It is easy to see that MPC + MPS = 1. This is because any 1 unit increase in income can only be used for consumption or saving.

So, if we assume that autonomous consumption is 7 and the MPC is 0.8, then we can say that:

$$C = 7 + 0.8Y$$

where Y = personal disposable income and C = consumption.

This is nothing more than the equation of a straight line and it is drawn in Figure 11.2.

When income is zero, consumption is 7. This is the intercept. The slope of the consumption line is equal to the MPC and in this case 0.8. So, if income is 100, we can now say that consumption will be $7 + 0.8 \times 100 = 7 + 80 = 87$.

> The **MPC** (**marginal propensity to consume**) is the extra consumption generated by 1 unit of extra income. And the **MPS** (**marginal propensity to save**) is simply the extra saving generated by 1 unit of extra income.

Investment

Investment is the demand for capital products by firms, plus changes to firms' inventories, or stocks.

We have seen how income determines the consumption decisions of private individuals. But what drives investment decisions? The answer to this question is highly debatable, but in general, and in simple terms, economists begin by assuming that investment decisions are based on instinct. How managers feel about the future is a major factor when deciding to invest money. If managers think the future looks good, then they will be likely to invest. But if the future looks bad, they will cut back on investments. As

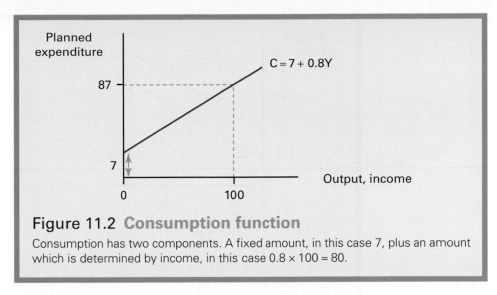

Figure 11.2 Consumption function

Consumption has two components. A fixed amount, in this case 7, plus an amount which is determined by income, in this case 0.8 × 100 = 80.

such, investment decisions taken now are not influenced by the current level of income. For this reason investment is also seen as autonomous. This means that, just like the 7 of consumption undertaken by consumers, firms set a base level of investment, say 50, but then there is no additional investment relating to increased income. The implications of this are shown in Figure 11.3, where the investment is set at 50 and remains constant at 50 for every level of income.

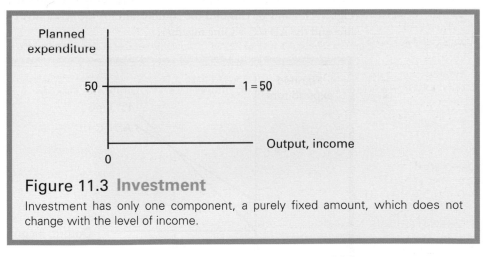

Figure 11.3 Investment

Investment has only one component, a purely fixed amount, which does not change with the level of income.

We can now add the consumption and investment together to arrive at aggregate demand or planned expenditure. This has been done in Figure 11.4, which, while looking complicated, is little more than an extension of Figure 11.2. From Figure 11.2 we have the consumption line, with 7 of consumption at zero levels of income and overall consumption of 87 when income is 100. We have then simply added in an additional 50 for investment. Aggregate demand, or planned expenditure, is now 7 + 50 = 57 at zero income, and overall planned expenditure, which is equal to consumption plus investment, is 87 + 50 = 137.

We started with the 45° line and said that equilibrium occurs where planned expenditure equals actual output. From Figure 11.4 we now have an understanding of

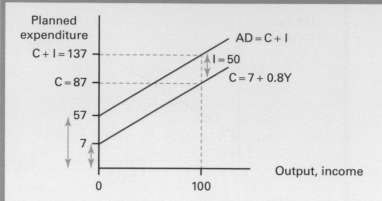

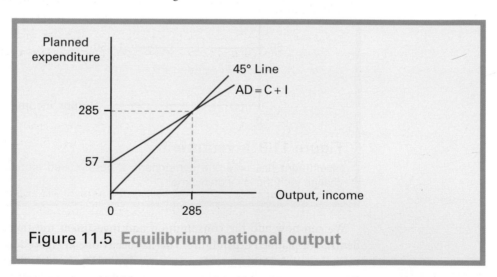

Figure 11.4 Aggregate demand: consumption plus investment

Adding investment to consumption simply increases autonomous expenditure by the increased amount of investment. In this case investment = 50, so at all levels of income spending has increased by 50. At zero income the level of consumption is 7; adding in investment of 50 simply means that planned expenditure = 57 when investment equals zero. Since autonomous expenditure does not change with the level of output then, even when income = 100, the difference between consumption and investment will still be 50.

expenditure in an economy. We, therefore, only need to introduce the 45° line into Figure 11.4 and we can find the equilibrium for the economy. Figure 11.5 shows the 45° line and the AD = C + I line together.

Figure 11.5 Equilibrium national output

In our example the equilibrium level of income is 285.

Proof:

AD = C + I, C = 7 + 0.8Y,

I = 50

AD = 7 + 0.8Y + 50

= 57 + 0.8Y

In equilibrium national output = aggregate demand, or $Y = AD$ (1)

Therefore $Y = 57 + 0.8Y$

Rearranging,

$0.2Y = 57$
$Y = 57/0.2 = 285$

(The review question 1 contains an additional example if you would like to test your ability to derive the equilibrium.)

Where the AD line crosses the 45° line must be the equilibrium, because this is where planned expenditure equals actual output.

At all output levels below 285, aggregate demand will be greater than national output. For example, if national output was only 200, then firms would not be producing enough output to meet the level of aggregate demand in the economy. Firms will have to meet the excess demand by using stocks held over from previous periods. Similarly, at all output levels above 285, national output will be greater than aggregate demand. For example, if national output is 300, aggregate demand will be less than the national output. As a result, firms will be left with excess stock.

Adjustment to the equilibrium

The economy will move to the equilibrium of 285 units by firms responding to changes in their stock levels. When output is below equilibrium, firms' stocks will reduce. Firms will interpret falling stock levels as an opportunity to expand production, because consumers are currently demanding more output than is currently being produced. In contrast, when output is above the equilibrium level, firms' stock levels will begin to increase. Rising stock levels will suggest to firms that current output is too high. Consumers are not demanding all that is being produced, hence the additions to stocks. Firms will, therefore, reduce output and the economy will shift towards the equilibrium.

In summary, adjustment to equilibrium occurs through firms reacting to changes in stock levels, where changing stock levels reflect differences between planned expenditure by consumers and actual output by firms.

The multiplier

Here is a simple idea. What would happen if firms decided that the economic outlook was favourable? We might expect them to increase their levels of investment from 50 to 100. But by how much would output increase? An extra 50? The answer rests on a very important insight known as the **multiplier**.

If the multiplier is 3, an increase in investment of 50 will lead to an increase in output of $3 \times 50 = 150$. But what determines the size of the multiplier?

The multiplier is directly related to the marginal propensity to save. In our example the MPS = 0.2. Consider the following: firms buy more computers and thereby increase investment by 50. The computer manufacturers receive the 50 and for the extra output pass this on in increased wages to their workers. The workers will use this to increase consumption by $0.8 \times 50 = 40$ and save $10 = (0.2 \times 50)$. So far expenditure has now increased by the initial 50 increase in investment plus the 40 in consumption by the workers. If the computer workers spent the extra 40 at supermarkets, then income of supermarket workers increases by 40. They will spend $0.8 \times 40 = 32$ on consumption and save 8.

The **multiplier** measures the change in output following a change in autonomous expenditure (the essential or basic amount of consumption plus investment).

We can keep going, but even at this stage we can see that an increase of 50 in investment has led to an increase in consumption of 40 and then another 32. So, overall, the change in investment of 50 has created 50 + 40 + 32 = 122 change in expenditure and therefore national output.

This is entirely linked to the circular flow of income introduced in Chapter 9. The 50 increase in investment is an injection into the circular flow. It moves round the cycle, 10 leaks out in savings and then 40 goes around again as consumption; 8 then leaks out in savings and then 32 goes around again. Indeed, if we did keep going we would find that the initial increase of 50 would create a total change in national output of 250, or 5 × 50. Why? Because the multiplier is calculated thus:

Multiplier = 1/MPS = 1/(1 − MPC)

So, if the MPS = 0.2, the multiplier = 1/0.2 = 5. So the size of the multiplier is entirely dependent upon the MPS. The higher the MPS, the faster the initial injection leaks out of the circular flow, and so less is left to go around again.

For example, if the MPS was 0.5, then 50 would go around the circular flow and 25 would leak out as savings with only 25 going around again as consumption. Then 12.5 would leak out, leaving only 12.5 to go around again. In total, because the multiplier is now only 1/0.5 = 2, the initial injection of 50 from investment would only result in output changing by 100.

11.3 Fiscal policy

What is so exciting about the multiplier? For the economist, the multiplier means that small changes in autonomous expenditure can generate big changes in national income. In order to see the importance of this insight we need to introduce the government sector.

If the government wishes to control the economy, such as moving the economy from a position of recession, then it only has to change autonomous expenditure by a small amount in order to generate a very large change in overall economic activity.

How might it do this? Asking firms to invest more is unlikely to be effective; firms invest because they want to, not because governments ask them to. But what about government spending? Could the government pump additional expenditure into the economy through its own projects such as health and education? We will answer this by examining **fiscal policy**.

Fiscal policy is the government's decisions regarding taxation and spending.

We will shortly see that fiscal policy can be used to control the economy, but the implementation of effective fiscal policy may be problematic.

Government, aggregate demand and equilibrium income

In the previous section we saw how planned expenditure, or aggregate demand, is equal to consumption plus investment, AD = C + I. In introducing the government we are creating a third source of spending within the economy. Aggregate demand is now calculated thus: AD = C + I + G, where G = government spending. Just like investment, government spending is also autonomous. It does not vary with the level of income. Governments take political spending decisions. How much should be spent on education and how much on roads. In the main, the level of income does not determine government spending.

In terms of our diagrammatic approach we simply add government spending into the analysis in much the same way that we dealt with investment. Government spending as an autonomous expenditure simply raises the aggregate demand line by the amount of government spending. In Figure 11.6, we have assumed that G = 20. With no government sector, as in Figure 11.4, we saw that when income was zero, spending equalled 57, which consisted of autonomous consumption equal to 7 and investment equal to 50. We can now add government spending equal to 20. So, aggregate demand when income equals zero is now 77.

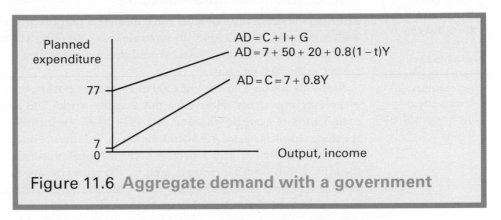

Figure 11.6 Aggregate demand with a government

However, we also need to address the impact of taxation. In Figure 11.4, without tax we simply argued that consumption, C = 7 + 0.8Y. But if individuals are taxed, we need to reduce their income, Y, by the amount of the tax. If the tax rate = t, then after tax income equals $(1 - t)Y$. It is this after tax income which individuals then use for consumption, or saving. So, if the MPC = 0.8, then consumers spend 0.8 of their after tax income. Therefore, taking account of tax we can now say that consumption is:

$$C = 7 + 0.8 (1 - t)Y$$

and not

$$C = 7 + 0.8Y$$

The MPC determines how steep the AD line is, because it determines the link between growth in income and growth in consumption. A higher MPC will result in a steeper AD line. Tax effectively reduces the strength of the link between consumption and income, because an increase in income will be taxed before individuals can use it to increase consumption. Therefore, tax makes the AD line flatter.

Taking tax and government spending together, we can now see that the AD line with a government sector is higher because of government spending, but flatter because of taxation.

What does this really tell us? The importance is in the consumption line being flatter. This means that when taxes are applied, an increase in income has a lower impact on consumption. This is because we have opened up another avenue for leakages. By introducing the government sector, income can leak out via savings and taxes. This is significant because we have seen that the multiplier was determined by the rate of leakages and, indeed, the multiplier is now:

$$Multiplier = 1/(MPS + MPT)$$

where MPS = marginal propensity to save, and MPT = marginal propensity to tax.

So, if MPS = 0.2 and the MPT = 0.22 = the UKs basic tax rate, then the multiplier = 1/(0.2 + 0.22) = 2.38

When we had no government sector savings the multiplier was equal to:

1/MPS = 1/0.2 = 5

Note that, introducing the government has decreased the size of the multiplier.

The balanced budget multiplier

The **balanced budget multiplier** states that an increase in government spending, plus an *equal* increase in taxes, leads to higher equilibrium output.

Reducing the size of the multiplier could mean that the government might actually make itself ineffectual. For example, the government could inject 100 into the economy and then take out 100 in higher taxes. Would the multiplier then be zero? Amazingly, the answer to this question is no.

Sounds fantastic. You can put £100 in everyone's pocket, then take it out again and make everyone richer! How does this actually work? The answer requires a close examination of aggregate demand, AD = C + I + G. An increase of 100 in government spending clearly increases AD by 100. However, the effect of increasing taxes by 100 does not reduce AD by 100. This is because of the marginal propensity to consume, MPC. As the MPC is only 0.8, an increase in taxes by 100 causes income to fall by 100; the change in consumption is therefore only 0.8 × 100 = 80. The net effect on aggregate demand is an increase in G of 100 and a reduction in consumption of only 80. Therefore, aggregate demand increases by 20.

The obvious question to now ask is, how do governments in practice use government spending and taxation to control the equilibrium level of output?

11.4 Government's approach to managing fiscal policy

The government's spending and taxation decisions are reflected in the government deficit. The projected expenditure and revenue sources for the government are available from the so-called Red Book. For the tax year 2006/07 the revenue and expenditure figures are shown in Figure 11.7.

The largest areas of expenditure are social security, health and education. Taken together these three areas represent more than 60 per cent of government spending. The largest sources of revenues come from personal taxation, national insurance contributions and VAT. It is perhaps surprising that revenues from corporation taxes are only £49 billion and represent only 9 per cent of total government tax revenues. Government borrowing is £36bn (£552 – £516bn), the difference between government expenditure and government revenues, and represents the government's deficit.

Deficits

The **government deficit** is the difference between government spending and taxation, or G – tY.

Government deficits as a percentage of GDP are plotted in Figure 11.8 for Germany, France, the US and the UK. Government deficits tend to display a cyclical pattern. Until 2001, most economies were running a surplus, rather than a deficit. As economies have fallen into recession, or slowed in growth, tax receipts have fallen behind expenditure levels and deficits have opened up. Members of the Eurozone are required to keep their budget deficits under 3 per cent of GDP. This has proved difficult. In the UK the government has pledged to have a neutral position over the cycle, but changed the start of the cycle in order to meet this criteria. The US has no formal restrictions on the size of its deficit.

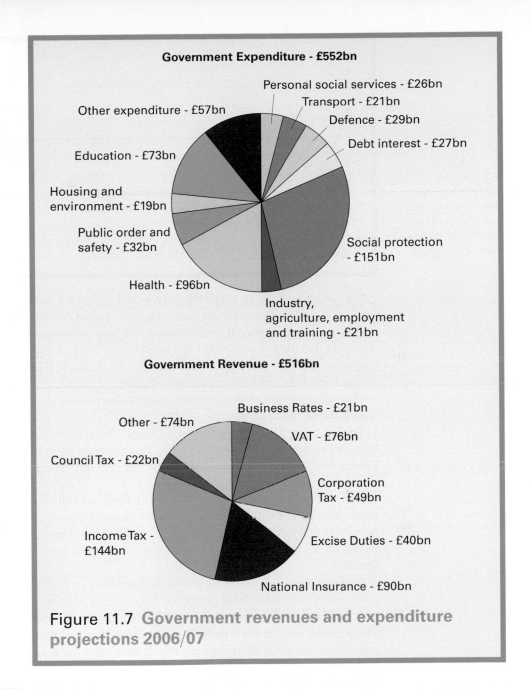

Figure 11.7 Government revenues and expenditure projections 2006/07

Fiscal stance

The government's **fiscal stance** is the extent to which the government is using fiscal policy to increase or decrease aggregate demand in the economy.

Unfortunately, the continual link between the government deficit and the business cycle makes it difficult to appraise the government's fiscal stance. For example, an expansionary fiscal policy would ordinarily consist of a reduction in tax and an increase in government spending, resulting in a larger government deficit. In a recession, tax receipts will fall and create a larger deficit. It is, therefore, difficult to use the government deficit as a measure of the government's fiscal stance. This is because the deficit can occur following an expansionary fiscal policy or, equally, because the economy is in recession.

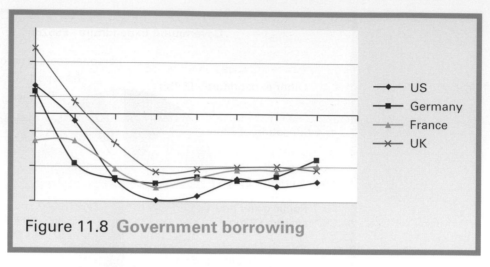

Figure 11.8 Government borrowing

We need, therefore, to adjust the government deficit for changes associated with the business cycle. We do this by calculating the government deficit if the economy was at its optimal, or full employment level of output. We keep government spending and tax rates the same, but then assume that the equilibrium level of the economy is at its full employment level. We are, therefore, assuming the economy is not in boom or recession. It is perfectly balanced between the two extremes.

This full employment budget position is then described as the structural budget, which is adjusted for the business cycle.

The UK currently pursues a balanced budget policy, with a stated aim of ensuring a balanced budget over the medium term. This has been referred to as Gordon Brown's Golden Rule. This is effectively arguing that the structural budget will be zero. In boom, we might expect a budget surplus; in recession, we could see a deficit; but on balance, the budget will be just that – balanced. Structural balance still allows a contractionary, or expansionary fiscal policy. During a recession the government can add spending into the economy, through tax reductions and increases in government spending. Similarly, during an economic boom the government can increase taxes and reduce government spending.

However, the important issue is to understand the degree of fiscal intervention by the government. Recently, fiscal policy has become less popular, reflecting the concerns of economists and politicians that fiscal policy can be destabilizing for the economy. This is not to say that fiscal policy is no longer used, rather that policymakers place less importance on fiscal interventions and at best see it as a supplement to monetary interventions. For example, recent low interest rates in the US have arguably been supported with tax cuts and increases in government spending. This reduced reliance on fiscal policy can be supported on a number of fronts, including automatic stabilizers, crowding out, uncertainty, inflation and potential entry into the single European currency. An analysis of each will now follow.

Less reliance on fiscal policy: why?

Automatic stabilizers enable the economy to adjust automatically to changes in aggregate demand.

If during a boom, income in an economy increases, tax receipts will increase, savings will increase and the government will cut back on social payments, such as unemployment benefit. This shows that the economy has automatic breaks built into the system that will help to control the rate of economic boom. Conversely, in recession, tax receipts will fall, savings will reduce and government payments will increase. This way the economy will automatically reduce the net rate of leakages and help to keep the economy moving.

Because such stabilizers work automatically then, from a fiscal position, the economy can be placed on autopilot. There is no need for the government to overly monitor economic activity and make policy changes. It can focus its energies on other matters, such as health and education.

Fiscal policy and implementation problems

There are additional reasons for believing in the virtues of automatic stabilizers and these relate to the problems associated with actively managing fiscal policy.

Time lags

In order to actively manage fiscal policy the government needs to know when aggregate demand is falling and when it is rising. This can only be achieved with a lag. Government statisticians collect data on economic activity, but they are only able to report and, perhaps more important, confirm either a slow-down or an increase in economic activity three to six months after the event. The government then needs to consider a policy response and then introduce the response. This all takes time. Once the policy is introduced, say a cut in taxation to offset falling demand in an economy, the economy may have moved on, showing signs of economic growth. The tax stimulation is then inappropriate because it will be adding to a boom, rather than assisting a recessionary problem.

Uncertainty

Assume an economy is in recession. The equilibrium level of income is £10 billion, but currently output is around £5 billion. The multiplier is 2. The economy has an output gap of £10bn − £5bn = £5bn. With a multiplier of 2 the government needs to increase aggregate demand by £2.5 billion.

Unfortunately, this example has benefited from complete certainty. We know the equilibrium level of output, the current level of output and the size of the multiplier. In practice the government and its advisers do not know any of these values with certainty. Now let us assume that all of the factors above are estimates. We could even be generous to the government and say that it guessed the size of the multiplier and the current level of GDP accurately. But the equilibrium level of income is only £8 billion, not £10 billion. Therefore, by overestimating the optimal level of output and injecting £2.5 billion into the economy the government will push the economy straight into a boom. It simply swaps a demoralizing recession for an equally unpalatable bout of inflation.

Offsetting changes

If the government pursues an expansionary fiscal stance, it will tend to take on more debt in order to finance its spending. At some point in the future this debt has to be serviced and perhaps even repaid. In the presence of very large mountains of public debt, sensible private individuals may predict that in the future tax rates will have to rise in order to fund the current lax fiscal position of the government. In order to offset these future higher taxes, individuals might save more now. Therefore, higher government spending and reduced taxes now could generate higher levels of offsetting autonomous savings.

The government's fiscal stance is effectively neutralized by the response of higher savings from the private sector.

Actively managed fiscal policy sought to manage the business cycle by adding demand during a recession and reducing demand during a boom. Due to problems of timing, uncertainty and offsetting, such policy responses have been ill-timed, misjudged and at best ineffective.

Deficits and inflation

We saw in Chapter 9 that inflation can erode the value of debt. If you borrow £100 and inflation is 10 per cent then, in real terms, at the end of year one you will only owe £90. You as a private individual have very little control over the rate of inflation. But for a government the case is very different. If a government runs up a mountain of debt, the temptation to let the rate of inflation increase and erode the real value of the debt is very tempting.

This has two important implications. First, if a government is trying to manage individuals' inflationary expectations, then it needs to manage the size of the government debt. Being seen to reduce debt and fiscal deficits reduces the need to stoke up inflation. As a consequence, inflationary expectations will be lower and inflation should turn out to be lower. Second, as we see in Chapter 13, within a fixed exchange rate system such as the European single currency, harmonizing inflation across member states may aid economic convergence among those states. Therefore, as entry into the system draws nearer, the UK government needs to bring fiscal policy under control.

Crowding out

Crowding out
occurs when
increased
government
spending reduces
private sector
spending.

Crowding out relates back to the business problem at the beginning of this chapter. If government takes an expansionary fiscal stance, then it can achieve this by spending more public money on health and education. But this policy runs the risk of robbing productive resources from the private sector. For every nurse employed in a hospital, a worker is effectively removed from the private sector. This is known as crowding out, because public expenditure by government crowds out private expenditure by firms. The extent to which this occurs is debatable. When there are lots of workers without jobs, an increase in government spending will not crowd out private expenditure. Employment will rise, output will grow and income will increase. But when productive resources such as labour are all fully employed, then increasing public expenditure is likely to rob the private sector of its resources. Employment stays constant, at best output stays constant and so does income. An expansionary fiscal policy has no net impact on national output.

Summary

Given all of these problems, it is not surprising that economists and governments have begun to move away from active fiscal management of the economy. Instead they have recognized the benefits of automatic stabilizers and moved focus to monetary and supply side policies. Fiscal policy was popular from the 1930s through to the 1970s, a period during which a global depression in the 1930s meant there was no crowding out. Economic change occurred at a more sedate and predictable pace and concerns regarding inflation were less important. All this has obviously changed. With modern economies developing with great pace and complexity, inflationary aversion is everywhere and high levels of employment ensure that crowding out is a real problem. However, the effectiveness of fiscal policy could return. As we will see when we discuss monetary policy, low inflation and low interest rates can make monetary policy potentially ineffective. Therefore, fiscal expansionism could soon be back on the agenda.

11.5 Foreign trade and aggregate demand

So far in our examination of aggregate demand we have only considered economies which do not trade with the rest of the world. While we will focus on issues of exchange rates and globalization in Chapters 13 and 14, it is worth incorporating the impact of international trade on aggregate demand.

Exports are generally expressed as X and imports as Z.

Economists generally talk about net exports, or the trade balance, which is clearly X – Z. If exports are greater than imports, the economy has a trade surplus, but if imports are greater than exports, the economy has a trade deficit.

We now need to think about incorporating X and Z into our existing analysis of aggregate demand. In fairly simple terms exports are UK products purchased by foreign consumers; Scotch whisky produced in the UK, but sold in the US would be an example. So, exports add to UK aggregate demand. Imports work in the opposite direction. These are foreign products purchased by UK consumers; BMW cars made in Germany, but bought in the UK would be an example. Therefore, aggregate demand can now be defined as AD = C + I + G + X – Z.

However, as with the introduction of the government sector, we need to address the factors that determine exports and imports. First, the level of UK income does not influence exports; instead, US consumers' willingness to purchase UK products is influenced by US income. As income rises in the US, consumers are willing to search out more expensive imports from overseas, such as Scotch whisky. Therefore, exports are autonomous, or independent, of the UK's level of income. In contrast, the level of UK income influences imports. As our income increases, we are willing to buy more expensive products from overseas.

We therefore have a marginal propensity to import (MPZ), which is the increase in income allocated to import products.

In terms of aggregate demand, exports are grouped with the other autonomous expenditures: autonomous consumption, investment and government spending. As such, exports represent a potential injection into the circular flow of income. Rising income levels in the US, or the European Union, are likely to result in additional UK exports to these economies. Conversely, as these economies move into recession, demand for UK products will fall.

Exports add to the complexity of planning UK domestic policy because, in order to keep aggregate demand at the equilibrium level, the government has to understand the level of domestic consumption, domestic investment and how the business cycle in Europe and the US might influence UK exports.

This argument is picked up in Box 11.2, with falling demand from the US leading to a fall in UK exports. Therefore, as the US and other economies move into recession, reductions in demand within these domestic economies are transmitted to key trading partners. Falling economic activity in the US leads to reduced UK exports and a reduction in UK economic activity.

Should we be troubled by a rising trade deficit? The answer is 'yes' because imports represent a leakage from the circular flow of income. Leakages reduce the size of the multiplier. With imports, injections leak out of the economy more quickly and, therefore,

Box 11.2 Oil imports fuel record trade gap

Surging oil imports have propelled Britain's trade deficit with the rest of the world up faster than expected, to a new record for November

Adapted from the Office for National Statistics and the Scotsman, 11 January 2006

The trade gap in goods and services widened to £5.96bn ($10.45bn) from a deficit of £5.05bn in October, said the Office for National Statistics (ONS). The November figure was more than £1bn higher than economists' forecasts. The goods trade gap with non-EU countries also widened to £3.02bn in November from £2.28bn in October.

Economists had forecast a deficit of about £2.5bn. In November, the UK was a net importer of oil for the fifth month running, the longest period since monthly records began in 1980. 'It's a disappointing set of numbers' said Philip Shaw, economist at Investec.

less money is left in the circular flow to go through the next cycle. In an open economy with a government sector the multiplier is:

Open economy multiplier with government sector = $1/(MPS + MPT + MPZ)$.

Imports, therefore, increase the economy's leakages and in so doing can reduce the size of the multiplier.

In terms of fiscal policy, the open economy creates real practical problems for the government. For example, if the government increases government spending, then this represents an autonomous injection into the economy. With an open economy, however, there is a distinct possibility that this additional expenditure could leak out as imports, resulting in zero impact on the level of aggregate demand. For example, increased spending by the UK government on healthcare can now be used to pay for operations undertaken in French hospitals. The money spent on extending the UK's airport capacity could be spent by workers on foreign holidays.

Summary

Fiscal policy, in the main, relies on the power of the multiplier to provide the government with an effective tool for managing the economy. As the world's economies become more globally integrated, the scope of international leakages increases and the multiplier decreases in size and effectiveness. Moreover, fiscal policy requires timely and accurate information. The complexity of modern economies, including increasing globalization, makes these informational requirements difficult to attain. Attention has switched to monetary policy and a concern with inflation targeting. Following the business application for fiscal policy we will consider monetary policy.

11.6 Business application: fiscal policy

If business is seeking tax breaks or additional spending from government, it can think again. The ability of many leading European economies to bolster economic activity through fiscal policy is limited. The discussion in Box 11.3 even brackets the previously

Box 11.3 Business and fiscal policy

More prudence, European commissioner tells Gordon Brown as UK breaches deficit

Adapted from an article by David Gow and Ashley Seager, in the Guardian, 12 January 2006

The UK came under renewed pressure from the European Commission to raise taxes or cut government spending. The UK, which is normally prone to lecturing its fellow members for their sorry performance: now faces embarrassment.

The government said 'The UK continues to have the lowest average debts and deficits of any other major European economy ... We make no apologies for investing in vital public services'. Even so the UK will be lumped with France, Germany and Italy – serial sinners against the guidelines.

The Commission took issue with the UK by saying that the Commission's assessment was that the deficit would be 3.1% in the coming fiscal year and could no longer be considered temporary – nor the result of a severe economic downturn or unusual events.

So, although the UK budgetary position is less worrying than that of others in the EU – in particular as far as its debt position is concerned – the Commission recommends that the UK deficit be declared excessive and the UK asked to correct the situation.

prudent UK government with the serial sinners of the Euro zone. A key concern for all of these governments is to keep fiscal policy relatively tight. Whether fiscal policy is capable of influencing aggregate demand is debatable, especially with timing problems and off-setting behaviour. However, by the use of public humiliation and the imposition of fines the European Commission seeks to enforce a tight fiscal policy across Europe.

In the long term this maybe beneficial for business. There should be a lack of boom/bust economics, where economies move from recession to boom and back again. Instead, fluctuations in economic activity should be more moderate. This should help to stabilize employment and output, leading to improved consumer and business confidence. Consumption and investment expenditure may increase and the economy should grow steadily. For business the impact of government on the economy has changed. It has gone from being a short-term interventionist, altering spending and taxes, to being a source of stability which will (it is hoped) emanate out across the economy.

While the management of the macroeconomy through fiscal policy is the prerogative of government, the use of such policies, in both the short and long run, can have very real consequences for business. It is important for business to understand the beneficial and negative impacts the government can deliver upon the economy.

11.7 Monetary policy

Such is the importance of monetary policy that interest rate changes in the US, the Euro zone and the UK are dealt with as major news events. But why is interest rate policy such a significant part of economic policy?

The answer is complex and, in order to develop your understanding, we need to examine the market for money. We will achieve this by answering the following questions: (i) What is money? (ii) Why do individuals demand money? (iii) How is money supplied? (iv) How is the equilibrium price of money, namely interest, changed?

What is money?

Money facilitates exchange. Consider an economy with no money, generally referred to as a 'barter economy', where goods are swapped for other goods.

We are specialist economic textbook authors. That is what we produce. You might flip burgers or drive a taxi. This book could be worth 30 burgers, or one taxi ride to the airport. We do not like burgers, but we do fly, so we need a taxi. But will the taxi driver want our economics textbook in return for a trip to the airport; and if the burger flipper wants our book, do we want 30 burgers in return?

You can see the problem: without money a so-called **double coincidence of wants** is required in order to exchange goods.

As textbook authors we need to find people who want our book, and are offering goods we want in exchange. Money solves this problem. We can pay the taxi driver £30 cash and they can then use this money to buy goods which they desire, such as food, petrol or coffee; they do not have to accept the textbook.

A central role of money is that it is recognized and accepted as a medium of exchange.

Money also has other functions. It is generally seen to be a *unit of account*. All prices are expressed in monetary terms. A BMW is £20 000, not 100 cows. Furthermore, money should be a *store of value*. This way money can be used in the future. For example, milk is not a good store of value, because it deteriorates quickly and goes off. Money, as metal coins and paper bank notes, does not perish and, therefore, acts as a store of value.

Government-backed money, in the form of notes and coins, has a number of beneficial aspects associated with it. It is legally recognized as a medium of exchange and is culturally accepted as such. People are willing to exchange goods for money. Paper notes and coins are cheap to make (see the mass production techniques employed by the Royal Mint in Box 11.5). A £10 note does not require £10 of resource in order to make it. In contrast, a £10 gold nugget would represent £10 of resource. Government-backed money economizes on scarce resources. But here is the problem: because a £10 note can be produced for less than £10, forgers can make a profit. Therefore, forgery has to be outlawed and enforced.

> A **double coincidence of wants** occurs when two people trade goods and services without money. The first individual demands the good offered by the second individual, and vice versa.

 Box 11.4 Making money

Rolling in it!

Source: Royal Mint

The Royal Mint boasts some of the most advanced coining machinery in the world. In the foundry, strips of metal are drawn from large electric furnaces, reduced to the required thickness in a tandem rolling mill and transferred to large blanking presses where coin blanks can be punched out at the rate of 10 000 per minute. The blanks are softened and cleaned in the Annealing and Pickling Plant before the final process in the Coining Press Room. Here the blanks are fed into coining presses where the obverse and reverse designs, as well as the milling on the edge, are stamped on to the blank simultaneously. The Royal Mint's latest presses can each strike more than 600 coins per minute, making it impossible for the human eye to separate the individual pieces as they pass through the press.

But what determines the supply of money in the economy? This is a difficult question to address, as not all money is represented by notes and coins. In order to understand this issue further we need to introduce the idea of credit creation.

Credit creation

Credit creation is the process of turning existing bank deposits into credit facilities for borrowers. The process can result in an increase in the money supply.

Consider a business with which many of you will be familiar – clubbing. You go to the club and pay for drinks. In the morning the manager of the club (being more sensible than you) awakens earlier and pays the previous evening's takings into the bank – let us say £1000. When your hangover subsides, around two in the afternoon, you realize that the really good night out was extremely expensive. You go to the bank and join the queue for an increase in your overdraft.

The bank is sitting on £1000 from the club and assumes that only £100 will be paid out in the near future as wages. The bank thinks it can safely lend out the remaining £900 in overdrafts. You and your fellow borrowers take the £900 and head straight back to the club for another big night out. In the morning, while you skip another lecture, the club manager returns to the bank and pays in the £900. The bank manager awaits your call for another advance on your overdraft.

The banks are playing a very clever trick: the club manager thinks he has £1000 in the bank. But then the bank also lets you and your fellow borrowers think you have an additional £900 in the bank by lending part of the club's money to you. When you spend this drinking and enjoying yourself, the club manager pays the next night's takings into the bank, and he now thinks he has £1900 in the bank. We can, therefore, see that an initial £1000 in notes and coins was converted into another £900 of money, via overdrafts. This is then paid back into the bank and the process occurs again. Just as we have a fiscal multiplier, we can now observe banks, through credit creation, developing what is known as a money multiplier.

We clearly have to make a distinction between how much *money* people think exists and how much *cash* actually exists.

We formally refer to cash as the **monetary base**, or the stock of high-powered money, which is the quantity of notes and coins held by private individuals, or held by the banking system.

The amount of money, or the money supply, is the **monetary base** plus deposits at the bank. We will see shortly that this definition can be broadened, but it clearly includes the amount of cash in circulation and the amount people think they have in the bank.

The money multiplier is, therefore, the ratio of the money supply to the monetary base.

Size of the money multiplier

The size of the money multiplier is determined by two factors: (i) the willingness of individuals to deposit money in the bank, rather than keeping it in their pockets; and (ii) the level of reserves held by the banks. For example, the credit creation process will become greater as more individuals provide banks with cash. So, as people switch from holding money in their pockets, to storing it at the bank, the more banks can create credit. Second, if banks reduce reserves from 10 per cent to 5 per cent of deposits, then more credit can be created; for example, for every £100 paid in, the banks can lend out an additional £5 by reducing reserves from 10 per cent to 5 per cent.

So, if cash deposits and reserve levels are central to the process of credit creation, what influences each of these important factors? The level of reserves is directly influenced by regulation. Governments, or central banks, may insist that banks keep a minimum level of reserves in order to meet deposit holders' cash withdrawals. This merely reflects an interest by governments to avoid bankruptcy among the banking sector. Clearly banks also wish to avoid bankruptcy and many will use treasury management teams to build complex models capable of predicting cash flows into and out of the bank on a daily basis. The more confident the bank is that cash flows in will exceed cash flows out, the more they will be willing to lend. The less predictable these cash flows become, the more dangerous it becomes to lower reserves and lend more money.

The willingness to hold cash on deposit, rather than in your pocket, has in recent times been influenced by technological change in the financial services industry. Many firms only pay salary and wages into bank accounts. Wages are rarely paid in cash any more. Loans, mortgages and mobile phone contracts will only be offered if direct debits can be set up on your bank account. Utility suppliers – gas, electricity and water – will offer discounts if monthly direct debits are set up. Couple all these changes with the popularity of credit cards and the overall requirement for cash in your pocket, rather than at the bank, has significantly reduced. As a consequence, more cash is in the banking sector and banks using treasury management are becoming more adept at modelling its flows and taking opportunities to create credit.

Measures of money

We saw above that measuring the money supply requires a distinction between high-powered money (cash) and money on deposit. The government has used this distinction to develop a number of money measures ranging from **M0**, a narrow measure of money, to **M4**, a broad measure of money. The intervening measures of M1, M2 and M3 have become less relevant.

The previous intervening measures of M1, M2 and M3 simply took M0 and then added in sight, time, or building society deposits. The argument now is that financial products have become so blurred and substitutable, as banks and building societies compete directly against each other, that it makes sense to simply draw a definite distinction between narrow M0 and broad M4. Table 11.1 contains data on the relative size of narrow money M0 and the additional components of M4.

M0 is a measure of the monetary base: cash in circulation outside the banks, cash in the banks and the bank's own accounts at the Bank of England. M0 is, therefore, a narrow measure of money.
M4, takes M0 and adds sight deposits at banks, time deposits at banks, and deposits at building societies. M4 is, therefore, a broad measure of money.

Table 11.1 Narrow and broad UK money (£bn) Dec 2005

	Wide monetary base M0	44
−	Banks' cash and balances at bank	−6
+	Cash in circulation	38
+	Banks' retail deposits	707
+	Building societies' deposits and shares	172
+	Wholesale deposits	344
=	Money supply M4	1305

Source: Bank of England

11.8 Money market equilibrium and monetary policy

The previous discussion provides an understanding of money supply. However, before we begin to consider how the government might effectively control the money supply, we also need to consider the demand for money. By integrating demand and supply for money we can then analyse the money market equilibrium that the government, or central bank, needs to manage.

Demand for money

Do not confuse a demand for more money with a demand for additional income. We all want more income, but may not want more money. For example, if you receive £1000 in income the question is, how much of this £1000 will you hold in money and how much in other financial securities such as bonds or equities?

Economists identify three motives for holding money: the **transaction motive**, the **precautionary motive** and the **asset motive**.

The transaction motive

The **transaction motive** for holding money recognizes the need that money payments and money receipts are not perfectly synchronized.

We hold money because we have to pay for goods and services at various points after we receive income payments. Consider the following scenarios: (a) you are paid on Friday and carry out all your shopping on Friday; and (b) you are paid on Friday and shop each day for food, clothes, fuel, etc. Under scenario (a) your payments and receipts of money are perfectly synchronized; under (b) they are not. Therefore, you need to hold more money in scenario (b) than in (a).

As the value of our transactions increases and as the degree of synchronization between receipts and payments deteriorates, the greater becomes the transactional motive for holding cash. Moreover, we need to state that demand is for real money balances, where the demand is adjusted for inflation. So, if inflation doubles, the nominal value of our receipts and payments will also double, and we will have to hold double nominal money balances, but in real terms our demand for money will remain constant.

The precautionary motive

The **precautionary motive** for holding money reflects the unpredictability of transactions and the need to hold liquid funds in order to meet these payments.

We also hold money because we are unsure when transactions will occur. For example, we might hold some money in case of emergencies. The car develops a fault and needs repairing, or we might have spare cash in order to take advantage of special offers in the shops as and when they occur.

As uncertainty increases, the precautionary motive for money will also increase. In addition, as income increases, the value of potential transactions also increases. For example, someone who owns a Ferrari needs to hold more money to fix a fault with the Ferrari, than someone who owns a Fiat Uno (assuming each are equally reliable).

Under the **asset motive**, individuals hold money as part of a diversified asset portfolio. Some wealth is held in equities, some in bonds, a portion in property and some in money.

The asset motive

Individuals hold money as part of a diversified portfolio of assets. Equities are risky assets, with values going down as well as up. Bonds are financial instruments, where a firm offers to make specified repayments in the future to the bondholder. The risk is that the firm will default on the payments. Money is a low-risk asset. Aside from the exchange rate, the value of money is only affected in real terms by the inflation rate.

Clearly the more wealth is held in cash, the more an individual is foregoing the potential higher returns from holding other financial assets such as bonds. Indeed, bonds pay a rate of return, or interest. We can argue that the higher the rate of interest on bonds, the higher the opportunity cost of holding real-money balances. Therefore, as the interest rate increases, individuals will demand fewer real-money balances.

We can now think about the money market equilibrium. In Figure 11.9 we have the demand for real money balances, LL_1 and the supply of money, L_1. The supply of money is perfectly inelastic. As the interest rate, or price of money, increases, then the supply of money remains unchanged. This, as we will see shortly, is because the government (or central bank) adds to or reduces the money supply as it sees fit. Its decision is not influenced by the interest rate. The demand for real-money balances is not perfectly inelastic and reflects the asset motive for holding money.

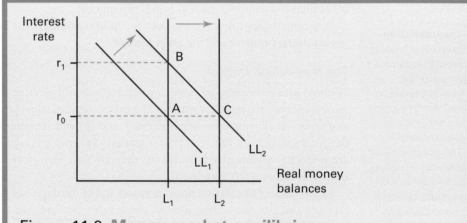

Figure 11.9 Money market equilibrium

Money demand LL is interest responsive, reflecting a trade-off between holding non-interest-bearing money and alternative interest-generating assets such as bonds. Money supply L is perfectly interest inelastic. In equilibrium money demand equals money supply. An increase in money demand will lead to a higher equilibrium interest rate, while an increase in money supply will lead to a lower equilibrium interest rate.

As interest rates on bonds increase, individuals find holding money too expensive and reduce their holdings of real money balances.

At the equilibrium A, the demand for real money balances is equal to the money supply at an interest rate of r_0.

We can consider a change to the demand for real-money balances. If income increased, or uncertainty increased, then either the transaction motive or the precautionary motive for holding money would increase. In both instances the demand for real money balances would shift out to the right at LL_2. If money supply remains unchanged, the equilibrium moves to B and the interest rate rises to r_1.

If the central bank increased the money supply from L_1 to L_2, by printing more bank notes, then the supply of money would move out to the right. At the higher level of money demand, LL_2, the equilibrium moves to C and the interest rate returns to r_0. Clearly, if the central bank reduced the amount of money in the economy, then the interest rate would increase.

Controlling the money supply

We have seen that the money supply is composed of cash in circulation, plus money on deposit at the banks. In attempting to control the money supply, it is clear that the central bank has two options open to it. First, the credit-creation process undertaken within banks could be regulated by the central bank. Second, the amount of notes and coins in circulation could be controlled.

Managing the credit-creation process requires regulation of the reserve requirements run by banks. Increasing the reserve levels reduces the ability to lend money. Unfortunately, many banks in the 1980s found ways around these controls. By setting up operations in the US and other European countries, where the reserve requirements were less, banks could then lend money back to UK-based companies, effectively bypassing UK regulation.

The second approach is to control the amount of notes and coins in circulation, or manage the monetary base. **Open market operations** are a known way of trying to control the monetary base.

> **Open market operations** occur when the central bank buys and sells financial assets in return for money.

The central bank might sell government bonds in the market place. If you bought such a bond, you would write a cheque and transfer money from your account to the central bank. This takes funds out of the banking system and limits the credit-creation process. Put into reverse, the central bank could print new notes and use these to buy back the government bonds. As it does so, this cash is transferred from the central bank into private bank accounts. The credit-creation process can then expand.

However, there is a recognized problem with trying to control the monetary base. Banks can exploit the position of the central bank. As the lender of last resort, the central bank will always try to bail out a bank in financial distress. The implications of one bank going bust can be substantial for a financial system and the rest of the economy. However, because the central bank will ordinarily rescue a stricken bank, it is possible to run risks as a lending bank, knowing that there is a safety net to catch you. Hence, when the central bank tries to control the monetary base, private banks will be tempted to push lending and the central bank will always pump in more notes and coins in order to keep banks financially solvent.

Controlling the interest rate

So, rather than control the money supply, central banks have now moved to controlling the interest rate. Interest rates are declared and then however much money is demanded at the official base rate is how much money is supplied to the market. Indeed, in markets where the demand for money is particularly unstable, it is best to set interest rates, rather than money supply. For example, if the money supply is managed, then changes in money demand will lead to instability in interest rates. If the interest rate is set, however, changes in money demand simply lead to instability in money supply. If control of the economy operates more through interest rates than through money supply, it is of no surprise that policy has shifted from managing money supply to managing interest rates.

11.9 Issues in monetary policy

Monetary policy is no easy mechanism for controlling economic activity; and like fiscal policy, monetary intervention is also beset with problems and policy considerations. These can include timing problems, considerations of inflation targeting and central bank independence.

Box 11.5 No mercy now, no bail-out later

Adapted from an article by Ambrose Evans-Pritchard, the Daily Telegraph, 23 March 2006

As Ben Bernanke, the head of the US Federal Reserve, knows all too well, monetary policy is like pulling a brick across a rough wooden table with a piece of elastic. Tug, tug, tug: nothing happens. Tug a little harder: it leaps off the surface and knocks your teeth out.

A garrulous professor, he could scarcely have taken charge of the US Federal Reserve at a more hazardous moment, just as the credit cycle nears it peak. The departing Fed chairman Alan Greenspan has done the easy work, lifting US interest rates to 4.5% in 14 brisk steps from the aberrantly low – perhaps fatally low – level of 1% in June 2004. This may be near the 'neutral' level, or not.

A mistake now could put millions out of work, or worse, and since it takes a year or more (the Swiss National Bank says three years) before the full effects of monetary policy are felt, Mr Bernanke will not find out until it is far too late.

Timing problems and monetary transmission

The **transmission mechanism** is the channel through which monetary policy impacts economic output.

In simplistic terms, interest rates affect consumers' willing to borrow for consumption and firms' willingness to borrow for investment. Unfortunately the **transmission mechanism** is not instantaneous. The Bank of England's monetary committee works on the assumption that interest rate changes take one year to affect economic output and two years to affect prices. These are rules of thumb reflecting more practical considerations of economic adjustment, rather than hard precise rules predicted by economic theories.

The time lag for economic output could reflect pre-committed expenditures. You may book the family summer holiday in January. But between January and the summer, interest rates may rise. Because you are pre-committed to spending the money, the interest rate rise is unlikely to alter your expenditure, or overall aggregate demand, but it may curb the amount of expenditure you pre-commit to next year's summer holiday. The same may be true of house purchases and investment in production or retail facilities by firms, where an interest rate change takes place between the decision to spend and the actual point when the transaction takes place. The transactions will still take place, because the parties are committed to the sale process. It is only in the longer term that the volume of sales and the amount of investment will reflect the new higher interest rates. In a similar manner, a fall in interest rates is unlikely to lead to an immediate increase in additional expenditures, because the expenditure for the coming year has already been planned out and committed. It is only next year that you may upgrade your holiday expenditure, while within firms with strict budgetary control and annual planning cycles, additional expenditure will not occur for another twelve months.

The two-year time lag for inflation is likely to reflect the prevalence of annual wage negotiations and the evolution of inflationary expectations. For example, if interest rates are increased to fend off higher inflation, it is not clear how this policy will alter inflationary expectations. In the short term the higher interest rate may have little impact, with consumers and firms wondering about the credibility of the monetary authorities to fight inflation. Only if rates are kept high for a period of six to twelve months will inflationary expectations change. Once these changes in expectations are made, they will not impact wages and prices until wage negotiations take place. These tend to be conducted annually. So, given that interest rates take a year to effect output, the ability to change prices and wages to the new equilibrium output level may take up to one year longer.

The problem with such long time lags is that some other problem may hit the economy in the intervening period – for example, war, terrorist attack, avian flu, stock market crash, oil price increase. All of these are very real, immediate and significant threats to economic stability.

Inflation targeting

The EU, UK and US all follow different interest rate policies. The European Bank targets inflation less than 2 per cent. The Bank of England targets inflation of 2 per cent on average. The US Federal Reserve has no inflation target (yet). The differences are important. The Eurozone is strictly anti-inflation. Fighting inflation is central to economic stability. The UK is less stringent and takes a slightly more flexible view, arguing that inflation needs to be controlled, but it may be sensible to have a period of above-average inflation in order to facilitate expansion of aggregate demand, say during a recession; or to accommodate a supply side shock, such as increase in the oil price. The US is most flexible and believed until recently that targeting GDP was preferable to targeting inflation, thereby enabling monetary policy to accommodate any shock at the expense of inflation targeting.

This leads to a trade-off under monetary policy: target inflation and keep inflationary expectations under control, but suffer long-term adjustment in economic output; or enable the accommodation of economic shocks and keep output high, but suffer higher inflation and the risk of falling international price competitiveness and a corrective recession.

Central bank independence

A final consideration is the independence of monetary policy from political motives. A fear with fiscal policy is that governments will face incentives, particularly near to elections, to alter taxation and spending for electoral gain rather than for economic stability. The same can be true for monetary policy except it is easier to place monetary policy with a non-government agency such as the central bank. Furthermore, providing the bank with an inflation target reduces the political link and boosts the economic driver of monetary policy decisions. However, the appointment of key monetary decision makers, at most central banks, is a government decision. So, decisions may still be taken in the light of political patronage.

11.10 Fiscal or monetary policy?

The answer to this question is highly debatable and for many economists it is fundamental to their very existence. However, broadly speaking, in terms of controlling aggregate demand, Keynesians believe in the effectiveness of fiscal policy, while monetarists believe in the effectiveness of monetary policy.

Keynesians do not have a strong regard for the crowding-out argument. Instead, they believe that during recessions economies face an abundance of under-utilized economic resource, such as unemployed workers. This creates a very elastic aggregate supply line. In Figure 11.10 when aggregate demand AD_1 shifts to the right, following an increase in government spending, GDP grows without any increase in inflation. The extra demand simply mops up the idle resource.

Monetarists do not accept these arguments. Instead, they think crowding-out is important and as such an economy often does not face an abundance of economic

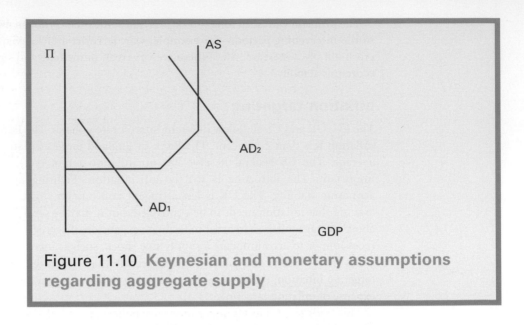

Figure 11.10 Keynesian and monetary assumptions regarding aggregate supply

resource. Instead, even in downturns, the economy is still somewhere near to its full employment level. As such the economy faces an almost perfectly inelastic aggregate supply line. If fiscal policy is used to stimulate aggregate demand, then AD_2 in Figure 11.10 shifts to the right, GDP remains constant and inflation rises. The extra expenditure on public goods and services not only crowds out the supply of private goods and services but it also bids up their prices driving higher inflation.

The monetarists are also associated with the quantity theory of money which states that:

$$MV \equiv PY$$

where M is the money supply, V is the velocity of circulation, P is the price level and Y is real GDP. Since real GDP is nominal GDP deflated by the price level, then nominal GDP must be PY. The velocity of circulation is the number of times money circulates around the economy. For example, if the money supply is £50 billion and nominal GDP, PY is £500 billion, then V must be 10, that is, £50 billion in notes and coins must change hands ten times in order to facilitate £500 billion of expenditure.

Since monetarists believe that an economy is at or near its long-run, full-employment level then Y is assumed to be constant. In addition monetarists believe that in the long run V is reasonably constant. These two assumptions are very important because on the left-hand side of the equation we have a constant V and a variable M. On the right-hand side we have a constant Y and a variable P. Therefore, if the money supply increases, V and Y will not change, they are constants. Instead, P must increase by the same amount as M. It should now be clear that within this monetarist model, inflation is driven by an increase in the money supply. For the monetarist inflation management is simple: control the growth in the money supply. While Keynesians reject the quantity theory of money, and while targeting money supply growth is no longer popular, major central banks in the EU, the UK and the US maintain a watchful eye over growth in the money supply.

For businesspeople the debate between Keynesians and monetarists is perhaps purely academic and, therefore, of little relevance. Of greater importance is how the various policies are currently mixed.

At present, in the UK monetary control has been allocated to the Bank of England, with the explicit aim of keeping inflation at an average rate of 2 per cent. The government has retained its control over fiscal policy. Consider Figure 11.11. If the government introduces a policy of fiscal expansion through tax reductions and increased government spending, aggregate demand increases. As this process occurs the equilibrium level of output and prices increases. If nothing is done the economy will experience an inflationary boom. However, the Bank of England has been tasked with keeping inflation at 2 per cent. Seeing the inflationary pressures within the economy, the Bank of England increases interest rates. Aggregate demand is reduced and the economy remains at its initial equilibrium, with constant GDP and prices. Central bank independence, tasked with controlling prices, effectively neutralizes active fiscal policy. It is no surprise that the chancellor talks about fiscal prudence. Indeed, we might be forgiven for thinking that keeping government spending and taxation in balance are the sole criteria for economic success. In reality, it does not really matter what the chancellor says about fiscal policy. It is more the case that he has no option but to be prudent.

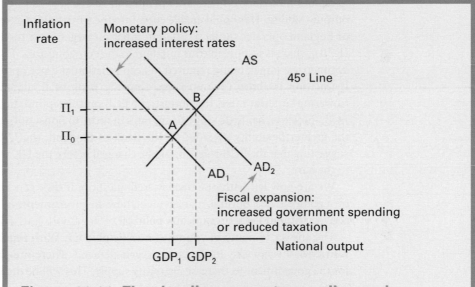

Figure 11.11 Fiscal policy, monetary policy and prudence

Increasing fiscal policy by either increased government spending or reduced taxation leads to an increase in aggregate demand, shifting rightward from AD₁ to AD₂. At equilibrium B, GDP is higher but so too is inflation. The central bank reacts to the inflationary stimulus by increasing interest rates and reducing aggregate demand from AD₂ to AD₁. The equilibrium returns to A, lowering both inflation and GDP.

Similar arguments apply to the eurozone. Domestic governments are required to keep their budget deficits below 3 per cent of GDP. If large economies such as France and Germany, or if collectively many governments breach this limit, there will be a concern that the additional spending will eventually lead to higher inflation. The European Central Bank will then have to raise interest rates to curb the excess aggregate demand, induce a slow-down in economic growth and bring inflation under control. Therefore, under fiscal expansion eurozone interest rates may have to be higher; and those countries that abide by the spending limits will also be affected by the higher costs of borrowing.

It is important to understand why the governments have arrived at a situation where monetary policy in the hands of central banks constrains the use of fiscal policy. In terms of Figure 11.11, the government is pursuing stability in prices as opposed to stability in output. Prior to this, governments have given greater importance to stability in output, rather than prices. It is perhaps the view of the government that targeting stability in prices lays the foundations for stability in output. Low and stable inflation provide businesses and consumers with the confidence to commit to spending and investment plans. In contrast, targeting output simply leads to boom–bust economics. Politicians mistime policy changes and simply make the economy unstable. By targeting inflation and keeping prices stable, the real economy can then operate in an environment of price stability and develop with greater stability.

Moreover, in terms of potential entry into the euro, interest rate policy would be handed to the European central bank; as we will see in Chapter 13 on exchange rates, keeping inflation under control is central to the success of the euro. In the case of the UK, fiscal and monetary policies are operated in such a way as to ensure price stability and output stability. This could enable entry into the euro, but it has to be noted that the Bank of England operates under a different inflation target from the European Central Bank (ECB), which is responsible for inflation in the eurozone area. The Bank of England has a symmetrical target, being required to keep inflation at 2 per cent over the medium term. If inflation is above (below) 2 per cent the Bank of England must consider raising (lowering) interest rates. In contrast, the ECB must keep inflation below 2 per cent. The ECB, therefore, has little scope to cut rates in order to boost output (and inflation). Given the greater flexibility awarded to the Bank of England, the UK government has been suggesting that the ECB rules should be changed before the UK will consider committing to the euro.

We are now left with one unanswered question. If they generally succeed in elections on a platform of economic management, how do governments influence macroeconomic activity without fiscal or monetary policies?

The answer to many of you must now be obvious. With monetary and fiscal policies restricted, it is not easy to change aggregate demand. Therefore, the only game in town is for the government to increase aggregate supply. This will be discussed in Chapter 12.

11.11 **Business application: monetary policy**

Interest rates and investment

Debt is a complementary good for firms seeking to invest. Just as car users need to buy petrol, firms when investing in new plant and machinery often need to purchase loans. If the interest rate falls, loans become cheaper. As a result, demand for investments increases. However, it is important to recognize that it is the real price of debt which is important. If inflation is higher than the interest rate, then negative real interest rates apply and debt is very attractive to borrowers. If prices are falling, so-called 'deflation', then it is impossible for an economy to enjoy negative real interest rates. This is the situation described in Box 11.6; and it can become very difficult to drive investment and consumption growth through lax monetary policy.

Box 11.6 **Bratwurst and sushi**

Why Europe's monetary policy needs to tighten and Japan's doesn't

Adapted from an article in The Economist, 24 November 2005

EUROPE'S interest rates, stuck at 2% for 30 months, have not increased in more than five years. So the expected rise is being condemned as imprudent and premature. Many European politicians argue that a rise in rates could snuff out the euro area's economic recovery. Indeed, some commentators fret that a rise in interest rates risks repeating Japan's past policy mistakes, and will tip the euro area back into recession.

Fashionable though it is to compare the euro zone to Japan, their economies are no more alike than bratwurst and sushi. The euro area's inflation is running at 2.5%. Even with zero interest rates, Japan's real rates were already positive before the BoJ pushed them higher. In contrast, the euro area has enjoyed negative real interest rates for most of the past two and a half years. In sharp contrast to Japan in 2000, the euro area's monetary policy is unusually loose. After all, both the money supply and bank credit are growing at an annual pace of more than 8%.

Investment and business confidence

The cost of the loan is not the only factor that influences a firm's decision to invest. The interest rate reflects a cost of investing, but what about the benefits? If an economy is in recession, consumption of goods and services is falling. If a firm cannot sell the output generated by new investments, the benefits of investing are very low. A recession is, therefore, likely to reduce business confidence. If businesses are not confident about being able to sell products, or make a profit because of recession, they are likely to delay investment decisions. Reductions in interest rates are unlikely to boost investment rates.

However, cutting interest rates could have two additional benefits. First, consumers may take advantage of the cheaper debt and use credit to expand consumption. Second, as we will see in Chapter 13, a falling interest rate can also reduce the exchange rate value of the currency. If, for example, the UK pound drops from €0.66 to €0.60, then UK products become 10 per cent cheaper for consumers in Europe holding euros. If UK exports do grow, UK firms should be willing to invest in order to meet the increased demand. Therefore, reducing interest rates may boost business confidence by promoting consumer spending and/or export growth.

Investment under low inflation and low interest rates

A more fundamental question surrounds the issue of low inflation and low interest rates. The price of loans is the real interest rate, which is the nominal rate minus the inflation rate. If inflation sticks to the 2.5 per cent level, then interest rates can only be cut to 2.5 per cent before real interest rates become negative (the bank pays you for taking out a loan!). So, with low interest rates and low inflation, the scope for providing a monetary stimulus to the economy is very limited.

Low inflation, stability and investment rates

Moreover, what are the effects of low inflation on the economy and, in particular, on business? Constantly low inflation should bring increased stability. Businesses seeking to invest millions of pounds over many years will be assured by increased price stability. Predictions regarding costs and revenues are much easier to make and firms face less uncertainty when assessing investment risks. If low inflation reduces uncertainty, active monetary policy, leading to low inflation, may boost investment because of stability issues, rather than because of cheaper borrowing.

Alternatively, low inflation may reduce the need, or desire, to invest. High wage inflation increases a firm's production costs. In order to recover these cost increases firms may seek to raise the final price for their products. In such a scenario firms have a clear incentive to swap increasingly expensive workers for capital equipment. But in recent times price inflation has been low. Wage demands have reflected the new lower rates of inflation and, as a result, firms have potentially less need to deal with an expensive workforce by investing in machinery.

It is, therefore, very clear that monetary policy and the pursuit of low inflation have many varied implications for business. Interest rates may influence investment simply by changing the cost of borrowing. However, the impact of interest rates on economic activity, business confidence and especially consumer spending and export growth may play a greater role in investment decisions. Finally, the use of monetary policy in targeting low inflation and economic stability may influence investments in different ways. Increased stability may make firms more willing to invest simply because it is easier to assess the relative costs and revenues from investment. However, without rising inflation and a consequential rise in labour costs, the need, or desire to substitute capital for workers will be diminished.

✐ Summary

1   The use of government spending and taxation to affect aggregate demand are examples of fiscal policy.

2   Aggregate demand is composed of consumption, investment, government spending and net exports.

3   In equilibrium planned expenditure equals planned output. In the Keynesian Cross the equilibrium is characterized by the 45° line.

4   Expenditure which does not change with the level of income is known as autonomous expenditure. Increases in autonomous expenditure lead to higher equilibrium levels of output.

5   The marginal propensity to consume (MPC) measures the increase in consumption from an increase in income. The marginal propensity to save (MPS) measures the increase in savings from an increase in income.

6   If a £100 million increase in autonomous expenditure leads to a £500 million increase in GDP, then the fiscal multiplier is 5. The multiplier is dependent upon the rate of leakage from the circular flow of income. In a closed economy the multiplier is equal to 1/MPS. But in an open economy with a government sector, the multiplier is reduced by the marginal propensity to tax (MPT) and the marginal propensity to import (MPZ) and so equals 1/(MPS + MPT + MPZ).

7   Fiscal policies can act as an automatic stabilizer on the economy. Rising incomes in a booming economy will be constrained by increasing tax receipts.

8   Active fiscal policies where the government seeks to pursue an expansionary, or contractionary fiscal policy can be problematic. Problems surrounding timing, uncertainty, offsetting behaviour, crowding out and inflationary inducing deficits can create instability in the economic system.

9   Monetary policy is the use of interest rates, or money supply, to control aggregate demand.

10 Money has a number of characteristics. It has to be a store of value, a unit of account and accepted as a medium of exchange.

11 The money supply is composed not only of notes and coins, but also deposits within the banking system. The narrow and broad measures of money, M0 and M4, attempt to take account of these differences.

12 Credit creation occurs when the banks create additional money supply by lending out money on deposit. This increases the money supply.

13 There are three motives for holding money: the transaction, precautionary and asset motives.

14 Increases in income lead to an increase in demand for real money balances and reflect the transaction and precautionary motives for holding money. The speculative motive reflects how changes in the interest rate lead to changes in demand for money.

15 In money market equilibrium the demand for money equals the money supply.

16 Governments, or central banks, now seek to set the interest rate and then provide sufficient money supply in order to make the market clear. It is the transmission of this market clearing price/interest rate to the rest of the economy that influences aggregate demand.

 Learning checklist

You should now be able to:

◆   Use Keynesian Cross diagrams to find the macroeconomic equilibrium output

◆   Calculate the size of the fiscal multiplier

◆   Explain why the multiplier might assist fiscal policy

◆   Assess the government's fiscal stance

◆   Explain the potential problems associated with using fiscal policy

◆   Explain the key features of money

◆   Provide an explanation of how banks create credit

◆   Explain why we use both broad and narrow measures of money

◆   Explain the three motives for holding money

◆   Discuss money market equilibrium using a suitable diagram

◆   Address how fiscal and monetary policy are related in the UK

◆   Explain how business activities are influenced by fiscal and monetary policies

❓ Questions

Fiscal policy

1 In a closed economy with no government sector consumption, $C = 20 + 0.8Y$, investment $I = 40$. What is the equilibrium level of income Y?

2 When examining fiscal policy, should business be more interested in taxation policy or government spending?

3 If entry into the euro by the UK improves trade with our European partners, what may happen to the size of the UK multiplier?

4 What problems are associated with the implementation of fiscal policy?

Monetary policy

1 The Bank of England controls the money supply by deciding how many notes and coins to produce. True or false?

2 UK business has prospered from rising consumption financed by rising personal debt. But how might this hamper business in the future?

3 How will low inflation and low interest rates influence the level of investment by firms?

4 Why is central bank control of interest rates a control on overexuberant fiscal policy? Is such a situation beneficial for business?

Exercises

1 True or false?
   a) In equilibrium planned expenditure will equal planned output.
   b) The fiscal multiplier is equal to 1/MPC.
   c) The following are autonomous expenditures, investment, government spending and net exports.
   d) Credit offered by banks is backed by cash deposits.
   e) Keynesians believe that inflation is a monetary problem.
   f) If aggregate supply is perfectly inelastic a reduction in interest rates will lead to higher inflation.

2 Table 11.2 shows some data on consumption and income (output) for the economy of Hypothetica. Planned investment is autonomous, and occurs at the rate of $60 billion per period.
   a) Calculate savings and aggregate demand at each level of income.
   b) For each level of output, work out the unplanned change in inventory holdings and the rate of actual investment.
   c) If, in a particular period, income turned out to be $100 billion, how would you expect producers to react?
   d) If, in a particular period, income turned out to be $350 billion, how would you expect producers to react?
   e) What is the equilibrium level of income?
   f) What is the marginal propensity to consume?
   g) If investment increased by $15 billion, what would be the change in equilibrium income?

h) Using the data of exercise 2, use graph paper to plot the consumption function and aggregate demand schedule.

i) Add on the 45° line and confirm that equilibrium occurs at the same point suggested by your answer to 2(e) above.

j) Show the effect on equilibrium of an increase in investment of $15 billion.

Table 11.2   Income and consumption in Hypothetica (all in Hypothetical $billion)

Income (output)	Planned consumption	Planned investment	Savings	Aggregate demand	Unplanned inventory change	Actual investment
50	35					
100	70					
150	105					
200	140					
250	175					
300	210					
350	245					
400	280					

3 Refer to Box 11.1 when considering the following questions:

a) Using a Keynesian cross diagram illustrate how an increase in exports would alter the equilibrium output for an economy. What evidence is there that Germany is benefiting from an export boom?

b) Identify all the evidence in support of an increase in consumption and investment expenditure.

c) Explain the variety of ways through which an increase in interest rates by the ECB would impact the German economy.

Chapter 12
Supply side policies and economic growth

Chapter contents

Learning outcomes

By the end of this chapter you should understand:

Economic Theory

- How economic growth is linked to growth in long-run aggregate supply

- The neoclassical model of economic growth

- The convergence hypothesis

- The endogenous growth model

- The types of policies used to develop economic growth

Business Application

- What determines the rate of innovation and the effectiveness of implementing innovation within an economy?

- China's economic growth is unprecedented, but what factors would increase the risk of a slowdown in China's economic growth?

Supply side policies and economic growth at a glance

The issues

Different economies grow at different rates. How do economies grow and how can governments involve business in developing economic growth?

The understanding

Economic growth can be linked to the development of long-run aggregate supply. The output potential of an economy is fixed if aggregate supply is perfectly inelastic. Changes in aggregate demand only alter the inflation rate. Therefore, in order to make the economy grow it is essential to increase the level of aggregate supply. At a simplistic level improving aggregate supply can be achieved by either increasing the availability of factor inputs, such as labour, or by increasing the productivity of factor inputs, so that more output can be produced with more input. However, a more interesting question relates to how fast an economy can grow. Neoclassical theory argues that growth will converge across economies to a common rate. Endogenous growth theory counters this view, suggesting that governments can develop policies which will enable the economy to grow at faster rates.

The usefulness

The growth rate of an economy has important implications for business. First, sales and revenue growth will, in part, be related to economic growth. Second, government policies designed to improve productivity within an economy may aid a firm to reduce its costs.

Economic growth is measured as the percentage change in GDP per year.

12.1 Business problem: assessing economic growth

The growth rate for the UK economy from 1999 quarter 1 to 2005 quarter 3 is presented in Figure 12.1. Annual growth (for the preceding four quarters) is shown in the top line. The rate of growth has varied from a maximum of 4.4 per cent in 1999 to as little as 1.6 per cent in 2005. While there is a variation in the growth rate, the average appears to be around 2.5 per cent.

The importance of growth rates becomes more apparent over time. For example, assume that we have an economy and the level of GDP is 100. The economy now grows at four hypothetical growth rates, 1 per cent, 2.5 per cent, 4 per cent and 10 per cent. The amount of GDP in each year, for each growth rate, is tabulated in Table 12.1.

The amount of GDP in year 10 is vastly different depending upon the growth rate of the economy, varying from 110 under a growth rate of 1 per cent, to 259 under a growth rate of 10 per cent. Therefore, over time the growth rate of an economy has enormous implications for the generation of individuals' incomes and the potential for companies to grow. As a consequence, governments, workers and firms are extremely interested in the projected growth rates for an economy.

For example, through a simple examination of the circular flow of income, economic growth is associated with growth in the flow of income between households and firms. More products are produced, more income is paid to workers/households and more

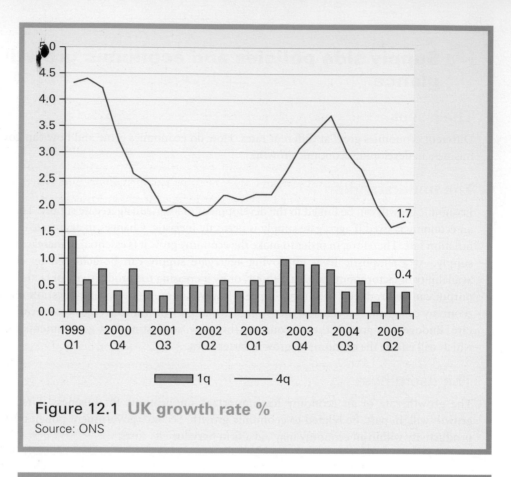

Figure 12.1 UK growth rate %
Source: ONS

Table 12.1 Impact of different growth rates

| Year | Growth rate | | | |
	1%	2.5%	4%	10%
0	100	100	100	100
1	101	103	104	110
2	102	105	108	121
3	103	108	112	133
4	104	110	117	146
5	105	113	122	161
6	106	116	127	177
7	107	119	132	195
8	108	122	137	214
9	109	125	142	236
10	110	128	148	259

products are sold. As a result, the faster an economy grows, the faster incomes rise and sales increase. While this makes economic growth an attractive opportunity for business, an additional consideration also has to be examined.

In the main, governments try to make the economy grow through developments in aggregate supply, providing firms with the ability, or incentive, to supply more output. Firms will supply more if the marginal costs of production fall. Policies designed to reduce companies' costs and, moreover, boost productivity are central to developing aggregate supply and economic growth. This means that economic growth and the development of sales is not the only benefit for firms. Policies designed to aid economic growth may also aid the cost structures faced by firms. Companies that understand why economic growth is important and how growth might be achieved are better placed to understand government policy and exploit the opportunities offered by economic growth. This chapter will provide you with an overview of supply side theories and economic growth.

12.2 Growth and aggregate supply

Making the economy grow through fiscal and/or monetary policy is difficult. Whenever the government increases aggregate demand through fiscal expansion, central banks may reduce aggregate demand through a monetary contraction. Therefore, we can only envisage real economic growth occurring if aggregate supply increases. We can even make this argument more compelling if we assume that aggregate supply is perfectly inelastic. In Figure 12.2 with perfectly inelastic aggregate supply, aggregate demand begins at AD_1. The equilibrium level of output is GDP_1 and the rate of inflation is Π_0. Following a fiscal or monetary stimulus, aggregate demand increases to AD_2. At the new equilibrium of B, GDP remains unchanged at GDP_1, but inflation has increased to Π_1. We can say that when aggregate supply is perfectly inelastic, increases in aggregate demand will be entirely inflationary. In contrast, if aggregate supply increases to AS_2, then the economy moves to equilibrium C, GDP increases to GDP_2 and inflation falls to Π_2. Therefore, growth through improvements in aggregate supply seems preferable.

Perfectly inelastic aggregate supply means that any increase in prices does not result in an increase in supply. In Chapter 9 we argued that aggregate supply will be perfectly inelastic if nominal wages fully adjust to inflation, resulting in a constant real wage. If the real wage remains constant, firms face no incentive to hire more labour and increase output. We can also provide additional arguments for why the aggregate supply curve is perfectly inelastic.

In the long run all factor resources – land, labour, capital and enterprise – that are available for employment, or production, will be utilized. All workers who want a job will be employed, and all machines and offices that have been acquired by companies will be fully utilized. From Chapter 4, when we examined markets, we know this to be true. This is because in the long run markets clear. The market prices for labour, capital and raw materials will be the equilibrium prices. As such, the demand for workers will be equal to the supply of workers; similarly for capital and raw materials. Importantly, the economy will be operating at **full employment**.

Full employment occurs within an economy when all markets are in equilibrium.

Full employment can be related back to the production possibility frontier presented in Chapter 1. Full employment occurs when the economy is operating on the frontier. The maximum possible production by the economy has been achieved. Because of full employment, aggregate supply cannot respond to an increase in aggregate demand. No more supply is currently possible. Therefore, with fixed supply, the only way to deal with increased demand is for prices and inflation to rise.

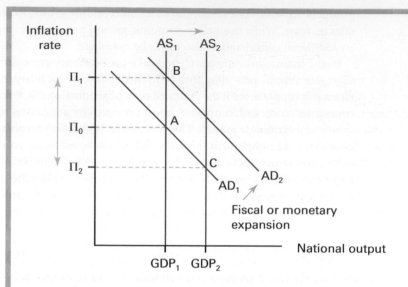

Figure 12.2 Inelastic aggregate supply and changes in aggregate demand

With perfectly inelastic aggregate supply, a fiscal or monetary stimulus, leading to an increase in aggregate demand will be purely inflationary. At equilibria A and B GDP is constant at GDP_1. While at A inflation is Π_0, but at B, following the increase in aggregate demand, inflation has increased to Π_1.

In contrast, an increase in aggregate supply from AS_1 to AS_2 moves the equilibrium from A to C. GDP increases to GDP_2 and inflation falls to Π_2.

Clearly, if economic growth is desirable, then moving aggregate supply, or increasing the potential productive output of the economy, is key. Government policy has moved towards a consideration of increasing aggregate supply in the long term with a particular emphasis on developing productivity, especially amongst high-value-adding workers. In the case of China this has led to an unprecedented acceleration in the provision of MBA education as discussed in Box 12.1

Supply and productivity

We argued in Chapter 3, when examining the cost curves of individual firms, that the marginal cost curve (above average variable cost) is the firm's supply curve. Therefore, at the macroeconomic level, aggregate supply must be the sum of all firms' marginal cost curves (above average variable cost).

The firm is only willing to supply more output at any given price if its marginal costs decrease. Box 12.2 provides details of the UK's GDP per capita gap with other developed economies and then breaks this gap into two sources, labour utilization and productivity. For example, the gap between UK and French GDP per capita is very small. But the means of producing this level of GDP per capita are very different. The utilization rate of French labour is 25 per cent less than in the UK, but this is offset by French workers being 30 per cent more productive than their UK rivals. If the UK could raise its labour productivity, then at the same utilization rate GDP per capita would accelerate beyond that of France and perhaps some of the other countries in the table.

Box 12.1 China's B-School Boom

Adapted from an article in BusinessWeek, 9 January 2006

Walk into any classroom at one of China's elite business schools and what you are likely to see is not all that different from what you would find at Harvard, Wharton, or MIT's Sloan School. Indeed, in most cases the MBA programs attended by China's top students are very much the product of Western educational institutions, which in recent years have rushed to establish programmes on the mainland. The idea: to tap into the enormous demand for talent created by China's white-hot economy.

The colossal effort by the central government of China to educate the nation's next generation of managers is unprecedented. The need could not be more urgent. Twenty-five years into China's transformation into a market economy, the nation faces a critical shortage of well-trained managers. After two decades of explosive economic growth, many Chinese managers run regional or national companies, yet they lack the sophisticated skills they need to compete effectively.

For US companies, the emergence of China's new managerial class has positive and negative implications. For those seeking to penetrate China's massive market of 1.3 billion people, the graduates of the nation's new MBA programs will supply a steady stream of local talent with in-depth knowledge of China, something their Western managers cannot provide. But as Western management ideas take root in the nation's corner offices, multinationals could find themselves confronting a newly powerful adversary: Chinese companies suddenly in possession of the management know how needed to go head to head with global giants. Those same ideas – about efficiency, productivity, profitability, and growth – hold vast potential to ignite China's already blistering economy, raise living standards, and transform the nation from a low-cost manufacturing centre to a make-or-break battleground for the global economy.

 Box 12.2 The UK productivity gap and sources of income difference

Source: OECD 2005.

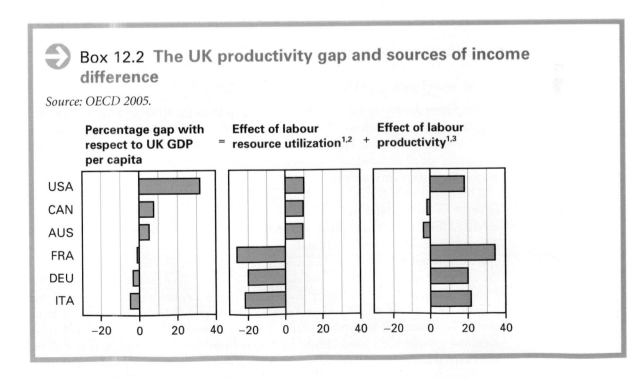

The key to improving marginal costs is developing productive efficiency. Therefore, if economic growth across the entire economy is seen as desirable, developments in productivity seem essential. We will examine this idea in detail by exploring **neoclassical exogenous growth theory** and the competing alternative of **endogenous growth theory**. These will then provide the theoretical background for a review of government initiatives designed to improve UK productivity.

12.3 Neoclassical growth theory

Assume we have a simple model where the economy's output is determined by three things: (i) technical progress, (ii) capital and (iii) labour. There are simple but appealing features of this approach. If we allow the number of workers to increase (our population grows) but keep capital constant, then from Chapter 3 we know that the economy will run up against the law of diminishing returns. Extra workers will not continue to improve the rate of productivity. Indeed, marginal productivity might become negative, driving down total productivity. This problem was first recognized by Rev. Thomas Malthus in 1798, who predicted that with a fixed supply of land, adding additional workers to the land would result in slower growth of food output than growth rates in population. Essentially, diminishing returns would ensure that at some point the population would outgrow its supply of food and begin to starve. (Reflecting this point, economics is still known as the dismal science, which for professional members of the subject is less worrying than the term 'Armageddon'.)

Clearly in the developed world we have not starved. So, the law of diminishing returns has been held back. This has been achieved by either (i) improving technical progress in agriculture or (ii) the employment of more capital. We can see evidence of each. Technical progress has developed with improved knowledge of fertilizers, insecticides and herbicides, improved irrigation systems and, more controversially, genetic modifications. Capital in the form of tractors and combine harvesters has also helped to improve the productivity of land and workers.

How long can growth keep improving?

Robert Solow developed a model of economic growth in the 1950s and the fundamental insight from his approach was that economic growth would not increase forever. Rather, it will reach a steady state. In growth rate equilibrium, or the steady state output, labour and capital are all assumed to be growing at the same rate. Hence, capital per worker and output per worker are constant.

If the labour force is growing at 10 per cent, then capital also has to grow at 10 per cent in order to keep capital per worker constant. Increases in capital are funded out of increased investment. Banks provide loans for investment from savings. In order for a 10 per cent increase in investment funds, income or output must grow at 10 per cent in order to guarantee a 10 per cent increase in savings. Essentially, labour growth rates set the tempo for capital investment and economic growth. Indeed, a common fallacy is that higher savings will lead to higher investment, higher capital per worker and higher growth. This is only true for short-term economic growth rates. In the short term, providing all workers with more productive capital improves productivity and raises economic growth; but a blank cheque has also been written for the future, in that all the extra capital has to be maintained. Increased maintenance requires a greater proportion of economic output to go into the renewal of existing capital, rather than the development of new additional capital. As a result, economic growth slows and reverts back to the steady state growth rate.

This has a fundamental and particularly troublesome conclusion: growth rate **convergence**.

> The **convergence hypothesis** states that poor countries grow more quickly than average, but rich countries grow more slowly than average.

If a country has a low ratio of capital per worker, then it does not take much output to renew existing capital. Therefore, more resource can be put into the production of additional capital per worker. However, if capital per worker is high, then more effort is put into renewing existing capital and less resource is available for creating additional capital per worker. Therefore, economic growth rates in modern economies will fall, while growth rates in developing economies will grow. We, however, see little evidence of either. On average the world's richest and most developed economies exhibit persistently higher growth rates than the world's poorest developing economies.

12.4 Endogenous growth theory

> **Endogenous growth theory** considers models in which the steady state growth rate can be affected by economic behaviour and policy.

The neoclassical model is problematic: convergence is not observed and growth is determined by either labour force growth or, at best, by developments in technology. However, neoclassical economists see even developments in technology as being exogenous, or determined outside the model.

For neoclassical economists growth is determined by technological development, but technological development is not affected by economic growth.

For example, technological development occurs with mad professors staggering out of their labs, the air filled with smoke and the word 'eureka' being proclaimed. These dotty individuals who stumble across new insights of economic importance, such as plastic, computers, nuclear power and the Internet, find such knowledge by chance. None of these discoveries are based within economics. Clearly nuclear physics, biology and chemistry are different subjects; but surely within an economy, government and the economic system can provide structures, incentives and institutions that foster and promote technological development. Leaving such a beneficial activity to chance, in the hands of dotty individuals, is not good policy.

However, endogenous growth theory has to make a brave assumption: that of constant returns to capital (or something similar), such as knowledge. The Solow model does not allow increasing growth rates from increased capital accumulation because of diminishing returns. Nor does it allow increasing returns; if it did, growth rates would explode exponentially and that is not observed in reality. But how might we envisage a situation of constant returns to capital? Investment by individual firms in capital will still exhibit diminishing returns. But if investments by one firm have positive externalities, then constant returns to capital are possible. For example, if one firm invests heavily in broadband infrastructure for the Internet, then all other firms who wish to use the Internet to deliver media, online shopping and even teaching materials, will also receive a positive boost to their online investments. This way, an increase in investment from one firm leads to increases in productivity across many firms. The economic growth rate can now increase over time through positive externalities.

The more fundamental point is that governments now have a role in developing how the economy grows over time. Under the neoclassical model, growth was determined by labour force growth and chance inventions. In the endogenous world, governments have the potential to increase technological developments and direct economic decision-makers to investment activities with positive externalities. For business this is important because industrial planning, initiatives for training and tax breaks for R&D become critical components of government's desires to increase potential output and, therefore, aggregate supply.

12.5 **Supply side policies**

Education markets and long-term growth

Governments around the world are keen to widen participation in higher education. Universities have been tasked with taking in students from poor and deprived areas. Such a policy is political and economic. Bringing a broader and larger number of individuals into higher education widens the skill base of the workforce. This has positive externalities. With higher cognitive skills among the workforce, more advanced productive capital can be employed by firms. This is not about employing more machines per worker, it is about utilizing more productively advanced machines per worker. In addition, a university education enables people to learn for themselves and think critically. If people can learn for themselves, then they might react better to change. So, when new ways of operating come along, firms adapt quicker and exploit new ideas more readily. Also, by thinking critically, managers can develop new means of operation more rapidly. In this way education comes to the core of technological improvement. The higher the income level of the economy, the greater scope the economy has for funding educational improvements. More education, the greater the rate of technological development, both within university labs and the workplace.

An important point is to establish the optimal mix of skills for an economy. It is perhaps not desirable to allocate resources to the provision of a university education for all workers. Box 12.3 provides a comparison of skill levels for many developed economies.

The UK's (GBR) problem is not in the provision of university education. If anything the UK has one of the workforces with the highest percentage of graduates. Rather, the UK's problem is its large percentage of low-skilled workers. Where it would be more desirable to transfer these workers to the upper secondary and tertiary level of skills, those UK individuals who do not enter university are not receiving the same skills training as they do in countries such as Germany and France. It appears, therefore, that the UK has many educated managers, but an underskilled set of workers. This can be very problematic. If managers wish to pursue innovative products, or employ advanced production techniques, then workers are ill-equipped to respond. They simply do not have the skill base to exploit advanced technologies. The argument may be a generalization, but the points for government are simple. Higher education in the UK is doing well. Attention now needs to be paid to the development of skills within those individuals who choose not to attend university. Moreover, these individuals and their employers need to be provided with incentives to engage in skills development.

Labour markets and long-term growth

For managers to be capable of exploiting innovative ways of operating, or taking advantage of new capital machinery, labour markets have to be accommodating. The existence of strong trade unions and legislation that either limits redundancies, or raises redundancy payments, will constrain the ability of firms to exploit new developments. Trade unions will seek to protect their members' interest and perhaps block changes that result in redundancies. Therefore, throughout the 1980s there was a strong impetus from government to reduce the power of trade unions and make it easier for firms to make workers redundant. Two things have happened. First, trade unions have begun to work with, rather than against, companies. Developing greater collaborative relationships seeking, for example, to help businesses improve productivity by raising workers' views of

→ Box 12.3 Skill levels

Educational attainment of the population aged 25–34 years

Source: OECD 2005.

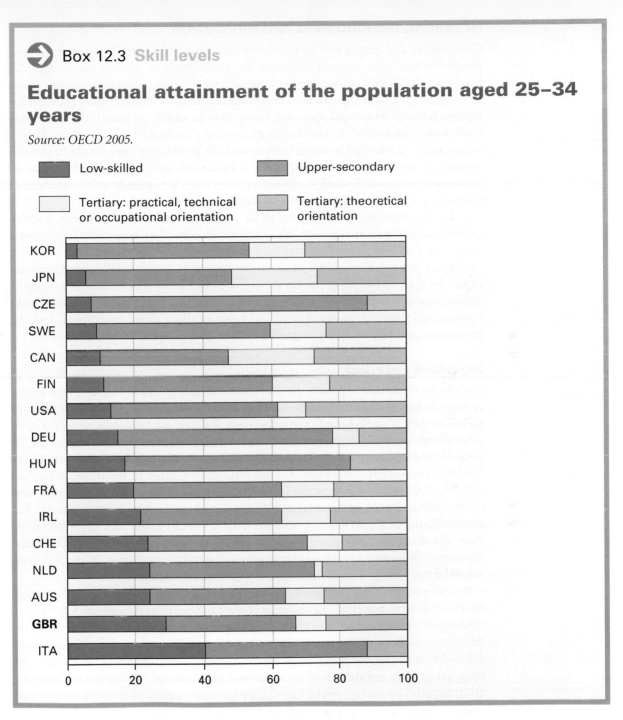

inefficient practices and perhaps even supporting the development of skills and education within the current workforce. Second, the rise of the stakeholder perspective argues that firms are a collection of interest groups including consumers, workers, managers, shareholders and government and each needs to work with and recognize the needs of others. Therefore, cultural change and regulatory change in the labour market free up the rapid redeployment of economic resource and can improve labour efficiency and economic growth.

Research, development and innovation

Government can play a role in providing incentives to undertake research in new productive processes, or even encourage the exploitation of existing knowledge. Tax breaks for R&D expenditure can be a useful incentive to undertake research. More recently the government announced tax breaks on directors' remuneration packages for high-technology industries, the idea being that in order to attract the most able individuals from around the world, very attractive pay packages had to be offered. Highly valued skills are attracted into the economy and it is hoped, over time, local workers will observe, learn and develop similar skills. If such skills are based in high-technology industries, which will flourish in the future, then the UK is attracting the right type of economic expertise in order to survive in the future.

Industrial networks are also seen as an important means of developing positive externalities and economic growth. Local regions are beginning to specialize in particular industries: Yorkshire in food production, Cambridgeshire in technological development, London in finance, Oxfordshire in motor racing and Manchester in higher education. Again, for these industries to sustain the engine of economic growth, they need support industries and it is better to plan for this than hope that they appear. Managers need training and financial resources need to be put in place to aid investment, and the government can help to deliver each of these through regional development agencies.

Financial services

A common discussion of growth theories relates to savings and investment, with higher savings leading to higher investments. This misses a number of points. High levels of savings in the UK could be lent to firms overseas. Further, the financial services industry, as an intermediary between savers and borrowers, may enhance growth. For example, by being experts in investment appraisal, financial services firms can more effectively screen out poor investment opportunities. Therefore, development in the financial services sector can lead to better investments within the economy. With higher, rather than lower, quality investments being undertaken, the capital stock can become more productive and economic growth should improve. Moreover, the existence of insurance can protect firms from the financial consequences of risks, such as fire, earthquake, etc. Therefore, insurance can be seen as necessary for expensive capital accumulation. Without it firms would be less willing to invest, leading to a reduction in growth rates.

A clear question for governments is, how do you generate economic growth through the financial services sector? The answer at present appears to be through the legal system. If banks take savers' money and lend to firms for investment purposes, then in order for this system to flourish the courts need to be able to enforce payments of outstanding debts. In countries where the legal environment is very supportive of lenders, the financial services industry (and the economy) grows faster. Where the law provides greater protection for borrowers, financial development and economic development are slower.

Other policies

Tax cuts

In the 1980s the UK and US governments reduced personal taxation rates, arguing that such policies provided incentives for individuals to work longer and raise productive output. However, most evidence tends to suggest that many individuals recognized that with the tax cut they could actually reduce the hours they worked and still earn the same amount of income as they did under the higher tax rates. A possible explanation for this behaviour is that individuals valued leisure time more than they did income. Therefore, following the tax cuts, individuals decided that, rather than seek higher income levels, they would retain the current income level and instead opt for more time spent with family and friends enjoying various leisure activities.

Privatization

Privatization was also popular in the 1980s and 1990s. Previously, water, telephone, gas and electricity were all supplied by government companies operating as so-called 'nationalized' industries. Rail services were also nationalized, as was British Airways and the UK airports. Most nationalized industries acted as monopolies and were deemed to be inefficient through lack of competition. Furthermore, any increase in investment by nationalized industries had to be funded by the taxpayer. Such a system limited funds, because the government had competing projects such as health and education to invest in; and it was not clear how financial performance would be ensured. Privatized companies can access the London finance markets and raise significant sums of money. Furthermore, unlike the government, private investors would be keen to ensure that the privatized industries operated at a profit and similarly only invested in profitable and productive assets. Therefore, as the privatized industries were and are important components of the national infrastructure, it is easy to see how increased investment and improvements in operational efficiency could have positive externalities for the rest of the UK economy – particularly if productivity improvements occurred in communications and transport. Reflecting these arguments, the government privatized these nationalized industries and enabled new companies to compete in these markets.

The growth of competition has been slow to develop. In the case of tele-communications, economies of scale created an effective entry barrier. However, as technology changed and mobile communications became more popular, new companies found it easier to enter the market. In terms of utilities, we can now buy gas from electricity producers and vice versa. The market appears far more competitive, at least for those customers who wish to shop around. Therefore, if competition is increasing in these markets, then prices should be falling and firms will be seeking new and innovative ways of operating. In the long term, important factor inputs for other companies, such as communication, energy and transport, all become cheaper and overall supply in the economy improves.

Developing market forces through competition was a key aspect of the privatization programme. Without the safety net of the government, privatized companies would have to manage costs and understand customers' needs better than their rivals in order to survive. A key question is how to bring the benefits of competition to industries such as health and education, which are politically difficult to privatize. In response the government has been very active in promoting independence among healthcare providers. Primary healthcare trusts are generally a collection of many general practitioners who decide how to spend their allotted budget with competing hospitals. The potential creation of foundation hospitals enables hospitals to react to the primary healthcare trusts by deciding what forms of treatment (health product markets) they wish to compete in. So, even without privatization it may be possible to bring market forces to bear on organizations in the pursuit of operational efficiencies.

Summary

There are clearly many possible policy prescriptions for economic growth but, broadly speaking, governments seek to develop labour productivity, capital productivity or technological progress. More fundamentally, governments are beginning to return to the idea that they can *design* an economy, which will outperform in terms of growth. The neoclassical model advises governments to sit back and wait for the economy to develop. The endogenous growth theory directs governments to think about how businesses relate to the educational system, how financial services relate to the development of business and how the labour market reacts to the needs of business. Economic policy has moved to an understanding of how to enhance the whole economic system by thinking about how the individual parts work together and in particular how positive externalities can be generated throughout the economic system.

12.6 Business application: innovate or die

We have seen that economic growth is associated with productivity gains and innovation. Exogenous growth models suggest that innovation occurs on a random basis, while endogenous growth models propose that innovation rates are a reflection of the level of economic activity and the characteristics of the economy. As such innovation rates will vary across economies. The discussion in Box 12.4 tends to supports this view, with only a few European economies being able to match the innovation rates of the US and Japan, while countries such as the UK, France and Italy lag behind.

 Box 12.4 The EU is 50 years behind the US for innovation

Adapted from an article in the Financial Times, 13 January 2006

Additional data taken from:

www.trendchart.org/scoreboards/scoreboard2005/index.cfm

The EU's record on innovation is so poor that it would take more than 50 years to catch up with the US, according to a survey released by the European Commission. Measuring the innovation inputs and outputs listed in the table below, the Commission said the study was important because it looked beyond R&D spending to analyse the ability to transform basic research into marketable products, and thence into jobs and economic growth.

The study found that only four countries Sweden, Finland, Denmark and Germany can compete with the US and Japan, while the UK, Italy and France were only average performers. Although the UK economy grows and joblessness is at an all-time low, it still faces major challenges for knowledge creation. The slow improvement in the R&D base could be a cause for the negative trends for high-tech exports and employment in medium-tech manufacturing.

INPUT – Innovation drivers

S&E graduates per 1000 population aged 20–29
Population with tertiary education per 100 population aged 25–64
Broadband penetration rate (number of broadband lines per 100 population)
Participation in life-long learning per 100 population aged 25–64
Youth education attainment level (% of population aged 20–24 having completed at least upper secondary education)

INPUT – Knowledge creation

Public R&D expenditures (% of GDP)
Business R&D expenditures (% of GDP)
Share of medium-high-tech and high-tech R&D (% of manufacturing R&D expenditures)
Share of enterprises receiving public funding for innovation
Share of university R&D expenditures financed by business sector

INPUT – Innovation & entrepreneurship

SMEs innovating in-house (% of all SMEs)
Innovative SMEs co-operating with others (% of all SMEs)
Innovation expenditures (% of total turnover)
Early-stage venture capital (% of GDP)
ICT expenditures (% of GDP)
SMEs using non-technological change (% of all SMEs)

OUTPUT – Application

Employment in high-tech services (% of total workforce)
Exports of high technology products as a share of total exports
Sales of new-to-market products (% of total turnover)
Sales of new-to-firm not new-to-market products (% of total turnover)
Employment in medium-high and high-tech manufacturing (% of total workforce)

OUTPUT – Intellectual property

EPO patents per million population
USPTO patents per million population
Triadic patent families per million population
New community trademarks per million population
New community designs per million population

Such findings are clearly important for long-term economic growth within these various economies. Higher innovation rates can enable the economy to grow quicker. Even if the increase in growth brought about by innovation is small, we saw at the beginning of this chapter that the compound effect over many years will create a marked acceleration in GDP.

This is important for business in at least two broad respects. First, innovation which leads to growth will create greater economic activity, higher living standards, improved sales, greater profits. Second, innovation can provide firms with a competitive advantage over their international rivals. Products which are more advanced and provide greater utility to end users have more value added. This will be reflected in higher premium prices, better wages for workers and higher profits. Moreover, innovation can act as a barrier to entry. UK companies which lack innovative capacity may find it difficult to enter high-technology markets. Instead, they may appear to be locked into medium-technology markets which can be entered by companies from many economies across the globe.

While innovation appears to be important, the crucial step is the transformability of innovation. The UK performs reasonably well in the creation of innovation and its innovative inputs are respectable. The problem is in generating innovative outputs. If innovation and knowledge creation occurs in universities and companies' own research labs, there needs to be the skill base to convert such knowledge into profitable products. While the UK has a preponderance of graduates who run and manage companies, it lacks the secondary and technical skills which are needed to either manufacture high-technology innovative products, or use innovative high-technology techniques in the production process. Therefore, while we saw in Chapters 5 and 6 that a firm's commercial success depends upon its costs and revenues, it also clearly depends upon the nature of the economic resources that it can access. Moreover, economies which are better at enhancing the quality of their economic resources over time may present their companies with enhanced competitive advantage.

12.7 Business application: How long can the Chinese economy grow at rates of 10 per cent per annum or more?

The growth of the Chinese economy has been one of the major economic miracles of the past 25 years. Compound growth rates of 9.7 per cent per annum over such a time period are impressive and unmatched by many economies, except perhaps India.

Concerns over a Chinese take-away, where business in Europe and the US is out-competed by cheap Chinese imports, is perhaps blinkered. Cheap Chinese imports have undoubtedly helped to keep inflation low in Europe. In addition, the booming Chinese economy has also sucked in many commodities, investment capital and skills and services from the developed world, creating export and business opportunities galore. In recent years China through its demand for exports has helped to keep the developed economies of the world out of recession. But for how long can businesses in developed economies either rely on export demand from China, or seek out growth opportunities within China?

In simple terms the Chinese economy is at present reasonably unconstrained in its access to economic resources; it faces what is in essence a relatively elastic aggregate supply line. As more workers migrate from agricultural jobs located in China's interior to industrial employment located near China's coastal areas, aggregate supply can expand to meet the increasing growth in demand. Figure 11.12, used to compare Keynesianism and Monetarism, is repeated in Figure 12.3

When aggregate demand increases in China, it is met with additional aggregate supply, the economy grows and GDP rises by 10 per cent per annum or more. We are clearly considering an increase in AD_1, where aggregate supply is elastic. The issue for policymakers in China and business people around the world is to understand the factors that will lead to China hitting a situation of inelastic supply, or when it will have reached a situation of long-run full employment.

The discussion in Box 12.5 might shed some light on this. To date China's growth has been reliant on the supply of reasonably abundant commoditized economic resources. These have included, steel, copper, cement and low-skilled workers. The rise in economic prosperity has, however, now channelled this new-found wealth into the demand for services: leisure, banking, insurance, real estate, property developers, designers and private hospitals. These types of service require a different type of labour, generally better educated and more skilled. The supply is less abundant. As we saw in Box 12.1, China is witnessing a boom in business school education, but it will be a number of years before the economy is self-sufficient in business education and the supply of qualified managers.

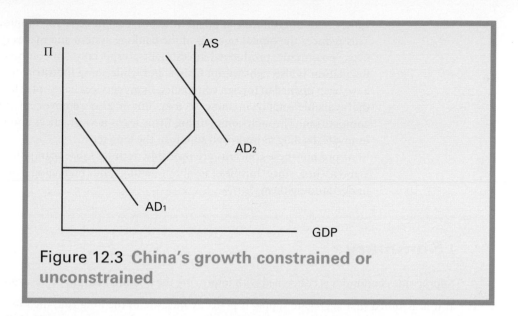

Figure 12.3 China's growth constrained or unconstrained

→ Box 12.5 Are you being served?

Adapted from an article in The Economist, 12 January 2006

China, the world's factory, it turns out, has a sizeable canteen attached, not to mention an office block and shopping mall. Last month's official revision of China's gross domestic product revealed an economy worth $1.9 trillion in 2004, an increase of 20% and now the world's seventh largest economy. By 2007 China should be bigger than France and the UK. The biggest increase came form the service sector which jumped by nine percentage points, to 41%, compared with 46% for manufacturing and 13% for primary industries (mainly agriculture and mining).

Where has all this extra activity come from? As people grow wealthier, they want more restaurants and bars, clothes stores, car dealerships, bookshops, private hospitals, English language classes and beauty salons.

Li Deshui, commissioner of China's National Bureau of Statistics, confirms that most of the new GDP comes from three categories. The first is wholesale, retail and catering; the second, transport, storage, post and telecommunications. The third activity is real estate. Property development has, in turn, boosted demand for architects, decorators, do-it-yourself stores and other building services.

Recent years have seen a surge in media and technology services, including the Internet; in financial services such as leasing; and in education and leisure. China's rapid economic growth is fuelling demand for accountants, lawyers, bankers and all manner of consultants, as Chinese companies expand and restructure. Specialists in marketing, advertising and public relations advise on the relatively new area of marketing products and developing brands. The new wealth has other consequences, too. China now has nearly 1m security guards. And it can offer its new rich everything from cosmetic surgeons to pet salons.

So, this change in the required skill set may present a bottleneck in the growth trajectory of the economy, and in the near future China may move nearer to a situation of inelastic aggregate supply, where increases in aggregate demand feed directly into higher inflation, as would be the case with an increase in AD_2 in Figure 12.3.

Skills may not be the only constraint facing China. Concern has been expressed about the quality of its banking sector. Many banks have provided soft loans, lending to projects which were uneconomic and had little prospect of repaying monies lent by the banks. This reduces the capital reserves of the banking system and makes it difficult to finance new, potentially productive investments, especially in commercial infrastructure. Regulation is also tight within China, and while some industrial manufacturing sectors have been opened to foreign companies, many services have not. This not only constrains the available supply in these sectors, but it also removes an important source of competition. Through competition, firms learn new practices and can be motivated to innovate, leading to improved supply in the long term.

At present these concerns are probably nothing more than potential risks to China's growth, but since business is about taking and managing risks, it is worthwhile understanding them.

 Summary

1   Supply side economics is concerned with improving the potential output of the economy.

2   If it is assumed that aggregate supply is perfectly inelastic in the long run, then increasing aggregate supply is the only way of generating additional economic output without raising inflation.

3   Neoclassical growth theory asserts that diminishing returns will lead to a natural growth rate for an economy. Any increase in the natural growth rate can only stem from technological progress, or an increase in the number of workers.

4   Neoclassical growth theory leads to the conclusion that all economies will converge on a common growth rate. Empirical evidence does not support this idea.

5   In response to neoclassical growth theory, endogenous growth theory asserts that diminishing returns to capital in one firm, or industry, might generate constant returns to scale across the entire economy. In essence, investments in capital by one firm, or industry, have positive externalities for the rest of the economy. Economies can now grow at different rates, rather than converge, depending upon the generation of productivity-enhancing positive externalities.

6   Under endogenous growth theory the government has a role in facilitating growth. Developments in education, financial services, levels of R&D and freer labour markets should all lead to higher future growth rates.

 Learning checklist

You should now be able to:

♦   Explain how economic growth is linked to growth in long-run aggregate supply

♦   Provide a review of the neoclassical model of economic growth

♦   Explain and evaluate the convergence hypothesis

♦   Explain the endogenous growth model and highlight how and why it is different from the neoclassical growth model

♦   Explain and evaluate the various types of policies used to develop economic growth

♦   Explain how and why business can be central to economic growth and policies designed for economic growth

? Questions

1   What improves supply within an economy?

2   Does neoclassical growth theory provide an adequate understanding of economic growth? Is endogenous growth theory any better than the neoclassical approach?

3   Why is business important for economic growth?

4   Will government supply side policies always be in the interests of business?

Exercises

1   True or false?
    a)   An annual growth rate of 2 per cent p.a. leads to a sevenfold increase in real output in less than a century.
    b)   Sustained growth cannot occur if production relies on a factor whose supply is largely fixed.
    c)   In the neoclassical growth theory, output, capital and labour all grow at the same rate.
    d)   Higher savings enables a higher long-run rate of growth.
    e)   Given the convergence hypothesis, we can expect all poor countries to catch up with the richer countries.
    f)   Growth may be stimulated by capital externalities: that is, higher capital in one firm increases capital productivity in other firms.

2   Which of the following policy suggestions are appropriate for improving economic growth in an economy?
    a)   The encouragement of R&D.
    b)   A reduction in marginal tax rates to increase labour supply.
    c)   Investment grants.
    d)   The establishment of training and education schemes to improve human capital.
    e)   An expansion of aggregate demand to increase the level of employment.
    f)   The encouragement of dissemination of new knowledge and techniques.

3   Refer to Box 12.4 when considering the following questions:
    a)   From the table, select two items under each heading and explain their relevance to innovation.
    b)   Managing actual GDP is a UK economic success story, managing potential GDP is not. Discuss.

Section V
Global economics

Chapter 13
Exchange rates and the balance of payments

Chapter contents

Learning outcomes

By the end of this chapter you should understand:

Economic Theory

- Fixed exchange rates
- Floating exchange rates
- The performance differences between fixed and floating exchange rates
- How to evaluate fiscal and monetary policy under different exchange rate regimes
- Optimal currency zones
- Issues relating to European monetary union

Business Application

- Why is it important for business to understand the role of China's savings held in the US.
- How hedging can be used to reduce exchange rate risk and create speculative investments

Exchange rates at a glance

The issues

There are many currencies in the world. The US dollar, UK sterling and the Euro are all examples of important currencies. Over time the strength of the US dollar against UK sterling or the Euro varies. When the dollar is strong, it can be exchanged for more Euros than when it is weak. This generates issues for business and government. What price will businesses receive for their goods and services when they are exported overseas? Also why is it beneficial for a number of economies to share a currency, such as the Euro?

The understanding

In order to understand exchange rate movements and the potential benefits from being a member of the Euro, it is necessary to understand the balance of payments, as well as floating, versus fixed, exchange rate regimes. Once this knowledge is in place, it is possible to address the effectiveness of domestic fiscal and monetary policy under the Euro.

The usefulness

In part, trading overseas is determined by how internationally competitive an economy is. The Euro, by fixing the exchange rate across all member economies, requires greater price flexibility within member economies. Firms need to understand these issues. Furthermore, by understanding hedging, firms can understand how exchange rate volatility can be managed.

13.1 Business problem: should the UK be a member of the euro?

There are myriad issues associated with whether, or not, the UK should adopt the euro, but not all of them have business implications. For example, many individuals see the pound as a symbol of 'Britishness'. The pound as a currency and the picture of the sovereign on notes and coins are seen by many as key aspects of their nationality. Indeed, this deep cultural affinity with the national currency is not a uniquely British view. Upon adopting the euro, the French held a day of national celebrations and mourning in a sign of respect for the French franc.

For business the euro is not a cultural identity problem because, as many businesspeople will tell you, 'business is no place for sentiment'. Rather, the euro has simple operational implications and profound macroeconomic consequences. Changing prices from pounds to Euros and cutting back on the need for currency conversions are simple operational implications. The macroeconomic implications are far greater. Consider the following by way of a brief introduction to the issues.

Imagine boats in a harbour bobbing up and down. Each boat represents an economy, UK, France, Germany, Spain, Italy and so on. The waves are the business cycles. When each economy had its own currency, the boats were connected together with ropes. So, as the wave hits the first boat it is able to rise up and then fall. The next boat then moves up and down and so on. Each boat, or each economy, has some flexibility in dealing with the business cycle. Under the common currency of the euro, Germany, France, Spain and

Italy and all other members have swapped the ropes for an iron bar welded across the front of all their boats. In the face of the business cycle the eurozone members now move together. The flexibility of the ropes has been swapped for the size and stability of a huge integrated eurozone economy. The question for the UK is whether it wishes to swap its flexible rope for a stable but relatively inflexible weld to the rest of Europe?

The answer to this problem rests on two broad areas: (i) an understanding of the trade-off between flexibility and stability; and (ii) an understanding of how strong the welds are between the different boats. This chapter will provide answers to these questions, highlighting how the international environment, through exchange rates and intra-national economic policies, affects business.

13.2 **Forex markets and exchange rate regimes**

Forex markets are where different currencies are traded.

Whenever you travel abroad you convert pounds sterling into euros, US dollars, etc. Since we are talking about a **forex market**, the item being traded must have a price. The price of currency is simply the rate at which it can be converted. In Table 13.1 various exchange rates for the pound are listed. For example, £1 will buy 1.4624 euros, or 203.45 Yen.

Table 13.1 Forex rates for the UK pound

euro	1.4624
Japan – Yen	203.4500
USA – dollar	1.7556
Hong Kong – dollars	13.7703

If these are the prices from the forex market, then the obvious question is, how does this market work? Who is demanding and selling currency?

The answer is fairly simple: individuals and firms buy and sell currencies whenever they undertake transactions with other economies. For example, whenever an import into the UK occurs, pounds have to be exchanged for another currency. Similarly, whenever an export out of the UK occurs, the foreign purchaser needs to sell their own currency in exchange for pounds. We can, therefore, think of imports as generating the supply of pounds in the market and exports as generating the demand for pounds in the market. In Figure 13.1 we have a traditional demand and supply curve for pounds.

If we begin in equilibrium with Q_S equal to Q_D, then the exchange rate is e_0 or £1 can be converted to €1.5. If exports from the UK to Europe rise, then European consumers will need to demand more UK pounds. The demand curve for pounds shifts from Q_D to Q_{D1}. The exchange rate for pounds appreciates, with £1 being converted into €1.7. If exports fall, demand shifts from Q_D to Q_{D2} and the value of the currency depreciates, with £1 being converted into only €1.2. Similarly, if UK consumers import more goods into the country, they will have to supply more pounds in exchange for euros. We could also envisage a change in supply. If the supply of pounds shifted to the right, the pound would fall in value. But if supply shifted to the left, the pound would rise in value.

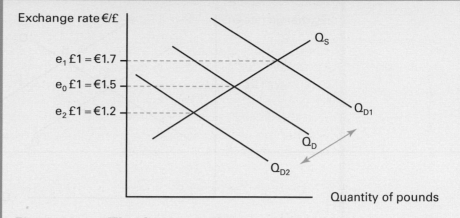

Figure 13.1 The forex market

As the demand for pounds increases, the exchange rate appreciates. When the demand for pounds falls, the exchange rate depreciates.

Exchange rate regimes

The exchange rate market can be characterized as operating under two extreme regimes.

In a fixed exchange rate regime the government sets an exchange rate and then uses the central bank to buy and sell currency to keep the market rate fixed.

Under a floating exchange rate regime the exchange rate is set by market forces, with holders of foreign currency demanding and selling various currencies.

We will examine how each system works and then provide an analysis of their relative strengths and weaknesses.

Fixed exchange rate

In Figure 13.2 we adapt our previous figure and illustrate how a fixed exchange rate works. For simplicity assume the government sets the exchange rate at e_0. If demand and supply meet at this rate, then the market is in equilibrium and there is no need for any market intervention. However, if, in accordance with an export boom, there is an increase in the demand for pounds, the demand curve will shift to Q_{D1}. The market would like to be in equilibrium at B, with an exchange rate of £1 equals €1.7. But the government is fixing the price at £1 equals €1.5. The government is effectively pricing below the equilibrium price and, as we saw in Chapter 4, this leads to market disequilibrium. At the fixed rate of £1 equals €1.5, the willingness to supply pounds is A, but the willingness to demand pounds is C. Therefore, in the market there is an excess demand for pounds equal to the distance A to C. The government, or the central bank, has to meet this excess demand by supplying an additional AC pounds to the market. The extra pounds are effectively swapped for US dollars, euros, etc. and are added to the central bank's foreign currency reserves.

In Figure 13.3 we can consider what happens if the demand for pounds falls to Q_{D2}. Now there will be an excess supply of pounds equal to AE. The central bank now needs to buy the excess supply of pounds. In order to buy pounds it has to offer something other than pounds in return. When the central bank was selling pounds it will have received euros and other currencies in return. These were added to the bank's currency reserves. It now uses these reserves to buy back the pounds.

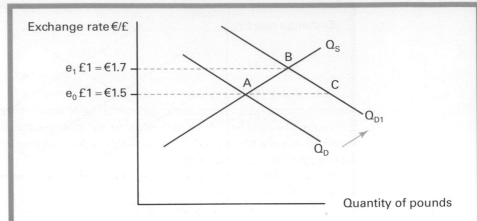

Figure 13.2 Increased demand under fixed exchange rates

As the demand for pounds increases, the market would like to move from A to B. But the government has fixed the price at £1 equals €1.5. It, therefore, has to supply the additional AC pounds in order to keep the price at £1 equals €1.5.

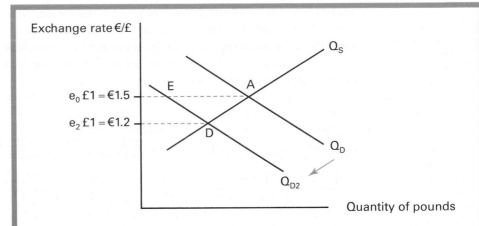

Figure 13.3 Reduced demand under fixed exchange rates

As the demand for pounds decreases then at the fixed exchange rate of £1 equals €1.5, supply is greater than demand by the amount AE. In order to maintain the fixed exchange rate the government has to purchase the excess supply of pounds using its foreign currency reserves.

However, there is a critical problem for the central bank. It is feasible for the central bank to keep supplying additional pounds to the market, because as the central bank it can ask for more pounds to be printed. Unfortunately, the central bank cannot commit to an indefinite purchase of the pound because in order to do this it has to have an infinite supply of foreign currency, such as US dollars and euros. Since the US federal reserve bank controls the supply of dollars and the European central bank controls the supply of euros, the Bank of England will soon run out of foreign currencies with which to buy the pound.

Devaluation

If the currency is being continually supported by the central bank, it is probably the case that the fixed exchange rate has become vastly different from the long-term market rate for the currency. The correct policy response is not to keep buying the currency. Instead, the currency should be allowed to devalue. In our example, the fixed exchange rate of £1 equals €1.5 is abandoned and the government seeks to manage the exchange rate at the new equilibrium of £1 equals €1.2.

This potential for devaluation creates a fundamental weakness within fixed exchange rates: they are open to **speculative attack**.

> A **speculative attack** is a massive capital outflow from an economy with a fixed exchange rate.

If the government has fixed the exchange rate at £1 equals €1.5, but you think it will soon have to devalue to £1 equals €1.2, then the best thing to do is take pounds and convert them into euros: £1 million will buy you €1.5 million. If many people do this, massive capital outflows will be observed. Note that people are cutting demand for pounds and instead demanding euros. This means the government has to offer more support to the pound at £1 equals €1.5. It will soon give up and when it devalues to £1 equals €1.2, you can take your €1.5 million and convert them back into €1.5m/1.2m = £1.25m. So, by changing your money into euros and then waiting for a devaluation you have made £0.25 million, or a 25 per cent return on your investment.

Floating exchange rates

> Under a **floating exchange rate** system there is no market intervention by the government or the central bank.

As demand increases and falls for the currency, the equilibrium rate moves from E through to B. There is no impact on the central bank's foreign currency reserves as there is no intervention in the market place.

In the long run, floating exchange rates *should* obey **purchasing power parity**.

Consider the following example. Assume the exchange rate is £1 equals €1.5. We will also assume that a pair of designer jeans cost £50 in London and €75 in Paris. With the current exchange rate the price of the jeans is identical in London and Paris (£50 × 1.5 = €75).

> **Purchasing power parity** requires the nominal exchange rate to adjust in order to keep the real exchange rate constant.

Now assume that inflation in Paris is zero, but inflation in London is 10 per cent. At the end of the year the jeans in London have increased in price by 10 per cent and so now cost £55. The jeans in Paris have stayed the same €75. If the exchange rate is still £1 equals €1.5, then we can save £5 by buying the jeans in Paris and bringing them back to the UK. Clearly £5 is not much of a saving, but if we were in business and set about buying 1000 pairs of jeans, then it might be worthwhile importing from Paris.

However, as we begin to import jeans we have to sell pounds and demand euros. As we (and everyone else) do this, the value of the euro will rise. In fact, it will rise to £1 equals €1.36. Why? Well if we now convert the price of the jeans in Paris back to pounds we have €75/1.36 = £55. All that happens is that the nominal exchange rate adjusts so that the price of jeans in Paris is identical to the price of jeans in London. The real exchange rate is constant and as a result we have purchasing power parity – it costs the same to buy goods in London as it does in Paris.

Clearly this is an extreme illustrative example. Consumers need to be aware of the price differences between Paris and London. The price difference has to be big enough to make consumers interested in exploiting the price differential. Finally, the cost of moving the goods from Paris to London has to be lower than the price difference.

The Economist magazine has for a number of years used the price of a Big Mac to assess purchasing power parity. Details of this are provided in Box 13.1. While the limitations of this approach are discussed, it should be noted that the Big Mac index has been surprisingly accurate in predicting future exchange rate movements.

 Box 13.1 The Big Mac index

McCurrencies

25 May 2006

From The Economist print edition

The Economist's Big Mac index is based on the theory of purchasing-power parity (PPP). The Big Mac PPP is the exchange rate that would leave burgers costing the same in America as elsewhere. Thus a Big Mac in China costs 10.5 yuan, against an average price in four American cities of $3.10 To make the two prices equal would require an exchange rate of 3.39 yuan to the dollar, compared with a market rate of 8.03. In other words, the yuan is 58% 'undervalued' against the dollar. In contrast, using the same method, the euro and sterling are overvalued against the dollar, by 22% and 18% respectively.

The index was never intended to be a precise predictor of currency movements, simply a take-away guide to whether currencies are at their 'correct' long-run level. Curiously, however, burgernomics has an impressive record in predicting exchange rates: currencies that show up as overvalued often tend to weaken in later years. But you must always remember the Big Mac's limitations. Burgers cannot sensibly be traded across borders and prices are distorted by differences in taxes and the cost of non-tradable inputs, such as rents.

	Big Mac prices in local currency	in dollars	Implied PPP of the dollar	Actual dollar exchange rate 22 May, 2006	Under(−)/over(+) valuation against the dollar, %
US	$3.10	3.10			
Australia	A$3.25	2.44	1.05	1.33	−21
Canada	C$3.52	3.14	1.14	1.12	+1
China	Yuan 10.5	1.31	3.39	8.03	−58
Euro area	€2.94	3.77	1.05	1.28	+22
Hong Kong	HK$12.0	1.55	3.87	7.75	−50
UK	£1.94	3.65	1.60	1.88	+18

Exchange rates in practice

As indicated at the beginning, fixed and floating exchange rate regimes are extremes. The UK pound floats. Occasionally when interest rates are set by the Bank of England's Monetary Committee some recognition of the likely impact on the exchange rate is made. But it is rarely an overriding consideration. Until recently the Malaysian Ringit was fixed to the US dollar. The Chinese Yuan is fixed in the short term against a basket of currencies including the US dollar, the euro, the Japanese Yen and the UK pound. The euro floats against all other currencies, but at its point of conception it effectively fixed all the rates between the member countries forever. Finally, the forerunner to the euro, the European exchange rate mechanism, was a hybrid system. Currencies were allowed to float between certain bands, which were fixed. If the currency stayed within the bands there was no government intervention. Once the market wanted to move outside the bands, then the central banks stepped in.

13.3 **Fixed versus floating exchange rates**

Given that both fixed and floating exchange rates are used by different governments, it should be expected that each system must have benefits and drawbacks. These are generally related to **exchange rate volatility**, **robustness** and **financial discipline**.

Clearly under a fixed exchange rate there is no volatility in the short term. The government fixes the exchange rate. In contrast, floating exchange rates are volatile. The value of the exchange rate changes on a daily and even hourly basis. A sense of the volatility is shown in Figure 13.4, illustrating the changing exchange rate between the US dollar and the pound sterling.

Volatility is a measure of variability. In the case of exchange rates, a concern over volatility is a concern over how much the exchange rate changes.
Robustness is a concern with flexibility, or the ability to accommodate change.
Financial discipline is the degree to which a government pursues stringent monetary policy and targets low inflation.

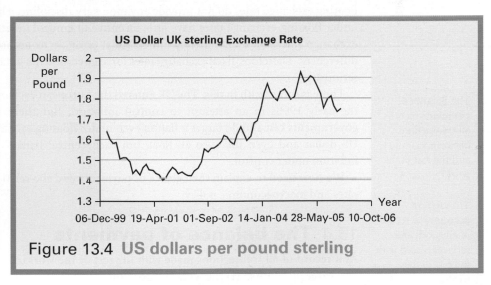

Figure 13.4 **US dollars per pound sterling**

However, we also need to consider long-term volatility. In Figure 13.3 we could begin at equilibrium A under a floating exchange rate. The demand for the currency begins to shift to Q_{D2}. Over time there is a gradual adjustment to the new equilibrium at D. The exchange rate slowly moves down and firms and consumers wishing to exchange money slowly adjust to the changing exchange price. In contrast, under a fixed exchange rate the government is committed to supporting the equilibrium at A. If under pressure from a speculative attack and the government decides to stop supporting the currency and allows it to devalue to the equilibrium at D, then there is a sudden and dramatic change in the exchange price. Such changes can be more dangerous than gradual adjustment. Indeed, currency devaluations often lead to volatility in the rest of the financial markets, such as stock markets.

So, from the perspective of business, floating exchange rates create short-term uncertainty due to their volatility, but they provide gradual adjustment in the long run, which may be preferable to dramatic one-off changes offered by fixed exchange rates.

Consider our example of the boats in the harbour. The boats connected by ropes are the economies with floating exchange rates. They are flexible and able to accommodate environmental changes. In the case of the boat this was the rise and fall of the waves. We witnessed above, when examining purchasing power parity, that environmental change might exist in the form of inflationary differences between economies. If the UK inflation rate is 10 per cent and the US rate is 0 per cent, then it becomes attractive for UK consumers to buy US products, rather than UK products. As they do this they sell pounds and demand dollars. The value of the pound will fall, reflecting the inflationary differences between the UK and the US. When full adjustment has occurred, US products cost the same as UK products.

Under fixed exchange rates there is no scope for exchange rate adjustment; purchasing power parity does not hold. Instead, UK companies become increasingly uncompetitive against US companies. Imports increase, demand for domestic UK produced goods falls, and the UK moves into recession. The recession will be expected to reduce inflation within the UK.

Therefore, under a fixed exchange rate purchasing power parity is gained through changes in domestic prices, rather than exchange rate changes.

As we have seen above, floating exchange rates can accommodate inflationary differences between economies. This has led to some individuals taking the view that floating exchange rates do not provide any monetary discipline. Therefore, governments under floating exchange rates have little incentive to control inflation. In contrast, fixed exchange rates, by their inherent inflexibility, struggle to accommodate inflationary differences. Therefore, fixed exchange rates force governments to take financial discipline seriously.

There is some truth in this. The UK entered the European exchange rate mechanism in the early 1990s in an attempt to control inflation. But there is also the view that governments can and do target inflation even under floating exchange rates. The pound, US dollar and even the euro all float, but each central bank is tasked with keeping inflation under control.

We now need to explain the balance of payments and the relationship with exchange rates and macroeconomic policy.

13.4 **The balance of payments**

The **balance of payments** records all transactions between a country and the rest of the world.

The **current account** is a record of all goods and services traded with the rest of the world.
The **capital account** records, among other things, net contributions made to the EU.
The **financial account** records net purchases and sales of foreign assets. (This was previously known as the capital account.)

As a record of all transactions made with the rest of the world, the balance of payments has three accounts: (i) the **current account**; (ii) the **capital account**; and (iii) the **financial account**.

The current account measures imports and exports and can be further divided into visible and invisible trade. Visible trade is the export and import of tangible or visible products. Exporting a car is clearly an example of visible trade. Invisible trade captures intangible services. A London-based business consultant working for a German client is an example of an invisible export. Added together, visible and invisible trade make the trade account. After adjusting for net transfer payments, such as interest and profits on foreign assets, we get to the current account.

Payments by the UK towards the Common Agricultural Policy would be included in this account. It is worth pointing out that such payments were until recently included in the current account. The capital account was used as the heading for what is now the financial account. Changes were made to the construction of the UK balance of payments in order to bring it into line with other countries.

If a UK company decides to operate in another country, it has to invest there. It might buy a local company or it might instead build its own facilities. Either way there is a transfer of assets from the UK to the 'other' country. Similarly a private individual might decide to invest in shares quoted on the New York Stock Exchange. Again, financial resource has to be transferred between the two countries. The capital account records these types of purchase and sale.

In summary, the current, capital and financial accounts seek to record all transactions, whether they be goods, services or purely finance, which take place between a country and the rest of the world. Indeed, we will see shortly that as long as the exchange rate is floating, the three accounts will sum to zero. That is, the balance of payments will be zero. Clearly the three accounts are only measured with a limited degree of accuracy; and the smuggling of alcohol, cigarettes and drugs represent aspects of international trade that go unrecorded. As a result, the balance of payments are generally shown with a so-called 'balancing item', which corrects for any statistical mistakes in measuring the three accounts.

Balance of payments and exchange rates

Under a floating exchange rate the balance of payments must equal zero.

This stems from equilibrium in the forex market. In equilibrium the demand for UK pounds must equal the supply of UK pounds. In the current account we have individuals demanding and supplying pounds as they import and export goods and services. In the financial account we have individuals supplying and demanding pounds as they buy and sell international assets.

Therefore, if the forex market is in equilibrium, then the demand and supply of pounds from the current and financial account must also be equal.

Under a fixed exchange rate the situation is vastly different. In Figures 13.2 and 13.3 (p. 298) we saw that points C and E were points of disequilibria in the forex market. At point C in Figure 13.2 the demand for pounds is greater than the supply of pounds at the exchange rate of e_0. We can explain this excess demand for pounds by reference to the current and financial accounts. For example, if UK exports are greater than imports, then foreign consumers demanding pounds to pay for the exports will outweigh UK consumers supplying pounds to pay for imports. If UK investors do not wish to buy foreign assets at the existing exchange rate, then the supply of pounds will be less than the demand. In contrast, if we consider point E in Figure 13.3 the supply of pounds at the fixed exchange rate of e_0 led to an excess supply of pounds. We can again explain this excess supply of pounds by reference to the current and financial accounts. For example, if UK imports are greater than exports, then the supply of pounds will increase. But if foreign investors are not willing to buy British assets at the exchange rate of e_1, then the demand for pounds will be less than the supply.

Therefore, under a fixed exchange rate, the balance of payments will not necessarily be zero.

In order to make the balance of payments zero, we have to incorporate the concept of **official financing**.

Official financing is the extent of government intervention in the forex markets.

We know that in order to keep the exchange rate at its fixed level, the government must buy up the excess supply of pounds. This is called official financing and is added into the balance of payments as the final balancing item. It represents the extent to which the government has changed its foreign currency reserves by either buying up the excess supply of pounds or, alternatively, adding to its reserves by selling pounds in the forex market.

If we examine Table 13.2 we can see the actual values for each of the three accounts during 2001 and 2002. It is clear that the balancing item, or net errors and omissions, for 2002 is very large. In fact, it is bigger than the current account balance. It might be worth checking the figure in the future to see if the government revises its estimates of the three accounts. Information on the trade of goods and services or assets might have been recorded slowly, with correct figures not becoming known for some time. As a result, the figures provided by the government are only an initial estimate.

Table 13.2 UK balance of payments 2001–02

		2004 (£bn)	2005 (£bn)
1	Current account	−9.0	−10.2
2	Capital account	0.2	0.3
3	Financial account	14.3	13.4
4	Net errors and omissions	−14.5	−13.7
	Balance of payments (1 + 2 + 3 + 4)	0	0

Source: Office for National Statistics

Table 13.3 UK exports and imports of goods and services with EU and non-EU countries, £m

EU				
Year	Export goods	Export services	Import goods	Import services
2000	107 990	30 652	111 261	33 249
2001	109 710	31 351	115 096	33 882
2002	109 129	30 226	118 276	34 852
2003	110 589	*37 998*	136 417	41 878
2004	110 898	*41 537*	141 722	43 542
Non-EU				
Year	Export goods	Export services	Import goods	Import services
2000	79 946	46 547	107 001	32 112
2001	80 340	46 332	108 464	32 501
2002	76 719	53 122	101 966	32 974
2003	78 026	55 618	100 062	34 856
2004	80 035	61 479	109 625	38 038

Source: Office for National Statistics

It is often argued that the UK trades more with the EU than it does with the rest of the world. Table 13.3 lists the amounts of trade in goods and service for the UK with EU and non-EU countries. In terms of the export of goods it is clear that the UK has a stronger link to the EU than non-EU countries. But the export of services to non-EU countries is more important than the export of such services to the EU. More goods tend to be imported from the EU than non-EU, but the importation of services appears to be equally split between the EU and non-EU.

13.5 Exchange rates and government policy

We can now begin to consider the effectiveness of fiscal and monetary policy under fixed and floating exchange rate regimes. While this is theoretically interesting, it also has practical implications. The UK currently operates a floating exchange rate regime. If it were to enter the euro, then the exchange rate with all euro members would be fixed forever. Before we consider fiscal and monetary effectiveness we need to understand two further points: (i) the real exchange rate and (ii) perfect capital mobility.

Real exchange rate

The **real exchange rate** is the relative price of domestic and foreign goods measured in a common currency.

International competitiveness depends upon the real and not the nominal exchange rate.

Real exchange rate =
(€/£ exchange rate) × (£ price of UK goods/€ price of eurozone goods)

If the nominal exchange rate appreciated, then UK goods would become more expensive than European goods. European consumers would have to change more euros into pounds in order to buy UK goods. If the price of European goods rose quicker than the price of UK goods, because inflation was higher in Europe than in the UK, then the UK would become more competitive. So, even if the nominal exchange rate stays constant, but inflation is 10 per cent in Europe and only 5 per cent in the UK, the real exchange rate will appreciate by 5 per cent.

In summary, international competitiveness is influenced by the nominal exchange rate and the relative price level between the two countries.

Perfect capital mobility

Under **perfect capital mobility** expected returns on all assets around the world will be zero. If interest rates are 5 per cent higher in New York than in London then, in order to compensate, the exchange rate will rise by 5 per cent, making dollars more expensive to buy. Therefore, the expected rates of return in London and New York are then identical. Or, in economic terminology, interest parity holds.

If you had £1000 to invest in a savings account you might visit a finance site on the Internet and ask for a ranking of savings rates offered by leading banks and building societies. If you are not concerned about when you get access to the money, you might sensibly choose the bank offering the highest rate.

Now we will assume that you are richer and have £1 million to invest. It is now worth thinking beyond the UK: what are the interest rates being offered by banks in the UK, US, Germany or Japan? If the rates in New York are 10 per cent, but only 5 per cent in all other countries, then you can double your interest by moving your money to New York. Or can you? A slight problem exists. In order to invest in the US you need to sell your pounds and demand dollars. As more dollars are demanded, the price or exchange rate must appreciate. At the extreme, if financial capital is free to move around the world, then interest parity must hold and there is no incentive to move your money.

Fiscal and monetary policy under fixed exchange rates

Monetary policy

If interest parity holds, then movement in the exchange rate will offset any differential in interest rates between countries. However, this all assumes that exchange rates are floating. What happens when the exchange rate is fixed? Any difference in the interest rate between the two countries will now represent a guaranteed profit. As a result financial capital will flow to the country with the highest interest rate.

The only way to stop capital flows putting pressure on the exchange rate is to set a single interest rate for both countries. This is a loss of monetary independence for at least one of the countries.

Fiscal policy

If we begin by backtracking to Chapter 11, in a closed economy, if the government increases aggregate demand through a fiscal stimulus, the Bank of England will increase interest rates and cut aggregate demand in order to keep inflation under control. But under a fixed exchange rate there is a loss of monetary independence. The Bank of England seeks interest parity and so cannot change the interest rate from that set by its international trading partners. Therefore, any increase in fiscal policy will not be constrained by a tightening of monetary policy.

Fiscal policy is, therefore, seen as being more powerful under fixed exchange rates.

We can even go one step further and examine what would happen if the central bank tries to increase interest rates. Because interest parity does not hold, financial capital will flow into the UK. There will be an excess demand of pounds in the forex market. The Bank of England is committed to printing more money in order to meet the excess demand. But an increase in the supply of money leads to a reduction in the equilibrium price of money. The price of money is the interest rate. So an initial increase in the interest rate leads to a future reduction in the interest rate. Monetary policy is ineffective.

Why enter into a fixed exchange rate?

Aside from the stability offered by a fixed exchange rate, a very powerful benefit can be found in the real exchange rate, which is a measure of international competitiveness. The government is only fixing the nominal exchange rate. International competitiveness can be achieved by improving the real exchange rate. This is achieved by keeping the inflation rate in the UK at, or below, the inflation rates of its key trading partners. If inflation in the UK averages 2.5 per cent, but its international competitors are suffering 5 per cent inflation, then each year the UK becomes 2.5 per cent cheaper.

As such, fixed exchange rates can have a strong disciplinary effect on domestic inflation.

This disciplinary effect can exist in a number of forms. First, individuals under the economic consequences of a fixed exchange rate have lower inflationary expectations. Second, if inflation rises at a faster rate in the UK, then UK goods become less competitive. Exports fall, aggregate demand falls and employment falls. Wages and prices in the UK fall, inflation is reduced and UK goods become competitive again.

Fiscal and monetary policy under floating exchange rates

Monetary policy

We will now see that monetary policy is more powerful under floating exchange rates and fiscal policy is less effective. If we begin with monetary policy, a reduction of interest rates will boost internal demand. Individuals will consume more and companies will raise investment levels. Furthermore, if interest parity holds, then a reduction in the interest rate must be offset by a reduction in the exchange rate. This reduction in the exchange rate leads to an improvement in the level of international competitiveness. UK products are now cheaper for foreign consumers and so exports will rise.

Monetary policy under floating exchange rates is reinforced. A reduction in interest rates stimulates domestic and international demand for UK products.

Fiscal policy

If the government introduces a fiscal stimulus, then aggregate demand will increase and so will inflation. In order to control the inflation, the Bank of England will raise interest rates. In order to ensure interest parity the exchange rate must also rise. UK products now cost more abroad. The rising exchange rate has reduced the international competitiveness of the UK. Exports fall and the initial fiscal stimulus provided by the government is offset by falling external demand.

Under floating exchange rates, fiscal policy is neutralized by rising interest rates, a rising currency and falling exports.

We can use the ideas developed within this section to examine European monetary union.

13.6 European monetary union

> Monetary union is the permanent fixing of exchange rates between member countries.

In the case of European **monetary union**, conversion rates for French francs into euros, German marks into euros, Italian lire into euros, etc. were agreed and then carried out. On 1 January 2002 everyone in the euro zone only had euros to spend. At the same time, management of national currencies by national central banks stopped and the European Central Bank began managing the euro and setting one interest rate for the whole of the euro zone. We can understand this because we know that fixed exchange rates lead to a loss of monetary independence. But what are the major implications of euro membership for the UK and for businesses generally across the EU?

Starting with the simple, but less than obvious, the nominal exchange rate between each of the member states is fixed at 1 euro for 1 euro. The more serious issue is the real exchange rate and international competitiveness. Remember the real interest rate is the nominal exchange rate adjusted for the relative price level between countries. So, even though everyone in the euro zone has fixed the nominal exchange rate, differences in inflation rates will lead to changes in the real exchange rate and international competitiveness. For example, if Germany manages to keep German inflation at 2.5 per cent, but Italy can only manage to keep inflation down to 6 per cent, then even though they use the same currency, Italy will become less competitive over time.

If we now start to think through the points we can begin to see a fundamental issue for the euro. A single interest rate is set by the ECB for the entire euro zone. So, the ECB cannot help Italy by raising interest rates, without penalizing Germany. Fiscal policy is more powerful under a fixed exchange rate, so the Italian government could decide to create a recession in Italy in order to reduce inflationary pressures and improve international competitiveness. But if Italy is pushed into a recession, when the rest of the euro zone is growing, Italy's business cycle will no longer be synchronized with all other members and the one-size-fits-all interest rate policy from the ECB will not help Italy.

Maastricht criteria and the stability pact

It is, therefore, of no surprise that strict conditions were placed on potential members of the euro, through the so-called 'Maastricht criteria'. These conditions have now been imposed as continuing conditions as part of the stability pact. In summary, the criteria seek to create macroeconomic harmonization between the member states and ensure continuing harmonization.

Before entry, potential adopters of the euro had to have low inflation and low interest rates. In the previous two years no devaluation of the national currency was allowed. This prevented countries from seeking any early real exchange rate advantage. Furthermore, on the fiscal side, government budget deficits were to be around 3 per cent of GDP and overall debt to GDP ratio should be 60 per cent. These rules were also imposed in an attempt to control fiscal stances and prevent a build-up of inflationary pressures within member countries. The stability pact of 1997 was a further agreement that the Maastricht criteria would continue to operate even after entry.

Optimal currency zones

The Maastricht criteria and the stability pact were and are attempts to keep all member economies moving together. But a more theoretical set of conditions for the success of a currency zone, such as the euro, were put forward by Robert Mundell in the 1960s.

Mundell began to think about the factors that would lead to an **optimal currency zone**. Three criteria were put forward as important for the success of a currency zone.

An **optimal currency zone** is a group of countries better off with a common currency, than keeping separate currencies.

Trade integration

The first is the degree of trade between member countries of the currency zone. Trade integrates economies. However, perhaps more importantly, highly integrated economies have the most to gain from a temporary devaluation of their currency against their partners' currency. A single currency is basically a credible commitment to co-operate, rather than starting an international price war through exchange-rate adjustments.

Similarities in industrial sectors

The second criterion concerns how the economies will deal with macroeconomic shocks. The more similar the industrial structure across all the member countries, the more likely they are to stay synchronized. For example, if all members have similar industries, an external shock, such as a rise in the oil price, or in the case of Europe, a recession in the US leading to a reduction in export growth, will lead to similar effects in all economies. No one country will suffer more than another. In contrast, if only one member country was very reliant on oil, or the US, then that economy would go into recession, while all the other countries would remain unaffected.

Flexibility and mobility

If all else fails, then there is the final safety net criterion. Factor resources such as labour and capital should display mobility and price flexibility. If an economy suffers a specific shock and goes into recession, then the quicker domestic prices adjust, the more rapid is the adjustment to international competitiveness. Furthermore, the more willing resource, such as labour, is to move throughout the currency zone to find employment, the less important is the need for specific national governments to deal with domestic problems. The single monetary policy of the central bank will suffice.

Clearly, if a country is not integrated through trade, industry or factor resource transfers, the greater the need for it to keep its own currency and its own monetary independence.

Is Europe an optimal currency zone?

In terms of Europe, the evidence tends to suggest that the euro zone is integrated to a degree; and so could represent a successful currency zone. But perhaps the more important issue is one of continuing integration and stability brought about by the euro. The longer the euro succeeds as a common currency, the more closely integrated the member economies will become. The euro promotes price transparency. Goods priced in Germany can be compared directly with goods priced anywhere else in the euro zone. First, this promotes trade, which is the first criterion for an optimal currency zone. Second, currency stability and transparency makes cross-border investments more certain. In the absence of currency exchange rate risks, companies will be more willing to operate in other member states. The structural or industrial mix of each economy will, therefore, merge; this is the second criterion. Third, price transparency promotes competition and, therefore, an increased need or willingness for workers, employers and producers to keep prices under control and pursue international competitiveness, which is the third criterion.

UK entry into the euro

The UK government has set five tests that must be met before the UK can enter into the euro. These are listed and explained in Box 13.2. Following our discussion of the stability pact and the key factors supporting an optimal currency zone, it is easy to see why the government has chosen tests of economic convergence and flexibility. These are the key factors that would facilitate the UK's entry into the euro. If the UK economy converges with the other euro economies, then the interest rate, set for Europe by the ECB, will be similar to the interest rate that would have been set by the Bank of England for the UK. If the UK manages to diverge from other euro economies, then flexibility in product and labour markets will enable internal adjustment. Finally, the tests of investment, financial services, employment and growth relate to the economic benefits from being a member of the euro; and without benefits there would be little reason for entering.

In assessing whether the UK should join the euro, we can return to our analogy of the boats in the harbour. The question rests on whether, or not, the UK wishes to retain a floating exchange rate between the pound and the euro, and in effect keep a flexible rope between itself and Europe? Or will the UK economy move close enough to the rest of Europe, in terms of its economic cycle, price levels and productivity rates, to make a solid weld between the UK and the euro area? Making a decision based on these questions would provide a structured approach to entry and is clearly how the government would like to proceed.

However, it is also possible that delaying the decision to enter the euro until all the five tests have been met could be damaging to the UK economy:

Lost trade

The euro, as a shared currency among member states, facilitates cross-border trade by

Box 13.2 **The five economic tests for the Euro**

Should the UK join the Euro?

Source: The UK Treasury

The Chancellor said in his October 1997 statement that the five economic tests will define whether a clear and unambiguous case can be made. In May 2003 it was decided that the UK had not yet passed all five tests. The five tests are:

- sustainable *convergence* between Britain and the economies of a single currency
- whether there is sufficient *flexibility* to cope with economic change
- the effect on *investment*
- the impact on our *financial services* industry
- whether it is good for *employment*

Convergence in the past has been limited; interest rates have been higher in the UK than in the euro area. Business cycles are more volatile in the UK, reflecting the greater importance of oil, the housing market and company finances.

Flexibility is important for both labour and product markets. Firms need to be flexible in pricing, reacting to increased competition and the greater needs of consumers. Wages need to increase in line with productivity growth and workers need wide-ranging skills to accommodate potential changes in the job market.

Lower levels of inflation, enabling firms to plan and invest in confidence, should improve investment. Furthermore, investment should be capable of responding to companies' increased needs for funds in the face of increased investment opportunities.

Financial services will be profoundly effected by the euro. With financial services representing around 8% of GDP, the acceptance of the Euro needs to be beneficial for London's financial centre.

The euro needs to improve employment and economic growth. However, this clearly depends upon the flexibility of the UK economy and the convergence of the UK with the rest of the euro zone.

making pricing easier and reducing the need for currency transactions. Evidence suggests that the euro has raised cross-border trade between eurozone members by as much as 30 per cent.

Lower foreign investment

Companies wishing to operate in the EU are more likely to invest in the eurozone than in the UK, because without the euro the UK is a more costly option, particularly in terms of exchange rate volatility. Lower investment will lead to reduced employment and perhaps even lower wages as UK labour endeavours to become more internationally competitive.

Weaker financial markets

As a powerful world currency, financial services companies will be keen to locate their operations in the eurozone, rather than in the UK. This will reduce employment in the UK and damage London's position as a leading financial centre.

Reduced competitiveness

The euro is perhaps already improving competitiveness in the eurozone. With greater price transparency, price dispersions for the same product across the eurozone have fallen since its inception, particularly for large consumer items such as electrical goods.

Convergence

It is not clear that the UK will converge with the eurozone. In fact the members of the eurozone are more likely to converge and become increasingly integrated as a result of the euro. In terms of convergence, the UK may end up chasing a moving target.

Euro policy and politics

To debate reform of euro fiscal and monetary policy you have to be a member. As an outsider the UK cannot direct the future of the euro.

All of these points relate back to our boats in the harbour. As the UK bobs up and down with a rope connecting it to the eurozone, trade and investment are more difficult with Europe. To be located on the stable platform that is the eurozone, with boats all welded together, makes trade more possible. The eurozone economy is bigger and financial services will view the large economy of the eurozone as more attractive than the smaller UK economy. Finally, if you are sitting in a small boat bobbing up and down in the harbour, you only have yourself to talk to. On the large platform that is the eurozone you can engage in many important debates relating to the euro.

13.7 Business application: China's saving rate and world currencies

A saving rate of 50 per cent of GDP is extremely high. Admittedly not all of this saving comes from China's consumers. Firms and government account for half of China's overall saving. But still at 25 per cent of GDP, saving by Chinese households is vastly higher than the sub 5 per cent and 10 per cent rates achieved in Europe and the US.

Chinese saving is high for a variety of reasons. First, Chinese consumption has not kept pace with growth in incomes. The Chinese have yet to adjust fully to their new found level of economic wealth. This is perhaps not surprising given that the rate of change has been so dramatic and the distribution of wealth is highly skewed. Much of the rise in China's GDP has been captured by a small percentage of the population. There are only so many plasma TVs, Porsche Cayennes and overseas trips that can be consumed. So the surplus income is saved. In addition, China has poor provision of social security and health care. In response households have increased savings to meet future eventualities. Finally, education and the growing importance of a university education also generates savings, since much of the provision is fee based.

In terms of the commercial sector, increased levels of exports to the US and Europe has helped to fuel the growth in profits. The distribution of these profits has been limited. Holding shares in China's (family-orientated) companies is not the norm; and where it is, corporate governance tends to be weak. Therefore, Chinese companies are awash with cash which needs to be saved.

Other than the size of China's saving rate, why the interest, especially for business? Vitally, China's saving rate has enormous macroeconomic consequences for other world economies, in particular the US.

Box 13.3 The frugal giant

Adapted from an article in The Economist, 22 September 2005

Thanks to rocketing economic growth, the Chinese are spending a lot more than they used to. But Chinese saving is growing even more rapidly. Since 2000, the country's overall saving rate – already the world's highest by far – has risen sharply, to nearly 50% of GDP. Even though China is investing at the staggering rate of 46% of GDP, it is still running a net saving surplus.

China may still be poor, but it has become one of the world's biggest exporters of capital. And its impact on the allocation of global capital is even bigger. This is because it recycles a lot of savings from other countries and redirects those funds towards America. China is a big recipient of foreign investment and even more speculative capital has flowed in as investors have been betting on a rise in China's currency, the yuan.

Rather than allow these capital inflows to strengthen the currency, China's central bank has chosen to pile up foreign-currency reserves, many of which are invested in American Treasury bonds. Thanks to its own saving surplus and its recycling of savings, China had $711 billion-worth of reserves at mid-year.

According to Box 13.3 China holds over $700bn of investments in US treasury bonds. China is effectively helping to fund American indebtedness, where the debt stems from a government budget deficit and a current account deficit. With China playing the role of supplier of capital, their increased willingness to supply means the US equilibrium interest rate can be lower. This lax monetary policy in the US is helping to fuel domestic consumption on cars and homes. In addition, since China is demanding the US dollar, then the exchange rate of the dollar is higher than expected given the size of its trade imbalance. With the dollar higher, US consumers see non-dollar-denominated imports from China and Europe as relatively cheap. So, China's saving matters because it helps to underpin other economies around the world, notably the US.

The problems relate to when this funding arrangement slows. US interest rates will have to rise to attract the financial capital needed to fund US indebtedness. These higher rates will curb borrowing, leading to a fall in consumption at home and overseas, while the fall in demand for dollar assets by the Chinese will lead to a depreciation of the dollar, making it more expensive for the US to import goods and services from overseas. Therefore, if the US economy helps to regulate economic activity in Europe and other regions of the world, the relationship between the US and China becomes immensely important for the level of economic activity across the globe.

Obviously, such problems can be avoided if the US reduces its willingness to borrow and begins to save more. Unfortunately, just as in Europe, consumerism is rampant, capital markets are deregulated and relative stability in economic activity all lead to higher consumer and business confidence. The willingness to take on additional credit and the ease with which it can be done are very high.

The importance for business people is to see how the macroeconomic environment of one country can be transmitted around the world through an understanding of trade and financial flows. The intricacies of the world economy are sometimes difficult to unravel, but when one economy has a $700 billion investment in the world's leading economy, it is often best to understand why and what might happen next.

13.8 Business application: hedging

The value of currencies changes every minute. Over a month, or indeed a year, the value of a currency could change by a large amount. This represents an exchange rate risk to exporters and importers, and as discussed in Box 13.4 can have important implications for a company's profits. To provide a numerical example, a UK company might agree to buy steel from a French company for the next year. The price of the steel is agreed and fixed at the beginning of the contract in Euros, say €1000 per tonne. If at the beginning of the contract €1 is worth £0.66, the company is paying £666 per tonne. However, if over the year the Euro becomes stronger and is worth £0.80, then the price of the steel increases to £800 per tonne. The Euro price of the steel has not changed, but the change in the exchange rate makes the steel more expensive in pounds. So how do you protect yourself against such risks? The answer is you **hedge**.

Hedging is the transfer of a risky asset for a non-risky asset.

Box 13.4 **For whom the euro tolls**

Adapted from an article by Beth Carney in BusinessWeek, 13 June 2005

European companies with few operations in the US will be helped by the currency's slide. Others will be clobbered. Here are five on each side

In terms of earnings development for Corporate Europe, the weaker euro has been a good thing. Most European companies will be helped rather than hurt by the shift. Although by historical standards the 12-nation currency remains strong against the dollar, its recent trend continues downward.

WINNERS AND LOSERS

How does a weakening euro affect European companies? 'In such an environment,' says Davina Curling, a European fund manager at F&C Asset Management in London, 'there are obvious winners and losers.' Broadly, any company that exports to the US gets a lift when the euro declines against the dollar. The companies that suffer include those importing goods from regions with currencies that follow dollar movements or those that have high dollar-denominated commodity costs.

BusinessWeek Online asked some experts to come up with specific examples of companies that gain or lose when the euro falls. The winners are:

- **Porsche:** The German luxury carmaker generates 35% of its sales in dollars, yet produces all its cars in Europe. Unlike carmakers such as DaimlerChrysler, which sells a significant number of cars in the US but also has factories here generating dollar-denominated costs, Porsche 'has no natural hedge', he says. Simply put, when the euro weakens, the company's US sales are worth more, and its European costs are worth less. 'Porsche is a big one', Higgins says. 'It's very, very sensitive to the dollar.'

- **LVMH:** LVMH Moët Hennessy Louis Vuitton's luxury goods – including Dom Perignon champagne, Fendi handbags, and Givenchy fashion – are well known in the US. American buyers account for 31% of its sales, and the company has 'no significant' production facilities in the US. Although it uses currency options on goods sold between its subsidiaries, LVMH is not completely protected against currency fluctuations, which means a weaker euro boosts euro-denominated profits and sales.

- **Sanofi-Aventis:** Since the US is the world's most lucrative drug market, the European pharmaceutical industry is one of the sectors most affected by shifts in the exchange rate. 'The classic beneficiaries [of a stronger dollar] are always drug companies, because they have the greatest exposure to the US,' says Stewart Adkin, senior pharmaceutical analyst at Lehman Brothers.

According to Lehman Brothers, the euro-zone drugmaker with the most sensitivity to currency fluctuations is the region's biggest: Sanofi-Aventis, which was formed in 2004 from the merger of the French Sanofi-Synthélabo and Franco-German Aventis. By the bank's calculations, in 2004 every 5% strengthening of the US dollar would have yielded a 1.6% earnings increase for Sanofi and a 2.5% boost for Aventis.

The stocks that might be hurt the most are:

- **Ryanair and easyJet:** European airlines have been somewhat protected from high oil prices by the strong euro, since oil is priced in dollars, says Curling. So a weaker euro means fuel is more expensive for European companies. For low-cost carriers the move is especially important, since fuel represents a bigger proportion of their total costs than it does for flag carriers (typically state-controlled or state-aided airlines). Unlike major European carriers that fly across the Atlantic and in doing so book some of their revenue in dollars, the discount players only fly within Europe, leaving them further exposed.

- **Puma and Adidas:** These sporting-goods makers have headquarters in Germany, and they sell plenty of soccer cleats and track suits in Europe. However, most of their products are made in Asia, where the currencies tend to be closely linked to the US dollar and have been weaker against the euro in the past few years. 'When the dollar was weak, they had an advantage.' Now, however, with the euro sliding, 'it's going the other way around'.

- **Hennes & Mauritz:** The recent success of the Swedish retail chain known as H&M has not been just a function of its trendy fashion sense. It imports more than half its goods from dollar-based regions, mostly in Asia. It also locates the vast majority of its stores in Europe. 'Earnings growth over the last three years has been hugely supported by expanding margins on the back of a shrinking cost base.' Now that the euro is the currency that is getting weaker, the group's margins will also shrink: 'This will hit the profits if it carries on.'

In the forex market there is ample opportunity to hedge. In Table 13.4 we have the exchange rates for a variety of currencies with the pound. The exchange rate is known as the spot price. This is the exchange rate now, i.e. the exchange rate that you might get 'on the spot'. The next set of columns list the forward prices. These are the exchange rates at which people are willing to sell a currency at one month, three months, or one year into the future. If we take the euro, the spot price is €1.4485 per £1; but the one-year forward price is €1.4281 per £1, or 2.1 per cent less. This difference reflects expectations about how the currency will move over the next year and a reward for taking the risk of agreeing to sell at an agreed price in the future.

Table 13.4 Spot and forward exchange rates for pound sterling

Currency	Spot price	One month	Three months	One year	% change
US dollar	1.7728	1.7721	1.7716	1.7747	1.1
Euro	1.4585	1.4537	1.4495	1.4281	−2.1
Japan	203.13	202.318	200.714	193.905	−4.5

Source: Financial Times, 27 January 2006

Our steel importer can now hedge its exchange-rate risk. Rather than facing the risk of the pound falling against the euro, it can agree in the financial markets a rate for the next month, the month after and even for one year into the future. Its future payments then become less risky; it has hedged the currency risk.

Speculation

We have argued that businesses might seek to reduce risk by hedging exchange rate movements. It is also the business of some individuals and companies to make money out of hedging. They do this by speculating that the forward price is wrong. For example, if the one-month forward price for converting pounds into US dollars is £1 = $1.5, but you think that in one month the spot price will fall to £1 to $1, then you can potentially make a very large profit.

Consider the following scenarios: a company goes to the bank and borrows £1 million. It then converts this into US dollars at the spot price of £1 to $1.5. The company now has $1.5 million. Assume that the one-month forward price for converting pounds into dollars is also £1 = $1.5 and the company also buys the forward rate.

What happens if the forward rate is correct?

If the forward rate is correct, then the spot price at the end of the month is also £1 for $1.5. The company can enter into the following (and profitless exercise). Change its $1.5 million into £1 million and use the forward contract to change its £1 million into $1.5 million. It is no better off.

What happens if the forward rate is wrong?

If after one month the spot price has fallen to £1 equals $1, then the company can take its $1.5 million and convert it into £1.5 million. It can then pay off its £1 million loan and it still has £0.5 million left. It then uses the forward contract to further increase its investment returns by converting the remaining £0.5 million into $0.75 million. It started owing £1 million and ended up with $0.75 million cash in the bank! Before you go out and borrow lots of money and try this strategy for yourself, remember this is high risk. The spot price could just as easily move in the other direction and then you would end up owing more than you initially borrowed.

 Summary

1 The foreign exchange market is where currencies are traded.

2 In a floating exchange rate the value of the currency reflects changes in the supply and demand of the currency. When demand increases, the currency appreciates in value. When demand falls, the currency falls in value.

3 Under purchasing power parity the price of goods in one economy are the same as the price of goods in another economy when converted into the same currency.

4 In the long run a floating exchange rate will adjust to ensure purchasing power parity holds.

5 Under a fixed exchange rate regime the government commits to managing the value of a currency at a set price. If the market shows signs of wishing to move above the fixed price, the government supplies more currency to the market. In contrast, if the market shows signs of wishing to move below the set price, the government supports the currency by increasing demand for the currency.

6   Fixed exchange rates do not ensure purchasing power parity and in the long run the prospect of devaluation can lead to speculative attack.

7   Most major currencies, such as the pound, the US dollar and the euro, float. Some minor economies fix their exchange rate to the dollar; Argentina was an example.

8   When considering the virtues of fixed and floating exchange rates it is sensible to consider volatility, robustness and financial discipline.

9   Floating exchange rates are more volatile than fixed exchange rates. But the prospect of speculative attacks and devaluations can make fixed rates sources of wider economic uncertainty and volatility.

10 Floating exchange rates allow economies to adapt to external changes such as inflationary differences. Fixed exchange rates require economies to be highly integrated, as they cannot accommodate change within the fixed rate.

11 Because of the inflexibility of fixed exchange rates they are seen as promoting financial discipline and the pursuit of low inflation.

12 The balance of payments records the transactions undertaken by a country with the rest of the world. It has three main accounts: the current account, the capital account and the financial account. The current account measures the trade of goods and services. The capital account measures the flow of transfer payments such as UK government payments to the EU commission. The financial account measures the investment flows.

13 Under a floating exchange rate the balance of payments balance. The equilibrium market price of the currency means that the demand and supply of the currency that stems from the transactions recorded in the current, capital and financial accounts must balance. Under a fixed exchange rate, equilibrium in the forex market is only achieved by the government intervening. Therefore, for the balance of payments to balance, the level of intervention has to be included. This is called official financing and simply measures the use of the foreign currency reserves.

14 Monetary policy is more powerful than fiscal policy under a floating exchange rate system. Fiscal policy is more powerful than monetary policy under a fixed exchange rate system.

15 European monetary union is a fixed exchange rate system between all member countries: 1 euro in Germany is worth 1 euro in Italy. However, the euro floats against all other national currencies, such as the pound and the US dollar.

16 The success of the euro depends upon whether its member economies represent an optimal currency zone. For such a zone to exist, trade between members has to be high, the economies need to respond to external economic shocks in a similar way and price flexibility or factor mobility has to be high. In essence, economies have to be either highly integrated and synchronized, or must be capable of quickly adapting to differences through price changes.

17 The euro zone is reasonably integrated and as the system progresses it is likely to become more synchronized. The use of a single interest rate policy from the European Central Bank and the control of fiscal expenditure through the criteria set down in the stability pact should force economies to cut internal levels of inflation and synchronize their business cycles.

18 By fixing the nominal exchange rate between member economies of the euro, international competitiveness is strongly linked to the cost and productivity of factor inputs. Euro zone economies with low labour costs and high productivity growth rates should attract increased attention from businesses seeking to enhance their cost effectiveness.

19 Currency markets and the volatility within them represent business opportunities for speculators. Firms that do not like risk will try to hedge currency risk by purchasing forward rates, which guarantee the exchange rate in one month, three months or one year. Speculators, in contrast, will seek to buy forward when they expect the forward and spot rate to be different.

 Learning checklist

You should now be able to:

♦ Explain how fixed exchange rates work

♦ Evaluate fixed versus floating exchange rates

♦ Explain the power of fiscal and monetary policy under fixed and floating exchange rate regimes

♦ Explain the features of an optimal currency zone

♦ Understand the importance of China's saving rate in the development of macroeconomic conditions around the world.

♦ Explain hedging and how firms might use hedging within forex markets

❓ Questions

1 A country has a current account surplus of £6 billion, but a financial account deficit of £4 billion. (a) Is the exchange rate system fixed or floating? (b) Is its balance of payments in deficit or surplus? (c) Are its foreign exchange reserves rising or falling? (d) Is the central bank buying or selling domestic currency? Explain.

2 Under fixed and floating exchange rates, which type of policy is most effective, fiscal or monetary? Why does the eurozone have one interest rate set by the European Central Bank?

3 Why is flexibility among business and workers a desirable feature of the UK economy prior to entry into the euro?

4 Should the UK be a member of the euro?

Exercises

1 True or false?
  a) The US dollar is a floating currency.
  b) The Chinese Yuan is a managed float.
  c) A rise in the real exchange rate reduces the competitiveness of the domestic economy.
  d) After converting into euros the price of Chanel perfume in Singapore is the same as in Schiphol airport; this is an example of purchasing power parity.
  e) If the current account is in surplus and the balance of payments is not zero, then a floating exchange rate regime is in existence.
  f) Monetary policy is more effective under a floating exchange rate.

2 Figure 13.5 shows the position in the foreign exchange market: DD is the demand schedule for sterling and SS the supply schedule. Assume a two-country world (UK and the eurozone):

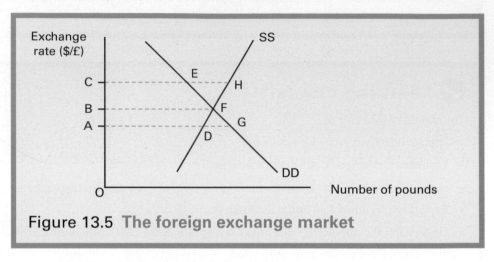

Figure 13.5 The foreign exchange market

a) Explain briefly how the two schedules arise.

b) Identify the exchange rate that would prevail under a clean float. What would be the state of the overall balance of payments at this exchange rate?

c) Suppose the exchange rate were set at OA under a fixed exchange rate regime. What intervention would be required by the central bank? What would be the state of the balance of payments?

d) Suppose the exchange rate was set at OC. Identify the situation of the balance of payments and the necessary central bank intervention.

e) If the authorities wished to maintain the exchange rate at OC in the long run, what sort of measures would be required?

3 Refer to Box 13.4 when considering the following questions:

a) Draw an average revenue and average cost diagram for Porsche depicting the impact of a change in exchange rates on Porsche's profits.

b) Draw an average revenue and average cost diagram for H&M, depicting the impact of a change in exchange rates on H&M's profits.

c) Advise both of these companies on the relative merits of hedging their exchange rate risk.

Chapter 14
Globalization

Chapter contents

 ## Learning outcomes

By the end of this chapter you should understand:

Economic Theory

- The cultural, political and economic drivers of globalization

- The concept of comparative advantage

- The use of tariffs and quotas

- How to assess the rise in international trade

- The reasons behind the rise and fall in foreign direct investment

Business Application

- Understanding the impediments to an exploitation of comparative advantage

- Understand the sources of international competitiveness in the IT sector

Globalization at a glance

The issues

The world economy is becoming increasing integrated, with more and more products being sold across national boundaries and firms operating in more than one economy. The issues for business are numerous, but include: why is globalization happening, what opportunities does it present; and what threats might develop from globalization?

The understanding

The increase in cross-border trade and the number of firms operating in more than one country can be related to a number of issues. In recent times barriers to international trade, such as tariffs, have fallen. The World Trade Organization has played an important role, but so has the development of trade blocs, such as the EU. Falling transportation costs and developments in communications technology have also made international trade and international operations more feasible. But this only explains why trade is easier. Why trade occurs is related to an important economic concept known as 'comparative advantage'.

The usefulness

In understanding why globalization is occurring and where it is occurring, business can begin to understand where opportunities in the global economy exist for the enhancement of costs and revenues. Similarly, as globalization is a double-edged sword, an understanding of the implications of globalization will help to highlight where threats of increased competition are likely to come from in a global economy.

14.1 Business problem: how do we take advantage of the global economy?

The world has changed. As little as ten years ago taking a holiday in Spain was common, but taking a holiday in the Caribbean, the Far East or even Australia was something very different. Now backpacking around the world by students, and the retired, is reasonably common. Given this trend in travel it is of no surprise that one airline alliance decided to call itself 'One World'. Perhaps part of the mystique associated with international travel was the inaccessibility of the traveller. Communications back home generally took the form of a post card, which invariably arrived home after the traveller. In recent years improvements in the integration of telecommunications networks has allowed mobile phones to work almost anywhere. Text messages, video messages and voice calls mean that someone on holiday in Thailand is just as accessible as someone on the other side of town.

World travellers and international telecommunications are not the only changing features of the world. Once you are abroad there are now many commonalities. For example, have you ever been abroad and failed to find a McDonald's, or a Starbucks? This relentless march of global brands has its benefits. You can walk into a McDonald's anywhere and know what you are going to receive. The brand provides comfort and certainty in its continued deliverance of a Big Mac and fries. But the power of the global brand can be felt just as much at home as it can overseas. Take a quick look at yourself. Is there a Samsung phone in your pocket, a pair of Nike trainers on your feet and a pair of Levi's on your bum? There is a reasonable chance that you have one of these, or at least something similar.

What does all this mean for business? Globalization provides opportunities and threats for business. The willingness of consumers in faraway markets to consume international products, such as Big Macs, provides opportunities for McDonald's to grow. But at the same time, by operating overseas, McDonald's gains potential access to cheaper labour, cheaper raw materials and cheaper finance. In contrast, noodle shops in Hong Kong and fish and chip shops in the UK now face international competition from the likes of McDonald's. The fast food market is a clear and tangible example of globalization and increased competition. But the influences of globalization are far-reaching. Speak to almost any businessperson and they will recognize the importance of globalization. Read any business paper, or magazine, and you will find an article on globalization. Businesses are actively seeking out cost advantages by using the global market to source labour, finance or raw materials. They are then using these advantages to proliferate their brands around the world.

In this chapter we will examine the economic rationale behind globalization and highlight some of the main drivers of globalization in recent times. An examination of global products and operations, and global labour and financial markets will provide an understanding of this important trend in the modern business environment.

14.2 **Why is the global economy developing?**

There are many potential drivers of globalization, ranging from the economic, through the political to the cultural. In this section we will examine each in turn in an attempt to provide a working knowledge of globalization and the future developments for business.

Culture

The process of globalization must to some extent be facilitated by a convergence of cultures. For example, St Patrick's Day is a celebration of the patron saint of Ireland. Yet the day itself is now celebrated by many other nationalities the world over. Admittedly, many of the Irish have at some point emigrated to other parts of the world, but this does not explain the extent to which other cultures are willing to assume the St Patrick's Day celebrations.

Anthony Giddens, a leading sociological writer on globalization, has argued that globalization is the cultural suspension of space and time. If space is a cultural reference point for geography and national identity, the willingness of many other cultures to celebrate St Patrick's Day surely reflects a suspension of cultural space. Individuals from the UK, Australia and the US in celebrating the Irish patron saint's day are suspending, in part, their cultural attachment to their own national culture.

If national cultural identity was important in the past, what is leading to a suspension of time and space under globalization? Some of the answers to this question lack any firm empirical support, but they do seem plausible.

Travel

Increased international travel promotes an acceptance of other cultures. Travel facilitates experimentation with different types of food, language and customs. The old adage of 'when in Rome act like a Roman' can be an enlightening and enjoyable experience for many travellers. When they then return home they periodically like to consume products from these distant places.

Film and media

Hollywood and the American entertainment industry are successful industries. They produce films, TV sit-coms and a variety of music that are enjoyed not only by Americans, but also by many people around the world. The portrayal of American lifestyles, the types of cars driven, the use of coffee shops, the consumption of burgers, pizzas, doughnuts and soft drinks, and the belief that opportunity exists for everyone, can all be viewed and absorbed while watching such movies, or TV programmes. So, if viewers around the world enjoy watching, or listening to American culture, then perhaps they will also enjoy partaking in, or consuming, American culture? If this is true, then American media are an important facilitator of US companies selling their brands around the globe.

Technology and communications

The ability to communicate with anyone, at anytime, anywhere in the world increases the perception of a global village, as opposed to a large fragmented global system. Financial centres in Tokyo, London and New York probably helped to develop the first impressions of a continuous, integrated global financial system. In recent times, global news providers, such as the BBC, Sky and CNN, have developed formats built around the 24-hour clock, with the news rooms moving between continents as the sun and daylight move around the world. This, in the terminology of Giddens, enables individuals to suspend time and space. A suspension of space is evident by the view that the global economy is everywhere, not somewhere. Similarly, time is a human concept, which slices up the day. But time is continuous; it has no beginning and no end. The continuous, ever-rolling nature of 24-hour news, financial centres and global business provides the opportunity for individuals, wherever they are in the world, to suspend time. It does not matter if it is midnight here. Somewhere in the world, it is 10.00 a.m. and, therefore, someone is making news and someone is making a profit. The global person and the global business are not constrained by time, or space.

While telecommunications and the media have made the world feel smaller, transport technologies have made the movement of people and products more affordable. Jumbo jets make the transport of individuals between continents cheap, fast and reliable. Similarly, the invention of the container vessel in the 1960s, carrying many steel box containers with various cargos, meant that one ship could exploit economies of scale, whereas previously a single exporter with a small cargo would have had to hire a small ship to transport their product around the world. Furthermore, the development of land-based infrastructure such as deep-sea ports, motorways and rail networks has helped to make the movement of goods around the world and overland much more feasible and affordable. Such have been the improvements that estimates by the World Bank suggest that transport costs are now 80 per cent less than a century ago.

Culture and politics are facilitators of globalization. They enable firms and consumers to buy, sell and even produce on a global basis. But there has to be a motive for firms and consumers to act globally. Why do they wish to take advantage of a political freedom to act internationally and the global appetite of consumers?

Economic rationales

> The **law of comparative advantage** states that economies should specialize in the good that they are *comparatively* better at making.

The economic answer begins with an analysis of what is known as **comparative advantage**.

The key word is *comparatively*. We can highlight its importance with the following example. In Table 14.1 we have the required hours to produce one car, or one TV. In the EU it takes 30 hours to make a car and 5 hours to make a TV. The EU is more productive than the UK in the case of cars and TVs. If we had said that each economy should specialize in what it is good at, the UK would make nothing and the EU would make everything. This is not a good idea because the UK could make something and add to world output. This is why we employed the word 'comparative'.

Table 14.1 Output and opportunity costs

		Hours to make one unit	Opportunity cost
EU	Cars	30	6 TVs
	TVs	5	1/6 car
UK	Cars	60	10 TVs
	TVs	6	1/10 car

In the last column of Table 14.1 we have the opportunity cost. In this case the opportunity cost is how many cars (TVs) have to be given up in order to produce one more TV (car). In the case of the EU, if workers were transferred from TVs to cars, then the cost of making one more car is the loss of 6 extra TVs.

We can now compare the relative cost of providing cars and TVs in the EU and the UK. The EU can produce cars more cheaply than the UK. The EU only sacrifices 6 TVs for each extra car; the UK has to sacrifice 10 TVs. In the case of TVs the EU has to sacrifice 1/6 of a car for each extra TV, but the UK only has to sacrifice 1/10 of a car for each extra TV. The UK can produce TVs more cheaply than the EU. We can now say that the EU has a comparative advantage in car production and the UK has a comparative advantage in TV production. Therefore, if the EU specializes in cars and the UK in TVs, total output will be greater than if both were to try to produce cars and TVs for themselves. For example, if the UK gives up 6 cars and produces 60 extra TVs, the EU can make the extra 6 cars by only giving up 36 TVs, providing a net addition of 24 TVs. Similarly, if the EU makes 10 more cars and gives up 60 TVs, the UK makes these extra TVs for the loss of only 6 cars, thus providing the world with 4 extra cars.

Terms of trade

While trade between the EU and the UK will lead to higher output, it needs to be profitable for trade to actually occur. Since the EU is comparatively better at producing cars it will be an exporter of cars, or it will provide an international supply of cars. This is illustrated in Figure 14.1 with the upward sloping supply curve. If the EU did not trade with the rest of the world, the price of cars (in TVs) would be 6. Once the international price of cars begins to rise above 6, the EU is willing to supply additional amount of cars, or effectively increase its export of cars.

In contrast, the UK has a comparative disadvantage in the production of cars. If it did not trade with the rest of the world the price of a car in the UK would be 10 (TVs). However, if the international price for cars is less than 10, the UK would increase its willingness to demand cars. In effect the UK would be importing cars. Since the EU is willing to export at prices above 6 TVs and the UK is willing to demand at prices below 10 TVs there must be an equilibrium international price for cars which in Figure 14.1 is P_{cars}. The actual value for P_{car} will depend upon the elasticities of supply and demand for cars in the international market.

We could draw a similar figure for TVs, but this time the UK would be exporting and the EU importing. Again the equilibrium price for TVs would lie between the opportunity cost of dishwashers in the UK and the EU, at a price of P_{TV}.

A country's terms of trade measure the price ratio of exports to imports, in this case the terms of trade would be the ratio P_{TV}/P_{TV}. More generally it is a weighted average of a country's export prices to its import prices, $P_{exports}/P_{imports}$.

If a country's terms of trade improve, then the price of its exports is rising relative to the price of its imports. It has to export less in order to fund its imports. This can happen if the either the exchange rate changes, or the equilibrium price for exports or imports changes.

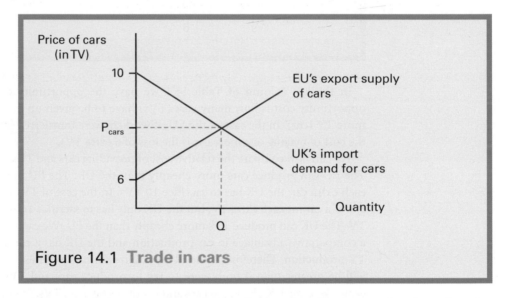

Figure 14.1 Trade in cars

This example is more commonly described as the gains from trade, where the gains from trade are the additional output of some goods with no loss of other goods.

The fundamental importance of comparative advantage

Comparative advantage and the gains from trade are very powerful arguments and have provided many governments with a rationale for freer international trade. However, it must be remembered that comparative advantage is not simply an international matter. The decision-making and behaviour of many ordinary individuals conforms to comparative advantage. Families increasingly take their children to daycare, rather than one parent leaving paid employment. Why? Because the daycare centre, when looking after many children, can exploit economies of scale which the single family cannot. The daycare centre has a comparative advantage in the care of children. With cheaper daycare, the opportunity cost of going to work is now less than the opportunity cost of staying at home and looking after the children. Similarly, why do some people specialize as decorators, doctors, academics, or bank managers? Because they have a comparative advantage in their chosen vocation. Painting a wall is fairly straightforward, but in taking the time to do this an academic, doctor or bank manager has to give up some possibly very lucrative fee-paying work, or a large amount of free time. It is, therefore, more efficient to employ a decorator who is a specialist and can do the job much more quickly.

The overriding message is that comparative advantage applies to all of us. The idea of comparative advantage and international trade is nothing more than an extension of these ideas, but crucially it is being argued that factor inputs, such as labour and capital, should be employed where they have a comparative advantage. As such we should not look at the individual, as in the case of a decorator or doctor; nor should we look at an individual economy such as the UK. Rather, we should be looking at the global economy and seeking ways that enable resources to be allocated to their most productive ends. In this way globalization is a natural consequence of comparative advantage. Economies do not seek to produce all the products that they need. Instead they produce what they are comparatively good at and then trade it for products in the global economy that they are not good at making. In this way globalization is simply like the doctor hiring a decorator to paint their house; and a decorator hiring a doctor to cure their illness. But what are the sources of comparative advantage?

Factor abundance

Think of a country and then think what products it is famous for. Table 14.2 contains some obvious examples.

Table 14.2 Countries and their exports

Country	Product
France	Wine
Germany	Cars
Saudi Arabia	Oil
Canada	Wheat
India	Textiles
Holland	Plants
Australia	Sheep
Barbados	Holidays

Clearly, France is famous for more than just wine, but each product listed above is known to come from each of the countries. France is good at wine because it has the right land and the right climate for making the grapes ripen at just the right rate in order to concentrate the flavours required for good wine. Germany is good at cars because it has a highly skilled workforce that is required for the production of high-quality manufactured goods. Saudi Arabia has land with good oil reserves. India has lots of workers, who are required for the labour-intensive production of textiles. Australia has lots of open places required for grazing sheep; and Holland as a very flat country is good for growing plants that do not like to be shaded from the sun by hills and valleys. Barbados, situated just above the equator, is excellent in providing year-round tropical holidays; it is also fairly good at bananas and sugar.

Economies, therefore, appear to produce goods for which they have an abundance of a key factor input.

Britain does not export tropical holidays, or wine. It does not have the factor inputs for such products. France and Barbados do. It is, therefore, comparatively cheap for France and Barbados to produce these types of product. The UK has an abundance of history. Castles, battlefields, the monarchy and parliament all attract visitors. We can produce history better than most and, in exchange, France provides us with wine, India with textiles, Australia with sheep and Barbados with tropical holidays.

Comparative advantage is clearly linked to the endowment of resources within an economy.

Two-way trade

The observant will have spotted that some countries trade the same product. For example, the UK sells cars to Germany in the form of Rovers, Jaguars and even Peugeots! Germany exports cars to the UK in the form of BMWs, VWs and Mercedes. The UK also exports more cheese than it imports. Why does it not stop exporting cheese and import less? The reason, as in the case of cars, is to do with tastes. Some individuals like different features. Some consumers like German cars; some like French cheese. It is the difference in tastes that generates two-way trade between economies. Furthermore, the ability of Jaguar, Rover and Peugeot to trade internationally enables economies of scale to be exploited. Producing for the UK is likely to be very low scale. But producing for the whole of Europe enables manufactures to operate nearer to the minimum efficient scale. So, international trade can lead to lower cost production and increased variety.

Trade restrictions

Despite the accepted benefits of comparative advantage, international trade has in the past been impeded by various governments around the world.

A problem with comparative advantage is that it raises economic output for the world. But this does not mean it improves economic prosperity for all individuals.

For example, in trading with the US, if the UK decided to abandon car production and specialize in TV production, workers in the car industry would become unemployed and there is no reason to suggest that they will be happy making TVs. So, in this case, UK car-makers do not find comparative advantage particularly attractive.

However, uncompetitive industries do not have to simply roll over and die. If the industry has political influence, perhaps stemming from the number of voters that they potentially employ, then the government can be asked to provide so-called **protectionist measures**.

Protectionist measures seek to lower the competitiveness of international rivals.

Tariffs are examples of trade protection. A tariff is a tax on imports and, therefore, raises the price of imports.

For a more in-depth example of tariffs we can examine Figure 14.2. Without imports for this good, UK supply and UK demand would form an equilibrium at A. However, the world price for this product is much lower at £10. UK supply at £10 is only Q_s and UK demand is much greater at Q_d. This excess of UK demand over UK supply is met by imports. If the government imposes an import tariff of £5, then the world price effectively rises to £15. UK firms now raise supply from Q_s to Q_{s1}. But because the product now costs more, UK demand falls from Q_d to Q_{d1}. The level of excess demand is now much less and as a consequence the level of imports falls.

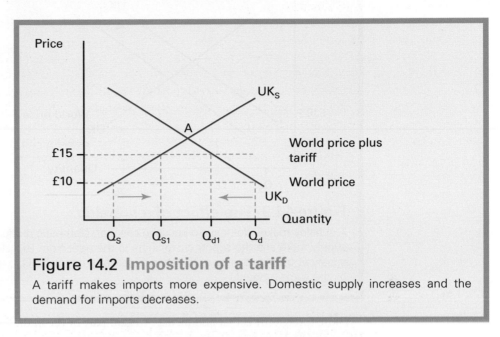

Figure 14.2 Imposition of a tariff
A tariff makes imports more expensive. Domestic supply increases and the demand for imports decreases.

In the face of tariffs, imports fall and domestic supply increases.

When tariffs are removed, international competition leads to a reduction in domestic supply and an increase in imports.

The case for tariffs is limited. They are a form of government intervention that simply supports inefficient domestic producers. Furthermore, tariffs in the main support domestic producers, and not domestic consumers. UK consumers under a tariff have to pay more for the good, via a tax to government, than they would if no tariff existed.

An alternative form of support for domestic producers could take the form of a subsidy. This is illustrated in Figure 14.3. A subsidy makes production cheaper for the domestic industry. The industry is more willing to supply and the supply curve shifts to the right. The domestic consumer pays the international price for the product, but a reduction in imports is brought about by the increase in domestic supply.

However, there is a question regarding how the government will fund the subsidy. Governments finance themselves principally through taxation. So increased domestic subsidies must lead to higher taxes. However, while a tariff is a tax paid by the consumer buying the product, subsidies can be funded by taxing everyone. Funding a subsidy via increased taxation spreads the burden of supporting the domestic industry. But why should some people support an industry that they perhaps do not buy products from?

Non-tariff barriers

Governments can restrict trade in other ways.

A **quota** restricts trade by limiting the amount of a product that can be imported into a country. For example, a steel quota might limit the importation of steel to 200 million tonnes a year.

Since quotas restrict international supply, then the price in the domestic market must increase.

A **quota** has the same effect as a tariff. It makes goods more expensive for consumers and it raise the profits of inefficient domestic firms.

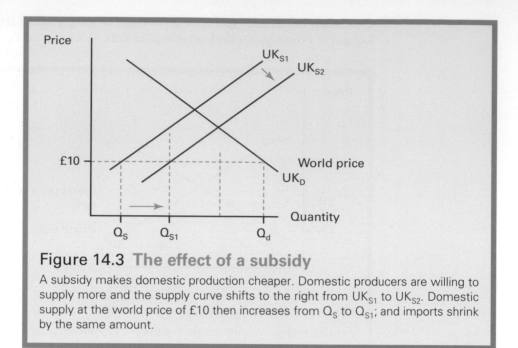

Figure 14.3 The effect of a subsidy

A subsidy makes domestic production cheaper. Domestic producers are willing to supply more and the supply curve shifts to the right from UK_{S1} to UK_{S2}. Domestic supply at the world price of £10 then increases from Q_S to Q_{S1}; and imports shrink by the same amount.

Those foreign firms that also manage to gain part of the quota can also sell inside the UK at the higher price. Under a tariff domestic consumers paid a tax to government. Under a quota some of the price increase leaks out of the economy to foreign firms.

Other methods include the application of standards. The EU is infamous for asserting that a banana must show a certain curve to its overall shape. The cynical view is that bananas from certain parts of the world are not 'curvy' enough. The EU can then proudly claim to reduce trade barriers on bananas. Those that are not curvy enough are not bananas, so the trade barrier still exists. Red tape required for import licences, driving on the left-hand side of the road, and an outright ban on British beef even after the BSE scare has vanished – all can be viewed as means of restricting international trade.

Reasons for protecting trade

While the protection of domestic industries from international competition appears to be very contentious, a number of arguments are still put forward for creating barriers to trade.

Defence or national interest

Governments may wish to support an industry that has strategic value. Steel is very important to the UK economy and the government would not wish to see the economy dependent upon another economy for steel, the fear being that at some point in the future we manage to fall out with the steel supplier and our access to steel is terminated. But why not provide incentives for the steel producers to become more efficient, rather than pricing international competition out of the domestic market with tariffs?

Infant industry

Sometimes an industry might seek government protection. During the period of protection the industry is expected to develop its capabilities to a level where it is capable of competing internationally. But if a company is capable of making profits at some point in the future, then why does the capital market fail to provide it with funds? Is it the case, perhaps, that the industry is incapable of ever becoming internationally competitive? Domestic wages, the price of raw materials, or the level of technology may mean that the industry will never catch up. Furthermore, during the five years that it might take to develop the industry, what are the international competitors going to be doing? They are unlikely to be doing nothing. Instead they will be looking to develop their competitive advantage, through improvements in production and operating efficiency. The case for infant industries can become continual, with industries asking for extensions to the period of protection, with no real hope of protection ever being withdrawn.

Way of life

The UK and perhaps even the French place an economic value on the attractiveness of the countryside. If French and UK farmers are internationally uncompetitive then, over time, they will stop farming. This *could* lead to a reduction in the management of the countryside. If true, then it might be desirable to think about protecting farmers from international competition. In so doing, trade protection also protects society from the loss of a positive externality, a well-managed countryside. This argument is sometimes used in support of the Common Agricultural Policy.

Politics

A main driver of globalization has been the merging of political and economic views on international trade. We have seen that economists are keen to promote the ideas of international trade based on comparative advantage. Economists also find it hard to support trade restrictions: first, because trade restrictions prevent comparative advantage and, second, because tariffs and quotas support inefficient domestic producers at the expense of consumers, or taxpayers. Politicians have now also recognized the economic arguments against trade restrictions.

International institutions

This recognition of the importance of international trade can be traced back to the end of the Second World War, when political leaders of the time decided that stability in the world would be enhanced by greater political and economic integration. As a result, a number of supra-national institutions were set up, for example, the United Nations, the World Bank and the World Trade Organization (WTO, formerly known as the General Agreement on Tariffs and Trade, or GATT).

GATT, formed in 1947, was an international institution that brought countries together to negotiate reductions in tariffs. Various rounds of negotiations were held and each round lasted many years. The Tokyo Round began in 1973 and ended in 1979, with an average tariff reduction of 33 per cent. The Uruguay Round began in 1986 and ended in 1993. While this again reduced tariffs, the round also agreed the creation of the World Trade Organization. While GATT was a place for countries to come together and discuss trade barriers and disputes, the WTO is an organization with power. Countries can now ask the WTO to rule on trade disputes and even impose fines on countries that fail to uphold international trade.

A **trade bloc** is a region or group of countries that have agreed to remove all trade barriers among themselves.

Trade blocs

In 1965 the Treaty of Rome led to the development of what is now known as the European Union. As an area of free trade between member nations it can be described as a **trade bloc**.

Aside from the EU, there is also, for example, the North American Free Trade Area (NAFTA), a trade bloc promoting trade between the US, Canada and Mexico, while in South East Asia there is ASEAN, the Association of South East Asian Nations.

The importance of political institutions, such as the UN, and trade blocs, such as the EU, is that politicians increasingly recognize the economic importance of international trade and economic integration. Without international competition, domestic producers might not seek to innovate, drive down costs and keep prices low. Without access to international markets, domestic companies might not gain access to the cheapest, or most productive factor inputs. These arguments are extremely persuasive, as evidenced by the continued success of the EU and the eagerness of other countries to join the EU. However, the balance of power between regional trade blocs and true internationally free trade engendered by the WTO is beginning to shift. Box 14.1 highlights how economies could retreat from globalization into regionalization unless the Doha round is successful.

 Box 14.1 **The WTO's Shaky Common Ground**

Adapted from an article by Frederik Balfour in BusinessWeek, 12 December 2005

When trade ministers met in Doha, Qatar, not long after the September 11 attacks in the US, they aimed for talks that would boost global living standards and political stability by bringing poorer nations into the global trading system. But the so-called Doha Round of negotiations have foundered time and again on disputes over rich countries' farm subsidies and import barriers in nations such as India and Brazil.

Europe is increasingly isolated on subsidies for its farmers. Brussels wants far higher levels of tariff protection for agricultural products than most of the rest of the world. If the WTO fails, other regional bodies could prosper. ASEAN, which includes 10 countries of Southeast Asia with a combined population of more than 500 million, is planning to expand its free-trade area to include China and South Korea. North America has NAFTA, with trade agreements with Chile, Singapore, and Vietnam. The danger is that the least developed countries, especially those in sub-Sahara Africa, stand little chance of joining trading blocs, so they're likely to miss any potential gains from free trade.

14.3 A closer look at the EU

The EU has its origins in the European Community which was established among six economies in 1957. These were West Germany, France, Italy, The Netherlands, Belgium and Luxembourg. By the 1990s membership had expanded and included most of the economies of Western Europe. Finally, in 2004, EU enlargement added a further ten Eastern European economies including the likes of Poland and the Slovak Republic. The EU now comprises 25 member countries.

Table 14.3 shows that the EU in terms of GDP and population is now bigger than the US. While China has a bigger population, economic growth has not yet caught up with the EU, US and Japan, but with three times as many individuals the potential to close the gap is possible.

An important feature of the EU is the limited presence of internal trade barriers. Tariffs and quotas between member states have been abolished leading to an increased movement of internal free trade. The creation of the euro facilitated further the ease with which trade could occur by removing the difficulty of price comparisons and the need to convert competing currencies.

Table 14.3 Comparing the EU, 2004

	EU	US	Japan	China
GDP (US$ billions)	12 700	11 700	4620	1650
Population (millions)	455	294	128	1296

Source: World Bank

Regulatory harmonization in labour markets, tax regimes and patent systems have eased the administrative burden faced by firms wishing to operate beyond their national boundary. Furthermore, financial deregulation, principally in banking and insurance, has ensured that companies licensed to operate in one member economy are free to operate throughout the EU. The intention is to reduce domestic oligopolies and increase cross-border competition. Many of these initiatives were associated with the creation of the Single European Market in 1992, where the EU market was envisaged to be free of national regulations, taxes or informal practices.

Benefits of the EU

The strength of the EU economy is arguably greater and deeper than the sum of its parts. This is because the size, scope and diversity of the member states leads to increased competition, the realization of economies of scale and the improved attainment of comparative advantage.

We have already argued that increased trade enables economies to specialize in the production of goods and services in which they have a comparative advantage. This allocation of scarce resources to the production of goods with the lowest opportunity cost raises the combined output of trading partners. With 25 member economies the opportunities for pursuing comparative advantage are enormous. Especially when such economies are geographically disperse, have differing factor endowments and are at differing stages of economic development.

Furthermore, a producer who is restricted to their domestic market may face an overall market size which is smaller than the minimum efficient scale in production. Whereas access to larger international markets facilitates the attainment of scale economies, leading to reduced production costs and perhaps improved pricing for consumers.

While natural scale economies may lead to the development of oligopolies in national economies, the removal of trade barriers leads to increased cross-border competition and a reduction in natural entry barriers. All of these can lead to increased levels of competition. This competition may generate lower prices, innovation in the pursuit of cost efficiencies and the development of new products. These are factors which can improve the economic performance of the EU economy.

There is evidence to support these economic arguments, at least in terms of increased consumption. Table 14.4 reports estimated gains for a number of member countries. The results indicate that smaller economies gained more than larger ones; and also the largest gains came where the most protected industries were opened up to competition. The results reflected the consumption gains following a one-off permanent shift in aggregate supply. However, they fail to reflect any ongoing endogenous growth effect, where, for example, increased competition drives further innovation and economic growth.

Therefore, the gains from EU trade and competition could be both higher and more persistent than suggested by the estimates in Table 14.4.

Table 14.4 Consumption gains from the single market

Range of Estimates (% of GDP)	Countries
2–3	France, Germany, Italy, UK
2–5	Denmark
3–4	The Netherlands, Spain
4–5	Belgium, Luxembourg
4–10	Ireland
5–16	Greece
19–20	Portugal

Source: C. Allen, M. Gasiorek, A. Smith 'The competition effects of the single market in Europe', *Economic Policy*, 1998

A consequence of increased trade and competition has been the emerging corporate strategy of being a pan-European company. One simple manifestation of this is the swapping of Internet country designations such as www., ... co.uk, .fr and .de, for the more regional designation of www., ..., .eu. Coupled with this geographic rebranding exercise has been the growth of cross-border mergers, especially the fragmented industries of telecommunications, banking and energy, which until recently have been fairly immune from the effects of the Single European Market. Spain's Telefonica acquired the UK telecommunication company O_2, creating the largest telecommunications company in the Western world. The French water and electricity company Suez looks set to merge with Gaz de France, to preempt a bid by the Italian electricity company Enel for Suez.

These two examples raise interesting contrasts within the EU. The UK has witnessed a number of high-profile acquisitions of its leading companies, especially by European companies. But there has been no political backlash. In the case of Suez, the threat of an Italian takeover provoked the French government into engineering a merger between Suez and Gaz de France with the objective of creating a national champion. The French government is not alone. The Italian, Spanish and Polish governments have all promoted similar strategies in the pursuit of national champions. The reasons are simple. Within the EU economy super-large companies which can exploit economies of scale are likely to be the most competitive. As such, consolidation and horizontal merger is likely. The Single Market therefore brings with it benefits and risks. Trade, competition and consolidation bring cost reduction, but may place national economies at the mercy of super-regional companies. The perceived balance of these risks and benefits, coupled with national pride are likely to dominate the development of corporate mergers and takeovers for some time to come.

Issues facing the EU

The Common Agricultural Policy, CAP, was until 2003 a system of subsidies which provided price support for agricultural produce. It has now been modified to become a system of direct income payments to farmers, thereby enabling farming to survive, but not creating a direct price distortion in the market for produce. The CAP represents €40 billion of expenditure, or 40 per cent of the EU's budget. France is the biggest recipient, receiving almost €9 billion, followed by Spain with €7 billion, Germany with €6 billion and the UK with €4 billion.

The CAP is strongly defended by the French who view the French farming sector as a key aspect of their national identity. In particular, the reputation of French gastronomy rests on its ability to grow and create the finest cheese, meat, vegetables and wine. In addition, the beauty of the French countryside is arguably protected by the continued presence of farmers.

There is strong opposition to the French. In particular, the UK has questioned the wisdom of the CAP. With agriculture representing less than 2 per cent of EU GDP, why does 40 per cent of the EU budget go to support this sector? Would it be more sensible to allocate a significant portion of the EU budget to education and science, thereby, building knowledge capital and generating opportunities for further economic growth?

Outside the EU world trade negotiations have stalled on the unwillingness of the EU to remove the CAP and its agricultural trade barriers to non-member countries. However, within this a subtlety exists. According to the World Bank it would be more beneficial for world trade if the EU reduced external tariffs, rather than dismantling the CAP. The reason is that the CAP reduces the price of agricultural products in the EU and beyond. Removing the CAP would make it more expensive for countries in Africa, the Middle East and elsewhere to import EU agriculture. However, removing trade tariffs would make it easier for such countries to export to the EU.

The issues surrounding the CAP are unlikely to be resolved in the near future, since in 1992 the EU agreed that no further changes to the CAP would occur before 2013, and the French appear keen to hold everyone to that agreement.

EU enlargement

The addition of ten new members in 2004 was the single biggest expansion of the EU. However, there are more countries awaiting membership. Romania and Croatia are awaiting final approval; while Turkey is still signaling its eagerness to join. Enlarged membership brings benefits as well as problems. Each new country opens up yet more markets for member countries to compete in without any trade barriers. In the case of the new accession countries it also presents an ample supply of cheap, yet reasonably skilled workers, offering manufacturing companies the opportunity to relocate and exploit cost savings. This has been illustrated most obviously by the automobile industry with the likes of Volkswagen and Ford moving European production to the new member states.

The problems brought by these new member nations reflect their transition economy status, moving from communist state planning to free market economics. Privatization programmes, poor legal infrastructure, weak bank finances, plus a need to invest heavily in transport and communications infrastructure, education and health, mean that many of these new economies face a constraint on their growth. Longstanding EU members from Western Europe have recognized the need to divert development spending into the new member states. But change will take time and will also come at the expense of development expenditure in the economies of Germany, France, the Netherlands and the UK.

Undoubtedly, the EU is a successful trade bloc and a model for others such as NAFTA and ASEAN. Its ongoing problems are small when compared with the size of its economy, the amount of cross-border trade and the degree of corporate competition. While national politicians may disagree on the way to deal with the issues presented by the EU, few would wish to sacrifice the economic power and benefits derived from being a member.

14.4 To what extent are markets becoming global?

Globalization occurs at many levels. Firms can export overseas or even operate overseas. They can exploit cheaper labour, capital or finance overseas. An examination of globalization requires an analysis of numerous issues.

Global product markets

In considering global product markets we will concentrate on trading internationally, as opposed to operating internationally. Trading internationally is the export and import of goods and services from domestic locations to international markets – for example, BMW selling cars to other countries. McDonald's operating in Hong Kong is operating internationally. We will consider this later.

Indices for world merchandized exports and world GDP are plotted in Figure 14.4. The values for world exports and GDP were set to equal 100 in 1950. This does not mean that world GDP and world exports were equal in 1950. Instead, by setting GDP in 1950 = 100 we can examine the growth in GDP over time and, similarly, we can examine the growth in world exports. For example, the index value for world GDP in 2000 was around 300. Therefore, between 1950 and 2005 world GDP grew by $(300 - 100)/100 = 200\%$. In contrast, the index for world exports was over 600 by 2005. As a result, we can say that between 1950 and 2005 world exports grew by $(600 - 100)/100 = 500\%$.

Looking at Figure 14.4 the growth of world GDP has been fairly constant throughout the period 1950–2005. The GDP line increases at a fairly steady rate throughout the period. In contrast, world exports initially grew at the same rate as world GDP and then,

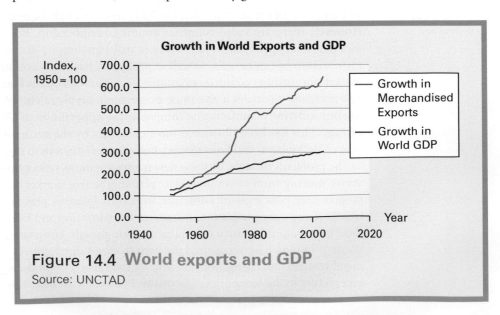

Figure 14.4 World exports and GDP
Source: UNCTAD

in the late 1970s the slope of world exports becomes much steeper and the acceleration in world exports becomes evident.

Since exports are a component of aggregate demand and, therefore, GDP, we can now say that from the early 1980s a growing proportion of world GDP was being exported.

This is clear evidence that the development of GATT, the WTO and the various trade blocs, such as the EU, have been extremely successful in promoting international trade. But we still need to ask whether product markets are become increasingly global.

In Table 14.5 we have the world's ten biggest exporters and importers. They are the same countries. This should not be a surprise. A country that is a significant importer needs to finance its consumption and it can achieve this by also exporting a great deal. A more productive approach is to assess where each country is trading. In Tables 14.6 and 14.7 the exports and imports of the US and the EU with various regions are shown.

Table 14.5 Leading exporters and importers, 2005

Rank	Exporters	Value	Share	Annual percentage change	Rank	Importers	Value	Share	Annual percentage change
1	Germany	912.3	10.0	21	1	United States	1525.5	16.1	17
2	United States	818.8	8.9	13	2	Germany	716.9	7.6	19
3	China	593.3	6.5	35	3	China	561.2	5.9	36
4	Japan	565.8	6.2	20	4	France	465.5	4.9	17
5	France	448.7	4.9	14	5	United Kingdom	463.5	4.9	18
6	Netherlands	358.2	3.9	21	6	Japan	454.5	4.8	19
7	Italy	349.2	3.8	17	7	Italy	351.0	3.7	18
8	United Kingdom	346.9	3.8	13	8	Netherlands	319.3	3.4	21
9	Canada	316.5	3.5	16	9	Belgium	285.5	3.0	22
10	Belgium	306.5	3.3	20	10	Canada	279.8	2.9	14

Source: UNCTAD

It is very clear that the vast bulk of trade occurs between developed countries, or regions of the world. Little if any trade from the US is with the Middle East or Africa. The EU displays a similar pattern, but it also conducts little trade with Asia. Therefore, it is reasonable to argue that, while world trade has increased, it is not global. Rather, trade has increased between the developed economies of the world. It has not included the less-developed economies of the world.

Global operations

Exports are the sale of domestic production to overseas markets. Globalization is more than this. Many leading firms around the world have operations in more than one country.

Multinational enterprises are usually large companies with production and/or sales operations in more than one country.

Table 14.6 US trade with various regions, 2005

	Exports		Imports
Region		Region	
World	100.0	World	100.0
North America	36.7	Asia	36.6
Asia	26.5	North America	27.4
Europe	23.1	Europe	20.8
South and Central America	7.4	South and Central America	6.9
Middle East	2.9	Middle East	3.6
Africa	1.6	Africa	3.2
CIS	0.6	CIS	1.0

Source: UNCTAD

Table 14.7 EU trade with various regions, 2005

	Exports		Imports
Region		Region	
World	100.0	World	100.0
Europe	74.0	Europe	71.8
North America	9.0	Asia	11.9
Asia	7.4	North America	5.9
Middle East	2.5	CIS	3.0
Africa	2.5	Africa	2.7
CIS	2.2	South and Central America	1.8
South and Central America	1.3	Middle East	1.6

Source: UNCTAD

The **transnationality index** is an average of three ratios: foreign assets/total assets, foreign workers/total workers and foreign sales/total sales for the firm.

The United Nations Conference for Trade and Development has developed an **index of transnationality** that seeks to measure a firm's exposure to non-domestic markets.

Selected companies are shown in Figure 14.5. Many of us probably find it very easy to understand why Nestlé, a Swiss chocolate confectioner, is the most globally integrated company in the world.

When multinational enterprises operate overseas, they have to invest in foreign markets. This might be represented by the purchase, or building, of a production facility. Or, alternatively, the company may decide to acquire an existing company in the foreign market and use them as the foundation for international expansion.

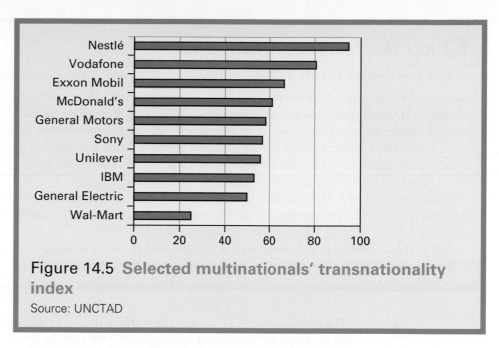

Figure 14.5 Selected multinationals' transnationality index

Source: UNCTAD

The purchase of foreign assets is commonly known as **foreign direct investment (FDI)**.

As we saw with international trade, **FDI** has exhibited rapid growth in the last 25 years. The amounts of global FDI for various years are shown in Figure 14.6. 2000 was characterized by some very large global mergers and acquisitions, such as Time Warner and AOL, which perhaps overinflate the figure. But a decline has been in evidence since. This has reflected increased reluctance to operate overseas in the face of political and terrorist risk and a reduced ability to raise financial capital following the collapse of stock markets in the early years of this millennium.

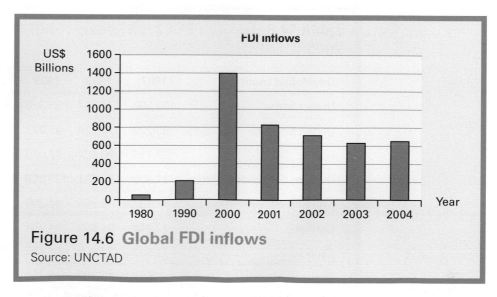

Figure 14.6 Global FDI inflows

Source: UNCTAD

However, as Box 14.2 indicates, companies are still willing to search the world for products, which can be marketed on a global basis. It does not seem to matter how good the beer is, it is simply the concept that it comes from Brazil which is captivating. As long as domestic consumers are entranced by the variety and exotic image of foreign lands, global brands will continue to drive foreign direct investment.

Box 14.2 More beer from Brazil

Adapted from an article by Andy Holloway, 24 April–7 May 2006 issue of Canadian Business magazine.

Molson Coors Brewing Co. couldn't get anyone to drink its Brazilian import, but that hasn't stopped Labatt Breweries of Canada from rolling out its own version this spring. Brahma supposedly fills a gaping hole in Labatt's lineup: an 'international player in clear glass,' says spokesman James Villeneuve. Apparently, beers are no longer categorized by style or price, but by bottle colour and location. That's understandable, since Brahma doesn't exactly offer an exotic taste explosion. Indeed, Labatt seems proud that Brahma, the world's sixth-best-selling beer, has a 'clean flavour' and 'no aftertaste'.

Molson tried selling A Marca Bavaria using a tacky television ad that boasted 'there are no sins below the equator'. It also positioned the beer as 'super premium', even though it was clearly neither of those things – especially in Brazil, where it is considered a poor man's brew.

With Brahma, which is broadly targeted at a younger market, Labatt is taking a more low-key approach that emphasizes Brazil's ginga lifestyle, which loosely translates as 'effortless flair'.

The distribution of FDI around the world is also very interesting. In Tables 14.8 and 14.9 we have the ten largest recipients of FDI split by developed and developing economies. The US and Europe are much bigger recipients of FDI than the rest of the world. In developing economies, China is the largest recipient of FDI. But in 2004 with only US$47 billion of FDI, China was only sixth overall, behind the Netherlands. So, as with international trade, FDI also appears to be large, but not entirely global. Most foreign direct investment appears to be attracted into a small number of economies, many of which are developed, as opposed to developing.

Table 14.8 Top ten FDI host (developed) economies in 2000 (US$m)

Developed countries	1997	1998	1999	2000	2001
United States	103 398	174 434	283 376	300 912	124 435
United Kingdom	33 229	74 324	87 973	116 552	53 799
France	23 174	30 984	47 070	42 930	52 623
Belgium and Luxembourg	11 998	22 691	133 059	245 561	50 996
Netherlands	11 132	36 964	41 289	52 453	50 471
Germany	12 244	24 593	54 754	195 122	31 833
Canada	11 527	22 809	24 435	66 617	27 465
Spain	7697	11 797	15 758	37 523	21 781
Italy	3700	2635	6911	13 377	14 873
Sweden	10 968	19 564	60 850	23 367	12 734

Source: UNCTAD

Table 14.9 Top ten FDI host (developing) economies in 2001 (US$m)

Developed countries	1997	1998	1999	2000	2001
China	44 237	43 751	40 319	40 772	46 846
Mexico	14 044	11 933	12 534	14 706	24 731
Hong Kong, China	11 368	14 770	24 596	61 938	22 834
Brazil	18 993	28 856	28 578	32 779	22 457
Bermuda	2928	5399	9470	10 980	9859
Poland	4908	6365	7270	9342	8830
Singapore	10 746	6389	11 803	5407	8609
South Africa	3817	561	1502	888	6653
Chile	5219	4638	9221	3674	5508
Czech Republic	1300	3718	6324	4986	4916

Source: UNCTAD

Why do firms become global?

There are a variety of reasons why firms become global, but essentially these reasons relate to costs and revenues.

Revenue growth

A company's growth is constrained by the size and growth of its domestic market. If we take a company like Wal-Mart, which already dominates the US grocery market, its opportunities for growth are limited by the size of the US market. But if it operates overseas, as it does in the UK through the Asda chain, then its sales can increase. Sales growth in overseas markets may also be cheaper. Consider the adverts of many leading global companies, particularly mobile phone operators and car-makers. The advert often has no voice-over. The advert is usually images and music. This is because if the advert is made for the UK market, then it can also be screened in other markets as well. Different economies can offer different growth rates, especially if sales are income elastic. For example, in highly developed economies, such as the US and Western Europe, the demand for insurance products is income inelastic, a 10 per cent rise in income will generate a less than 10 per cent rise in demand for insurance. However, in the Far East insurance is income elastic, with a 10 per cent rise in income leading to a bigger than 10 per cent rise in the demand for insurance. Therefore, in the developed world insurance is set to become a smaller proportion of national income, while in the Far East insurance is set to become an increasing proportion of national income. As a consequence, large insurance companies have rushed to set up operations in the Far East.

Costs

Firms may operate overseas because they have an international cost advantage and can compete effectively in foreign markets. Alternatively, firms may be seeking international expansion in order to gain a cost advantage.

Sources of international competitiveness

Sources of international competitiveness can be categorized as national, industrial or firm-specific.

Most obviously, comparative advantage resulting from the factor endowments of the economy (such as labour, raw materials or capital) can provide firms with an international competitive advantage. Operating overseas enables a firm to exploit these advantages.

Additional sources of national competitiveness may stem from macroeconomic conditions. Inflation may be falling, making prices internationally competitive. Supply side policies, such as increased levels of education and training, improved communications infrastructure, plus better functioning capital markets may provide firms with an improved ability to operate internationally, by creating the workers and capital needed, to manage overseas operations, with capital markets providing the necessary finances in order to fund such investments.

Industrial sources of international competitiveness stem from the competitive structure of the domestic market.

In Chapters 5 and 6 we introduced perfect competition, monopoly and oligopoly as different types of market structure. The characteristics of these structures may aid international competitiveness. For example, a monopoly in the domestic market may provide a firm with the necessary financial resources to invest in an overseas operation. Similarly, if economies of scale are an important cost advantage in the domestic market, such scale economies may provide the firm with the competitive advantage to move into the international markets. For example, the US, being a very large market, enables many of its domestic suppliers to be operating at the minimum efficient scale. With low costs many of these producers can consider developing operations overseas.

Firms may have knowledge, or expertise, in any aspect of their operations, for example, design, production, distribution or marketing. With a lack of national- or industrial-based advantages, **firm-specific** competencies may provide a firm with an advantage over its rivals. For example, Tesco and Sainsbury's both operate in the same UK supermarket business. They have access to the same factor inputs and benefit from the same industrial structure, so why have Tesco outperformed Sainsbury's? Tesco must have some firm-specific advantage over Sainsbury's. The advantage could stem from a brand name, management know-how, logistics technology, or even being able to build stores quicker and cheaper than rival operators. Clearly, since the advantage lies within the firm it is firm-specific. The asset may not be tangible, but it is an advantage that is specific to the firm.

Economies of scope, specific assets and internationalization

This specific nature of the asset is essential for an understanding of internationalization by a firm. If, as discussed in Chapter 7 when analysing growth strategies, the firm's specific advantage generates economies of scope, internationalization provides a way of exploiting scope economies. Investment in a brand for the domestic market may present an economy of scope if the brand can also be used to enter an international market, thereby saving on the cost of developing a new brand. Research and development associated with a new product such as a microprocessor, a drug, or a plasma TV could represent an economy of scope if the product can be launched in more than one market. But should a firm exploit its own brand or new product development itself? Or, instead, sell rights to use its brand name or product development to an operator in the international market? This is the make or buy decision also discussed in Chapter 7. If the asset is specific, then the transaction costs of selling access to the brand or product knowledge to a third party may be very high. A hold-up problem could occur where the third party threatens to damage the brand, or provide competitors with access to the product knowledge. In order to reduce the transaction costs, it is better for the firm to exploit firm-specific assets internationally within its own operations, rather than selling access rights to other firms.

In summary, if a firm has a specific asset such as knowledge, or branding which provides it with a competitive advantage, the best way to exploit that asset is to retain control. Expanding the firm's operations into international markets enables the firm-specific competitive advantage to be exploited. Transferring the asset to a third party is likely to increase transaction costs.

Accessing international competitiveness

Companies can operate overseas to exploit cheaper factor inputs, such as cheaper labour, lower raw material cost and better capital equipment. But cheap labour may not be productive labour, or it may be labour with a poor level of skills. So, the quality of labour also needs to be considered. Operating in international markets also cuts down on transportation costs. Products need not be transported around the world. Instead, they can be produced and sold in the local market.

A common concern regarding multinational enterprises has been the exploitation of workers. Wages in developing economies tend to be less than in developed economies. Firms are tempted to move overseas in order to reduce labour costs. If developing economics are also associated with more relaxed employment laws, then the use of child labour, long working hours and limited holidays may also make such places look attractive to large multinational enterprises. However, if multinational enterprises do exploit workers then, referring back to Tables 14.8 and 14.9, it is worth considering why FDI is more prevalent in the developed world, rather than the developing world.

A basic observation and answer to this question would be that FDI measures investment in capital, not labour. For example, a Japanese company investing in a Plasma TV manufacturing plant in Wales is investing in high-technology capital equipment to produce products for the developed world. A UK clothing retailer hiring workers in South-East Asia to make clothes is unlikely to invest very much in capital. FDI may, therefore, not be a good measure of the extent of global operations.

14.5 Business application: globalization – exploiting comparative advantage

Nothing is ever as easy as it sounds. The reduction in trade barriers around the world has arguably freed up world business and enabled the most competitive firms to flourish. However, even within the EU a supposed model of internal free trade is characterized by anti-competitive regulations. As discussed in Box 14.3 Kelloggs has to produce four varieties of cornflakes to meet the various nutritional legislation in member states of the EU. Such production complexities help to negate any economies of scale and competitive advantage which may stem from access to a larger market. Such barriers and impediments to trade are but one example of a myriad of problems faced by businesses operating overseas:

Box 14.3 **Europe grapples with a market that isn't as unified as it hoped**

Adapted from an article by G. Thomas Sims, 1 November 2005 The Wall Street Journal

European countries have been trying to build a unified market for close to 50 years. In theory they completed the task in 1993. However, Kelloggs has to manufacture four different varieties of corn flakes and other cereals for its European markets, with each variety tailored to the different dietary regulations on vitamin D consumption in Denmark, the Netherlands, Finland the UK and so on. Caterpillar trucks have to install a louder horn for the German market and move the headlights to a different location. John Deere its competitor does not bother to supply some models in Europe because of the regulatory hurdles.

A single pan-European market was meant to throw open doors for trade investment and growth. Economists say persistent national differences saddle companies with extra costs and hinder enterprise and expansion. Companies say it is difficult to mass produce in any economy of scale.

Communication and co-ordination

First, there is the matter of communication and co-ordination among suppliers, workers and customers. Language is an obvious barrier to good communication. Ordering raw material supplies in a foreign language for your production facility is fairly easy to master, especially with the aid of an interpreter. Explaining complex technical processes, however, or trying to justify recruitment procedures, marketing plans, operational procedures, or financial control through budgeting will require an understanding of local culture, traditional business practice and perhaps even an awareness of the local law. Therefore, communication and co-ordination of the international operation requires a great deal of specialist expertise in running international operations.

Legal issues

Second, local laws may differ substantially from those of the home base. Employment law could be different, resulting in higher redundancy payments and longer periods of notice before employment can be terminated; there might be stronger trade union representation, leading to more industrial disputes; environmental controls could be harsher, leading to cleaner but more costly production; contract law could differ and the legal system could be ineffective at enforcing contracts. Even import restrictions might apply. For example, companies operating in the EU, but from non-EU countries, are required to source more than 70 per cent of their production inputs from within the EU.

Quality of inputs

Third, input factors can have varying quality across countries. Labour is an obvious example, with basic skills such as literacy and numeracy varying across developed and developing economies. Such skills are essential for training staff, developing staff and managing staff. Furthermore, such skills are essential for staff that are required to use machinery in the production process, particularly machinery that is computer controlled and might require adjustments to be made to it. If the supply of staff with the appropriate levels of skills is limited, then development of the local workforce may well be necessary. While enhancing skills might be seen in a favourable light by the local community, no one will be more grateful than other local firms, which in the fullness of time will be seeking to poach the international company's highly productive workers.

Image and brand

Finally, there is the issue of image. Well-known global companies have come under extreme scrutiny. Clothing and footwear suppliers, such as Nike, have been criticized for exploiting cheap labour in the developing world. If using cheap labour from the developing world provides a comparative advantage, then the negative press associated with such activities is perhaps not what shareholders desire.

Oil producers have also been criticized for operating in countries with poor human rights records, for polluting the environments in which they work, for paying bribes to local governments and for doing little to improve the local economies from which they profit. In response, BP, the UK's leading oil producer and leading global company, has developed a global ethical policy in which it has promised to support human rights, help to reduce pollution, not pay bribes and to help the development of local economies within which it operates. A social responsibility stock market index has been launched in the name of FTSE4Good. Companies are included in the index if they conform to guidelines of environmental and management practices. The list currently includes the likes of ABN AMRO, British Airways, Carrefour, Unilever and Vodafone. Nestlé were removed following concerns over their marketing of powdered baby milk in Africa.

Therefore, as firms seek out competitive advantage in the global economy, they have to become increasingly aware of the wide and serious demands placed upon their management teams, especially in terms of protecting the brand image.

14.6 Business application: sources of international competitiveness

It is important for business people the world over to understand the crucial difference between competitive advantage and a sustainable competitive advantage. A competitive advantage may provide you with some short-term strength over your rivals. But if your advantage can be mimicked, then you do not have a sustainable competitive advantage. In Box 14.5 Bangalore as a location clearly has a competitive advantage in outsourcing IT, data processing and call centre services. Much of this advantage stems from a reasonable IT and telecommunications infrastructure; and reasonably skilled staff who speak English and who are willing to work for much less than similar staff in the US and Europe.

Unfortunately, Bangalore does not necessarily possess a sustainable advantage. Now that it is known that large corporations are willing to outsource business services, many locations around the world will seek to copy Bangalore's low-cost strategy. In fact, even some regions in the EU which are in need of economic regeneration could place themselves in direct competition with Bangalore. The clear problem for Bangalore is that its strategy can be copied. Therefore, it is substitutable and that means it faces elastic, or price-sensitive consumers. However, as incomes rise, wages rise, it will become ever more difficult to remain internationally competitive.

So how do you continue to reap the benefits from globalization? You must find a strategy which is sustainable. One which other locations, or companies find very difficult to copy. In the absence of imitators, firms face fewer and less-intense price competition. While the availability of cheap labour within a location can be copied, industrial and or firm level characteristics are much more differentiated. Silicon Valley has been a success for a variety of reasons, but none that relate to cheap labour.

Silicon Valley benefits from economic clustering, the co-location of supportive and competitive firms. Competition between rivals spurs innovation, while the co-location of supportive industries enable innovation. Silicon Valley may provide industry level

Box 14.5 **What Bangalore should aim for**

Adapted from an article by Satyam Cherukuri, in BusinessWeek, 24 November 2005

If the Indian city is to sustain its position as a center of technology, it must emulate Silicon Valley and encourage innovative risk takers.

Bangalore is the city of dreams. It is the city where failure is a stranger, and expectations climb as high as the booming Indian stock market. Bangalore today accounts for a large slice of India's revenues in outsourced services and offers a model that cities around the world are emulating. Many American companies view it as a place to pursue innovation, while American knowledge workers see it as a threat to jobs.

The ugly truth is that, while this southern Indian city of 7 million may be a global center of information technology and other services, business in Bangalore is essentially a 'me, too' activity with little true innovation. Multinational corporations come to reduce their costs, and the Indian companies set up shop to offer services to anyone who wants to reduce risk as well as cost.

It is a comfortable and, so far, highly profitable arrangement. But it is not what India needs in the long run. The growth rate for such services as information technology and business-process outsourcing cannot be sustained. The cost pressures on outsourcing and offshore providers from a booming local economy, combined with competitive price pressures from rivals in many parts of the world, will slow the expansion.

The first reaction to slower growth will be to lower prices, but the pressure on margins will demand more creative solutions. How can Bangalore sustain its strong position beyond 2007, and what is the right model for other regions and cities aspiring to a winning place in the race towards the globalization of innovation?

The answer lies in vigorous, robust, and innovative tech companies that can develop new products for the world. These companies will be a new breed, with the ability and nerve to generate ideas and then use science, technology, and engineering to produce high-value results.

Silicon Valley is the benchmark example for this concept of serial innovation. The micro economy running from San Jose, Calif., to San Francisco has given birth to generations of risk takers who have taken technology to market and, in the process, changed the world. The globally recognized names of Hewlett and Packard, Wozniak and Jobs, Page and Brin, are representative of the many individuals at smaller companies who engage in innovation risk as a way of life.

sources of international competitiveness by the concentration of similar companies in one area. Skilled technical and scientific workers are attracted to the area and can move between projects and companies without having to move home. Moreover, important support services such as banking and venture capital are likely to locate in the area and develop expertise in financing specialist IT innovation companies. As firms within Silicon Valley develop, firm-specific routines around developing innovation strategies and commercializing knowledge creation begin to develop. These industrial and firm-level characteristics are much more difficult to copy and as such lead to the development of higher value-added services, where the advantage is unlikely to be competed away on price.

The challenge for Bangalore is not that difficult. It has entrepreneurial spirit, it has cash resources to invest in innovation and it has the engineering and technical skills to develop a sustainable competitive advantage. Moreover, the lessons from Bangalore are appropriate for many national economies and companies faced with global competition. The very existence of competition suggests a lack of entry barriers, substitutability and low prices. Profits, wages and economic wealth will never be generated in such industries. It is therefore important to move to less competitive positions within the value chain. We are already beginning to observe automotive companies, such as Volkswagen, locating their assembly lines in Eastern Europe where wages are lower but productivity is comparable with Western Europe. In contrast, design, engineering, product development and marketing have remained within the home economy. These are much more involved complex tasks which are difficult to copy by low-wage economies, leading to lower competition and a higher rate of return to this section of the value chain. Box 14.6 provides an example of so-called 'near sourcing', where developed economies use resources located in nearby emerging economies. The very fact that firms are willing to pay £1 to £2 extra for fast fashion is suggestive of greater value added when compared with China. The garments from Eastern Europe and China are easily substitutable, but the quick service offered by firms located in Eastern Europe is not. It cannot be copied by the Chinese.

So globalization offers opportunities and threats, working out how to maximize the opportunities and tame the threats is the art of business management, but through an understanding of micro and macro business economics you should now be prepared to meet the challenge.

 Box 14.6 **The rise of nearshoring**

Adapted from an article in The Economist, 1 December 2005

Ex-communist Europe is grabbing a lucrative niche in the global outsourcing business.

The region's most obvious advantage, low labour costs, is diminishing, so leading companies are hunting much harder for lasting advantages based on talent and geography.

In the garment industry 'fast fashion' – ordered and manufactured in speedy response to sales trends – is booming. Fast fashion is a pound or two more per piece from central and eastern Europe, but customers are prepared to pay. The product cycle for garments from China is about three months with four weeks of that time spent at sea. From eastern Europe, by contrast, it is just four to six weeks, including a day or two for delivery by lorry.

 Summary

1 The reasons for increasing globalization are numerous but include the cultural, technological, economic and political.

2 Comparative advantage is an important economic reason behind the rise of globalization. Comparative advantage states that countries should specialize in the goods and services of which they are comparatively better at producing.

3 Comparative advantages are most likely to arise from an abundance of a particular factor resource. France is good at wine because it has an abundance of productive land and climate. Germany is good at producing high-quality cars because it has an abundance of highly skilled labour and high-quality capital equipment.

4 Two-way trade in the same product between countries may still exist even in the face of comparative advantage. Cars are an example. The UK and Germany may trade cars with each other, but the types of cars will be different. This simply reflects differences in taste and preference among German and UK car drivers and not comparative advantage in production.

5 In the past, countries have tried to protect industries from international competition by imposing trade barriers. Tariffs and quotas are common examples. Unless the industry is of strategic, or defensive importance to the economy, then economists generally agree that trade restrictions are against the public interest.

6 The leading political reasons for globalization have been the acceptance of the economic importance of comparative advantage and a willingness to reduce trade barriers. The formation of trade blocs such as the EU and the work of GATT and the WTO have been important in the process of reducing trade restrictions.

7 Following the successes of GATT and the WTO, the trade of goods and services across national boundaries has grown faster than world GDP. This would suggest that the provision of goods and services is more globally integrated than ever before.

8 However, when examining the pattern of international trade flows, it is apparent that the vast majority of international trade occurs between a small number of developed economies. So, while trade has increased, it is questionable as to what extent trade is actually global.

9 Companies operating in more than one country are known as multinational enterprises.

10 Foreign direct investment (FDI) occurs when a company invests outside its domestic base. Throughout the 1990s FDI grew rapidly. But in recent years it has shown a marked decline.

11 Firms may begin to operate overseas for two basic reasons: (i) to increase sales and (ii) to reduce costs.

12 However, international operations incur specific problems, such as language problems, legal issues, co-ordination problems and possible damage to the global brand. As a consequence, some multinational enterprises are beginning to reappraise their global activities, as evidenced by the falling levels of FDI.

 Learning checklist

You should now be able to:

◆ List and explain the main drivers of globalization

◆ Explain comparative advantage and identify potential sources of comparative advantage

◆ Explain the impact of tariffs and quotas on domestic prices, firms and consumers

◆ Explain the reasons why trade restrictions have fallen

◆ Assess whether the rise in international trade is global

◆ Provide reasons for the growth in FDI

❓ Questions

1 What factors have promoted the globalization of business?

2 In a global economy is it possible for the UK to become uncompetitive in every product market?

3 Is globalization a threat, or an opportunity for business?

4 What problems might a firm face when managing global operations?

Exercises

1 True or false?
   a) Comparative advantage reflects international differences in the opportunity costs of producing different goods.
   b) The need to protect infant industries is a power argument in favour of protectionist measures.
   c) The imposition of a tariff stimulates domestic demand
   d) The purchase of a share in Microsoft by someone who is not a citizen of the US is an example of foreign direct investment.
   e) Comparative advantage could stem from an abundance of factor endowments.
   f) The increase in world merchandise trade has not been entirely global.

2 This exercise examines the gains from trade in a two-country, two-good model. To simplify matters for the time being, we assume that the two countries share a common currency; this allows us to ignore the exchange rate. The two countries are called Anywaria and Someland; the two goods are bicycles and boots. The unit labour requirements of the two goods in each country are shown in Table 14.10; we assume constant returns to scale.
   a) Which of the countries has an absolute advantage in the production of the two commodities?
   b) Calculate the opportunity cost of bicycles in terms of boots and of boots in terms of bicycles for each of the countries.
   c) Which country has a comparative advantage in the production of bicycles?

Table 14.10 Production techniques

| | Unit labour requirements (hours per unit output) | |
	Anywaria	Someland
Bicycles	60	120
Boots	30	40

Suppose there is no trade. Each of the two economies has 300 workers who work 40 hours per week. Initially, each country devotes half of its resources to producing each of the two commodities.

d)   Complete Table 14.11:

Table 14.11 Production of bicycles and boots, no trade case

	Anywaria	Someland	'World' output
Bicycles			
Boots			

Trade now takes place under the following conditions: the country with a comparative advantage in boot production produces only boots. The other country produces sufficient bicycles to maintain the world 'no-trade' output, devoting the remaining resources to boot production.

e)   Complete Table 14.12 and comment on the gains from trade:

Table 14.12 Production of bicycles and boots

	Anywaria	Someland	'World' output
Bicycles			
Boots			

f)   On a single diagram, plot the production possibility frontier for each country. What aspect of your diagram is indicative of potential gains from trade?

3   Refer to Box 14.5 when considering the following questions:
   a)   Identify the competitive strengths and weaknesses of Bangalore as a centre for off shore business services.
   b)   A common complaint is that 'Bangalore is stealing all our jobs'. Is this really a problem?

Answers to end-of-chapter questions

Chapter 1 Economics for business

1 Goods or services competing for your income might include rent, food, heating and travel. Activities competing for your time might include studying, work, sleep and leisure activities, such as the cinema, drinking and sport.

In assessing whether you minimize your opportunity costs you need to examine what you decided to do, or consume, and compare these with what you decided not to do, or consume. If you minimized your opportunity costs, then you have chosen all the things that provide you with the maximum amount of benefit.

2 (a) The price of cars is a microeconomic issue. It is an issue associated with one market, or sector. (b) Inflation is the rise in prices across the entire economy and, therefore, represents a macroeconomic problem. (c) Strong sales in the housing market are a micro issue as they relate to a single market. However, the housing market is linked to the macroeconomy and, in this example, has led to the Bank of England holding interest rates constant. As interest rates are set for the whole economy, then this is a macroeconomic issue.

3 Firms operate within markets. If product markets are a collection of firms supplying products and consumers buying products, then it is important for business to understand how consumers and firms interact in markets. Furthermore, firms will also be interested in understanding how competing firms interact in markets. Business also buys its inputs, such as labour, from markets, so the costs of firms are, in part, determined within markets. Therefore, understanding markets can lead to an understanding of profitability.

4 Firms also operate within economies. Governments seek to control economies. Understanding how government economic policy will influence consumers' ability to spend, firms' ability to invest and the level of international trade and competition are all important issues for business to comprehend.

5 (a) Asserts an opinion without any supporting theory. It is, therefore, a normative statement. (b) In contrast, this asks a question that can be answered using economic theory. It is, therefore, a positive statement.

6 The plot of house prices against year shows a positive relationship; year and house prices increase together:

House prices against year

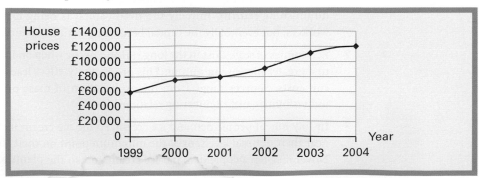

House prices, index and percentage increases

Year	Index	% increase
1999	80	–
2000	100	25
2001	107	7
2002	120	13
2003	147	22
2004	160	9

Chapter 2 **Consumers in the market place**

1 Elastic products – a price increase leads to a big drop in demand – any product that faces lots of competition, so pizzas from competing shops, different brands of beer.

  Inelastic products – a price increase leads to a small drop in demand – cigarettes, beer as a market, gas, water, electricity, cars, petrol, insurance, medicine.

2 At any given price consumer surplus is greater under inelastic demand. In the extreme case of perfectly elastic demand every consumer pays the market price and is only willing to pay the market price, so consumer surplus is zero.

3 Elasticity is influenced by the proximity of subjects. You could, therefore, reduce the number of substitutes by acquiring one or more of your competitors. Or, alternatively, you could try to differentiate your product. Coca-Cola and Pepsi are very similar products, but their brand differentiation would have you think otherwise.

4 During an economic boom you need products that have a positive income elasticity, or so-called normal goods, as consumers will be willing to buy these. During a recession you need products that have a negative income elasticity, or so-called inferior goods, as consumers will buy more of these as their incomes fall. Therefore, by producing both normal and inferior goods you will have a portfolio that balances the effects of economic boom and recession. Your sales of normal goods increase during a boom, but your sales of inferior goods increase during a recession.

Chapter 3 **Firms in the market place**

1 In the short run capital is fixed and, as a result, costs are determined by the law of diminishing returns. Initially the fixed capital is being exploited as we add more workers, but eventually the capital becomes overutilized and costs begin to rise.

2 Economies of scale exist in the long run and occur when an increase in all inputs leads to a greater increase in output. This productivity effect leads to a reduction in long-run costs. Sources range from the exploitation of mass production techniques to indivisibilities and engineering relationships.

3 In July lots of people demand ice cream, so the ice cream factories will be operating near their optimal levels, or at the minimum point on their short-run cost curves. In November few people demand ice cream and so the plants are operating below the

optimal level. By reducing the price, ice cream firms are trying to sell more output and thereby move nearer to the minimum point on their cost curve.

4   Ordinarily a firm may only be expected to operate at price levels that are below average variable cost. However, it may go lower if it was keen to force a rival out of the market, or it could cross-subsidize its losses from another market.

5   If economies of scale are large, then competitive advantage could be gained by operating at the minimum efficient scale. But if the nature of the industry changes, then economies of scale may be no longer relevant. Banks traditionally operated with 2–3000 branches, representing significant economies of scale. Internet banking makes such a structure obsolete.

Chapter 4 **Markets in action**

1   An increase in the supply of celebrities is likely to reduce the market price for celebrities. Chat shows and magazines can choose among many celebrities, so higher competition reduces the fees that will be paid. However, if the public's demand for celebrities continues to rise, then the price could stay high.

2   A rise in income is likely to increase demand for homes and, therefore, the price could increase and home-builders may then make more money. But what will happen if interest rates increase? Would increased mortgages, a complementary good for homes, cut the demand for homes? Furthermore, will the supply of house-builders increase in the future? If so, prices will fall and lower profits will be made.

3   Yes, you are undertaking a degree because you have the capability to pass the course in three years. Someone with less capability might fail one or two years, resit and take four to five years to pass. This is too expensive in time and lost earnings, so they do not go to university. Hence, a degree signals something special about your abilities.

4   **Supply and demand of healthcare**
The supply of healthcare treatment is set by the government. It is not influenced by price and is therefore perfectly inelastic. At zero price, the amount of healthcare treatment demanded by UK patients is greater than the amount of treatment supplied. This shortage of healthcare treatment results in waiting lists. A controversial solution would be to charge the equilibrium price P1. Then demand would equal supply and there would be no waiting lists. A more politically acceptable solution is to shift the supply of healthcare to the right and aim to meet demand at zero price.

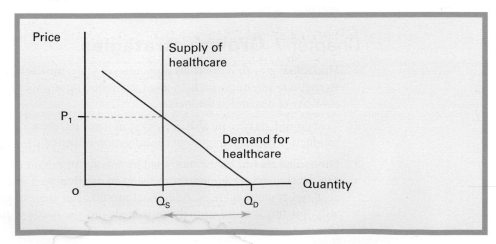

Chapter 5 **Market structure and firm performance**

1 No market is perfectly competitive, as this is the ideal. But some markets come near. Stock markets and commodity markets such as oil, copper and wheat are all reasonable examples. Microsoft is a monopoly supplier of some computer software. BT was a monopoly supplier of telecommunications in the UK. And at the extreme the Beckhams are a monopoly supplier of their life stories and celebrity parties.

2 As demand increases, the price rises and firms are more likely to make profit. Next year farmers will plant more fields with wheat, the supply will increase and prices will fall. Hence in the long run only normal profits will be earned.

3 See Figure 5.11 on page 107. Figure 5.11 illustrates an increase in costs. Your diagram should be the reverse.

4 Without competition there is little to discipline monopolies. They could operate inefficiently, increase cost and eventually operate at a loss. Many nationalized monopolies did just this. So, monopoly is no guarantee of profits.

Chapter 6 **Strategic rivalry**

1 If the advert is for a new product, or the start of a sale, then we might say it is primarily informative. But many adverts are simply brand-development exercises and, as such, more closely represent the creation of entry barriers.

2 Morally the answer is no. Economically the answer is it depends. If you are playing the game once, that is, the lecturer will not be teaching you again, then they are likely to cheat by taking your £100 and not guaranteeing a 70 per cent, and of course you would not be daft enough to tell the Dean! If they are teaching you for another module later in the course, then they might be open to repeat co-operation.

3 It appears to be competition and it may well be. But it is also a good way of co-ordinating pricing. Indeed, suspicion can be aroused by some small print that lists the retailers with which they will match prices. If it is competition, surely they would be willing to match any retailer's prices?

4 You would cheat if: (i) the other companies had cheated in the last round, (ii) you had discovered that the next round is going to be the last, (iii) you suddenly acquired a competitive edge where it was now in your interests to compete, because you could outcompete your rival and gain the monopoly position for yourself.

Chapter 7 **Growth strategies**

1 Horizontal growth is driven by economies of scale, the learning curve and a desire to strengthen revenues; perhaps even by reducing competition and reducing the elasticity of demand in the market.

2 Cost considerations are also important motives for vertical growth. But, aside from production costs, an important consideration is the reduction of transaction costs.

3 Diversified growth can be motivated by a desire to exploit economies of scope. This can develop new revenue streams using an existing asset and, therefore, represents cost and revenue motives. Additional motives can stem from a desire to diversify risk. But this is more strongly associated with the needs of managers, rather than shareholders.

4   Growth provides the opportunity to grow in size relative to other rivals in the same market. Advantage stems from an improved ability to reduce costs and control pricing and revenues. Lower competition may also lead to an increased ability to organize a cartel. Vertical integration could bring control of an essential up- or downstream asset for the industry. Rivals may be forced to buy raw materials or distribution from one of your operating divisions. Diversification can bring greater strength through the exploitation of an asset in many markets. The potential for cross-subsidization can provide the ability to leverage competitive advantage gained in one market to the other operations of the company.

Chapter 8 **Governing business**

1   Profit maximization requires MC = MR. It is often difficult to measure MC and MR. Aside from these technical difficulties it is possible that, due to the separation of ownership from control, managers can pursue their own objectives. These might be (i) expense preference behaviour, (ii) sales maximization or (iii) growth maximization.

2   A management buyout should decrease agency costs. When an owner/shareholder hires managers this creates agency costs. But when managers decide to buy out shareholders, they are effectively moving from being agents to principals. Managers are becoming the owners. Hence, no agency costs.

3   Negative externalities: air pollution, sound pollution, litter, not having a wash. Positive externalities: studying for a degree, planting roses in the garden, being vaccinated, buying an energy-efficient appliance.

4   **The effect of a subsidy on rural and semi-rural train travel**
    If trains improve the movement of workers and shoppers both from and into rural and semi-rural areas, leading to positive externalities for employers and retailers, the MPB could be less than MSB of train travel, providing a subsidy to rail users lowers the private cost (MPC) of using the railway, thereby leading to an increase in the number of rail passengers.

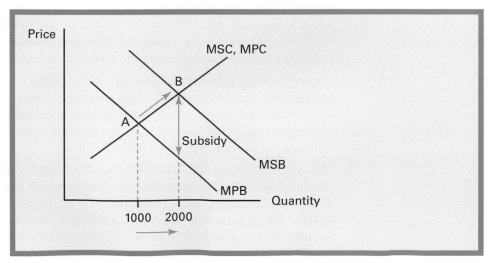

5   To deal with externalities it is common to use *taxes* to reduce output when private output is higher than the socially optimal level, whereas *subsidies* are used to increase supply when the socially optimal level of output is higher than the private level of output.

Chapter 9 **Introduction to the macroeconomy**

1 A rise in aggregate demand with aggregate supply remaining constant will lead to an increase in GDP and inflation, leading to a so-called inflationary boom.

2 With an influx of additional workers, households can supply firms with extra workers. Firms will only demand more workers at lower wage rates. So, if we can assume that wages fall, then the flow of resources from households to firms will increase within the inner ring of the circular flow of income. With more productive resource, firms can increase the flow of goods and services in the outer ring.

   With more resource supplied to firms at a lower cost, firms are more willing to supply output. The aggregate supply curve shifts to the right, with firms willing to provide more GDP at all levels of inflation.

3 Demand for normal goods increases when income rises, while demand for inferior goods increases when income declines. Income will tend to rise during a boom and decline during a recession. So, producing normal and inferior goods may be a good strategy for dealing with the business cycle. But consumers' understanding of the brand may be confused. In order to prevent this problem it may be better to offer two brands, e.g. Ferraris and Fiats.

4 If sales have been rising, then profits may have been increasing. But increased profits will have attracted other firms into the market or, alternatively, existing players in the market may have already invested in additional capacity, leading to an increase in supply. Increased competition generally leads to an increase in supply and a consequential decrease in the market price. With a falling price, margins are squeezed; therefore, now is perhaps not the best time to invest.

Chapter 10 **Measuring macroeconomic variables and policy issues**

1 GDP per capita is high in Luxembourg, so the ability of consumers to spend is good. But how many consumers are there in Luxembourg? Clearly not as many as the US, which is second in the list. Moreover, how is the income distributed among the inhabitants of Luxembourg? Equally, or disproportionately? If much of the income resides in a few hands, then the ability to spend on the business products is limited.

2 Assume the firm's products (and all other products in the economy) increase in price by 3 per cent. Then by agreeing to a 5 per cent pay rise, the firm will be raising its real wage cost by 2 per cent (5 − 3). However, if the firm can ask for a 2 per cent increase in productivity, its real wage will remain constant. Workers will be funding their increased real wage through higher levels of output.

3 Why is unemployment high in the area? Does the unemployment represent frictional, structural, demand deficient or classical unemployment? If it is structural, then will the skills in the area be useful to the firm? If it is classical unemployment, will the workers still expect a wage above the equilibrium? However, if unemployment is demand deficient, then by the firm moving to the area it will be bringing demand into the job market.

4 A government may try to control its balance of payments problem by deflating the economy, reducing prices and thereby seeking international competitiveness, where exports can outpace imports. The issue for the firm is whether it can suffer a period of

economic slowdown, while waiting to see if international competitiveness is attained in the longer run.

Chapter 11 Economic stability and demand side policies

Fiscal policy

1   In equilibrium, actual output must equal planned expenditure. Therefore Y = PE.
     Planned expenditure = C + I = 20 + 40 + 0.8Y = 60 + 0.8Y
     In equilibrium Y = 60 + 0.8Y
     Rearranging for Y,
     0.2Y = 60, therefore Y = 300

2   Firms should *not* concentrate on taxation or spending; rather, they should examine the net effect of government spending, less taxes, which is the government's fiscal stance. The fiscal stance should not be overly expansionary, nor lead to too great a contraction in the economy. An excessive fiscal stance could lead to greater instability in the economy, creating higher inflation, greater economic uncertainty, lower consumption and reduced investment by firms.

3   If entry into the euro promotes trade with our European partners, then leakages from the UK circular flow of income will increase through higher imports. Therefore, the multiplier will reduce. However, exports may also increase, which will provide higher levels of autonomous expenditure in the UK. Moreover, following entry into the euro, firms may be more willing to invest in the UK, again increasing autonomous expenditures.

4   Problems of timing, uncertainty regarding the size of the multiplier, the size of the output gap, offsetting changes and inflationary-inducing deficits make fiscal policy problematic.

Monetary policy

1   False. Notes and coins in circulation are only a 'narrow' measure of the money supply. A 'broad' measure also includes money on deposit at banks and building societies. Critically, through the process of credit creation banks and building societies can expand the size of the money supply by lending out money deposited with them by other customers. More practically, the central bank sets interest rates and passively supplies whatever money is demanded at the current interest rate. So, the Bank of England does not control the money supply.

2   First, the level of personal debt will have to be paid back in the future. When this occurs, consumption will slow (as income is transferred from consumption to debt repayments). Second, the increasing availability of debt is a reflection of the credit creation process. Suppliers of personal finance are boosting aggregate demand and *could* be a source of inflationary pressures. Inflation could be destabilizing for the economy and for business.

3   Lower interest rates may boost investment by reducing the cost of borrowing. But if investments are more closely related to the level of business confidence, then investment is likely to be interest inelastic. A more interesting question is whether low

inflation and stable inflation boost investment through greater economic stability. Or, whether low inflation reduces the need to be innovative and exploit capital technology in order to deal with rising costs levels.

4   Expansionary fiscal policies can lead to inflationary pressures. If the central bank is tasked with keeping inflation low, then any fiscal expansion likely to generate inflation will be counteracted by the central bank raising interest rates and cutting demand in the economy. By acting as a restraint on the government's use of fiscal policy, the Bank of England may aid business by helping to create a more stable economy.

Chapter 12 **Supply side policies and economic growth**

1   Supply is determined by the amount of economic resource including land, labour capital and enterprise. Supply is also governed by the productivity of these resources. More capital may improve the productivity of labour, as might education. Technical advances may improve the productivity of capital and the discovery of new resources such as oil, minerals, etc. may all contribute to growth in supply.

2   Neoclassical growth theory views economic growth as dependent upon the growth rate in labour and technical progress. Without randomly occurring technical progress, economic growth across the world will converge to a common rate. Convergence is not observed and it would appear sensible to assume that technical progress is not entirely random. The size of the economy and the involvement of the government, firms and the education system could all play a role in the progress of technology.

Endogenous growth theories assume that investments made by one firm, in some instances, can have positive externalities and improve the productivity of other firms. Furthermore, the rate of technical progress is not entirely random and can be reasonably influenced by government policies relating to R&D, the education system, the labour market and perhaps even financial services. However, a drawback of the endogenous approach is the assumption of constant returns, which appears to some as ad hoc and convenient, rather than determined by theory.

3   Economic growth is a long-run process. We have seen that in the long run, economic growth is associated with movements in the long-run aggregate supply. Since businesses are significant suppliers of goods and services, business is important for economic growth. In particular, how business develops productivity through investment in capital and skills is extremely important for growth.

4   Policies designed to aid investment in capital, or improve workers' skills may help business. But policies designed to increase competition in markets will push markets away from monopoly and towards perfect competition.

Chapter 13 **Exchange rates and the balance of payments**

1   The exchange rate must be fixed. Under a floating regime the balance of payments would be neither in surplus, nor deficit. The surplus is £2 billion. The central bank sells this amount of sterling and buys £2 billion of forex reserves to achieve forex market equilibrium at the desired exchange rate.

2   Monetary policy is most effective under a floating exchange rate regime. Fiscal policy is more powerful under a fixed exchange rate regime. Within the eurozone the exchange rate between all member countries is fixed at N1 for N1. With no ability for the exchange rate to adjust, interest rate parity is necessary if huge capital flows between member states are to be avoided. Hence, the eurozone has one interest rate set by the ECB.

3   Since the euro fixes exchange rates between member economies, purchasing power parity can only be achieved by adjustment in domestic price levels. (Under a floating exchange rate, adjustment in the exchange rate, or domestic prices, is possible.) In order for domestic prices to change quickly, it is important for business and workers to be able to adapt to market forces and reduce (or raise) prices and wages to the average level within the eurozone. Labour markets need to be flexible and firms need to be responsive to market signals.

Chapter 14 **Globalization**

1   Changes in culture, politics, technology and communications have been highlighted as leading drivers of globalization. However, companies tend to trade overseas when they have a competitive advantage, or differences in consumers' tastes facilitate two-way trade.

2   It is possible in the future for the UK to be the least efficient producer in the world. But it will still have a comparative advantage in something. This is the good with the lowest opportunity cost of production, i.e. the good that requires less of everything else to be sacrificed, in order to produce more. So, the issue is not about the UK being uncompetitive; rather, it is about making optimal use of the world's economic factor inputs in generating outputs.

3   Globalization is a threat and an opportunity. It enables firms to move overseas and exploit sales, or cost opportunities, but it also enables international competitors to do the same.

4   Communication and co-ordination, culture, law, differing skill levels and damage to the global brand are all problems associated with operating overseas.

Allocative efficiency This occurs when price equals marginal cost, or $P = MC$.

Average fixed cost This is calculated as total fixed costs divided by the number of units produced.

Average revenue The average price charged by the firm and is equal to total revenue/quantity demanded: $(PQ)/Q$.

Average total cost This is calculated as total cost divided by the number of units produced.

Average variable cost This is calculated as total variable cost divided by the number of units produced.

Barriers to entry These make entry into a market by new competitors difficult.

Ceteris paribus This means all other things being equal.

Circular flow of income This shows the flow of inputs, output and payments between households and firms within an economy.

Common values These occur in an auction where the value of the item is identical for all bidders, but each bidder may form a different assessment of the item's worth.

Competition Commission The Competition Commission investigates whether a monopoly, or a potential monopoly, acts against the public interest.

Complete contract Under a complete contract, all aspects of the contractual arrangement are fully specified.

Consumer surplus The difference between the price you are charged for a product and the maximum price that you would have been willing to pay.

Contestable market A market where firms can enter or exit the market freely.

Credible commitment A credible commitment or threat has to be one that is optimal to carry out.

Cross price elasticity This measures the responsiveness of demand to a change in the price of a substitute or complement.

Cross-sectional data The measurements of one variable at the same point in time across different individuals.

Demand curve The demand curve illustrates the relationship between price and quantity demanded of a particular product.

Disequilibria In situations of disequilibria, at the current price the willingness to demand will differ from the willingness to supply.

Diversification The growth of the business in a related or an unrelated market.

Diversified portfolio A diversified portfolio of activities contains a mix of uncorrelated business operations.

Economic growth This is measured as the percentage change in GDP per year.

Economies of scale Long-run average costs fall as output increases.

Economies of scope These are said to exist if the cost of producing two or more outputs jointly is less than the cost of producing the outputs separately.

Elasticity A measure of the responsiveness of demand to a change in price.

Endogenized If costs are endogenized then the firms inside the industry have strategically influenced the level and nature of costs.

Exit barriers These make exit from a market by existing competitors difficult.

Exogenous costs Exogenous means external, outside. The exogenous costs of the firm are outside its control.

Expectations Beliefs held by firms, workers and consumers about the future level of prices.

Externalities The effects of consumption, or production, on third parties. If production, or consumption, by one group improves the well-being of third parties, then a **positive externality** has occurred. If production, or consumption, by one group reduces the well-being of third parties, then a **negative externality** has occurred.

Factors of production Resources needed to make goods and services: land, labour, capital and enterprise.

Finite resources The limited amount of resources that enable the production and purchase of goods and services.

Fiscal policy The government's decisions regarding taxation and spending.

Fixed costs These are constant. They remain the same whatever the level of output.

Forex markets These are where different currencies are traded.

Full employment This occurs within an economy when all markets are in equilibrium.

Game theory This seeks to understand whether strategic interaction will lead to competition or co-operation between rivals.

Gresham's Law This states that an increasing supply of bad products will drive out good products from the market.

Hedging The transfer of a risky asset for a non-risky asset.

Hold-up problem The hold-up problem is the renegotiation of contracts and is linked to asset specificity.

Horizontal growth This occurs when a company develops or grows its activities at the same stage of the production process.

Imperfect competition This is a highly competitive market where firms may use product differentiation.

Income elasticity This measures the responsiveness of demand to a change in income.

Index numbers These are used to transform a data series into a series with a base value of 100.

Indivisibilities Assets that cannot be divided into smaller units.

Infinite wants The limitless desires to consume goods and services.

Input markets These are where factor inputs, such as land, labour, capital or enterprise, are traded.

Kinked demand curve The idea behind the kinked demand curve is that price rises will not be matched by rivals, but price reductions will be matched.

Law of demand The law of demand states that, ceteris paribus, as the price of a product falls, more will be demanded.

Learning curve The learning curve suggests that as cumulative output increases, average costs fall.

Macroeconomics The study of how the entire economy works.

Marginal cost The cost of creating one more unit.

Marginal private benefit The benefit to the individual from consuming one more unit of output.

Marginal private costs The cost to the individual of producing one more unit of output.

Marginal product The addition to total product after employing one more unit of factor input.

Marginal profit The profit made on the last unit and is equal to the marginal revenue minus the marginal cost.

Marginal revenue The revenue received by selling one more unit of output.

Marginal social benefit The benefit to society from the consumption of one more unit of output.

Marginal social cost The cost to society of producing one or more unit of output.

Market economy In a market economy, the government plays no role in allocating resources. Instead markets allocate resources to the production of various products.

Market equilibrium The market equilibrium occurs at the price where consumers' willingness to demand is exactly equal to firms' willingness to supply.

Market structure The economist's general title for the major competitive structures of a particular market place.

Menu costs These are associated with the activity and cost of changing prices in shops, price lists and, of course, menus.

Microeconomics The study of how individuals make economic decisions within an economy.

Minimum efficient scale (MES) The output level at which long-run costs are at a minimum.

Mixed economy In a mixed economy the government and the private sector jointly solve economic problems.

Models or **theories** These are frameworks for organizing how we think about an economic problem.

Monetary union The permanent fixing of exchange rates between member countries.

Monopoly A market place supplied by only one competitor, so no competition.

Moral hazard Occurs when someone agrees to undertake a certain set of actions but then, once a contractual arrangement has been agreed, behaves in a different manner.

Negative relationship A negative relationship exists between two variables if the values for one variable increase (decrease) as the value of the other variable decreases (increases).

Normal economic profits These are equal to the average rate of return which can be gained in the economy.

Normative economics This offers recommendations based on personal value judgements.

Official financing The extent of government intervention in the forex markets.

Oligopoly A market that consists of a small number of large players.

Opportunity costs The benefits forgone from the next best alternative.

Panel data This combines cross-sectional and time series data.

Percentage This measures the change in a variable as a fraction of 100.

Perfect competition Briefly, perfect competition is a highly competitive market place.

Perfect information Assumes that every buyer and every seller knows everything. No one has an informational advantage.

Piece rates These occur when a worker is paid according to the output produced. Under hourly wage rates, workers are paid for time at work.

Planned economy In a planned economy, the government decides how resources are allocated to the production of particular products.

Pooling equilibrium A market where demand and supply for good and poor products pools into one demand and one supply.

Positive economics This studies objective or scientific explanations of how the economy works.

Positive relationship A positive relationship exists between two variables if the values for both variables increase and decrease together.

Price expectations Beliefs about how prices in the future will differ from prices today.

Price taker If a firm accepts the market price it is a price taker.

Private values In an auction these occur where each bidder has a private subjective value of an item's worth.

Production possibility frontier The production possibility frontier shows the maximum amount of products that can be produced by an economy with a given amount of resources.

Productive efficiency This means that the firm is operating at the minimum point on its long-run average cost curve.

Protectionist measures These seek to lower the competitiveness of international rivals.

Rationalization This is associated with cutbacks in excess resources in the pursuit of increased operational efficiencies.

Revenue equivalence theorem states that under private values each auction format will generate the same level of revenue for the seller.

Satisficing The attainment of acceptable levels of performance. Maximizing is the attainment of maximum levels of performance.

Separating equilibrium This is where a market splits into two clearly identifiable sub-markets with separate supply and demand.

Short run A period of time where one factor of production is fixed. We tend to assume that capital is fixed and labour is variable.

Single period game In a single period game, the game is only played once. In a repeated game, the game is played a number of rounds.

Specific asset A specific asset has a specific use; a general asset has many uses.

Speculative attack A massive capital outflow from an economy with a fixed exchange rate.

Strategic interdependence Firms within an oligopoly are seen to be strategically interdependent. The actions of one firm will have implications for its rivals.

Subsidy A payment made to producers, by government, which leads to a reduction in the market price of the product.

Substitutes These are rival products; for example, a BMW car is a substitute for a Mercedes, or a bottle of wine from France is a substitute for a bottle from Australia.

Sunk cost An expenditure that cannot be regained when exiting the market.

Supernormal profits These exist if the return to investors or shareholders is in excess of normal economic profits.

Supply curve This depicts a positive relationship between the price of a product and firms' willingness to supply the product.

Switching costs The costs of moving between products.

Tangency equilibrium This occurs when the firm's average revenue line just touches the firm's average total cost line.

Time series data The measurements of one variable at different points in time.

Total costs These are simply fixed costs plus variable costs.

Total product The total output produced by a firm's workers.

Total revenue Price multiplied by number of units sold.

Trade bloc A region or group of countries that have agreed to remove all trade barriers between themselves.

Transaction costs The costs associated with organizing the transaction of goods or services.

Variable costs These change or vary with the amount of production.

Vertical chain of production This encapsulates the various stages of production from the extraction of a raw material input, through the production of the product or service, to the final retailing of the product.

Vertically integrated A company is said to be vertically integrated if it owns consecutive stages of the vertical chain.

Winner's curse This is when a winning bid exceeds the true value of the sale item.

Index